Italian Recipes

by Amy Riolo

Wine pairings by Dr. Sante Laviola
Italian research scientist, professional wine taster,
and sommelier

A Wiley Brand

Italian Recipes For Dummies®

Published by: **John Wiley & Sons, Inc.**, 111 River Street, Hoboken, NJ 07030-5774, www.wiley.com

For general information on our other products and services, please contact our Customer Care Department within the U.S. at 877-762-2974, outside the U.S. at 317-572-3993, or fax 317-572-4002. For technical support, please visit https://hub.wiley.com/community/support/dummies.

Wiley publishes in a variety of print and electronic formats and by print-on-demand. Some material included with standard print versions of this book may not be included in e-books or in print-on-demand. If this book refers to media such as a CD or DVD that is not included in the version you purchased, you may download this material at http://booksupport.wiley.com. For more information about Wiley products, visit www.wiley.com.

Library of Congress Control Number: 2022932611

ISBN 978-1-119-86270-3 (pbk); ISBN 978-1-119-86317-5 (ebk); ISBN 978-1-119-86271-0 (ebk)

SKY10032663_030422

Contents at a Glance

Recipes at a Glance

Primi/First Course Dishes

Secondi/Fish and Seafood Main Courses

Secondi/Egg and Poultry Main Courses

Secondi/Main Courses with Meat

Contorni/Vegetable Side Dishes

Insalate/Salads

Colazione/Breakfast

Fruit, Cheese, and Nuts

Dolci/Classic Desserts

Holiday and Special Occasion Treats

Bread, Pizza, and Focaccia

Table of Contents

Introduction

"Donne, ricette e mode, chi li capisce gode."

"Women, recipes, and fashions, who understands them, enjoys them."

~ ITALIAN PROVERB

Recipes have always been an integral part of my life. Much more than just technical instructions, both oral and written recipes have the power to create cultural bridges between ourselves and others. They narrow the distance between time and space and give us the opportunity to be in touch with people and places that we may not be able to physically reach. Whether we are preparing recipes of those loved ones who are no longer with us or those who live on another continent, the act of doing so brings us closer to them.

It was the desire to be with those I could no longer be with, and in places that I couldn't travel to, that fueled my passion for recipe reading, writing, and collecting as a young girl. Growing up in a family with Southern Italian (Calabrian) roots in New York state, food was our main link to our culture. Like many Italian-American families, and families of immigrants during those times, we lost many aspects of our culture due to the erroneous belief that assimilation was necessary for the good of our nation.

It is often said that food is the last component of a culture to be lost when people emigrate, and, in the case of our family and community, that is definitely true. I apprenticed under my grandparents on both sides of my family and my mother since I was three years old. Making bread, meatballs, cookies, pastries, and holiday recipes with them was the highlight of my life growing up. Later, I learned that the very same *Cuzzupe di Pasqua* (Calabrian Easter Bread), *Petrali* (fig cookies for Christmas), and other recipes that my beloved Nonna Angela taught me, were the same recipes that our family in Crotone, Calabria, still make for the same holidays. In fact, we often prepare them at the same time on the same days without knowing it! This means that a century after my great-grandparents emigrated to the United States, those recipes acted as edible time capsules that kept our family's culture connected in a way that's hard to explain. The Riolo family in the U.S. lost contact with their Italian relatives for more than four decades, yet our recipes lived on. What a joy it was to discover that we still had an edible connection to one another when we reunited.

Twenty-seven years after I first stepped foot in Italy and rediscovered my family in Calabria thanks to my cousin, Joyce Riolo, I am proud to say that I have lived and continue to work there. I am the Brand Ambassador for Ristorante D'Amore in gorgeous Capri, Italy. I lead cuisine, culture, and wellness tours to the majestic (yet still relatively unknown to tourists) regions of Abruzzo, Molise, and Calabria. I have a line of Amy Riolo Selections products that come from genuine single-estate producers in Italy, and I have maintained beautiful relationships with my relatives there. I also have formed a marketing company for Italian products called Italian Sensory Experience, LLC. I speak fluent Italian and often travel to Italy for personal reasons, for work, and to attend conferences on olive oil, wine, and other products. In the United States, I am the Brand Ambassador for the Pizza University and Culinary Arts Center, which enabled me to get pizzaiola certification with Maestro Pizzaiolo Enzo Coccia. I am also the chef at Casa Italiana Language School in Washington, D.C., and am very involved with Italian and Italian-American organizations throughout the world. Recently I became a founding member of the Italian non-profit association called A.N.I.T.A (Accademia Nazionale Italiana Tradizione Alimentari, or Italian National Academy of Food Traditions) whose vision is to promote healthful and sustainable Italian cuisine, traditions, and agri-culture in the world.

After spending so much time in Italy, researching the recipes, and seeing how "Italian" food is served around the world, I knew there was a need for a book with mass appeal that would help demystify genuine, regional, Italian cuisine and cul-ture, and so my eleventh book, *Italian Recipes For Dummies,* was born. The contents of this book are based on my Mastering Italian Certification Series that I have taught in cooking schools and institutions. The idea behind the book and the series is to give cooks the knowledge, tips, and strategies they need to create the best Italian foods.

While recipes are the easiest entry point into Italian cuisine, preparing them with passion and integrity can lead to a lifelong case of *Italophilia*, or love of all things Italian. Eating a traditional Italian diet, of mostly plant-based ingredients dressed with healthful doses of quality extra virgin olive oil and artisan vinegar, is as good for the body as it is for the palate and the psyche. May the recipes in this book bring you closer to those you love and connect you to your past and your future, as they do for me.

About This Book

You don't need to live in Italy to create great Italian food. You do, however, need to understand Italian meal patterns, some history and culture, and why foods are eaten and paired in a specific way. You're in luck! *Italian Recipes For Dummies* provides not only the recipes needed to make authentic dishes, but also many of the often unexplained strategies that housewives and restaurant chefs have employed and passed down for years. These strategies make even the most labor-intensive Italian recipes accessible for home cooks everywhere, and this book reveals them.

I understand that some days are busier than others, so this book outlines how to fit cooking into *your* life. Most importantly, though, it discusses the deep-rooted misconceptions about *getting* to cook (not just having to cook) that have deprived us of one of life's greatest pleasures. You learn why Italians, myself included, are so passionate about food, and you may be inspired to adopt some of the fervor! Whatever your cooking skill level, you will find recipes and tips that are perfect for you.

This book is a reference, which means you don't have to read it from beginning to end or commit it to memory. Instead, you can dip in and out of the book to find the information you need. Use the table of contents and the index to find the subjects you're looking for. If you're short on time, you can skip sidebars (text in gray boxes) and anything marked with the Technical Stuff icon.

When it comes to the recipes, keep in mind the following:

>> All temperatures are Fahrenheit. For conversion to Celsius, see the Appendix.

>> Vegetarian recipes are marked with the tomato icon (🍅) in the Recipes in This Chapter and Recipes in This Book lists.

>> I call for high quality extra virgin olive oil (EVOO) and unrefined sea salt in many recipes throughout this book. I recommend these varieties because there is a big difference among the types on the market today, and using the best quality ingredients ensures that they are better for you. Be sure to check out Chapter 5 for more info about why these items are important to me and, I feel, to Italian cooking.

>> If your budget allows, use organic ingredients whenever possible. But no matter what, buy the best-quality ingredients you can, from as close to where you live as possible — and enjoy them to the fullest.

>> In this book, my dear friend, Dr. Sante Laviola, Italian research scientist, Sommelier, and official wine-taster of the Slow Wine Guide (published by Slow Food Editore) has paired his wine suggestions with my recipes. I truly appreciate his opinions because he has a very unique and highly informed perspective on wine pairing. With a PhD in Physics of the Earth System, Dr. Laviola uses a distinct form of wine pairing that promotes natural wines and protects our environment while pairing wines with the proper *terroir* (or natural environment including soil, topography, and climate) to each plate. He uses a

geo-sensory wine-tasting approach when pairing; instead of smelling a wine's aroma, he tastes it and senses the tactile properties in order to pair it with the territory, which is an increasingly popular method of evaluating natural wines.

Of course, the wine pairings in this book are mere suggestions. You may opt to not drink with your meals, to pair your own favorite wines, or use different pairing parameters. Note that Dr. Laviola has shared the properties and characteristics of the wines he's paired with the recipes to make it easier to find a suitable substitute if needed.

Finally, within this book, you may note that some web addresses break across two lines of text. If you're reading this book in print and want to visit one of these web pages, simply key in the web address exactly as it's noted in the text, pretending as though the line break doesn't exist. If you're reading this as an e-book, you have it easy—just click the web address to be taken directly to the webpage.

Foolish Assumption

In writing this book, I made a few assumptions about you, the reader:

>> You've probably already fallen head-over-heels for classic Italian recipes such as pasta, pizza, and simmering sauces.

>> You have a desire to prepare and enjoy genuine Italian food.

>> You want to achieve great results in the kitchen without a lot of trial and error.

>> You are willing to put in a bit of effort to experience mouthwatering and nutritious meals.

If any of these describe you, you've come to the right book!

Icons Used in This Book

You'll find icons throughout the chapters that alert you to certain types of information.

TIP

The Tip icon marks shortcuts that can save you time or money or make Italian cooking easier and more enjoyable.

REMEMBER

Remember icons mark the information that's especially important to know. If you're short on time, siphon off the most important information in each chapter by skimming through to look at the text highlighted by these icons.

TECHNICAL STUFF

The Technical Stuff icon marks information that is interesting but not essential to your understanding of Italian cooking and cuisine. If you aren't into it, you can skip over these sections without missing out on the major focus of the chapter.

WARNING

Look out! The Warning icon tells you about information that could relate to your safety. It marks important information that may save you headaches or prevent you from being misled.

Beyond the Book

In addition to the book you're reading right now, be sure to check out the free online Cheat Sheet for tips on getting comfortable cooking Italian dishes, reading food labels to identify authentic, quality Italian products, and planning a traditional meal like an Italian. To get this Cheat Sheet, simply go to www.dummies.com and type Italian Recipes For Dummies Cheat Sheet in the search box.

Where to Go from Here

It's time to start planning your Italian culinary adventure! Start by reading the Table of Contents and look at all of the subjects this book has to offer. You can begin wherever you like, but I recommend setting aside some time to really read and absorb the chapters in Parts 1 and 2 before diving into the recipes in Part 3. If you take the time to do this, the recipes will make more sense. You will understand the ingredients and why they are used. You will learn to pair the foods together properly in authentic Italian meals. Best of all, you'll know how to stock your pantry, what to make when, and what to look for when buying Italian foods. It is imperative to know about the history and culture of Italian cuisine, so you know what to serve, when, and why. The concept of cooking seasonally is one that Italians take seriously, and it is better for our economy, health, and environment, so it's a good idea to become familiar with Chapter 4 as well. Chapter 5 gives you the tools you need to recreate delicious and nutritious Italian meals in minutes with the help of a well-stocked pantry and pantry recipe formulas.

Next, read through the recipes and create a course of action. First, I recommend stocking your pantry accordingly. Then spend some time making the base recipes.

Next, dabble with some sauces or try a beloved recipe when you have time to do so and enjoy yourself in the process. Little by little, try new recipes and experiment pairing them properly. When you have a particular type of produce you like that is in season, look up how to prepare it, or swap it out for an ingredient in another recipe. You'll be on your way to cooking like an Italian in no time!

Remember that genuinely mastering a cuisine takes decades of interest, discipline, and dedication, as well as travel and experiences. This book contains information that you would carefully absorb from witnessing your family this way while growing up in Italy, which takes at least eighteen years. It also contains a great deal of information that you would learn if you spent years in an Italian culinary school and had the opportunity to travel throughout the country. If you are able to appreciate and integrate a few recipes or a chapter every two weeks, for example, and with just a bit of patience and dedication, by this time next year, your Italian meals and the quality of your culinary life will be totally transformed.

The important thing to remember is that there is no race and that incorporating a few of these suggestions (when it feels best to you) offers pleasant and positive payoffs. Remember that authentic Italian cooking is a lifestyle, and the results will continue to multiply throughout your life, so there is no rush. To rush into anything is not the Italian way. "*Chi va piano arriva lontano,*" or "who goes slowly arrives far," as the Italian expression suggests.

May you savor every moment at the kitchen and the table!

1

Introducing the Art of Italian Cooking

Understand authentic Italian cuisine, its history, and culture.

Discover the importance of mastering time-honored traditions.

Enjoy cooking seasonally.

Build an Italian pantry and learn to cook from it.

Learn the art of *la bella figura* — how to make a good impression with food.

Recreate Italian base recipes that are the backbone of the kitchen.

Embrace Italian-style Sunday and holiday meals.

Master everything from traditional, typical meals to light dinners at home and meals on the go.

Become fluent in Italian culinary terms.

Chapter **1**

Cooking the Italian Way: That's Amore!

Love is the common denominator that binds the cuisine of each Italian region together to create a national treasure. Before discussing individual recipes and techniques, one must conjure up a sense of *amore* in order to be a great Italian cook. A deep sense of love for oneself, for those you're cooking for, for the recipes and the regions themselves, and for the producers of the ingredients – let them inspire you to place a premium on cooking and eating well in the first place. Keeping those topics close to your heart and mind will inspire you to cook Italian food well.

Even if you've never cooked Italian food before, there's no need to be intimidated. Despite Italy's long, rich, and varied culinary history, the tips and techniques in this book prove how simple, accessible, straightforward, mouthwatering, and healthful Italian food can be.

Appreciating How History and Geography Shaped Italian Cuisine

Italians take cuisine very seriously while enjoying it to the fullest. In addition to mere fuel for the body, food is viewed as a source of daily pleasure and culinary medicine that should be savored. Along with fashion, music, art, architecture, design, and other artisan crafts, authentic cooking and food products are important parts of the culture that are a source of pride for Italians. Italians believe that the more informed we are on where our food comes from (both in the historical and geographical sense), the more we will appreciate it and enjoy it. In addition, understanding the history behind a dish helps to preserve its place in history by creating a place for it on the culinary landscape that won't soon be forgotten. Taking the time to learn about Italian history and the unique features of its geography gives you the knowledge needed to serve the proper dishes at the right time of day and during the right season. It also enables you to pair foods together more easily and get the most out of seasonal produce. In short, knowledge of Italian history and geography helps to give you the mindset that an Italian naturally brings to the kitchen.

What Italians consider to be their cuisine varies greatly from how others around the world describe it. True Italian cuisine is recognized as the regional foods and recipes that make up the traditional classics that have been enjoyed for decades, centuries, and even millennia. There are a few ubiquitous and world-renowned creations that Italians claim as their collective own, such as pizza, pasta, risotto, gelato, and panettone. In the modern world, those recipes are carefully guarded, protected, and considered to be part of the culinary patrimony of the nation. These edible ambassadors make Italians proud when they are successfully recreated around the globe.

If you scratch a bit deeper beyond the surface, however, you will note that each of those dishes is linked to a particular place, such as the pizza of Naples, or they come from a larger category, such as pasta, which has different regional variations. Italians describe their own food by region, town, or city. *Ragù Bolognese* (from Bologna), *Torta Caprese* (from Capri), *Carciofi all Romana* (from Rome), and so on. As a result, to truly understand Italian cuisine, you must learn about Italy's regions, culture, and history.

Food in every Italian region is the most highly celebrated aspect of the culture. Appreciated for being a daily source of pleasure, joy, and health, Italian food is a way of life. Chapter 2 discusses how time-honored traditions in agriculture and in cooking have woven their way into the tapestry of Italian daily life. By reading that chapter, you get a better sense of the role that food plays, beyond fuel, in an Italian's life. By learning about highlights in Italian culinary history, you quickly can identify how the cuisines of various regions have both common denominators and unique qualities.

Regardless of which Italian region you spend time in, you'll be able to taste the layers of history that it has experienced. From ancient indigenous inhabitants, to foreign rulers, and fancy courts, many factors have contributed to make Italian cuisine a microcosm of the influences that have shaped the course of Mediterranean history. The mere notion of food as culture itself has, for centuries, enhanced Italian cuisine and enabled it to become the most popular cuisine in both the world and the United States today.

Many newcomers to "real" Italian cuisine from abroad are surprised to learn that some of their favorites — which may have been Italian-American dishes or just improperly prepared recipes — are actually not part of a true Italian repertoire. Others still are surprised to learn just how simple, straightforward, mouthwatering, and healthful Italian food can be.

REMEMBER

In the United States, only one-third of the Italian foods eaten actually come from Italy. The rest are either falsely advertised or adaptations. In many cases, even the foods that are imported from Italy are not prepared properly. For this reason, many Italian recipes have *disciplinari*, or production guidelines, on the ways in which they should be made correctly. Pesto sauce from Genoa and pizza from Napoli are two examples of such recipes.

Back to Basics: Applying Ancient Strategies in the Modern Kitchen

Some cooking trends that are perfectly in line with our modern, fast-paced, even urban lifestyles, believe it or not, began in antiquity! Ancient ways of adding flavor to foods, the notion of culinary medicine, building on base recipes, making smart use of leftovers, and using seasonal produce are a few of my favorites. Thousands of years ago, aromatics such as garlic, onions, and leeks along with fresh herbs and spices were the "go to" flavor enhancers for recipes. Since these ingredients were available, they were combined in ingenious ways to not only make food taste better, but also provide relief and protection from illnesses and disease. Long before "culinary medicine" was a recognized term, food was used to heal the body and keep illness at bay. This concept fits perfectly with modern trends and provides easy and inexpensive ways to flavor our recipes without excess calories or fat.

For centuries, good Italian cooks relied on base recipes. Many of these, such as stock and bread crumbs, were created by using kitchen leftovers efficiently. You can use these same methods to cut down on your carbon footprint while saving money and eating more wholesome foods. Up until very recently, Italian cooks did not have the "luxury" of using out-of-season produce. Forced to use what was local and seasonal, their diet was based upon the nutrients that their bodies craved the most during each season. Even though modern supermarkets provide just about any food any time of year, health experts agree that local and seasonal ingredients do our bodies the most good. The more that we can incorporate these types of "ancient" practices in our modern lives, the better off our wallets, waist-lines, and environments will be for it.

Building on base recipes

Chapter 3 discusses the importance of base recipes in Italian cuisine. It may sound boring to an avid cook, desiring to quickly recreate their favorite dishes, to take a few hours to create these "recipes," but I can attest that it is time well spent.

For millennia, Italian home cooks have been doing "inactive cooking" by simmering stock on the stove, soaking beans, and other activites while they were busy attending to other things. They saved leftover bread to make bread crumbs, crostini, and bruschetta. They also cooked beans and legumes on a weekly basis to be added to recipes as needed. By adopting these ancient practices, you can be sure to not only make good use of time and money, but create healthier and tastier dishes as well.

Enjoying the seasons at the table

Seasonality at the Italian table refers to two things. The first is the time of year and the produce and types of fish and meat that are available during that period. The second involves the role that seasonal foods play in celebrating Italian holidays and Sunday suppers. Thanks to open air markets, butcher shops, and fish markets or marinas in most Italian neighborhoods, the average person in Italy is keenly aware of what is in season and when, and it is those foods that are most sought after. Television cooking shows, cookbooks, and food magazines in Italy all discuss seasonality and feature seasonal items. Because Italian holidays fall during the same seasons each year, certain seasonal foods (such as artichokes, asparagus, and lamb at Easter) are always on the menu. Familiarizing yourself with what is in season will set you up for success in the Italian kitchen.

Featuring seasonal foods

Did you know that eating seasonal produce is actually better for your body than eating fruits and vegetables that are out of season? Italians are consistently ranked among the healthiest people in Europe, and their eating and lifestyle patterns are to be thanked. Chapter 4 teaches how our bodies actually crave (nutritionally) the foods that grow in various times of the year as well as how to prepare them and plan meals around them. Since ancient times, Italian menus have always been produce-forward and dependent upon the seasons. Learning to cook and meal-plan this way is good for your wallet and your waistline, while ensuring that you eat the most fully flavored produce.

Even if you've never planned meals seasonally before, the tips in Chapter 4 will enable you to make the most of spring, summer, winter, and fall menus. Because the seasons fall at different times of year in different places, and various locations have unique agricultural patterns, it is best to plan what works for your growing conditions. A true Italian cook can always adapt to the location by employing traditional techniques with the best produce on hand. They cannot, however, tolerate produce that isn't at its best.

Celebrating holidays big and small

To master authentic Italian cuisine, you must learn the basics of the *piano della domenice*, or Sunday lunch, still ritually enjoyed by 70 percent of modern Italians. This weekly highlight is as much a pleasure to prepare as it is to eat and share with family and friends. With a few tips to remember, you can transport yourself to Italy, at least to the table, with ease and joy.

Italian holiday menus and recipes are anticipated around the globe. Every joyous occasion, from Christmas and Winter holidays like Carnevale and St. Joseph's Day, to Lent, Easter, and the Spring holidays, all have traditional recipes that are like edible time capsules just begging to be recreated. You learn the easiest ways to recreate these eleaborate recipes, how to serve them, and the customs behind them. Whether you are having a light dinner at home, entertaining guests, or eating on the go, the menus in Chapter 4 enable you to experience them with Italian flavor and flair.

Get Ready, Get Set!

Head into your kitchen with confidence and the knowledge that you can make masterpieces with relatively little equipment and few ingredients. Just flour, water, and your hands can open up worlds of culinary creativity. That said, there are a few recipes which will be made much more easily with the aid of a few simple tools. If you're going to make fresh tomato sauce, ravioli, gnocchi, pesto sauce, or fresh pasta or bread, be sure to have on hand the items mentioned in this section.

Gathering the tools you need . . . and then some

Italian cooks are very innovative, and over the course of history they've made many substitutions to their list of kitchen equipment. However, I like to keep it as simple as possible — for example, I do not use an immersion blender at home or a pasta maker. I blend my soup and vegetables with a hand-cranked food mill as Italians have done for centuries, and I choose to roll out my pasta by hand with a rolling pin because it is the ancient way of doing it and it provides a more interesting texture. That said, once you have your basic needs covered (pots, pans, sharp knives, a pasta strainer, spatulas, ladles, and a rolling pin), having the following items on hand will make your life in the kitchen easier. Add them to your arsenal as desired, or come up with your own substitutes.

» Cannoli molds

» Dough scraper

» Food mill (for transforming tomatoes into the proper consistency for fresh sauce without the seeds)

» Food processor

» Immersion blender

» Meat hammer

» Moka espresso pot and demitasse cups for espresso

» Mortar and pestle

» Pasta machine

» Potato ricer (for prepping potatoes for gnocchi the proper way)

» Ravioli cutters

» Specific pans including large roasting pans and cake pans

Stocking important pantry items

Pantries are every bit as relevant today as they were 500 years ago. Whether you're tired at the end of a long day of work, or snowed inside on a stormy day, your access to nutritious and convenient food becomes more limited, just as it was for our ancestors when crops were less abundant. Why turn to fast food and delivery when you can create something better from your own cabinet? Chapter 5 arms you with the tools needed to make luscious and memorable meals right from your own pantry.

Chapter 5 also teaches you how to read Italian labels so you get the most for your money at the store. Ever wondered about the difference between a DOP mozzarella and one without the quality seal? Chapter 5 delves into the distinctions between Italian quality seals and what you need to know. You'll also boost your vocabulary with a concise Italian culinary glossary.

Keeping courses and food pairings in mind

Anyone embarking on mastering Italian cuisine needs to be able to plan menus, because there is a specific eating pattern that works in terms of flavor, seasonality, and health benefits.

If you're new to Italian cuisine, you may be overwhelmed, not knowing what to serve or when to serve it, but Chapter 2 explains how the courses are set up and ideas to keep in mind as you decide what foods to serve, and Chapter 4 provides the sample menus and inspiration you need to pair the appetizers, sauces, pasta dishes, other first courses with the second courses, side dishes, fruit/nut/cheese platters, and desserts in this book.

Get Cooking! Eyeing Authentic Italian Recipes

When you're ready to cook, Chapters 6 through 20 are where to turn. From appetizers to sauces, pasta, risotto, soups, gnocchi, meat, fish, poultry, and eggs, you learn the genuine Italian approach to all ingredients. Whether you're preparing a fruit and cheese platter, a decadent dessert, a special occasion baked good, bread, pizza, or *focaccia*, you can find a variety of recipes to take you from morning to night, all year long.

REMEMBER

It's no mistake that I saved the recipes for last. Although you may be eager to dive in to cooking, recipes are only one component of Italian cuisine. By taking a bit of time to familiarize yourself with the philosophy behind the food, you'll have a much more meaningful (and fun) time in the kitchen and at the table.

As you embark on your Italian cuisine journey, keep in mind these ideas and traditions:

>> **Take your time, and enjoy the process:** One of the biggest secrets to the Italian kitchen is the pleasure that people take in preparing the food. People actually look forward to making cherished recipes for themselves and their loved ones when they can. A new crop, the arrival of the first berries of spring, or foraging mushrooms in the fall can all be excuses to create something sensational. If you head to the kitchen begrudgingly to cook Italian food, you will never be successful. Preparing true Italian food is work, but it is a labor of love. The first step to being a good cook is adopting this mentality.

>> **Read through the recipe, and adjust if needed (to use more seasonal ingredients, for example); Italian recipes aren't set in stone:** In fact, making the proper substitutions is a typically Italian thing to do!

>> **Gather the kitchen tools and ingredients you need ahead of time to help ensure a relaxed experience:** No one wants to be harried in the kitchen. Traditionally, Italian kitchens weren't set up like design studios; they were functioning laboratories with pots hanging from racks and tools out for easy access (like a restaurant). If your equipment is neatly tucked away, locating it, along with your ingredients, prior to cooking will save time and help you to enjoy the cooking process.

>> **Share your labor of love:** Getting others involved in the cooking process, eating with others, or sharing your creations helps to make the experience more pleasurable, healthful, and worthwhile.

Chapter **2**

Pizza, Pasta, and So Much More: Appreciating Italian Tradition

M uch of what the world considers to be "Italian food" is either the food of Italian immigrants in foreign lands (which has been adapted to their new home countries) or regional dishes that Italians themselves would describe as being the food of a particular place in Italy instead of a national cuisine. Even Italy's most ubiquitous dishes — such as pizza, pasta, and bread — have origins that can be traced to specific towns or regions even though they are now embraced by the nation as a whole. In this chapter, you learn how to master time-honored traditions, discover how menus are structured, familiarize yourself with a bit of Italian culinary history, and discover the role of culture in Italian cuisine.

The Role of Culture in the Italian Kitchen

Food is such an integral part of Italian culture — regardless of the region — that it is impossible to speak of one without the other. One of the reasons why Italian food is so appreciated internationally is that Italians understand and respect its place in culture. It has been said that food is art, nutrition, philosophy, diplomacy, spirituality, science, medicine, culture, joy, spirit, and entertainment. In the case of Italian food, this is especially true and realized by the locals.

No one in Italy is ever accused of speaking about food "too much" or called "a foodie." Instead, a *buona forchetta,* or "good fork," is used to describe a person who appreciates good food (as they rightly should), and it's a compliment. Throughout history, we see the use of food in pagan culture, through antiquity, in Christianity, and now in our modern world with an almost sacred (and rightly so) appeal. The food we consume is one of the most powerful tools we have to affect our personal health and happiness. Prior to the 20th century, it was the philosophers and physicians who wrote about food, not the chefs themselves, which underscores the importance of the topic of cuisine. From Pythagoras's teaching of nutrition in Kroton (Crotone), to Apicius writing the first Roman cookbook, to the scholars of the Middle Ages to Pellegrino Artusi's 19th century writing classic, we can witness food being a highly appreciated form of culture.

Culture, in the Italian kitchen, is the knowledge that traditions were created for specific reasons (religious, seasonal, in commemoration of events); to recreate a recipe as it was customarily done is to promote the heritage of a particular region. In addition to the pleasure of eating mouthwatering specialties, this desire to uphold culture is the base of Italian cuisine. In many instances in the kitchen, shortcuts can be taken to save time and money. A true Italian cook, however, always opts for the traditional option, when possible, because they realize that losing customs is too great a price to pay and that spending a few moments to pass down heritage is time well spent.

Touring Important Events in Italian Culinary History

It's important to understand that Italy's long and varied culinary history deserves semesters of study. The overview in this section offers just enough info to whet your appetite for the history of Italian food and to enable you to appreciate just how diverse it is. Wheat and wine, for example, are two cornerstones of both ancient and modern Italian cuisine that originated in Mesopotamia, the area that is now modern-day Iran and Iraq. The Romans made the most significant contributions to the development and spread of viticulture, the study of grape cultivation, around the Mediterranean. Today, as a result, Italy is the largest producer of wine in the world. The Roman goddess of grain, Ceres, gave grains their common name today "cereal," which in Italian are called *cereali.*

Most English-language history books begin discussing Italian history with ancient Rome. Prior to the Romans, however, there were native inhabitants and foreign powers in the various areas that now make up modern Italy. Each of those tribes, of which only some are mentioned here, already had laid the framework for the cuisine of their regions. The Lucani, for example, were from modern-day Basilicata, which is believed to be home to the first human settlements in Italy. Many of their agricultural practices, including animal husbandry and cheese-making traditions, are still being practiced today. Indigenous ingredients such as herbs, pulses, meat, seafood, and grains are still part of the daily diet in this region.

From the Celts in the extreme North, to the Etruscans in modern-day Tuscany and Lazio, the Samnites in what is now modern-day Abruzzo and Molise, the Apulians in Puglia, the Sicani in Sicily, the Umbrians in Umbria, some Carthaginians, in addition to the Greeks in Sicily, the Sardi in Sardinia, and the Itali and the Oenotri in my ancestral homeland of Calabria, even regional Italian cuisine has a multitude of ancient influence. The word Italy actually takes its name from the Itali tribe, and the word *oenotria*, or "land of trained vines," was given to Calabria by the Greeks, who called the area's inhabitants Oenotrians (vine cultivators). Calabrian wine, in fact, was so revered by the ancient Greeks that they served it during Olympic ceremonies in Greece.

How Romans and Greeks laid the foundation for Italian cuisine

The Greeks considered Southern Italy, from Naples south, to be the promised land. From the eighth to the fifth centuries B.C.E., they began populating the entire region, beginning with the Italian island of Ischia. For this reason, there are more Greek monuments in Sicily today than there are in modern Greece, and the regions of Southern Italy became known as Magna Graecia, or "Greater Greece." The fertile land, access to additional trade routes, and beautiful terrain inspired the Greeks to set up *polis*, or city states, in Coastal Greek towns.

Napoli was one of the main cultural centers as were modern-day Reggio Calabria and Crotone, along with many others. The Greeks set up monuments to their gods. Even the Greek philosopher and Mathematician Pythagoras set up his school of mathematics, nutrition, philosophy, and music in Kroton, now called Crotone, Italy. An old adage says "When the Romans were still poor shepherds, Pythagoras was teaching in Crotone." These Greek influences did leave a footprint on the cuisine of the Italian south. Pythagoras, for example, was a strict vegetarian and asked his disciples to give up meat in order to study with him. Greek herbs and spices such as oregano, anise, and eucalyptus became widely used. Manners of preparing meat and wine varieties, such as Greco and Aglianico, for example, came directly from Greece.

When the Romans came into power, they did not want to turn their backs on Greek cultural traditions, which they greatly respected, but rather build upon them. Many Romans went to Naples to experience the Greek way of life. The Roman philosopher Virgil was known for saying that Naples was, in fact, a city where one could live and die in the manner of the Greeks. Even Roman emperors and public figures recited plays in Greek when performing and presenting at amphitheaters in Naples, since it was a Greek speaking city at the time.

Romans improved upon Etruscan and Greek wine-making and culinary techniques and began introducing both olive trees and vines to Gaul (modern-day France) and other areas in the empire. The Romans set up a network of trade that spanned from the modern-day United Kingdom, through Western Europe, into North Africa, the Middle East, Central Asia, and China. Sometimes, they used existing trade routes such as the Silk Road, the Incense trails, and those set up by the Vikings; other times, they constructed their own routes.

Regardless of which routes they used, Roman commerce set up a sophisticated structure of international commerce that we now refer to as *globalization.* Roman Emperors sent fleets out to various areas of the globe to procure the best ingredients. They knew, for example, when the best prawns were available in the Mediterranean and sent ships to fish for them off the coast of Libya. They procured enough wheat from North Africa to fund the entire empire. Elaborate murals and depictions from Pompei provide a glimpse into the daily lives of ancient Romans, the ingredients they had at their disposal and how they cooked and shopped.

Spiced wine, or mead, along with barley and wheat bread, grains and pulses, fresh fruit (figs, pomegranate, apples, grapes, quinces, and dates) and vegetables (cucumbers, lettuce, leeks, greens, broccoli, onions, and garlic) along with legumes such as chickpeas and fava were prepared in addition to poultry, foul, and meat by the ancient Romans. Food was heavily spiced because spices were a symbol of wealth and luxury as well as traditional medicinals. Roman cuisine is most often depicted using garum (a fermented fish sauce) as a condiment. The Romans taxed citizens heavily on salt and wheat, so they invented ingenious ways of flavoring food (such as with preserved fish) and mimicking a staple grain (such as burning the grain that came out of winnowers and grinding it again by hand, known as *grano arso*, or "burnt grain" in Italian).

Black pepper, imported from Asia, was coveted by the Romans both as a commodity and a seasoning. They imported so much of it into the Egyptian port city of Alexandria that in antiquity one of the city's entry points was known as "The Pepper Gate." One of the greatest resources available on Roman cuisine is called *On Cooking* or *De Re Coquinaria* in Latin. The first-century book was written by the Roman philosopher Apicius, who is said to be the father of all gourmands. Legend has it that when Apicius learned that he could no longer afford the delicacies his palate craved, he committed suicide. His book recounts recipes from not only Rome itself, but other parts of the empire as well, and it's still available for purchase today. Many international cooking schools, restaurants, and culinary centers are named after Apicius, and for years it was believed that he wrote the first Western cookbook ever found. In the middle of the fourth century B.C.E., however, the Greek gourmand Archestratus wrote "Fragments from the Life of Luxury" in Sicily.

How terrain and climate shaped regional cuisine

Both Italy's indigenous inhabitants and foreign rulers made the best of what mother nature offered them in terms of climate. It's hard for many people to imagine that a country the same size as a single American state could have so much variance in terms of weather, terrain, and climate, but the Italian landscape is very diverse. The Alps in the North and the Apennine Mountain range that cuts through the nation, combined with the effects of the Ionian, Tyrrhenian, Mediterranean, Adriatic, and Mediterranean Seas, combine to make the soil and climate unique in places that are often only a short distance apart from one another.

No matter whether you speak to a winemaker, a farmer, an olive grower, or a fisherman in Italy, you will hear of how the weather plays a role in their livelihood. Even the same varieties of grapes, for example, grown within a particular region, are often different (in terms of flavor, size, and time of maturation) from estate to estate because of the climate in the specific areas where they are grown. Italy is also home to many microclimates, such as the one in the mountains of Calabria in Aspromonte, which is the only place where Bergamot citrus can be grown.

Because of these climatic variances, prior to modernization and industrialization, it was difficult for the masses to enjoy foods from all areas of Italy. Those who lived in the North couldn't afford to have the lush citrus such as clementines, oranges, and lemons from the south on a daily basis. Instead, they became treats that were enjoyed at Christmastime as gifts. The rice used for risotto in the North was not shipped to the South, and was not a part of the local cuisine. Only in modern times is risotto eaten at homes and in restaurants in Southern Italy. Each Italian region had local dialects used in the kitchen (which are still used, but not exclusively), a terrain, and (in the coastal areas) water that determined ingredient availability, and a climate that allowed for specific crops to be grown. For these reasons, regional Italian cuisine developed.

How foreign powers influenced cuisine across geographic locations

As foreign rulers came into power in different places in Italy, they often left their imprint on regional cuisine and took local traditions back to their countries of origin. It's important to realize that some cities in Italy are closer to France or North Africa than they are to Rome — and each region's cuisine reflects this. Sometimes, tourists to Italy eat only in establishments that offer what we consider to be "Italian food," and at first glance they have a hard time distinguishing what is local and what is regional. Scratch a bit below the surface, however, and you will find many unique foods in each Italian region. Here are just a very few of them:

>> **Austrian influences in the Northeast:** In the areas around Venice, in the Veneto and places like Udine, as well as in Trentino Alto Adige where it is estimated that 40 percent of the inhabitants speak German as a first language, you will find local versions of pretzels, sauerkraut, rye bread, goulash, and Austrian-inspired pastries such as Viennoiseries.

>> **Provencal synergy in Genoa and Liguria:** The shared history between Southern France and the Italian Riviera has given way to many similar recipes – from focaccia (fougasse) to pesto (pistou) and the abundant use of chickpea flour.

>> **Greek and Arab influences in Sicily and port cities:** Two waves of Arab occupation — the Aghlabids and the Fatimids — beginning in the ninth and tenth centuries in Sicily introduced mulberries, gelato, lemons, oranges, eggplants, couscous, marzipan, and many other ingredients to the largest island in the Mediterranean. Because Venice, Istanbul (then Constantinople), and Cairo were once sister cities in the spice trade, Venice (along with other port cities such as Genoa) received a great deal of revenue from spices, and they became important in the foods of those regions. Saffron, nutmeg, cinnamon, cloves, and ginger were just a few. Eventually, the spices became synonymous with luxury and holiday dishes, and the ingredients were introduced to the rest of the country.

>> **French influences in Piedmont:** French was the official language of the court until the mid-19th century, and French influences can still be noticed today. Due to the similar terrain, corn, barley, wheat, rye, and oats are grown along with grape orchards, fruit trees, and vegetables. Home to 70 percent of Italy's rice production, along with trout and frogs from the mountain rivers and the presence of the white truffle, French cuisine lends itself to the region.

>> **Spanish Rule:** From the 16th to the 18th century, many Italian states (everyone except Venice) were ruled directly by Aragon, as is evidenced by the many Aragonite castles that dot the Southern Italian coastline. During this time, it

was Spanish, not Italian, interests which were protected in Italy. Many people believe that many modern Italian disparities are rooted in the type of absentee governing and land ownership that began during this time period. The prevalence of tomatoes, chocolate, peppers, corn, and other ingredients brought in by the Spanish from the New World to Europe are culinary staples that were introduced during these times.

>> **The Kingdom of the Two Sicilies:** From 1816 to 1860, from Naples down to Sicily, there was a Kingdom whose rule passed back and forth between the French and Spanish. The Italian south (especially its agriculture) was exploited by foreign influences until the 19th century. Nowadays the culinary influence can be seen very much in the patisserie of the area. Rum baba and brioche are both Neapolitan and French specialties. In Sicily, many Chefs still go by the name Monzu, which is a Sicilianized version of the word *monsieur,* because it was *en vogue* to have a French chef in Sicily during that period.

REMEMBER

It is important to note that the examples above are just a few of the countless ways in which Italy's cuisine was and still is influenced by foreign powers. Throughout the recipe chapters of this book, you also learn a few of the ways in which recipes from Italian regions, such as those of the Florentine courts, inspired other cuisines, such as the Grande Cuisine of Paris, and many others. One of the most beautiful aspects of gastronomy is that the food we eat is always changing, evolving, and adapting to our tastes and needs. The more we know about the history of various cuisines, the better equipped we are to create delicious food and to pass it down to future generations with the power to promote culture and fuel economies.

Mastering Time-Honored Italian Traditions

"La cucina di un popolo è la sola esatta testimonianza della sua civiltà."

"The cuisine of a people is the only true testimony of their civilization."
—ITALIAN PROVERB

Creating traditional Italian food is a respected form of craftsmanship, just as goldsmithing, pottery-making, weaving, playing music, singing, wine-making, painting, sculpting, designing clothes and textiles, and architecture are. Just as one wouldn't normally pick up a paintbrush or sing for the first time and become a master, neither would someone who made pasta or pizza. Mastering Italian cuisine takes desire, passion, commitment, practice, and patience.

Traditional Italian recipes have been perfected over centuries, sometimes even millennia, so it is important to treat them with the respect they deserve. Each Italian dish that we prepare gives us the opportunity to pass down generations of love, talent, knowledge, and culture. Italians believe that by creating the recipes of our ancestors, we continue to honor them even after they leave this world. Carefully adhering to culinary customs is a sign of respect to the community and cultures that created them.

While modern Italian chefs and cooks do take many creative liberties in the kitchen, they do so after mastering the basics and the reasons behind them. If you know, for example, how to make a true *Cacio e pepe* condiment to toss with pasta and its rich history of being prepared by shepherds in the Roman hills, then you are likely to update the recipe while maintaining its integrity. The Italian viewpoint on recipe makeovers is similar to how many people feel about remakes of popular songs. Unless the new version is as good as or better than the original, it's best to stick to tradition. Because Italian cuisine is already revered the whole world over for its taste and appeal, making it better than the original is no short order. Most of us, myself included, are delighted to be able to recreate many of our childhood favorites with as much accuracy and precision as possible.

La bella figura: Using food to make a good impression

If you've spent time in Italy or with Italians, you may have heard the term *la bella figura*, which literally means "the beautiful figure," but transliterated means "a good impression." Food is often intertwined with making a *bella figura* because it is an instrument to use to your favor when you are getting to know someone. If you are going to meet someone, or have been invited somewhere, you can bring an artisan food product, a good bottle of wine, or one of your handmade specialties to them to make a good impression. When entertaining, you should always offer your guests your best recipes, cooked with love. The foods you choose when entertaining (discussed in depth in Chapter 5) should be the best quality, best tasting, and best variety.

To make a *bella figura* when cooking for guests, you should either cook something very homey and close to your heart, or more elaborate dishes that you normally save for special occasions, in order to make a good impression and demonstrate your feelings for them. Doing this shows that you have invested a certain amount of time and care in preparing a meal for your guests, because their presence matters to you. Even a meaningful dish or two prepared with care or some thoughtful edible gift can go a long way in the hands of the receiver.

Staying the course: Italian meal planning

One of the biggest mistakes that non-Italians make when serving Italian food is not in the preparation of recipes themselves, but in the way that they are paired together. Fixed price "Italian" menus in the U.S. and United Kingdom, for example, often offer a soup as an appetizer and a pasta as a main course, which would never be done in Italy. Both soups and pasta dishes are considered first courses. Eating two together would not only be an overkill of calories and food groups, it would also take away from the integrity of each dish, which is meant to lead up to the second course.

These are the components of a traditional complete Italian meal, normally eaten at lunch (when the main meal of the day is eaten), but could also be eaten at dinner, especially if entertaining, or in a restaurant.

>> **Antipasto:** An appetizer begins the meal, although informal family meals and dinners at home might omit this course. Larger holiday meals or special occasion menus offer several appetizers.

>> **Primo:** A first course of pasta, gnocchi, risotto, or soup is always at lunch and sometimes at dinner. This is the heart of the Italian meal, and if you had to make only one dish and omit the rest, this course is it.

>> **Secondo:** A second course of seafood, fish, poultry, eggs, meat, or a vegetarian protein is usually served at lunch and dinner. On special occasions, there are several secondi, and at formal dinners you might have a few separate meat or seafood courses, starting with the lightest and ending with the more robust flavors.

>> **Contorno:** A side dish of cooked vegetables accompanies the secondo in the same course. Holidays and special occasions call for several contorni.

>> **Insalata:** A salad, most typically green or mixed, follows a meal at lunch or dinner.

>> **Frutta/Noci:** A plate of fruit, nuts, and/or cheeses usually follows the meal (sometimes by a few hours) and on regular days replaces dessert. In restaurants, this course is not as commonplace as it once was.

>> **Dolce:** A sweet dessert is usually not eaten at each meal at home, but always on Sunday and holidays and often in restaurants. At holidays and for special occasions, several types of desserts are served.

>> **Caffé:** An espresso coffee is considered to be the period at the end of a meal.

>> **Digestivo:** A digestive liqueur officially concludes a meal and helps to aid digestion.

Pairing complimentary dishes

In Italy a good meal is like a piece of beautiful classical music which requires each instrument and melody to be played in a specific time. The *crescendo*, or the highest point, lies at lunch time, either at the first course, or, if there is a second course, just as it begins. All of the other dishes need to play supporting roles, to either build up to the highest point or delightfully accompany the diner to the conclusion of the meal. From a nutritional standpoint, the various courses also offer more opportunities to showcase a wide range of nutrients from various food groups (protein, carbohydrate, and healthful fats) as well as antioxidant-rich produce.

In each chapter of this book, I give examples on how to pair dishes together so that the flavors build and complement one another. Most recipes have serving and pairing suggestions. A few points to remember — even though you are serving several courses in a meal, they should all go together in the sense that their flavors are complimentary. For example:

>> If you serve a first course with tomato sauce, then the second course is usually roasted, grilled, or pan-fried (but without sauce).

>> Saucy second courses are served with simply dressed first courses that don't overpower them.

>> Textures are also taken into consideration. Each meal should have a soft, saucy component, a fresh, crunch component, al dente pasta (if serving), as well as creaminess, which could come from a soup, a sauce, or a dessert.

REMEMBER

It is important to remember that to an Italian, eating well is a priority, a daily pleasure that we're able to enjoy often. For newcomers to a multicourse meal, it might seem intimidating. Once you begin experimenting, however, you will find an eating strategy that is as healthful as it is delicious.

Chapter 3

Base Recipes: The Backbone of the Italian Kitchen

The recipes in this chapter are hardly anything to brag about. Despite their simplicity, however, they truly are the backbone of the Italian kitchen and having them on hand sets you up for success. Whenever I teach my Mastering Italian Certification Series cooking classes, I always start with these.

In this chapter, you learn how to make fresh bread crumbs, crostini, bruschetta, stocks, beans and legumes, and to prepare fruits and vegetables in advance so you will be able to whip up marvelous Italian meals in minutes.

Introducing the BFFs of Italian Home Cooks

Base recipes like those included in this chapter have long been the best friends of Italian home cooks. Setting out to make every component of the more intricate recipes can be challenging, so savvy homemakers traditionally took advantage of breaks in their schedule to stock their kitchens with time-saving basics. Even though most Italians work outside of the home nowadays, they still rely on these recipes to enable them to pull together authentic dishes whenever the mood strikes.

Waste not: Making bread crumbs, crostini, and bruschette

Because bread is so integral to the Italian culture (see Chapter 21), it is considered sacrilege to waste it. Artisan and homemade breads don't last as long as commercially prepared breads do, because they are free of preservatives. After a day or two, real fresh bread should be hard, and then stale.

TIP

Use leftover bread to create bread crumbs, crostini, and bruschette. Making these items on your own saves time and money, while adding flavor to your recipes. In much less time than it takes to go to the store and purchase pre-made bread crumbs that are full of additives, you can simply put leftover bread in the oven and process it in a food processor. Homemade croutons taste better as well because they are fresher than what you buy in the store. In addition, homemade versions of these everyday items are free from unwanted chemicals and additives, so they are better for your health, too.

Note: Bruschetta is said to be the most mispronounced of all Italian words. The correct pronunciation is broos/KEHT/tah (not broo/SHEH/tah). It is also important to note that Italian words that end with the vowel "a" change to an "e" ending for the plural form. Bruschetta becomes bruschette when plural, pizza becomes pizze, and so on.

Savory stocks: The unsung heroes

Homemade stocks, known as *brodo*, are the unsung heroes of the Italian kitchen. Whether you would like to make an authentic risotto, homemade soup, stew, braised meat or seafood recipe, having healthful stock on hand enhances the flavor of your recipes.

Health-wise, homemade stock can't be beat. Purchased stocks contain a great deal of sodium (even the "low-sodium" varieties contain a hefty amount) and additives, but the homemade versions do not. Flavor-wise, fresh broth can make or break Italian recipes.

TIP

The good news is that stock is very easy and inexpensive to make. Whenever I have leftover skins from onions, carrot or celery tops, shrimp shells, roasted chicken or meat bones, I place them in double plastic bags and refrigerate or freeze them until I am ready to make stock. If you make a stockpot at a time, you can freeze portions in gallon size containers for later use. Each week, place a gallon or two in your refrigerator so that you have it on hand to make your recipes during the week.

The recipes in this book call for homemade stock, and Chapter 5 gives ideas of how a few pantry ingredients can be transformed into a wholesome dinner with the addition of stock.

Beans and legumes provide boundless possibilities

Per the Mediterranean Diet, we should be consuming ½ cup of cooked (¼ cup dry) beans or legumes per day. Many Americans fall short on this requirement, but luckily there are many tasty Italian recipes — from *minestre* and bean, chickpea, and lentil soups to side dishes such as *Cannellini brasati*/Braised Cannellini Beans and classics such as *Fave e cicoria*/Fava Beans with Chicory.

Throughout the centuries, beans and lentils were often dismissed as "poor man's food" and even nowadays are considered vegetarian protein sources that are meat substitutes. However, when we consider how good beans are for our health, how good they are for our environment, and the fact that they lend themselves to so many cooking applications, they should be enjoyed much more often.

In ancient times, lentils were actually a form of currency, and beans were used to count. The power of the ancient Egyptian empire depended upon revenue from lentils because it was the chief exporter of them to the Mediterranean. To this day, we eat lentils on New Year's in Italy to signify prosperity. Whatever your reason for eating them is, having precooked beans on hand makes cooking a cinch.

When purchasing dried beans and lentils, be on the lookout for DOP and IGP Italian varieties, which signal genuine ingredients coming from specific areas with certification from the Italian government. (Chapter 5 talks more about product labeling). For example, you might see *Fagioli Bianchi di Rotonda* DOP, *Fagiolo Cannellino di Atina* DOP, *Fagiolo Cuneo* IGP, *Fagiolo di Lamon della Vallata Bellunese* IGP, and *Fagiolo di Sarconi* IGP or heirloom versions that are being re-introduced to the market for flavor and quality. Otherwise, use your favorite kinds. In Italy, borlotti (Roman), cannellini, and white beans are used most extensively.

TIP

I like to cook beans once a week, at the same time I'm using up my leftover bits to make stock, bread crumbs, and crostini. This way, I know that I have them on hand for the week to add to soups, salads, and pasta dishes, or to purée and use to top crostini or as a bed for vegetables or seafood.

Note that beans and lentils come in many varieties. All dried beans need to be soaked overnight (or covered in boiling water for an hour) before they can be cooked. Lentils come in red, green, brown, and black varieties and do not require soaking before cooking. The red varieties can cook up in as little as 5 minutes — making them one of the most ancient forms of "fast food."

Fruits and vegetables for the healthy win

Having a multicolored selection of fresh fruits and vegetables on hand is paramount in an Italian kitchen. Frozen fruits and vegetables are a good plan B if getting to the market or store often is not an option for you. In addition, Italian cooks have turned to preserved vegetables, in extra virgin olive oil or vinegar, for years to help keep summer's bounty available year-round.

You can combine many different kinds of vegetables with the stock, bean, or lentil recipes in this chapter to make savory soups, or sauté them to top bruschette and crostini. Tossing your favorite mix of fresh vegetables into a salad topped with fresh croutons from the Fresh Bread Crumbs recipe in this chapter can also be a fun way to add a personalized touch to a healthful meal. The Roasted Red Peppers recipe in this chapter provides the perfect topping for bruschette and crostini – perhaps atop a bed of mashed Braised Cannelini Beans (recipe also in this chapter). And turn some tomato purée into tomato sauce that can be used to coat pasta or combined with homemade stock to make an authentic and savory tomato soup.

Molliche di pane/Fresh Bread Crumbs

| PREP TIME: 5 MIN | COOK TIME: 0 MIN | YIELD: 16 SERVINGS |

INGREDIENTS

1 (8-ounce) loaf dense, day-old country-style bread

DIRECTIONS

1 Cut the loaf of bread into 1-inch cubes and, working in batches, if necessary, place them in a food processor, being careful not to fill it more than halfway. Pulse on and off until the crumbs are as fine as possible.

2 If not using immediately, freeze breadcrumbs in a plastic freezer bag for up to a month.

TIP: Try using leftovers from one of the bread recipes from this book to make breadcrumbs. If you are using store-bought bread to make this recipe, it may take a few days for the bread to get hard enough to process into breadcrumbs. If that's the case, either leave the bread uncovered overnight to dry out, or place it in a 200-degree oven until it gets hard and begins to turn color. Allow it to cool, and then grind it.

Crostini

PREP TIME: 5 MIN	COOK TIME: 5 MIN	YIELD: 4 SERVINGS

INGREDIENTS

1 (8-ounce) loaf dense, day-old country-style bread

DIRECTIONS

1 Preheat the broiler to high.

2 Cut slices of Italian-style bread into thin, ¼-inch-wide slices on the diagonal, and place on a baking sheet.

3 Place under the broiler, and toast until golden, 1–2 minutes on each side.

TIP: Crostini can be used as a base for appetizers, placed on the bottom of a bowl as a base for hot soup, or cut into cubes and used as croutons, depending upon your needs.

NOTE: Some people get crostini and bruschetta confused. The main difference between them: Crostini are usually smaller (hence the suffix "ini" at the end of the word) and thinner. They are toasted without the addition of extra virgin olive oil, which is drizzled on them once they are toasted.

VARY IT! The sky is the limit when it comes to the type of crostini toppings you can have. Leftover bits of meat, cheese, seafood, and vegetables make excellent crostini toppers. Chopped fresh tomatoes with garlic, basil, and EVOO are a classic, but marinated seafood, mascarpone cheese with sausage or grilled vegetables, eggplant or bean purées with tomatoes or greens, salt-cod mousse, pesto with octopus, chicken livers, and caramelized onions with pecorino cheese are all great combinations.

Bruschetta

PREP TIME: 5 MIN   COOK TIME: 5 MIN   YIELD: 4 SERVINGS

INGREDIENTS

4 (½-inch) slices ciabatta or other light, crusty, country bread

2 tablespoons Amy Riolo Selections or other good-quality Italian extra virgin olive oil

DIRECTIONS

1   Preheat broiler to high or grill to medium–high.

2   Brush olive oil on both sides of the bread.

3   Grill the bread slices on both sides until grill marks appear, or place under the broiler until golden brown.

TIP: Prepare your toppings ahead of time so you can place them on the hot bread and enjoy the bruschette immediately.

VARY IT! If you use good-quality bread and olive oil, then plain, simple bruschetta can be a decadent snack or accompaniment to soup or salad. To serve them as an appetizer, use your favorite combinations of ingredients. I like to use ricotta cheese, grilled vegetables, or tomatoes and eggplant most often, but there are many options to choose from.

Brodo di verdure/Homemade Vegetable Stock

PREP TIME: 5 MIN	COOK TIME: 30 MIN	YIELD: 8 SERVINGS

INGREDIENTS

1 medium yellow onion, halved (not peeled)

1 carrot, trimmed and halved

1 stalk celery, trimmed and halved (can include leaves, if desired)

4 ounces cherry tomatoes

4 sprigs fresh basil, with stems

1 small bunch (approximately ¾ cup) fresh flat-leaf parsley, with stems

½ teaspoon unrefined sea salt

DIRECTIONS

1 In a large stockpot, place the onion, carrot, celery, tomatoes, basil, and parsley. Cover with 16 cups of water. Bring to a boil over high heat. Reduce the heat to medium-low. Add the salt, and simmer, uncovered, for 30 minutes.

2 Drain the stock, reserving the liquid. Discard the rest. If you're not using it right away, allow to cool and then store in the refrigerator for up to a week or freeze it for up to a month.

Brodo di pesce/Homemade Seafood Stock

| PREP TIME: 15 MIN | COOK TIME: 30 MIN | YIELD: 8 SERVINGS |

INGREDIENTS

1 medium yellow onion, halved (not peeled)

1 carrot, trimmed and halved

1 stalk celery, trimmed and halved

Shells from 2 pounds shrimp or fish bones, or a combination

½ teaspoon unrefined sea salt

1 dried bay leaf

1 tablespoon whole black peppercorns

DIRECTIONS

1 In a large stockpot, place the onion, carrot, celery, and shrimp shells/fish bones. Cover with 16 cups water. Bring to a boil over high heat. Reduce the heat to medium-low.

2 Skim off the residue that forms on top of the stock, and discard. Add the salt, bay leaf, and peppercorns. Simmer, uncovered, for about 30 minutes.

3 Drain the stock, reserving the liquid. Discard the rest. If you're not using it right away, allow to cool, and then store in the refrigerator for three days or freeze for up to a month.

Brodo di pollo/Homemade Chicken Stock

PREP TIME: 5 MIN	COOK TIME: 40 MIN	YIELD: 8 SERVINGS

INGREDIENTS

1 medium yellow onion, halved (not peeled)

1 medium carrot, trimmed and halved

1 medium stalk celery, trimmed and halved

1¼ pounds chicken bones or carcass from cooked chicken

1 teaspoon whole black peppercorns

1 dried bay leaf

½ teaspoon unrefined sea salt

DIRECTIONS

1 In a large stockpot, place the onion, carrot, celery, chicken bones, peppercorns, and bay leaf. Cover with 16 cups water. Bring to a boil over high heat. Reduce the heat to medium-low.

2 Skim off the residue that forms on top of the stock, and discard. Add the salt, and simmer, uncovered, for 40 minutes.

3 Drain the stock, reserving the liquid. Discard the rest. If you're not using it right away, allow to cool, and then store in the refrigerator or freezer.

Brodo di carne/Homemade Meat Stock

INGREDIENTS

1 medium yellow onion, halved (not peeled)

1 medium carrot, trimmed and halved

1 medium stalk celery, trimmed and halved

1¼ pounds roasted meat bones

1 teaspoon whole black peppercorns

1 dried bay leaf

½ teaspoon unrefined sea salt

DIRECTIONS

1 In a large stockpot, place the onion, carrot, celery, meat bones, peppercorns, and bay leaf. Cover with 16 cups water. Bring to a boil over high heat. Reduce the heat to medium-low.

2 Skim off the residue that forms on top of the stock, and discard. Add the salt, and simmer, uncovered, for 2 hours.

3 Drain the stock, reserving the liquid. Discard the rest. If you're not using it right away, allow to cool, and then store in the refrigerator or freezer.

Fagioli secchi/Dried Beans

PREP TIME: 1 HOUR | **COOK TIME: 30 MIN** | **YIELD: 8 SERVINGS**

INGREDIENTS

1 cup dried beans (any variety)

¼ teaspoon unrefined sea salt

DIRECTIONS

1 Place the beans in a stockpot, and cover with cold water; leave to soak overnight. (If you're short on time, place the beans in a stockpot, cover with boiling water, and leave to soak for 1 hour instead.)

2 Drain the soaked beans, and place them in a saucepan. Add the salt, cover the beans with water, and bring to a boil over high heat.

3 Reduce the heat to medium-low, cover, and let cook until the beans are tender, about 25 to 50 minutes. (It may take longer depending on the size of the beans.)

4 Drain and cool. If not using right away, store in an airtight container in the refrigerator for up to one week.

Cannellini brasati/Braised Cannellini Beans

PREP TIME: 5 MIN PLUS AT LEAST 8 HOURS FOR SOAKING	COOK TIME: 40 MIN	YIELD: 8 SERVINGS

INGREDIENTS

1 cup dried cannellini beans

4 rosemary sprigs, divided

1 tablespoon Amy Riolo Selections or other good-quality extra virgin olive oil

¼ teaspoon unrefined sea salt

DIRECTIONS

1 In a large bowl, add the cannellini beans and enough cold water to cover them by 4 inches. Let soak in a cool place or in the refrigerator for at least 8 hours or overnight.

2 Drain the beans and transfer them to a 2-quart saucepan. Pour in enough water to cover by 1 inch, and drop in two rosemary sprigs. Bring the water to a boil, and then lower the heat so the water is barely at a simmer. Cook until the beans are tender but not mushy, with just enough liquid to cover them, about 30-40 minutes. (If necessary, add more water, 1 tablespoon at a time, to keep the beans covered as they simmer.)

3 Remove the beans from the heat and gently stir in the olive oil, the sea salt, and the remaining two rosemary sprigs. Let the beans stand to cool and absorb the cooking liquid. The end result should be tender beans with a creamy consistency in just enough liquid to coat them. If you're not using them right away, store the beans in an airtight container in the refrigerator up to one week.

Lenticchie/Lentils

PREP TIME: 5 MIN	COOK TIME: 30 MIN	YIELD: 6 SERVINGS

INGREDIENTS

1 cup dried lentils (any variety)

¼ teaspoon unrefined sea salt

¼ teaspoon black pepper, freshly ground

1 bay leaf

DIRECTIONS

1 Rinse the lentils in a colander.

2 Place the lentils in a saucepan, and add enough water to cover them twice (you should have twice as much water as lentils). Add the sea salt, pepper, and bay leaf. Bring to a boil over high heat. Reduce the heat to low, and simmer, uncovered, until the lentils are tender, about 5–30 minutes depending on the variety. (Red lentils are the quickest-cooking variety, followed by green and brown, and then black.)

3 If you're not using them right away, store cooked lentils in an airtight container in the refrigerator up to one week.

JARRING THE PURÉE

True Italian cooks will not buy jarred tomato purée. Traditionally, many people enjoy the late summer ritual of jarring their own sauce when tomatoes are at their peak. If you'd like to start your own ritual, this is how it's done.

1. Sterilize the jars you need for the amount of purée you have.

2. Place two or three basil leaves in each freshly sterilized jar, and pour in the purée using a funnel. Fill almost to the edge, and close with a screw-on cap.

3. Select a pot large enough to accommodate the jars, fill it with water, and bring it to a boil over high heat.

4. Wrap each jar with a dishcloth, place it in the large pot, and ensure that the jars are covered in water up to the three-quarter mark.

5. Simmer over low heat for 30 minutes, and then let the jars cool in the water.

6. Once cold, remove the jars from the pot, dry them, and make sure the lid has been vacuum-sealed by pressing on the cap. If the lid is slightly concave, dipping in toward the center, the seal is good. If you hear a clacking sound, however, it means that the vacuum seal has failed. In this case, you'll have to start again from the beginning or freeze the purée.

7. When the seal is tight, with no "click-clack," your purée is ready. Place it in the pantry and look forward to savoring the intense and lingering taste of these tomatoes even in December, taking you back to the warm light of summer days.

Pepperoni rossi arrostiti/Roasted Red Peppers

PREP TIME: 5 MIN	COOK TIME: 40 MIN	YIELD: 4 SERVINGS

INGREDIENTS

4 red bell peppers (keep whole)

1 tablespoon Amy Riolo Selections or other good-quality extra virgin olive oil

DIRECTIONS

1 Preheat the oven to 500 degrees.

2 On a baking sheet, place the whole bell peppers. Bake until the skins are wrinkled and the peppers are charred, about 30–40 minutes, being sure to turn them each time a side is charred (approximately twice during cooking).

3 Remove from the oven, and cover tightly with aluminum foil to create steam. Set aside.

4 When peppers are cool enough to handle, after about 30 minutes, cut into quarters, peel off the skin, and remove the seeds. Add to your favorite recipe or, if not eating immediately, place the pepper pieces in a jar, cover with olive oil for additional flavor and nutrition, and seal with a lid; refrigerate up to 2 weeks. Before using, drain the oil from the peppers; reserve the oil in the refrigerator for another use.

Passata di pomodoro/Tomato Purée

PREP TIME: 5 MIN	COOK TIME: 30 MIN	YIELD: 6 SERVINGS

INGREDIENTS

2 pounds ripe San Marzano or other plum tomatoes

Handful of fresh basil leaves, washed and dried

DIRECTIONS

1 Wash and dry tomatoes, remove the stems, and cut them in half.

2 Fill a large stockpot three-fourths of the way with water, and place over high heat.

3 Bring to a boil, and carefully lower in tomatoes with a large spoon.

4 Boil, uncovered, until the skins start to break.

5 Drain and allow to cool enough to handle.

6 Put the tomatoes through a food mill in order to remove the skins.

7 If the tomato juice is very thin, return it to the stockpot and boil for 15-30 minutes until it has thickened slightly. Use immediately to make tomato sauce, or jar or freeze the purée for later use.

TIP: The water content in the tomatoes that you use makes a big difference in the thickness of your purée. While you could technically use any type of tomatoes that you prefer, I highly recommend firm, ripe, plum-style tomatoes that yield a better consistency for this purpose.

This recipe calls for a very small number of tomatoes, enough to be used in one recipe. You can use much larger quantities to make extra purée for jarring to use until the next year's tomato season. You can also freeze batches to use later.

NOTE: In Italy, people usually make purée once a year at the end of tomato season and preserve the tomatoes to use in all of their recipes throughout the year, so that they do not have to purchase purée from the store. Many families get together and make an annual event out of the tomato preserving process.

Chapter 4

Cooking with an Eye on the Calendar

Glancing through a calendar, an Italian cook won't just think about what they have to do, they'll also think about what they *get* to cook, and of course, serve and eat!

REMEMBER

There are three key factors to pay attention to when menu planning, and they are what I refer to as the three S's: seasons, Sundays, and special occasions (holidays).

In this chapter, you learn how and what to cook for the seasons, Sundays (or your day of rest), and special occasions, Italian-style with menus and suggestions using the recipes in this book exclusively. These menus are simple guides that demonstrate the progression of customary courses and the way ingredients are paired together and used seasonally. Feel free to alter them to suit your needs and tastes.

Seasonality in the Italian Kitchen

Given the international popularity of Italian food, the importance of seasonality often gets lost in translation. *Pasta al pomodoro* is available year-round, despite tomato season being in the summer, because of jarring methods (see Chapter 3) which have been used since antiquity. Thick, heavy sauces and rich lasagne that are normally reserved for wintertime Sundays and holidays in Italy can be found any day of the week abroad. To make matters worse, supermarkets offer many of the same types of produce all year round, so the average American doesn't really know what is in season and when, with the exception of a few favorites such as springtime berries and summer corn. It's no wonder, then, that Italian food lovers abroad get easily confused when planning seasonal menus.

The section below talks about what Italians typically prepare in various seasons. Keep in mind, however, that climates are different. While you never want to skimp on quality or freshness, any Italian cook will tell you it's better to recreate a recipe with seasonal ingredients in your area than to purchase out-of-season items just to recreate a recipe. Fresh, in-season produce is the best for our bodies because it contains the nutrients we need at that time of year. In addition, eating seasonal produce is better for the environment, and less expensive, so it's a good idea to incorporate it regardless of the cuisine you are creating.

Because the roots of Italian culinary history lie in antiquity, when agrarian gods were praised for bountiful crops, produce has made up the majority of the traditional diet. Fresh fruits, vegetables, and grains were supplemented with seafood and meat, which also varied from season to season. Over time, these culinary combinations became part of the Italian gastronomic imprint. For many people, recreating them is second nature. Most Italian cooks don't stop to think about why lamb and artichokes are eaten in spring, or how mushrooms and game are eaten in fall; it has been that way for ages. As we learn to master Italian cuisine, however, it's important to take these factors into consideration and to be aware of their existence. After we have done that, we can successfully adapt them to fit with our environs outside of Italy.

Sampling Everyday Menus for Every Season

To me, making menus is one of the most pleasurable experiences in life. In a well-planned menu, seasonality, nutrition, taste, texture, aroma, and terroir (flavors imparted by the local terrain) work together through a series of courses to create a perfectly balanced eating experience.

While it might sound intimidating to some, many of the principles of food pairing are so embedded in our memories that it seems as though certain foods just naturally go together. If you've never created a menu before, use the following guidelines until you are comfortable with the process. Notice how the elements of the

Italian meals you enjoy the most work together, and apply those principles in your own kitchen.

TIP

Here are a few tips:

>> Traditional, complete Italian meals consist of an appetizer, a first course, a second course with a side dish, salad, fruit and nuts or cheese, and/or a dessert and a cup of espresso followed by a *digestivo*, or after dinner liqueur (such as grappa, Amaro, Sambuca, or Limoncello) — served in that order.

>> In today's hurried culture, even in Italy, the full traditional meal is often only served on Sundays (when most Italians still participate in the ritual family meal), when entertaining, in fine-dining situations, or on holidays.

>> Workday lunches may now consist of a primo (first course), salad, and espresso (often omitting the second course).

>> Workday dinners may consist of a second course, side dish, salad, fruit and cheese, and espresso (often omitting the appetizer and first course).

>> Pasta, risotto, or gnocchi is typically present in Italian lunches.

>> Fresh, seasonal, local, organic foods are always preferred.

>> Pasta dishes are never preceded by soup. Soup can be enjoyed on its own, or as a first course instead of pasta.

A sample springtime meal

Springtime dishes in Italy consist of a symphony of fresh flavors. Gardens give way to certain varieties of artichokes, fava beans and legumes, baby potatoes and carrots, spinach, fennel, peas, and asparagus, just to name a few of the ingredients that are available. Apricots and citrus are also usually plentiful. In terms of meat, lamb, veal, and kid take center stage because, in the way they were traditionally raised, they were old enough to be slaughtered in the spring. For that reason, lamb and goat in the south are usually served at Eastertime, along with a variety of other fresh ingredients.

Keep in mind that you should always adjust the ingredients to reflect what's in season in your area in the springtime, but the techniques and recipes still work well.

Table 4-1 outlines a typical (non-holiday or Sunday) springtime meal with dishes that can be created from this book. I have replaced the dessert course with *frutta* options from the fruit, cheese, and nut course (see Chapter 17) because this is an everyday menu. If you wanted to turn it into a Sunday menu, simply add dessert and swap out the pasta and the main course for longer cooking items.

TABLE 4-1:

Springtime Meal Menu

Course	Recipe	Location
Antipasto	*Crostini con purea di cannellini/*Crostini with Cannellini Bean Purée	Chapter 6
Primo	*Spaghetti al limone/*Lemon-Infused Spaghetti	Chapter 8
Secondo	*Scaloppine di vitello/*Veal Cutlets	Chapter 13
Contorno	*Asparagi grigliati con balsamico bianco e parmigiano/*Chargrilled Asparagus with White Balsamic and Parmesan	Chapter 14
Insalata	*Insalata verde/*Green Salad	Chapter 15
Frutta	*Susine grigliate con ricotta e miele/*Grilled Plums with Ricotta and Honey	Chapter 17
Caffé	*Caffé/*Classic Espresso	Chapter 16

A sample summertime meal

Summer in Italy is all about keeping cool and the opportunity to head to the sea or the mountains to do so. Until the late 20th century, air conditioning was not used, and seasonal produce was used to promote cooling effects and the nutrients needed during the hot months. Many Italians who live in large cities own or rent homes at the beach or in the mountains, specifically for the purpose of spending time in the summer (especially August) away from the city heat.

Seafood, lighter meats, poultry, tomatoes, eggplant, peppers, fresh herbs, greens, zucchini, melons, and berries take center stage during the warmer months. Chilled soups, cool *carpaccios*, pasta and rice salads, and fresh, light sauces are part of summer repertoires. Heavy sauces, intense baking, and rich, intricate recipes are avoided in the heat. Pizza, though, is still enjoyed, especially so at the beach and during summer evenings. In terms of cooking methods, grilling, pan-frying, and raw foods are the most commonly used applications when warmer temperatures abound.

Table 4-2 outlines a typical (non-holiday or Sunday) summer meal with dishes that can be created from this book. I have replaced the dessert course with *frutta* options from the fruit, cheese, and nut course (see Chapter 17) because this is an everyday menu. If you wanted to turn it into a Sunday menu, simply add dessert and swap out the pasta and the main course for longer cooking items.

TABLE 4-2: ## Summer Meal Menu

Course	Recipe	Location
Antipasto	*Bruschetta con pomodori*/Tomato Bruschetta	Chapter 6
Primo	*Trofie al pesto*/Trofie Pasta with Pesto Sauce	Chapter 9
	OR	
	Dried pasta with same Pesto Sauce	
Secondo	*Polpo alla griglia*/Marinated Grilled Octopus	Chapter 11
	OR	
	Petto di pollo marinato/Marinated Chicken Breasts	Chapter 12
Contorno	*Verdure grigliate*/Grilled Mixed Vegetables	Chapter 14
Insalata	*Insalata di pomodori e peperoni*/Tomato and Roasted Pepper Salad	Chapter 15
Frutta	*Frutta estiva*/Summer Fruit Platter	Chapter 17
Caffé	*Caffé*/Classic Espresso	Chapter 16

A sample fall meal

Warm, cozy, Italian fall flavors conjure up images of foraging in the woods, heady herbal notes of sage and rosemary, and a cornucopia of autumn produce. Bright squash, pumpkin, root vegetables, apples, pears, raspberries, poultry, meat, and game are traditionally eaten during these months. Warm, comforting soups and more intricate pastas are also enjoyed as things in the kitchen start to heat up for the holidays.

Table 4-3 outlines a typical (non-holiday or Sunday) fall meal with dishes that can be created from this book. I have replaced the dessert course with *frutta* options from the fruit, cheese, and nut course (see Chapter 17) because this is an everyday menu. If you wanted to turn it into a Sunday menu, simply add dessert and swap out the pasta and the main course for longer cooking items.

A sample winter meal

Winter cooking in Italy is all about warmth, comfort, and reliving the kitchen memories we grew up with. Slowly pouring hot broth into risotto, kneading dough for pasta, and shaping breads into edible masterpieces before baking are nostalgic recollections that cold weather gives us the permission and inspiration to indulge in. During the winter months, Italians eat more nutrient-dense foods and spend more time cooking them.

TABLE 4-3:

Fall Meal Menu

Course	Recipe	Location
Antipasto	*Antipasti misti (salumi e formaggi)*/Antipasto Platter	Chapter 6
Primo	*Crema di castagna*/Cream of Chestnut Soup	Chapter 10
Secondo	*Scallopine di tacchino*/Turkey Cutlets	Chapter 12
Contorno	*Patate arrostite*/Roasted Potatoes	Chapter 14
Insalata	*Insalata mista*/Mixed Green Salad	Chapter 15
Frutta	*Vassoio di formaggi*/Cheese Platter	Chapter 17
Caffé	*Caffé*/Classic Espresso	Chapter 16

It's important to remember that in ancient times, winter recipes were prepared over open hearths, which helped to heat not only the food, but also families. Large, brick ovens and fireplaces helped keep our kitchen and home warm all winter long when I was young. Nowadays, obviously, modern homes have centralized heating, but there's still something undeniably cozy about indulging in the warmth of fire and slowly-simmering recipes on the stove and in the oven.

Table 4-4 outlines a typical (non-holiday or Sunday) winter meal with dishes that can be created from this book. I have replaced the dessert course with *frutta* options from the fruit, cheese, and nut course (see Chapter 17) because this is an everyday menu. If you wanted to turn it into a Sunday menu, simply add dessert and swap out the pasta and the main course for longer cooking items.

TABLE 4-4:

Winter Meal Menu

Course	Recipe	Location
Antipasto	*Crostini con purea di cannellini*/Crostini with Cannellini Bean Purée	Chapter 6
Primo	*Risotto allo zafferano*/Risotto Milanese	Chapter 10
Secondo	*Pollo in umido*/Chicken, Tomato, and Pepper Stew	Chapter 12
Contorno	*Finocchio in padella con scalogni e castagne*/Pan-fried Fennel, Shallots, and Chestnuts	Chapter 14
Insalata	*Insalata Siciliana con le patate*/Sicilian Salad with Potatoes	Chapter 15
Frutta	*Macedonia di frutta con noci*/Fruit Salad with Walnuts	Chapter 17
Caffé	*Caffé*/Classic Espresso	Chapter 16

Savoring Extended Sunday and Holiday Meals

Sundays and holidays provide an opportunity for families to rest, relax, congregate and eat well. Historically speaking, the day of rest was one in which people would save the best cuts of meat, prepare more time-consuming recipes, and share the bounty of their garden with their loved ones. Sundays are like a little holiday during each week where the old adage "a Sunday well spent brings a week of content" gets represented well in the kitchen.

Larger holidays offer a much larger culinary stage where we can showcase traditional recipes that are often prepared only once or twice a year, and awaited with much anticipation. Sundays and holidays are indeed a time when our schedule, budgets, and calorie counting are set aside to enjoy *la dolce vita* (the sweet life), and that, of course, starts in the kitchen!

Sunday suppers

According to a recent Italian news report, 70 percent of modern Italians still observe the traditional *pranzo domenicale* or Sunday lunch tradition. Customarily, Italians both in the United States and abroad congregate with their families on Sundays. Traditionally, this included not only the nuclear family, but also grandparents, aunts, uncles, and cousins. Being invited to a *pranzo domenicale* of a family other than your own denotes a deep level of friendship and a familial closeness.

Sunday lunches are usually held a bit later than the typical 1 p.m. and last for hours. Common times for the *pranzo della domenica* are 2-6 p.m. or 3-7 p.m. For that reason, the foods served on this occasion overlap lunch and dinner. Many of the customs surrounding this meal were based on Roman Catholicism. Families did not eat meat from Friday until after having taken communion on Sunday at mass. Slowly simmered *ragú* was the perfect after-church treat and has become ubiquitous on Sundays in Italy, as have meatballs (served as a second course), roasts, and stews.

Homemade pasta dishes, elaborate sauces, and homey, regional cuisine is often commonplace on Sundays in Italy. Even though the religious significance is no longer the main reason that many people eat this way on Sunday, it is still the culturally preferred way of eating, and many families continue to cook these types of meals on a weekly basis. Modern families also enjoy the *pranzo domenicale* in restaurants on occasion. Even though they are eaten outside the home, the spirit, conviviality, and family nature of the meals, as well as their length, are still the same.

TIP

People who cook Sunday and holiday meals, mind you, don't do it all in one day. They plan ahead. Preparing sauces and doughs in advance and having a game plan along with a menu can make the task much more fun and less complicated. Plus, thinking about the Sunday meal can be a fun diversion in the early parts of the week. To make your own Sunday meal, look at the suggested seasonal menus above and do some of these:

>> Add another appetizer or two.

>> Add a proper (sweet) dessert after the fruit course or purchase pastries from a local pastry shop.

>> Serve homemade or artisan bread with the meal.

>> In place of all first and second courses (with the exception of the heat of summer), serve *Tagliatelle Bolognese*/Tagliatelle with Meat Ragú with a seasonal appetizer, salad, and dessert.

Tables 4-5 through 4-8 provide example menus by season.

TABLE 4-5: ## Spring Sunday Menu

Course	Recipe	Location
Antipasto	*Crostini con purea di cannellini/ Crostini with Cannellini Bean Purée*	Chapter 6
Primo	*Tagliatelle con salsa di ricotta e basilico/*Tagliatelle with Basil Ricotta Cream Sauce	Chapter 8
Secondo	*Pollo al forno con patate e carrote/*Roasted Chicken with Potatoes and Carrots	Chapter 12
Contorno	*Verdure in aglio, olio, e pepperoncino/*Greens Sautéed in Garlic, Olive Oil, and Pepperoncino	Chapter 14
Insalata	*Insalata di cetrioli, fagiolini, ed olive/*Cucumber, Green Bean, and Olive Salad	Chapter 15
Frutta	*Fragole in aceto balsamico/*Strawberries in Balsamic Vinegar	Chapter 17
Dolce	*Torta Caprese/*Capri-Style Chocolate and Almond Cake	Chapter 18
Caffé	*Caffé/*Classic Espresso	Chapter 16

TABLE 4-6:

Summer Sunday Menu

Course	Recipe	Location
Antipasto	*Caponata*/Sicilian Sweet and Sour Eggplant Medley	Chapter 6
Primo	*Sugu alla norma*/Tomato Eggplant Sauce **OR** Fresh Tomato Sauce with FRESH pasta of your choice from Chapter 9	Chapter 7
Secondo	*Spiedini di pesce*/Grilled Fish Skewers **OR** *Pesce spada alla griglia*/ Calabrian-Style Grilled Swordfish	Chapter 11
Contorno	*Peperonata*/Roasted Mixed Pepper Medley	Chapter 14
Insalata	*Insalata di cetrioli, fagiolini, ed olive*/Cucumber, Green Bean, and Olive Salad	Chapter 15
Frutta	*Macedonia*/Fruit Salad	Chapter 17
Dolce	*Torta di ciliege, mandorle, ed olio d'oliva*/Cherry, Almond, and Olive Oil Cake	Chapter 18
Caffè	*Caffè*/Classic Espresso	Chapter 16

TABLE 4-7:

Fall Sunday Menu

Course	Recipe	Location
Antipasto	*Funghi ripieni*/Stuffed Mushrooms	Chapter 6
Primo	*Gnocchi di patate*/Potato Gnocchi **OR** *Farrotto*/Farro "Risotto"	Chapter 10
Secondo	*Filetto di manzo marinato*/Rosemary and Balsamic Marinated Filet of Beef	Chapter 13
Contorno	*Finocchio in padella con scalogni e castagne*/Pan-fried Fennel, Shallots, and Chestnuts	Chapter 14
Insalata	*Insalata di pomodori e peperoni*/Tomato and Roasted Pepper Salad	Chapter 15
Frutta	*Pere cotte al cioccolato*/Poached Pears in Chocolate	Chapter 17
Dolce	*Tiramisù*	Chapter 18
Caffè	*Caffè*/Classic Espresso	Chapter 16

TABLE 4-8:

Winter Sunday Menu

Course	Recipe	Location
Antipasto	*Polenta grigliata*/Grilled Polenta	Chapter 10
Primo	*Orzotto*/Pearl Barley Risotto with Radicchio and Taleggio Cheese Fondue	Chapter 10
	OR	
	Ravioli Capresi/Capri-Style Ravioli	Chapter 9
	OR	
	Cavatelli con sugo/Calabrian Cavatelli with Spicy Tomato Sauce	Chapter 9
Secondo	*Vrasciole*/Calabrian Meatballs	Chapter 13
Contorno	*Patate raganate*/Calabrian Potato Gratin	Chapter 14
Insalata	*Insalata di ceci*/Chickpea Salad	Chapter 15
Frutta	*Mele al forno con crema ed amaretti*/Roasted Apples with Cream and Amaretti	Chapter 17
Dolce	*Torta di nocciola*/Piemontese Hazelnut Cake	Chapter 18
Caffé	*Caffé*/Classic Espresso	Chapter 16

Christmas and winter holiday menus

The Christmas season in Italy starts, culturally speaking, with the first Sunday of Advent and lasts through Epiphany. In addition to Christmas Eve and Christmas Day, important Saints' Days such as Santa Lucia (December 13) and Santo Stefano (December 26) also fall in December. New Year's Eve and New Year's Day, are also celebrated joyfully. It is only after Epiphany on January 7 that the Christmas season ends. Additional winter holidays include San Valentino or St. Valentine's Day, and Carnevale (Mardi Gras) before Lent begins.

On the feast of Santa Lucia, various towns have their own sweet and savory baked goods that are enjoyed in addition to wintertime foods. *Occhi di Santa Lucia*/Santa Lucia's Eyes Cookies are a traditional sweet enjoyed for breakfast or dessert, dunked in coffee or sweet wine for the occasion. On Epiphany, *La Befana* is celebrated. *La Befana* is a good witch who not only rewards children for good (and punishes them for bad) behavior on the Eve of Epiphany, but is also credited with sweeping away negative energy from previous years. Italian children hang stockings for her to fill on December 6. Cutout cookies in the shapes of stars and stockings, cakes, and stocking-shaped *pizze* and *calzoni* are made in her honor.

Much like in the United States, Valentine's Day meals are all about the romance, and some cooks like to amp things up with aphrodisiac ingredients such as oysters, chili, spices, and chocolate. There are no set dishes for St. Valentine's Day, but fine dining and elegance are synonymous with the holiday based upon St. Valentine secretly marrying young Roman couples against the will of the government in Terni, Italy.

Christmas meals usually consist of a *cenone*, or a large meal, on Christmas Eve. Because people couldn't eat meat prior to midnight mass on Christmas Eve, the large meal typically consisted of seafood and is where the Italian-American tradition of the Feast of the Seven Fishes began. You can read more about this in Chapter 11, but keep in mind that you can have a lovely, authentic Italian Christmas Eve without seven different types of seafood; that's not a common practice throughout Italy today. Pasta with seafood and fish or a seafood-based second course will still be delicious, nutritious, and authentic. See Table 4-9 for an example Christmas Eve menu.

A Christmas Day meal is like a greatly amplified Sunday winter meal. Many families eat *Tortellini in brodo* as a primo, followed by roasted meats. Others eat lasagne, baked pastas, or other family favorites. The meal usually takes place mid-afternoon and lasts for a long time. Table 4-10 features dishes that my family likes to serve, but you can feel free to change things up. Note that it is not typical to serve fish on Christmas Day since that is what the Christmas Eve *cenone* is based on.

Obviously, several cookies and desserts are traditional at Christmas, just as in other places. Even though people usually don't eat all of them at one sitting, it is nice to have them on hand and to give as edible gifts. The *Biscotti di regina*/Calabrian Sesame Cookies are traditionally enjoyed at Christmas and Santo Stefano, which is the following day. On December 26, many Italian families take walks outside and go to visit extended family and friends that they couldn't be with on Christmas itself. Whenever you go to visit someone else, it is nice to have these treats on hand to offer them.

Lent, Easter, and spring holiday menus

Meat was traditionally not eaten from Friday until Sunday mass in the Catholic church, but nowadays it is usually only abstained from on Fridays and during Holy Week during Lent. In the past, sugar and dairy were often refrained from, so there are some historical recipes that do not include those ingredients, made specifically for Lent. Today, typical late winter and spring fare is consumed with special attention to eating seafood on Friday. There are no set Lenten menus.

TABLE 4-9:

Christmas Eve Menu

Course	Recipe	Location
Antipasto	*Giardiniera/*Quick Italian Pickles	Chapter 6
	*Insalata di mare/*Seafood Salad	
	*Gamberi al limone e rosmarino/*Lemon and Rosemary Scented Shrimp	
Primo	*Pasta con tonno e finocchio/*Bucatini with Fresh Tuna and Fennel	Chapter 8
Secondo	*Pesce in acqua pazza/*Neapolitan-Style Fish in Crazy Water	Chapter 11
	*Involtini di tonno e melanzane/*Fresh Tuna and Eggplant Roulades	
	*Cozze in brodo con pomodori e zafferano/*Mussels in Tomato Saffron Broth	
	*Capesante con salsa di balsamico bianco/*Scallops with White Balsamic Sauce	
Contorno	*Finocchio in padella con scalogni e castagne/*Pan-fried Fennel, Shallots, and Chestnuts	Chapter 14
Insalata	*Insalata di riso/*Sicilian Rice Salad	Chapter 15
Frutta	*Macedonia di frutta con noci/*Fruit Salad with Walnuts	Chapter 17
Dolce	*Struffoli/*Neapolitan Honey Drenched Fritters	Chapter 18
	Cannoli	Chapter 18
	*Petrali Cucidati/*Southern-Italian Fig Cookies	Chapter 19
	*Mostaccioli/*Chocolate Holiday Cookies	Chapter 19
Caffè	*Caffè/*Classic Espresso	Chapter 16

During Carnevale, there are several sweet treats such as *Pignolata* (which is similar to *Struffoli*), *Chiacchiere* (fried pastry fritters called "gossips"), and other sweet fried treats. *Zeppole di San Giuseppe/*St. Joseph's Day Cream Puffs are made in honor of St. Joseph (the patron saint of pastry chefs), along with a large meal including fava beans in some areas. St. Joseph's Day is also Father's Day in Italy.

TABLE 4-10: ## Christmas Day Menu

Course	Recipe	Location
Antipasto	*Antipasti misti (salumi e formaggi)*/Antipasto Platter	Chapter 6
	Vrasciole/Calabrian Meatballs	Chapter 13
	Suppli al telefono/Roman Risotto Croquettes	Chapter 10
Primo	*Lasagne classica*/Homemade Lasagna Bolognese-Style	Chapter 9
Secondo	*Filetto di manzo marinato*/Rosemary and Balsamic Marinated Filet of Beef	Chapter 13
Contorno	*Patate raganate*/Calabrian Potato Gratin	Chapter 14
	Peperonata/Roasted Mixed Pepper Medley	
Insalata	*Insalata Caprese*/Caprese Salad (shaped into candy canes)	Chapter 15
Frutta	*Ficchi secchi al cioccolato*/Almond-Stuffed Dried Figs in Chocolate	Chapter 17
Dolce	*Struffoli*/Neapolitan Honey-Drenched Fritters	Chapter 18
	Petrali cucidati/Southern-Italian Fig Cookies	Chapter 19
	Mostaccioli/Chocolate Holiday Cookies	Chapter 19
	Biscotti di Regina/Calabrian Sesame Cookies	Chapter 19
Caffé	*Caffé*/Classic Espresso	Chapter 16

On Easter, egg-based dishes such as *Frittate* and sweets as well as breads and savory pies made with eggs are traditional (see Table 4-11). Fresh spring vegetables such as artichokes, asparagus, fava beans, carrots, and baby vegetables are all featured. In Calabria, my family makes *Cozzupe di Pasqua*/Calabrian Easter Bread to eat at breakfast on Easter morning and to distribute, while the more well-known *Colomba*/Traditional Easter Dove Bread is eaten throughout the country and enjoyed internationally. The *Pastiera*/Neapolitan Easter Pie is a must in the Campania region, while others make *Zuccotto*/Florentine Cream-Filled Dome Cake and Sicilians make *Cassata Siciliana*/Sicilian Ricotta-Filled Cassata Cake for dessert. See Chapters 18 and 19 for more information on these sweet treats.

TABLE 4-11: ## Easter Menu

Course	Recipe	Location
Antipasto	*Frittata di carciofi, asparagi, e cipolle caramellate*/Artichoke, Asparagus, and Caramelized Onion Frittata	(An adaptation of *Frittata di verdure*/Mixed Vegetable Frittata in Chapter 12.)
Primo	*Ravioli Capresi*/Capri-Style Ravioli	Chapter 10
Secondo	*Capretto al forno*/Roasted Kid **OR** *Agnello al forno*/Roasted Lamb **OR** *Polpette d'agnello*/Lamb Meatballs	Chapter 13
Contorno	*Asparagi grigliati con balsamico bianco e parmigiano*/Chargrilled Asparagus with White Balsamic and Parmesan	Chapter 14
Insalata	*Insalata Siciliana con le patate*/Sicilian Salad with Potatoes	Chapter 15
Frutta	*Vassoio di formaggi*/Cheese Platter *Fragole in aceto balsamico*/Strawberries in Balsamic Vinegar	Chapter 17
Dolce	*Pastiera Napoletana*/Neapolitan Easter Pie **OR**	Chapter 19
	Zuccotto/Florentine Cream-Filled Dome Cake **OR**	Chapter 18
	Cassata Siciliana/Sicilian Ricotta-Filled Cassata Cake	Chapter 18
Caffè	*Caffè*/Classic Espresso	Chapter 16

Ferragosto and summer special occasion menus

August 15 is known as *Ferragosto* in Italy. This national holiday dates back to Roman times (18 C.E.) when the Emperor Ottaviano Augusto celebrated the harvests and the end of the main agricultural crop season. Everyone was granted a holiday, which they celebrated with vacations, food, and merrymaking.

Today, that spirit is still deeply embedded into the Italian culture and even the most diligent workers manage to escape. Vacations, family meals, and picnics are the top priority of most Italians today, and the *pranzo* or lunch of the *Ferragosto* is highly anticipated. There are no set menus for *Ferragosto*, or for other summer special occasions, so you can freely choose recipes and dishes that inspire you most. Table 4-12 features one of my favorite menus.

TABLE 4-12:

Ferragosto and Summer Special Occasion Meal Menu

Course	Recipe	Location
Antipasto	*Polpette di melanzane/*Eggplant Croquettes	Chapter 6
Primo	*Spaghetti al limone/*Lemon-Infused Spaghetti	Chapter 8
Secondo	*Cotolette d'agnello alla griglia/*Grilled Lamb Chops	Chapter 13
Contorno	*Verdure grigliate/*Grilled Mixed Vegetables	Chapter 14
Insalata	*Insalata di pomodori e peperoni/*Tomato and Roasted Pepper Salad	Chapter 15
Frutta	*Frutta estiva/Summer Fruit Platter*	Chapter 17
Dolce	*Tiramisù di fragole/*Strawberry Tiramisù	Chapter 18
Caffè	*Caffè/*Classic Espresso	Chapter 16

Chapter **5**

Stocking an Italian Pantry

The pantry, or *la dispensa*, has always been the soul of traditional Italian kitchens. As old fashioned as it may seem to some, pantries aren't just storage space for things that we purchase in bulk because they are cheaper that way. Until a century ago, kitchens all over the world needed pantries in order to be able to provide balanced meals on a daily basis. Nowadays a good pantry can set you up for cooking flavorful and nutritious meals in less time than it takes to order carryout or delivery.

In this chapter, you learn the Italian approach to creating a pantry as well as how to tailor yours to your personal tastes and needs. You learn about the ingredients you need as well as the cultural traditions and health benefits associated with them. See Chapter 4 for more information on meal planning.

Identifying Prized Italian Products

Much more goes into creating Italy's world-renowned cuisine than meets the eye. Strict geographic indicators (GIs) are enforced by the Italian government and are adhered to by producers, ensuring quality and authenticity. Using traditional, sustainable methods, they create products that are higher quality, a better value, and more nutritious.

Geographic indicators make a difference

Most people who have travelled to Italy agree that the same types of food served in Italian restaurants in the United States taste better in Italy. And there's a good reason for that. In order to make less-expensive counterfeit products appeal to consumers abroad, producers need to manipulate them. To replicate the sweet, rich taste of slowly aged balsamic vinegar, geographic indicators, or GIs, are used to distinguish quality in food products in many countries in the European Union and the United States.

When you buy Maine blueberries, Idaho potatoes, Parmigiano-Reggiano cheese, and Italian wine, for example, GIs make the difference between which products are authentic and which aren't. Nowadays many counterfeiters make a great deal of money by selling "false" products. Whether you are buying Italian, French, or American products, there are designations assigned to specific products that guarantee their authenticity.

If you know the producer, or are buying Italian products from small producers with *single estates* (or just one place of production versus co-ops or multi-national corporations), the quality of your purchase is easy to trace. There are countless small, single estate producers in Italy that create prized Italian products without ever bothering to get them certified, even when they qualify. For larger producers, however, and those who do greater volumes of business, registering and paying for the designations is an important part of their business.

You can look up the authenticity of a company or product on the Made in Italy website at www.madeinitaly.org.

Looking for other important labeling

It is estimated that only 30 percent of the "Italian" products sold in the U.S. actually come from Italy. Many of the others are overpriced fakes. To protect yourself as a consumer, you should know the labels that can help distinguish authentic products from fakes.

Today in Italy there are over 800 products with GI designations. More than 300 of them carry the DOP, IGP, and STG designation, and 526 Italian wines have DOCG, DOC, and IGT labels. Buffalo mozzarella, *Aceto balsamico di Modena*, olive oil, saffron, vinegars, and even basil can carry a quality seal. It is important to know that there are some quality products from smaller producers that meet the same standards — or maybe even exceed them — but do not have the designation. If the source isn't traceable, however, sticking with products that carry GIs takes the guesswork out of your purchases.

Here are some of the acronyms used to denote high-quality Italian products. These categories were designed by and are protected by European Union Law. They are directly enforceable in all EU countries and with third party countries that have agreements with the EU. Note that each product has its own specific set of very strict regulations that it must meet:

>> **DOP:** This acronym stands for *Denominazione di origine protetta* (Protected Designation of Origin, or PDO, in English). DOP is a designation used on the label of high-quality Italian foods to indicate that the product originated and was processed in a particular place and has special qualities that derive from that area.

>> **IGP:** This acronym stands for *Indicazione geografica protetta* (Protected Geographic Indication) and means the product originated in a particular place, has special qualities that derive from the area, and at least one part of its production took place in that area.

>> **STG:** This acronym stands for *Specialità tradizionale garantita* (Traditional Guaranteed Specialty). This certification guarantees that a product's quality is related to a process based on a traditional component or a traditional method. The ingredients don't have to originate or be processed in a specific place. This label is used for Neapolitan pizza and mozzarella.

Choosing a quality olive oil

Olio d'oliva is much more than a condiment or a "healthful fat," as it is often described in English in Italy. There, it is viewed as "liquid gold," a testament to tradition, culture, a way of life, and a constant connector between our past and our future.

Some Italian olive oils have the DOP label, which means the olive oil meets tough standards, such as limits on acidity levels and storage time of olives before processing. The IGP olive oil label means the product meets the basic standards, such as using only olives picked directly from the tree rather than the ground, but has looser origination requirements.

Here are some more things to keep in mind when reading EVOO labels:

The term *extra virgin* is about acidity. By definition, extra virgin olive oil must have an acidity rate of 0.8 or less. The lower the acidity rate, the higher the quality. Italian olive oil quality is denoted by the following geographic indicators:

>> **Varieties:** There are more than 1,200 varieties of olives. Increasingly, many smaller producers are offering single variety olive oils so that consumers can become familiar with the particular type and pair it with the appropriate foods. Keep in mind that different varieties have different colors and flavors, which make them perfectly suited for pairing with different varieties. Just like wine, each olive has different notes that play off the other foods that they are paired with.

>> **Polyphenols:** Polyphenols are important for your health. It is the variety of olive or olives in an oil that determine its overall polyphenol level. The antioxidant properties of polyphenols have been widely studied, and they are known to assist in the prevention of degenerative diseases. You can discover the strength of the polyphenols in an olive oil at home by taking a sip and then slurping it back. As you make the slurping noise, the oil coats your throat. After a few minutes, you should feel a burn. The stronger the burn, the higher the amount of polyphenols in the oil. Single estate producers usually post their polyphenol levels on their websites. In Greece and hopefully soon in other countries, the EVOO richest in polyphenols can get sold as "medical grade." Note that different cultivars naturally have different levels of polyphenols, and each year's harvest yields slightly different results. A Koroneiki variety, for example, generally has a high phenolic content, but each year it varies.

>> **Cold pressing:** Extra virgin olive oil normally should be made using a process called *cold-pressed.* "Cold" means that the olives are kept no higher than 81.9 degrees, and "pressed" refers to the method of extraction. This method indicates that no heat or chemical additives were used to extract the oil from the olives, which can alter and destroy the flavors and aromas of the olive oil. This way, the olive oil also retains its full nutritional value. Putting it on a label isn't really necessary because it is standard. "First cold-pressed" means that the olive juice was obtained from literally the first pressing of the olives. In the olden days, this was a big deal because those olives offered the most nutritional value. Nowadays, it doesn't mean anything because the olives are put in centrifuges to extract the oil.

>> **Filtration:** Many purists prefer the flavor and quality of unfiltered olive oil, but some are turned off by the sediment found at the bottom of unfiltered EVOO bottles. For this reason, many farmers are using a natural filtration method, which involves placing the oil in cisterns and switching it from tank to tank once a month and allowing the sediment to filter out naturally. This time-consuming process maintains the integrity of the oil without the undesired sediment.

Like everything else, if you want to be sure that you are consuming the best-quality olive oil, try to look for bottles where the producer is most traceable. Single-estate varieties, for example, can be traced right back to the source, and you know exactly what you're getting.

In Italian, there is a saying: *olio nuovo, vino vecchio*, which means "new oil, old wine." It's important to keep that phrase in mind when you are adding oil to your pantry, because you don't want to keep anything around from longer than the previous year's harvest. Keep in mind that if you keep extra virgin olive oil in a cool, dark place, it could stay safe to use for a few years. It takes a while for EVOO to go rancid, normally.

That said, just because it isn't rancid doesn't mean you want to consume it. The olive harvests generally take place in late October to November in most places in the Mediterranean. Some micro-climates have them earlier or later. The olives that make Amy Riolo Selections EVOO, for example, are harvested in November. By the time the production process is finished and they are ready to be exported to the U.S., it could take a few weeks, so that would be December. Then it takes a while for the container to arrive in this country, for the product to be shipped to the stores, and for it to be put on shelves. Best case scenario, it is usually January before we can get our hands on the latest "nata" or harvest's oil. That oil should be consumed by the next harvest, or within a year for the most health benefits and freshest flavor.

When you buy a commercial EVOO at the store, don't just look for the expiration date, look for the pressed-on date. If they don't have one, make sure you are purchasing something that is far away from the expiration date because sometimes those are up to three years after the actual pressing of the olives.

HEALTH BENEFITS OF GENUINE EXTRA VIRGIN OLIVE OIL

Basically, because of its anti-inflammatory benefits alone, extra virgin olive oil is good for reducing the root cause of all illness. Additional research on the topic includes this information:

- Extra virgin olive oil has been proven to prevent the formation of blood clots and lower the levels of total blood cholesterol, which is believed to be responsible for the low incidence of heart problems in Italy.

- The antioxidants found in olive oil are Vitamin E, carotenoids, and phenols such as hydroxytyrosol (known for its anti-inflammatory properties) and oleuropein (known for producing anti-bacterial effects).

- Epidemiological studies believe that olive oil is capable of protecting against malignant tumors in various places in the body and reduces the risk of breast, colon, and bowel cancer.

(continued)

(continued)

- Squalene, a natural 30-carbon organic compound found in olives, is believed to reduce the incidence of melanomas — malignant tumors associated with skin cancer.

- The primary function of the immune system is to defend the body against the negative effects of toxins, microorganisms, parasites, and other foreign substances. Olive oil has been shown to boost the immune system against the negative effects of foreign substances.

- Olive-oil-rich diets may prevent memory loss in healthy elderly people. A study showed a reduced risk of suffering age-related cognitive decline. The quantity of olive oil consumed was inversely proportional to age-related cognitive decline and memory loss, dementia, and Alzheimer's disease.

Weighing your wine options

Wine demand increased greatly with the beginning of the Christian Era in 300 B.C.E. Over the years, wine-making became a practice that farmers, business-men, and priests alike could partake in. Because of its sacramental significance in the Catholic church, many wineries and wine-making traditions were tightly guarded in monasteries. In addition to the sensual pleasure of drinking wine, its consumption also became a way to strengthen relations — with the divine, family members, friends, and new acquaintances.

Going with a good grape

The art of wine-making continues to gain even more appreciation in Italy. The country is currently host to more than 2,500-3,000 varieties of grapes that are used specifically for wine. Around 700 of them are estimated to be indigenous grapes that originated in specific areas in Italy itself. Italy has the second larg-est selection of native grapes, after the country of Georgia. Thanks to many government-sponsored initiatives, many wineries are dedicating portions of their land to the growth of indigenous grapes, which are on the verge of being extinct. It is exciting to experience both the common and the "new" varietals being produced to perfection.

Wine can make or break an Italian meal. Serving a properly paired wine will help to elevate the dining experience and bring the best out of both the food and the *vino*. Because wine can be pricy, it's important to understand the value of different types in order to get the most for your money. Just like with food products, the Italian government has set a list of acronyms in place which can ensure that you are buying quality wine.

If you purchase a wine from Italy, and it has one of these labels, you can rest assured that you are getting your money's worth.

>> **DOC:** This acronym stands for *Denominazione di origine controllata* (Controlled Documentation of Origin, in English) and means the wine was produced within a limited area, using precise grape varieties, and adhering to strict production controls.

>> **DOCG:** This acronym stands for *Denominazione di origine controllata e garantita* (Controlled and Guaranteed Documentation of Origin, in English) and is the finest-quality label given to wines subject to the strictest varietal, processing, and production controls.

>> **IGT:** This acronym stands for *Indicazione geografica tipica* (Typical Geographic Indication, in English) and means the wine was produced from approved grape varieties within a defined geographical region.

Pairing wine with your meal

Viticulture, or the study of grape cultivation, has been a way of life on the European continent since 6,000 B.C.E. In ancient times, the Greeks named the inhabitants of Calabria *oenotri,* or "the wine cultivators."

In the olden days, common table wine was usually eaten at regular meals while the more expensive or unique types of wine were saved for special occasions in Italy. Nowadays, however, pairing wine with specific meat courses and experimenting with different wines is commonplace at home meals — especially among younger generations.

While wine is only enjoyed with meals (preferably with others), it is water, not soft drinks or other sugar drinks, that consistently accompanies meals. Water is the sustainer of life and the drink that Italians consume most daily.

Professional wine-pairing rules are typically dictated by the A.I.S. or *Associazione Italiana Sommelier,* and some differ from pairing traditions in other countries. Italians, for example, tend to not pair wine with any course that has lemon juice or vinegar in it. The Italian Sommelier's Association has a specific wheel that is used to guide sommelier's suggestions.

In this book, my dear friend, Dr. Sante Laviola, Italian Research Scientist, professional wine taster, Sommelier, official wine taster of the Slow Wine Guide, published by Slow Food Editore, has paired his wine suggestions with my recipes. I truly appreciate his opinions because he has a very unique and highly informed perspective on wine pairing.

PRESERVING FOR PEAK PERFORMANCE

Because ingredients taste best when they are at their peak, jarring (or canning), drying, and even freezing them for later use is popular in Italy. Prior to refrigeration and freezers, foods needed to be pickled and preserved in order to be eaten out of season. Many kinds of produce have such huge bumper crops (think zucchini, eggplant, and tomatoes at the end of the summer) that it is impossible to eat them all at once. Instead of wasting them, wise housewives would preserve them in a variety of ways to be enjoyed throughout the year.

It makes me happy that so many Americans are embracing preserving and canning. The DIY trend continues to grow and is not only a fun hobby, but a way to eat more nutritious foods as well. Even if that isn't the type of activity you're interested in, you can still build an effective pantry with quality items that you purchase. It has never been easier to find top-shelf Italian ingredients that make stocking your pantry a cinch. By having them on hand, along with a strategy of when to use them, your pantry can become your best cooking partner.

For more information, pick up a copy of *Canning and Preserving For Dummies*, 3rd Edition, available at your favorite book retailer.

That said, the wine pairings in this book are mere suggestions. You may opt to not drink with your meals, to pair your own favorite wines, or use different pairing parameters. Note that Dr. Laviola has shared the properties and characteristics of the wines he's paired with the recipes to make it easier to find a suitable substitute if needed.

Cooking from the Pantry

Stocking a few of the right ingredients can help you take the pantry items to new heights. I also like to call the freezer the modern American pantry because people in the U.S. are typically much more comfortable using their freezer than people in the Mediterranean region are.

The "Using pantry recipe formulas to create meals in minutes" section later in this chapter provides easy strategies for putting the pantry, fresh, and frozen foods together for winning combinations at every meal regardless of your taste, schedule, or budget.

Keeping essentials on hand

It takes a little time to set up a pantry in the beginning, but the rewards are extremely worthwhile. Once you start, you'll enjoy the benefits.

It has never been easier to find great Italian products abroad. In the United States, I rely on organic markets, such as Whole Foods and others, which seem to carry increased amounts of Italian brands each time I go shopping. If you are lucky enough to have a local Italian market in your neighborhood, be sure to make regular trips, especially for the cheeses, flours, and other pantry staples. Due to the already large and growing popularity of Italian food, even chain supermarkets in the U.S. now carry quite a few authentic Italian ingredients. Online ordering is also a great option.

If the stores in your area don't carry Italian products, or if you prefer to shop online, check out specialty importers such as www.Ditalia.com and ItalianFood andStyle.com which sell not only my own products but a variety of authentic, artisan Italian goods.

Here's a list of items to keep on hand:

>> **Baking**
- Active dry yeast
- Almond extract
- Almond flour
- Anise extract
- Baking powder
- Baking soda
- Chocolate, Fair Trade Certified if possible
- Cornstarch
- Pure vanilla extract
- Semolina
- Unbleached all-purpose flour
- Unsweetened cocoa powder, Fair Trade Certified if possible
- Whole wheat flour
- 00 flour (or "double zero" flour used to make pasta and pizza dough)

❯❯ Beans and legumes

- Brown lentils

- Borlotti beans (dried and/or low-sodium canned)

- Cannellini beans (dried and/or low-sodium canned)

- Chickpeas (dried and/or no-salt-added canned)

- Cranberry beans (dried and/or low-sodium canned)

- Peeled fava beans (dried)

❯❯ Herbs (dried)

- Oregano

- Rosemary

- Sage

- Thyme

❯❯ Italian specialty

- Anchovy fillets (packed in olive oil)

- Artichoke hearts (frozen or canned)

- Bread crumbs (plain) (see Chapter 3 for a recipe)

- Canned diced tomatoes (low-sodium and fire-roasted)

- Canned tuna (packed in water)

- Capers (packed in water)

- Dried porcini mushrooms

- Espresso coffee

- Olives (oil-cured, green and black, Kalamata and Gaeta)

- Roasted red peppers (jarred)

- Sun-dried tomatoes

- Tomato paste (reduced-sodium)

- Tomato purée (reduced-sodium)

❯❯ Nuts and dried fruit

- Almonds (blanched and raw)

- Chestnuts (jarred or packaged, whole roasted or steamed)

- Hazelnuts

- Pine nuts
- Pistachios (shelled)
- Walnuts

» Oils and vinegars

- White balsamic vinegar
- Balsamic vinegar (preferably *Aceto Balsamico di Modena*)
- Extra virgin olive oil
- Red wine vinegar
- White wine vinegar

» Pasta (whole wheat or gluten-free)

- Couscous
- Ditalini
- Farfalle
- Fusilli
- Linguine
- Orecchiette
- Orzo
- Paccheri
- Pastina
- Penne rigate
- Spaghetti
- Ziti

» Rice and grains

- Arborio rice
- Barley
- Carnaroli rice
- Cornmeal/polenta
- Farro
- Spelt berries

>> **Spices**

- Anise seeds

- Bay leaves (dried)

- Cloves (ground and whole)

- Crushed red chile flakes (preferably from Calabria and Basilicata)

- Fennel seeds

- Nutmeg

- Pure cinnamon (ground and sticks)

- Saffron

- Unrefined sea salt

- Whole black peppercorns

A note about the products I prefer

Throughout this book there are a few ingredients that I mention consistently. You are, of course, free to use whichever version you prefer, but here are my reasons for using a few favs repeatedly:

>> **Amy Riolo Selections:** I have my own line of Italian products that I suggest throughout the book. I do so confidently because I know the producers and where the products come from, and I can attest to their superior flavor and quality. When one of my ingredient lists calls for a similar item from another producer, such as an extra virgin olive oil, for example, it is because I believe that the particular item pairs perfectly with the other ingredients in the recipe. My products are available at www.ditalia.com, and you can get a 10 percent discount off everything on the site by using the code "amyriolo10" at checkout.

>> **Fair trade chocolate:** Lots of shady practices occur in the global chocolate industry. By purchasing Fair Trade Certified chocolate, you are ensuring that farmers are treated ethically and fairly.

>> **Unrefined sea salt:** This is my go-to salt. It is relatively inexpensive and has not been processed or exposed to harsh chemicals. It contains a variety of the minerals and elements necessary for optimal health that are native to the area it comes from. It does not have added iodine, as most commercial brands of table salt do. There is no noticeable difference in flavor between unrefined sea salt and other salts, so kosher salt, table salt, and other sea salts can be used in its place in the recipes in this book.

Using pantry recipe formulas to create meals in minutes

There are countless ways that people put their pantries to good use. Keep this list nearby so you can whip up a tasty and nutritious meal anytime. These 20 items are those that can be made strictly from the pantry alone. After you add in fresh and frozen ingredients, the sky is the limit in terms of taste and creativity. Always have carrots, celery, onions, garlic, citrus, Italian cheeses, and fresh greens or vegetables on hand to stretch these meals even further.

» **Risotto:** Carnaroli rice + Stock + Saffron + Vegetable/Protein of your choice (if desired)

» *Pasta e fagioli*/**Pasta with Beans:** Beans + Rice + Tomato purée + Stock

» *Pasta con lenticchie*/**Pasta with Lentils:** Pasta + Lentils + Garlic + Tomato purée and/or Stock

» *Pasta con tuna*/**Pasta with Tuna (or other fish):** Pasta + Tuna + EVOO + Olives and/or Tomato sauce

» *Insalata di riso*/**Rice Salad:** Arborio rice + Olives + EVOO + Jarred vegetables + Beans

» *Insalata di pasta*/**Pasta Salad:** Short pasta + Olives + EVOO + Jarred vegetables + Beans

» *Crema di ceci*/**Chickpea Soup:** Chickpeas + Stock + EVOO

» *Minestra*/**Minestrone Soup:** Beans and/or Lentils + EVOO + Pasta or rice or other grain + Puréed tomatoes + Stock + Dried porcini mushrooms + Vegetables

» **Bean Soup:** Beans + Stock + Tomato purée + EVOO

» **Pasta and Beans:** Pasta + Beans + Stock + Tomato purée + EVOO

» *Minestre*/**Minestrone-Style Soups:** Pasta (or other grain) + Beans + Stock + Tomato purée + EVOO + Vegetables

» *Zuppa di lenticchie*/**Lentil Soup:** Lentils + Stock + Tomato purée + EVOO + Vegetables

» *Budino di riso*/**Rice Pudding:** Rice + Milk + Dried fruits and nuts + Honey or sugar

» *Insalata di tuna*/**Tuna Salad:** Tuna + EVOO + Borlotti beans

» *Insalata di ceci o fagioli*/**Chickpea or Bean Salads:** Chickpeas or beans + EVOO + Vegetables + Spices

» *Pasta al pomodoro con verdure*/**Pasta with Tomato Sauce and Vegetables:** Pasta + Garlic + EVOO + Chili paste + Tomato purée + Vegetables

» *Suppli*/**Risotto Croquettes:** Carnaroli rice + Stock + Saffron + Vegetable/ Protein of your choice (if desired)

» *Spaghetti all'aglio e olio*/**Spaghetti with Garlic, Oil, and Chilis:** Spaghetti + EVOO + Chili paste + Garlic

2

Appetizers and First Courses

Discover how Italians begin their meals.

Get easy-to-use terminology and definitions of authentic Italian dishes.

Recreate beloved recipes for traditional and modern appetizers, sauces, pasta dishes, homemade pasta, risotto, soups, gnocchi, and more.

Master the Italian ritual of the *aperitivo*.

Learn the difference between antipasti and first courses and when to serve them.

Chapter 6

Starting Meals the Italian Way: Antipasti/ Appetizers and Aperitivi

taly's 20 regions offer such diversity in terms of appetizer recipes that you can sample many of the world's best flavors simply by taking a bite of a crunchy bruschetta or breaking apart a mozzarella-filled *supplì* (risotto croquette) to discover a stringy piece of fresh mozzarella oozing from the center. That said, many home cooks who have become adept at cooking wonderful Italian creations for lunch or dinner are often at a loss when it comes to creating an appetizer.

Because Italians don't begin their meals with salad, many newcomers to the cuisine simply turn to cheese and *salumi* (cured meat) plates (which are also a good option) to fill in the gaps between guests arriving and sitting down to enjoy a comforting pasta or risotto recipe. Italian appetizers are worth mastering, however, because they offer another course — a deeper journey into the full Italian culinary experience.

In this chapter, you'll discover what constitutes an Italian appetizer and find authentic recipes to enjoy whenever the mood strikes. You'll also see how the Italian appetizer course fits into the whole meal and which dishes are best served when. You'll immerse yourself in the pleasures of the early-evening *aperitivi* — Italy's stylish alternative to happy hour — and learn to host them in the comfort of your own home.

Appreciating the Italian Appetizer

If you want to truly understand the cultural importance of the Italian appetizer, you must ponder the popular proverb "*L'appetito vien mangiando*," which means "Eating makes you hungry" but implies — and is often used with the double implication — "The more you taste, the more you want." Italians use the appetizer course to literally whet the appetite for what's to come while creating a flavor and texture base that blends, harmonizes, and even accentuates the beloved first courses that follow it.

The word *antipasto*, which is the Italian word for *appetizer*, confuses many people because the prefix *anti* is often used in English to denote being against something. But the Italian word was inspired by the Latin prefix *ante*, which means preceding, before, or in front of. The Italian word *pasto* means "meal" and also underscores the importance of pasta in the diet.

Nine times out of ten, when an Italian is planning a meal, they will start with the first course, or *primo*: the pasta, risotto, soup, or gnocchi. Seasonal produce determines which type of first course is served. On special occasions, such as a holiday when a certain type of meat or fish is ceremoniously served, they start with the second course, or *secondo*. While considering which appetizer to make, then, a cook starts after deciding which first and/or second course to make.

If it's pumpkin season, for example, and someone decides to make pumpkin-filled ravioli with sage sauce for a first course, they'd probably pair it with a poultry or game dish for a second course. Because the meal is already full of rich, complex, and woody flavors, the appetizer would need to be delicious and satisfying, but also light enough to lead up to the first course without overpowering it. In this example, a bruschetta topped with a mushroom medley, a cannellini bean purée with crostini, or small bites of frittata would make a great *antipasto*, or entry course, without taking the spotlight from the first and second courses.

Even the simplest *bruschette*, crudités with good-quality extra virgin olive oil (EVOO), stuffed vegetables, and *antipasto* platters make impressive appetizers when they're made with good-quality ingredients (see Chapter 5 for more information). Creative home cooks and restaurant chefs in Italy are highly skilled at transforming leftovers into tasty and creative appetizers. Equipped with the recipes and tips in this book, you'll have the same skill soon!

Noting Differences between Dining In (At Home) and Out in Italy

Some iconic Italian dishes such as *Tagliatelle alla Bolognese* are prepared in restaurants, especially in less formal *trattoria,* in much the same way that they are in the home. Many of Italy's most beloved recipes come not from chefs, but from grandmothers and what were once referred to as housewives, or *casalinghe* — so much so, in fact, that the term *cucina casalingha* (home–style cooking) is emulated in restaurants around the globe. When it comes to appetizers, however, this course (like the dessert course) can vary most between dining in the home and dining out.

Before I delve further into this topic, it's important to realize that not all Italian eating establishments are considered to be restaurants. Various types make up the Italian eating scene.

Enjoying antipasti at Italian eateries

These are the main types of restaurants in Italy:

>> *Trattorie:* Typical family-style restaurants that pride themselves on cooking foods in the homemade fashion. They usually offer the majority of regional and Italian classics.

>> *Enoteche:* Ancient Italian wine bars. The food is meant to accompany and elevate the wine experience in an informal, unpretentious way.

>> *Osterie:* Originally set up to host people who were traveling from another place and didn't have local relatives to dine with. They're extremely casual and normally serve local specialties. They usually operate without menus and recite their daily offerings the way that regular restaurants recite their specials.

>> *Ristoranti:* More-formal fine-dining restaurants that offer elegant appetizers, some of which typically aren't eaten in homes, such as *crudos* and *carpaccios* (thinly sliced pieces of raw meat and fish), truffles, and oysters.

If you were going to eat in a *trattoria*, your antipasto could be a platter of cheeses and meats with preserved vegetables, bruschetta, stuffed vegetables, and so on. Many *trattorie* also have antipasto bars, which look like salad bars, but each individual compartment contains a different appetizer, such as Caprese salad or roasted peppers in olive oil. Some establishments allow you to make your own plate; others have the waiter prepare it for you.

In an *enoteca*, the menus are usually much more limited than full restaurant menus and may be built around various types of wines or other inspirations. Many of the recipes incorporate wine. In addition, *enoteche* sell cured meats, cheeses, and other gourmet products. Traditionally known for having great food, they're becoming increasingly trendy in Italy. In terms of appetizers, they offer antipasto platters and typical yet creative dishes that pair well with wine.

Historically, an *osteria* has been the place to go when you want to get a taste for how the locals eat. Nowadays, the differences between *trattorie* and *osterie* are less obvious, but generally speaking, the food they serve is straightforward and very regional, and appetizers are of the no-nonsense variety, created to please the palate and put local olive oil, produce, and leftover bread to good use. The occasional stuffed vegetables might also be offered in season.

CICCHETTI: DELIGHTFUL LITTLE TIDBITS

Venice has a tradition that tourists — much to the chagrin of the Venetians — often describe as "Italian tapas," which is *cicchetti* (standard Italian) or *cicheti* in the Venetian dialect. Originally served to gondoliers and workers who needed to accompany their afternoon wine while keeping cool in the shade, the drink you have with cicchetti in Venice is therefore called an *ombra* (shade) and is served in a *bacaro*, the Venetian word for bar.

Cicchetti are now the crowning glory of the Venetian culinary landscape. They are served in *bacaro* (the Venetian *enoteca*), *osterie,* bars, and even hotel lobbies. Their name means "little things" in the local dialect and likely stems from the Latin word *ciccus*, which means "little," because they can include small meatballs, crostini, sandwiches, seafood, and vegetables prepared in a variety of ways. *Cicchetti* allow chefs to be creative in what is normally a very traditional food scene. Known for its many modes of making risotto and seafood, Venetian food also includes traditional polenta, meat, and game recipes, so cooks in Venetian restaurants must be able to reproduce scores of classics daily. *Cicchetti* also give them a chance to get creative and come up with new dishes on a whim. Although *cicchetti* aren't traditionally cooked in Italian homes, there's no reason why making a bunch of them to accompany wine wouldn't be a great way to entertain friends.

Welcoming guests with appetizers at home

Appetizers are rarely served in Italian home meals except when guests are present or special events are being celebrated. A handful of olives, an antipasto platter, and maybe a vegetable-based dish are about all you need to begin your multi-course meal. On Sundays, however, and especially on holidays, families usually get more creative. Plates of bruschetta, stuffed vegetables, crostini, and larger antipasto platters may grace the table.

One area of distinction is the tables of southern Italy. From Naples south to Sicily, appetizers are treated much in the way that they are in the Greek and Arabic cultures, which influenced the Italian south. If you've ever witnessed a Middle Eastern Mezza table, you know what I'm referring to. Depending on the occasion, who's coming to dinner, and how much time your host has to prepare, the appetizer spread in these areas could look filling enough to be the entire meal. In my ancestral homeland of Calabria, Italy, for example, it isn't uncommon to have a dozen appetizers laid out before important guests or on a holiday. Eggplant meatballs, preserved vegetables, stuffed zucchini, risotto croquettes, cured meat platters, cured olive platters, fried or grilled cheese, bruschetta, preserved mushrooms, roasted peppers, and stuffed savory pizzas are just a few of the many examples that might be offered.

Following the aperitivo ritual

The word *aperitivo* comes from the word *aprire*, which means "to open," and in the course of the Italian meal, it does just that. From a social standpoint, the *aperitivo* is pure genius. Celebrating an early-evening break in the day gives us not only sustenance to continue the day, but also a time to pause and visit with colleagues, friends, or loved ones. In addition, the *aperitivo* gives you room to shorten or expand your time with someone. You can invite a colleague or friend for an *aperitivo* after work and still be home with the family for dinner. Or if you want to extend your time with someone, you can invite them to have an *aperitivo* with you before dinner or instead of dinner.

Aperitivi are often enjoyed at bars (*caffés*) or *enoteche*; often, even hotels offer them to guests in their lobbies. Other than prosecco and wine, popular Italian cocktails such as *aperol* spritz are usually enjoyed at *aperitivo* time. Nuts, olives, panini, *tramezzini* (Italian tea sandwiches), cured meats, cheese, and potato chips are usually available. Guests who enjoy an *aperitivo* outside the home usually pay per person and enjoy several of the goodies, all of which are meant to build the appetite for dinner a few hours later. Very popular in Italy at the moment, both at home and outside, is the *apericena* — a more extensive *aperitivo* eaten instead of dinner (*cena*).

Inviting someone home for an *aperitivo* is also a nice option because you can go out for dinner later. If you're busy and don't have time to prepare a full meal, but want to enjoy having your friends over, an *aperitivo* is a low-time-commitment way of doing that, especially because Italians usually stock wine, spirits, and staple ingredients for casual entertaining on a whim. (This tradition is also popular in France.) Culturally speaking, you can invite someone over for an *aperitivo* and dinner or for just the *aperitivo*. This way, the guest knows that they are on their own for dinner, but it still gives you a time to get together.

TIP

To host your own *aperitivo* at home, be sure to have prosecco, your favorite wine, or ingredients such as *aperol* (soda water) on hand to make your own spritzes. Be sure to stock cheeses, olives, nuts, and ingredients for making some of the recipes from this chapter. A few of these favorites are sure to make your guests feel pampered with minimal effort on your part.

Making a delicious first impression: Antipasti recipes

Appetizers are the first impressions of the meals we serve. At the Italian table, they're the overture to an intricate symphony of flavors that are meant to go together. When you begin planning your meals, think of them as though they're a beautiful melody or a favorite song. In the case of music, the notes build to create a crescendo later, and a meal is the same way.

Whether your meal is simple or elegant, the flavors and textures introduced in the appetizer should always complement the next course. If your first course or *primo* is a soup, for example, it would be a good idea to have bread or salad components in your appetizer or *antipasto*. In that case, crostini and bruschetta topped with vegetables would be a great choice. Just as you wouldn't wear a top without considering a bottom, you must always keep the whole picture together when planning the appetizer. Chapter 4 is full of meal-planning ideas and suggestions.

The recipes in this chapter are straightforward and easy to create. Their popularity has stood the test of time, and they're easily adaptable to ingredients from various seasons. Because Italians have always had a zero-waste policy in the kitchen, each recipe allows you to incorporate leftovers and the little bits you have on hand in the cupboard and refrigerator.

Insalata di mare/Seafood Salad

PREP TIME: 10 MIN	COOK TIME: 10 MIN	YIELD: 8 SERVINGS

INGREDIENTS

4 vine-ripened tomatoes, chopped

1 carrot, thinly sliced

¼ teaspoon unrefined sea salt

⅛ teaspoon black pepper, freshly ground

Juice and zest from 1 large lemon

1 pound dry scallops

1 bay leaf

¾ pound shrimp, peeled and deveined

1 pound boneless, skinless cod, haddock, or other white fish, cut into 1-inch pieces

1 pound baby squid tubes, cleaned and sliced in small rings

½ cup Amy Riolo Selections or other good-quality extra virgin olive oil, divided

3 cloves garlic, peeled

1 pound mussels, scrubbed well

½ cup fresh flat-leaf parsley, finely chopped

Additional lemon slices, for garnish

DIRECTIONS

1 Place the tomatoes, carrot, salt, pepper, and lemon zest in a large bowl, and mix well.

2 Bring a medium-size pot ¾ full of water to boil over high heat.

3 Lower the heat to medium, and add the scallops and bay leaf. Cook, uncovered, until scallops are opaque, approximately 1 minute. Remove scallops with a slotted spoon to a dish lined with paper towels. Add the shrimp and fish to the water, and cook until opaque, 1–2 minutes. Transfer to another dish lined with paper towels. Add the squid and cook for approximately 40 seconds, until rings begin to tighten slightly. Remove with a slotted spoon into a colander. Immediately transfer squid to a bowl of very cold water to stop the cooking.

4 Add 2 tablespoons EVOO and garlic cloves to a large, wide skillet with a fitted lid over a medium-high flame. When oil is hot, add mussels, toss to coat, and add ½ cup water over the top. Cover and cook for 2–4 minutes until mussels are open (cooked). Remove opened mussels, and set aside. If any mussels fail to open after another minute or two of cooking, discard them.

5 In a small bowl, make the dressing by whisking the EVOO and lemon juice together until emulsified.

6 Add the seafood to a salad bowl, and stir to combine. Drizzle with dressing, and stir. Sprinkle with parsley, garnish with lemon slices, and serve immediately.

TIP: Reserve this recipe, a traditional Christmas Eve appetizer that can be enjoyed anytime, for a time when the freshest seafood and produce possible are available to you.

Pair this dish with a bottle of *Passerina di Offida* or similar. A white wine with a slender body, low alcohol, and a taste profile underlined by freshness, sapidity, and tropical notes.

Funghi ripieni/Stuffed Mushrooms

PREP TIME: 10 MIN | COOK TIME: 5 MIN | YIELD: 4 SERVINGS

INGREDIENTS

4 Portobello mushrooms, rinsed and rubbed dry

¼ cup Amy Riolo Selections or other good-quality extra virgin olive oil

½ cup fresh bread crumbs (see Chapter 3)

¼ cup Pecorino or Parmigiano-Reggiano cheese, grated

¼ cup mozzarella cheese, shredded

1 tablespoon fresh thyme, coarsely chopped

1 tablespoon fresh basil, chopped

Salt, to taste

Black pepper, freshly ground, to taste

2 cloves garlic, peeled and finely chopped

4 cups fresh baby arugula or other greens

Zest and juice of 1 lemon

1 tablespoon fresh parsley, coarsely chopped

DIRECTIONS

1 Preheat broiler to 500 degrees.

2 Trim stems off mushrooms, and chop the tender parts into fine pieces, reserving the tough bottom parts for use in stock or stew. Place mushroom pieces in a large bowl.

3 Pour 2 tablespoons EVOO into the bowl with chopped mushroom stems, and add bread crumbs, Pecorino, mozzarella, thyme, and basil. Stir to combine, and season with salt, pepper, and garlic.

4 If the undersides of the mushroom caps contain large brown gills, lightly scrape them away with the back of spoon and discard. Distribute the filling evenly among mushroom caps until full, and place on a baking sheet.

5 Place the sheet under the broiler, and bake for 3–5 minutes or until the mushrooms are golden and cooked through and the cheese has melted.

6 Remove the sheet from the oven, and plate the mushroom caps on a platter filled with arugula leaves. Drizzle the remaining EVOO over the top, along with the juice of the lemon. Use the lemon zest to garnish the dish, and top with parsley.

TIP: Stuffed mushrooms are one of my mother's specialties. She always stuffs them with sausage, but I prefer a vegetarian version. If you'd like to make the meat-lover's version, simply crumble or cut a link of your favorite sausage and brown it in a skillet before adding it to the recipe. Omit the bread crumbs and cut down on the cheeses to compensate for the flavors.

Pair this dish with a bottle of *Rosso di Montalcino* or similar. Called "Brunello's brother," this wine's sensory characteristics recall blackberry and black currant. The intensity of its aromas and less than 1 year aging make it the ideal combination.

NOTE: You can stuff the mushrooms a day ahead of time and bake them before serving. Leftover mushrooms taste great chopped and tossed in cooked pasta or risotto; you can also use them to make a frittata.

Giardiniera/Quick Italian Pickles

PREP TIME: 5 MIN	COOK TIME: 10 MIN PLUS 25 MIN COOLING	YIELD: 4 SERVINGS

INGREDIENTS

1 cup white wine vinegar

1 cup water

1 tablespoon sugar

1 bay leaf

½ teaspoon red pepper, crushed, divided

5 black peppercorns

½ teaspoon salt, divided

2 garlic cloves, peeled and thinly sliced

1 ½ cups bite-size cauliflower flowerets

1 stalk celery, thinly sliced

¾ cup carrot, cut into 1-inch rectangular pieces

½ cup red bell pepper, cut into 1-inch pieces

½ cup green bell pepper, cut into 1-inch pieces

1 ½ tablespoons Amy Riolo Selections or other good-quality extra virgin olive oil

DIRECTIONS

1 Combine vinegar, water, sugar, bay leaf, crushed red pepper, peppercorns, and salt in a large saucepan. Bring to a boil.

2 Add garlic, cauliflower, celery, carrot, and red and green bell pepper. Reduce the heat to maintain a lively simmer, and cook until the vegetables are tender-crisp, about 3–5 minutes. Remove from heat, and let stand for 5 minutes. Drain, reserving 3 tablespoons of the cooking liquid.

3 Transfer the vegetables to a medium bowl. Stir in EVOO, pepper, the remaining 1/8 teaspoon each crushed red pepper and salt, and the reserved cooking liquid. Refrigerate for at least 25 minutes to chill. Stir, and serve with a slotted spoon.

TIP: Serve this salad before large meals, as in Italy, because it stimulates digestion. In Naples, this dish is called *Insalata di rinforzio* (the "strengthening salad") and is served as part of the large Christmas Eve feast, but I can guarantee that it tastes great all year long.

Pair this dish with a bottle of *Grüner Veltliner* or similar. The rich antioxidants known as polyphenols offer floral-fruity aromas in a soft, full sip with a delicately spicy finish. A slight aging gives the sip greater complexity, enriching notes of dried fruit.

NOTE: The name *giardiniera* comes from the word *giardino*, which means "garden" and refers to a female gardener, who would preserve the harvest this way to enjoy the vegetables all year long. In addition to gracing antipasto platters and being part of appetizer spreads, this salad is a nice accompaniment to panini and other sandwiches.

VARY IT! Feel free to change the quantities and types of vegetables in this recipe to suit your taste. You can use the same mixture with jalapeños or other hot peppers to make your own peperoncini mixture.

Bruschetta con pomodori/ Tomato Bruschetta

PREP TIME: 5 MIN	COOK TIME: 5 MIN	YIELD: 4 SERVINGS

INGREDIENTS

2 fresh, ripe tomatoes (½ pound), diced

4 tablespoons Amy Riolo Selections or other good-quality extra virgin olive oil, divided

⅛ teaspoon unrefined sea salt, divided

4 (½-inch) slices ciabatta or other light, crusty country bread

1 garlic clove, peeled

¼ cup fresh basil, finely chopped

DIRECTIONS

1 Preheat broiler to high or grill to medium–high.

2 Toss tomatoes with 2 tablespoons EVOO and salt in a medium bowl.

3 Grill the bread slices on both sides until grill marks appear, or place under the broiler until golden brown. Rub the garlic clove along both sides of the bread, and top each piece with even amounts of the tomato mixture.

4 Drizzle with remaining 2 tablespoons EVOO, and sprinkle basil over the top. Serve immediately.

TIP: If fresh tomatoes aren't in season, substitute roasted peppers or mushrooms.

Pair this dish with a bottle of *Grillo Superiore* or similar. A great Sicilian white wine rich in floral aromas and citrus notes, it is characterized by a full-bodied, savory, and pleasantly citrusy sip with a delicate spicy note on the finish.

NOTE: Bruschetta are easy, crowd-pleasing appetizers. This tomato version is perfect for summer.

VARY IT! The sky is the limit when it comes to bruschetta recipes. A good recipe to remember is good-quality day-old or slightly hard bread slathered with something creamy (you could use ricotta or mascarpone or goat cheese instead of garlic) and other cooked sliced vegetables.

Caponata/Sicilian Sweet and Sour Eggplant Medley

PREP TIME: 20 MIN	COOK TIME: 20 MIN	YIELD: 6 SERVINGS

INGREDIENTS

½ cup Amy Riolo Selections or other good-quality extra virgin olive oil

¾ pound (1 large or 2 small) eggplant, cut into 1-inch cubes

1 small yellow onion, finely chopped

1 stalk celery, roughly chopped

¼ teaspoon black pepper, freshly ground

1 cup canned crushed tomatoes

½ cup green Sicilian olives (such as Castelvetrano), drained, rinsed well, pitted, and roughly chopped

¼ cup white wine vinegar

¼ cup golden raisins

2 tablespoons sugar

2 tablespoons unsweetened chocolate, finely grated

3 tablespoons fresh basil, finely shredded

¼ cup pine nuts

4 very thin slices Italian or gluten-free bread, rubbed with olive oil and grilled or toasted on one side

DIRECTIONS

1 Heat EVOO in a 12-inch skillet over medium-high heat. Working in batches, if necessary, add eggplant to skillet, and fry, tossing occasionally, until browned, about 3–4 minutes. Using a slotted spoon, transfer eggplant to a large bowl.

2 Add onion and celery to skillet, and season with pepper. Cook, stirring often, until vegetables begin to brown, about 10 minutes. Reduce heat to medium, and cook, stirring, until vegetables are caramelized, 1–2 minutes.

3 Add crushed tomatoes, and continue cooking for 10 minutes. Stir in olives, vinegar, raisins, sugar, and chocolate, and cook, stirring occasionally, until thickened, about 15 minutes.

4 Transfer mixture to bowl with eggplant. Add basil and pine nuts, and mix together. Let cool to room temperature. Serve over toasted bread slices.

TIP: *Caponata* is usually served at room temperature as a side dish, but it also tastes great served cold on top of tender lettuce leaves or tossed into hot pasta for a quick, delicious, and satisfying meal. I enjoy it the next day tossed into ditalini pasta or Israeli couscous, which isn't traditional but tastes great.

Pair this dish with a bottle of *Nero d'Avola* or similar. An excellent wine from southern Sicily, which has a light ruby color and delicately floral-fruity aromas. In the mouth it is expressed with freshness, medium body, and soft tannins.

VARY IT! This recipe should have the perfect balance of sweet and sour flavors. The sweetness of the ingredients you use and the amount of caramelization that they produce while cooking will determine how much sugar you need to add. Feel free to adapt the recipe to your own taste, the way Sicilians do.

Crostini con purea di cannellini/ Crostini with Cannellini Bean Purée

PREP TIME: 5 MIN	COOK TIME: 10 MIN	YIELD: 8 SERVINGS

INGREDIENTS

2 cups cooked cannellini beans (see Chapter 3)

¼ cup Amy Riolo Selections or other good-quality extra virgin olive oil, plus extra for drizzling

1 clove garlic, peeled and minced

Juice of 1 lemon

¼ teaspoon black pepper, freshly ground

Pinch crushed red chili flakes

8 (¼-inch) slices Italian bread

¼ cup sun-cured black Sicilian olives, pitted

DIRECTIONS

1 Preheat oven to 350 degrees.

2 Place beans, EVOO, garlic, lemon juice, pepper, and crushed red chili flakes in a food processor. Purée until smooth. Add a few tablespoons of water until mixture resembles a light purée. Set aside.

3 Place bread slices on a baking sheet. Toast 2–3 minutes per side in the oven.

4 Remove bread from the oven, and spread cannellini bean purée on top. Garnish each slice with an olive, drizzle more EVOO on top, and serve.

TIP: This easy appetizer makes good use of healthful Italian ingredients. Serve these *crostini* with your favorite soup or salad.

Pair this dish with a bottle of *Rambela frizzante* or similar. A niche wine produced from the white Famoso grape with delicate floral notes, ripe yellow fruit to exotic fruit sensations, completed in a velvety, fresh, and elegantly persistent sip.

NOTE: Cannellini and borlotti beans are the most commonly used beans in Italy, in addition to chickpeas. Cannellini are known to reduce the risk of colorectal cancer.

VARY IT! Substitute chickpeas or your other favorite beans in this recipe, or top the crostini with your own mix of vegetables, meat, or cheese.

Polpette di melanzane/Eggplant Croquettes

| PREP TIME: 10 MIN | COOK TIME: 10 MIN | YIELD: 4 SERVINGS |

INGREDIENTS

2 slices (about 2 ounces) day-old Italian bread, cubed

½ cup milk

1 eggplant, unpeeled, chopped into ¼-inch cubes

1 ¾ cups plain bread crumbs, divided

⅓ cup Pecorino Romano cheese, grated

3 tablespoons fresh Italian parsley, finely chopped

2 tablespoons fresh basil, finely chopped

¾ teaspoon kosher salt

½ teaspoon black pepper, freshly ground

2 cups Amy Riolo Selections or other good-quality extra virgin olive oil, divided

4 tablespoons Amy Riolo Selections Sundried Red Pesto or your favorite tomato or pesto sauce

DIRECTIONS

1 Place bread in a small bowl, and cover with milk.

2 Place eggplant in a large saucepan, cover with water, and simmer until tender, about 20 minutes.

3 Drain well, and place in a mixing bowl with 1 ¼ cups bread crumbs.

4 Squeeze milk out of bread, and add to the bowl. Stir in cheese, parsley, basil, salt, and pepper, and mix well. Mixture should be thick enough to form balls; if it's too thin, add more bread crumbs until it holds together.

5 Pour remaining ½ cup bread crumbs into a shallow dish, and form teaspoons of the mixture into 12 equal-size egg shapes.

6 Roll eggplant in bread crumbs to coat.

7 Heat the EVOO to 375 degrees in a large heavy skillet over medium heat.

8 Carefully lower the croquettes into the skillet, leaving spaces between them. Fry until golden, about 2–3 minutes per side.

9 With a slotted spoon, carefully remove the eggplant balls to a platter or tray lined with paper towels.

10 To serve, place croquettes on a platter, and drop ½ table-spoon of pesto on top of each one.

TIP: If you're opposed to deep frying, you can also pan-fry and bake these eggplant croquettes for great results.

Pair this dish with a bottle of *Catarratto* or similar. An almost forgotten Sicilian vine that is characterized by a typically floral scent with salty hints. In the mouth it is straight, savory, and dry with a delicate stringent note on the finish.

Antipasti misti/Antipasto Platter

PREP TIME: 15 MIN | COOK TIME: 0 MIN | YIELD: 8 SERVINGS

INGREDIENTS

¾ pound mozzarella balls

¼ cup Amy Riolo Selections extra virgin olive oil, plus more for drizzling

1 teaspoon parsley, finely chopped

2 teaspoons basil, finely chopped, plus a handful of fresh basil leaves for garnish

Unrefined sea salt, to taste

2 cups mixed Italian olives

½ pound cured meat or smoked salmon slices

¼ pound marinated anchovies, drained

½ pound roasted red peppers, drained

1 loaf fresh focaccia (see Chapter 20) or Italian bread

DIRECTIONS

1 Combine mozzarella balls with EVOO, parsley, and basil in a small bowl, and season with salt to taste.

2 Arrange the olives, cured meat or fish, anchovies, and red peppers separately and attractively in different sections of a large serving platter.

3 Garnish with fresh basil leaves.

4 Serve with good-quality Italian bread or focaccia.

TIP: If you want to host your own *aperitivo*, let this platter be the main attraction, with some other treats to go along with it.

Pair this dish with a bottle of *Gattunio* or similar. A historic blend of Barbera and Croatina which has a fresh, fruity flavor and delicate bitterness pairs well with the richness of aged meats and cheeses.

NOTE: This platter could be accompanied by a platter of different types of cheeses, from fresh to aged. Be sure to include goat, cow, and sheep-milk cheeses of varying ages.

VARY IT! The recipe for this platter is just a template. Feel free to add or substitute your favorites. Most traditional versions contain olives, cheese, red peppers, and a cured protein. The varieties that you choose are up to you!

Chapter 7

Dressing Dishes with Italian Sauces

S auces, or *salse* as they are known in Italian, have been used since pre-Roman times to add flavor, depth, and nutritional benefits to pasta, protein, vegetables, and other dishes in Italy. In order to master Italian cuisine, you need to know which sauce pairs best with which recipe, when to serve it, and its historical/cultural relevance as well as how to prepare it. There's no need to panic, though; studying and preparing sensational Italian sauces enables you to embark on a rich culinary journey from your very own kitchen.

When it comes to pasta, there are three words that are used to define sauces. *Salsa* (as in *salsa di pomodoro, salsa besciamella,* and *salsa verde*) is the "classic" Italian tomato sauce; *sugo* is a more elaborate sauce using *salsa di pomodoro* as a base, and then *condiment*, which means something you put on pasta. *Condimento* can be used to describe *salsa* or *sugo* or anything else that doesn't fit into those two categories, such as pesto.

In this chapter, you discover why sauces and their particular recipes are so important in the Italian culture. You'll identify which recipes are "official," or traditional, and which are modern spins on classics. Not only can you recreate your favorite restaurant classics with the recipes in this chapter, but you can combine them in traditional ways on your own as well.

REMEMBER

The recipes in this chapter don't include wine pairings because the final dish, not the sauce alone, gets paired.

A Delicate Balance: Combining Foods and Sauces

Preparing and serving authentic Italian sauces truly is an artform. In Italy, sauces are an integral part of many meals, yet they never get the praise they deserve in America. The Italian–American community bases its Sunday dinners around Sunday "sauce" or "gravy." In Italy, when a dish with sauce is described, the sauce is named after whatever it is paired with, such as *Fettuccine al ragù* or *Gnocchi al pesto*; in both cases, the fettuccine and the gnocchi are the main events, and the sauce, even though it defines the whole dish, is mentioned almost as if it were an accessory.

In order to master Italian sauces, it is imperative to use the word *"condire"* which means "to season," "to dress," or "to flavor." In the case of sauces, whenever the word *condire* is used in the kitchen, it means "to dress." When an Italian chooses to use a sauce, they see it as a means of dressing pasta, gnocchi, fish, vegetables, chicken, or whatever it is being served with. *Condire* is also the base word for *condimento*, which is where our English word condiment comes from, which underlines the principle that a sauce should not be used to smother the food; it is dressing, but merely to cover (dress), season, and flavor it.

The delicate balance of combining sauces with foods to season and flavor them while being careful to let the flavor and texture of what they are paired with shine through is one of the main tenants of an Italian kitchen. If an Italian sits down to anything that isn't a soup yet is swimming in sauce, they immediately lose their appetite. In the case of Italian cuisine, you can have too much of a good thing, and it is better to adapt a "less is more" attitude when dressing food.

REMEMBER

I often tell my cooking students that dressing a pasta is like dressing yourself. When accessorizing, designers recommend that you look in the mirror and take one thing off before leaving the house, in order not to be overdressed. The same idea applies to Italian sauces: Always use a light hand. If they are prepared following the ingredients and techniques used in this chapter, even a small amount delivers an abundance of flavor and enough of a silky texture to coat the pasta without overpowering it.

Preparing Traditional Sauce Recipes

It's hard to imagine that 500 years ago in Italy, *salsa di pomodoro* (tomato sauce) didn't exist. Olive oil, garlic, anchovy paste, herbs, and sometimes butter or eggs in opulent times, were what pasta was dressed in. On most regular days, pasta would be topped with toasted bread crumbs instead of cheese, and in some cases it still is today.

Tomatoes and peppers, along with potatoes, corn, chocolate, and many other ingredients became available in Italy after Columbus returned from the Americas. It wasn't even until the 19th century that *spaghetti al pomodoro* started to spread from Southern Italy to the North at the request of General Garibaldi, who claimed that it would be the dish that "would unite all of Italy." This is important to note because it reminds us that there is no such thing as an ancient "Italian Tomato Sauce" and that crushed red chili flakes were not used in recipes prior to this time.

Most of our "traditional" Italian sauces, therefore, are relatively new to the cuisine. Many of them have become so emblematic of Italian cuisine that we no longer even need to describe them in other languages. Because these sauces are so widely diffused, however, they often lose their authenticity. For this reason, various Italian consortiums issue *disciplinari* or "official" recipes of what ingredients need to be used, and what techniques need to be followed, in order to make them authentic.

Traditional sauces in this chapter include *Cacio e pepe, Pesto, Salsa besciamella,* and *Salsa verde.*

Introducing Tomatoes: Modern Sauce Recipes

By Italian standards, the recipes featured in this section — all based on tomatoes — would be considered "modern" not because they are 21st century gourmet renditions created by molecular gastronomists, but because pre-15th century, the tomato was unheard of in Italy. Since then, however, they have become emblematic of Italian cuisine all over the world. Best of all, they are simple, healthful, and easy to prepare.

Whoever said that "hunger is the best sauce" clearly never sampled classic Italian recipes created with love and a few top-quality ingredients. It is important to remember that in the Italian kitchen, the primary function of sauces is to dress our beloved pasta, the crowning glory of the meal. Just like a bridesmaid should never outshine the bride, the sauce should never take attention away from the pasta. It is used instead, to help the pasta achieve its ultimate destiny as a true culinary masterpiece.

A good sauce makes you appreciate pasta's flavor, texture, and appeal much more than if it was plain. Sweet, savory, and sweet-and-sour sauces have been around since antiquity. Used to accompany meat, fish, pasta, vegetables, poultry, and game, they have added flavor to dishes since the beginning of time. Author of *Il Cuoco Gentiluomo* (*The Gentleman Cook*), Livio Cerini Di Castegnate says (in Italian) that "Sauces are an idea made of composed flavors that have been brought to life in the hands of Pygmalion cooks." That truly sums up the Italian viewpoint on the role of sauces in the local cuisine.

In addition to ancient recipes still on hand thanks to the ingenuity of ancient Sumerians, Jews, Egyptians, Assyrians, Greeks, Romans, and indigenous cultures around the globe, sauces have stood the test of time and even grown in popularity in the relatively recent past.

CATEGORIZING SAUCES

Modern sauces were categorized by French Chef Antonin Carème and made internationally popular by one of the Ritz's co-founders August Escoffier. The work of Escoffier was highly influenced by the "father of Italian gourmands," Pallegrino Artusi, whose most famous work *La scienza in cucina e l'arte di mangiare bene* (*The Science of Cooking and the Art of Eating Well*), revolutionized the Italian culinary scene by including scientifically accurate recipes in a way that modern cooks could easily put to use. His books have become culinary history references for Italian chefs for centuries. He is also credited with being the first cookbook author in Italy to include recipes from all the different regions (since the country had just been unified) in a single cookbook.

Categorizing sauces into Mother Sauces (*Veloutè* Sauce, Hollandaise Sauce, Bechamel Sauce, Fond, and Tomato Sauce) and then scores of derivatives for each one became part of an international standard culinary education. In modern-day Italy, however, the sauces that are part of the classic cuisine were not born from this tradition, but rather the ritual of Italian home cooks. For centuries, prior to cookbooks and the Internet being popular household items, grandmothers passed recipes down to their grandchildren, and mothers to their daughters, and sometimes even sons. The original Italian restaurants were not created to try the gourmet dishes of professional chefs, but rather to attempt to emulate what female cooks made so beautifully in the home.

Tomato sauce and all its derivatives, such as the ones included in this chapter, were most coveted. All Italians and Italian-Americans have a fond memory of a sauce being simmered over the stove. To us, that very aroma conjures up images of Sunday suppers, warm holidays, and the rich experience of gathering with loved ones. To make these sauces is not just about following a recipe; it is to unleash our greatest memories and to create a culinary affirmation that all is well in the world.

Each of the modern recipes in this chapter has its own story, and its own preferred serving time. Make them when you want to be assured that great flavor and good nutrition can coexist.

Modern sauces in this chapter include *Salsa di pomodoro, Sugo alla Norma, Sugo all'arrabbiata,* and *Ragù alla Bolognese.*

Cacio e pepe/Roman Cheese and Pepper "Condimento"

PREP TIME: 5 MIN	COOK TIME: 15 MIN	YIELD: 6 SERVINGS

INGREDIENTS

1 tablespoon salt

1 pound spaghetti or fresh pasta of your choice (*tonnarelli* are typical)

2 tablespoons black pepper, preferably Telicherry, freshly ground

½ pound Pecorino Romano cheese, grated, plus extra for serving

DIRECTIONS

1 Bring 6 quarts water to a boil in a large pot, and add a tablespoon salt.

2 Drop the pasta into the boiling water and cook, stirring often with tongs until just al dente. Drain, reserving about a cup of the pasta water.

3 Meanwhile, set a large skillet over medium heat, add the pepper, and toast over low heat, stirring, until fragrant, about 20 seconds.

4 Add the cooked pasta and at least ¼ cup of the reserved pasta water to the pan with the pepper. Using tongs, toss to combine over medium heat until the pasta is well coated.

5 Quickly stir the cheese into the pan (adding a splash or two more of the reserved pasta water if necessary to loosen the sauce), and continue tossing to coat vigorously. Serve immediately, with additional grated Pecorino on the table.

TIP: The base of this sauce is the reserved water from cooking the pasta. It is imperative to mix it and the cheese quickly together to create an emulsified cream that perfectly coats the pasta.

NOTE: *Cacio* comes from the Roman word for cheese, and this recipe is said to have been created by shepherds in the Roman countryside who would bring pasta, chunks of cheese, and pepper with them to the hills to create a quick lunch over an open fire while tending their flocks. Many people still use *cacio* as an alternative word for cheese.

VARY IT! This dish has become very trendy in American restaurants where it is served in a variety of ways. In Rome, it is usually served with freshly made *tonnarelli* pasta, which is an egg-based pasta that is similar to spaghetti but slightly more square in shape, or dried spaghetti. Other shapes that work well would be *tagliarini* or *fettuccine.*

Pesto/Fresh Basil and Pine Nut "Sauce"

PREP TIME: 5 MIN	COOK TIME: 0 MIN	YIELD: 4 SERVINGS

INGREDIENTS

¼ cup pine nuts

1 clove garlic, peeled

3 cups lightly packed fresh basil leaves, preferably Genovese basil

¼ cup Anfosso extra virgin olive oil, or other Ligurian if possible, plus extra for serving

¼ cup Parmigiano-Reggiano cheese, freshly grated

Unrefined sea salt or salt, to taste

DIRECTIONS

1 Combine the pine nuts, garlic, basil, and olive oil in a large mortar or food processor, and grind or process until a smooth paste forms.

2 Using a spatula, scoop pesto out of the mortar or food processor and into a bowl. Stir in cheese and a pinch of salt, if desired.

3 Transfer the sauce to a plastic container, and cover with a layer of extra virgin olive oil to store or toss directly into fresh, hot pasta.

TIP: Italians never heat pesto sauce – it is either slathered onto bread or tossed into vegetables or pasta at room temperature. If serving on pizza, slather it on the cooked pizza dough after it has baked instead of before putting it into the oven.

VARY IT! While traditional pesto is only made in summer when basil is at its peak, variations can be made all year round. In winter, I substitute the pine nuts for walnuts or almonds and the basil for baby kale or arugula to make a delicious and nutritious sauce that brightens cold days.

THE "OFFICIAL" PESTO RECIPE

In the region of Liguria, on the Italian Riviera where pesto originates, there is a Consortium that dictates whether pesto sauce is authentic enough to boast the DOP (Documented Origin Protected) label. To qualify, the pesto must be produced within the Liguria region, with specific types of each of the ingredients listed in the nearby pesto recipe and in a certain manner. The official recipe is mandated to be made with a mortar and pestle, not with a food processor as is done in many modern homes and restaurants. To learn more, visit: https://www.mangiareinliguria.it/pesto-genovese/disciplinare-del-pesto-genovese.

Salsa besciamella/Béchamel Sauce

PREP TIME: 5 MIN	COOK TIME: 20 MIN	YIELD: 8 SERVINGS

INGREDIENTS

¾ cup butter

3 tablespoons flour

½ teaspoon nutmeg

4 cups whole milk, preferably fresh, local, organic

1 teaspoon unrefined sea salt

DIRECTIONS

1 In a small saucepan, add the butter and melt it over low heat.

2 Add the flour, and whisk it in with the butter to combine.

3 Allow to cook for 1 minute, or until slightly golden. Add the nutmeg, and whisk again.

4 In another small saucepan, bring the milk to a boil over medium heat.

5 As soon as it boils, add it into the other saucepan and whisk well until you have a thick, creamy sauce. If the sauce needs to be thicker, continue to cook it over low heat for a few minutes until it thickens and set aside.

TIP: *Besciamella* is a perfect sauce for winter dishes. For a fantastic baked pasta, mix this recipe with 1 pound of *rigatoni* that is cooked until very al dente (about 3 minutes less than if you were serving immediately). Preheat oven to 350 degrees. Stir in cooked vegetables such as squash or zucchini, if desired. Top pasta with freshly grated Parmigiano Reggiano cheese and bake for 30 minutes, or until golden.

NOTE: This recipe is often used to top savory Italian crepes (called *crespelle*) and in baked pasta dishes. Even though the world considers this to be a French sauce, it was actually introduced to France by Catherine de Medici of Florence, Italy, when she married Henri II. In the Bologna region of Italy, classic *lasagne* is made by layering fresh sheets of pasta with *Bolognese* sauce (see the Bolognese recipe at the end of this chapter) and *Besciamella* sauce before being baked.

VARY IT! In addition to this version, which is served in Italy, France, and the U.S., many cities around the world have their own variations. In Saudi Arabia, they add a few pieces of good-quality saffron to the *Béchamel* sauce and use it to top roasted fish. In Egypt, they often make the sauce with half the quantity of milk and the other half of chicken stock. It is then tossed into short pasta along with a meat sauce and baked. Eggs are stirred into the *Besciamella* sauce in Greece before it is used in the classic *Pastitsio* recipe.

Salsa verde/Green Sauce

PREP TIME: 5 MIN	COOK TIME: 0 MIN	YIELD: 4 SERVINGS

INGREDIENTS

¼ cup Amy Riolo Selections or other good-quality extra virgin olive oil

1 cup fresh, flat-leaf (Italian) parsley

3 anchovies

1 teaspoon capers

½ cup fresh mint

2 cloves garlic, peeled

Black pepper, freshly ground, to taste

DIRECTIONS

1 Place all ingredients in a blender or mixer, and blend on high speed until emulsified.

2 Pour over your recipe or store in an airtight container in the refrigerator for up to a week.

TIP: Since this sauce isn't cooked, fresh herbs are required. This is an ancient recipe which was created to take advantage of the flavor and medicinal properties of the fresh herbs. Dried herbs are used very sparingly in Italian recipes, usually in slow-cooked roasts and meat recipes.

NOTE: Salt was taxed heavily in Italy from ancient Roman times until the last century. For that reason, ingredients like salted fish (anchovies) and capers were used to add flavor and salt to recipes while avoiding the tax. This sauce originally hails from Piemonte, where it is served over the classic *Bollito misto,* or Mixed Boiled Meats, in the winter. It tastes great over chicken, fish, and meat dishes and makes a wonderful dressing for cooked vegetables as well.

VARY IT! If you cannot find capers or need to substitute them, add additional sea salt to the recipe and a bit of lemon juice if substituting capers.

Salsa di pomodoro/Fresh Tomato Sauce

PREP TIME: 5 MIN	COOK TIME: 20 MIN	YIELD: 6 SERVINGS

INGREDIENTS

2 tablespoons Amy Riolo Selections or other good-quality extra virgin olive oil

2 large garlic cloves, peeled and minced

1½ pounds strained (seeded and skinned tomatoes) boxed or jarred tomatoes, such as Pomi brand, or 2½ pounds fresh, ripe tomatoes (if in season) (see Tip for instructions)

Unrefined sea salt, to taste

Black pepper, freshly ground, to taste

4-5 leaves of fresh basil, oregano, or parsley

Parmigiano-Reggiano or Pecorino Romano cheese, freshly grated, for garnish

DIRECTIONS

1 Heat oil in a medium saucepan over medium heat. Add garlic, and reduce heat to low.

2 When garlic begins to release its aroma (before it turns color), add tomatoes.

3 Stir and allow mixture to come to a boil to create caramelization on the side of the pan.

4 Add salt, pepper, and fresh herbs; stir and cover. Reduce heat to low, and simmer for 10–20 minutes, or until it has thickened slightly. Taste and adjust seasonings. Serve with grated cheese.

TIP: If you are using fresh tomatoes, place them in boiling water until their skins peel (just a few minutes), strain, and allow to cool to touch. Peel them, remove the seeds, and cut them into chunks. Then use them in place of boxed or jarred tomatoes in Step 2 above.

Most Italians make large batches of this sauce so they can have one recipe on hand at all times in the refrigerator and a spare or two in the freezer. This sauce keeps in the refrigerator for up to a week or in the freezer for a few months.

NOTE: If you are serving this sauce with pasta as a first course, the second course should not contain tomatoes. Simple grilled or pan-fried chicken, veal, beef, or seafood are natural accompaniments. This simple sauce is the base for Italian tomato soups, as well as the *Arrabbiata, Norma, Amatriciana, and Aurora* sauces in this section. In addition to pasta, you can use it to top pizza, eggplant *parmigiana,* and keep a little extra on hand to dip meatballs and croquettes into.

VARY IT! If using fresh tomatoes, try experimenting with different varieties including heirlooms. You may be surprised how much the recipe changes with each new type. Stir leftover beans and vegetables into this sauce and toss with pasta for a quick weekday meal. My personal favorite variation is to stir in 1 cup heavy cream and 4 cups fresh baby arugula to the cooked sauce. I simmer it for another few minutes and toss it into *farfalle* or *penne*-shaped pasta with a handful of Parmigiano-Reggiano cheese.

Sugo alla norma/Sicilian Tomato and Eggplant Sauce

PREP TIME: 5 MIN	COOK TIME: 30 MIN PLUS 1 HOUR TO SALT THE EGGPLANT	YIELD: 6 SERVINGS

INGREDIENTS

1 large eggplant, sliced in ¼-inch thick rounds

4 tablespoons unrefined sea salt, plus extra to taste

1¼ cups extra virgin olive oil, preferably Sicilian, divided

2 cloves garlic, peeled and minced

1 box or bottle (26-ounces) strained tomatoes or tomato puree or equivalent fresh tomatoes, peeled, seeded, and chopped (see Fresh Tomato Sauce recipe earlier in this chapter for instructions)

Pinch of crushed red pepper flakes

6 fresh basil leaves, roughly torn

Black pepper, freshly ground, to taste

½ cup Pecorino Siciliano or Romano cheese, freshly grated, divided

1 cup ricotta salata cheese, grated, if desired for serving

DIRECTIONS

1 Place eggplant rounds on a large tray or baking sheet and sprinkle with 4 tablespoons salt. Allow to sit for 1 hour (the salt will draw moisture out of eggplant so that the rounds absorb less oil when frying). Rinse eggplant slices and dry thoroughly with paper towels.

2 Heat ½-inch olive oil (approximately 1 cup plus 2 teaspoons) in a large, wide skillet over medium heat. When oil reaches 365 degrees (it is important that it reaches this temperature so that eggplant does not get soggy), carefully lower a few eggplant slices at a time into the oil, being careful not to crowd the skillet. Allow to cook for a few minutes per side, or until light golden, turning with a slotted spoon at least once during cooking.

3 Using the slotted spoon, carefully remove the slices from the oil and place onto a large plate or tray lined with paper towels. Continue until all eggplant slices have been fried and set aside.

4 In another large, deep skillet, heat 2 tablespoons olive oil. Add garlic and cook until it begins to release its aroma; do not allow garlic to turn color.

5 Pour in tomatoes, and stir. Add crushed red pepper, basil, salt, and freshly ground pepper.

6 Cover, reduce heat to low, and simmer for 20 minutes.

7 When eggplant is cool enough to handle, stack 3 slices together, and chop into 1-inch pieces.

8 After sauce has cooked for 20 minutes, turn off heat, remove lid, and add eggplant pieces and Pecorino cheese, stir well.

(continued)

9 Cover and simmer sauce on medium heat for an additional 10 minutes. Mix everything together, and serve over your favorite pasta with grated ricotta salata cheese.

TIP: If you already have extra Fresh Tomato Sauce (see the recipe in this chapter) on hand, you can add the fried eggplant and Pecorino cheese to a full recipe's worth of it and make this traditional sauce in even less time. This sauce is typically served with *penne, fusilli, ziti,* or *rigatoni* pasta.

NOTE: The name of this simple and delicious recipe is a tribute to the opera "Norma" by Vincenzo Bellini. It is said that when playwright Nino Martoglio first tasted the culinary masterpiece in Sicily, he exclaimed *"Chista è 'na vera Norma"* ("This is a true Norma!"), and since then the term *"alla Norma"* has been used to describe things done well all over the Mediterranean's largest island.

VARY IT! To save on calories and time, you could skip the salting of the eggplant and simply brush the rounds with EVOO and grill them or put them under the broiler for a few minutes on each side until golden and then proceed with the rest of the recipe. Leftover grilled zucchini and roasted peppers also taste great in place of eggplant.

Sugo all'arrabbiata/Spicy Tomato Sauce

| PREP TIME: 5 MIN | COOK TIME: 20 MIN | YIELD: 6 SERVINGS |

INGREDIENTS

2 tablespoons Amy Riolo Selections or other good-quality extra virgin olive oil

2 large garlic cloves, peeled and minced

1 small fresh hot red chile pepper, rinsed, trimmed, and seeded, or 3 small dried red chilies, thinly sliced

1½ pounds strained (seeded and skinned tomatoes) boxed or jarred tomatoes, such as Pomi brand, or 2½ pounds fresh, ripe tomatoes if in season (see Tip for instructions)

Unrefined sea salt, to taste

Black pepper, freshly ground, to taste

½ cup fresh Italian parsley, finely chopped

Pecorino Romano cheese, grated, to garnish if desired

DIRECTIONS

1 Heat oil in a medium saucepan over medium heat. Add garlic and chilies, and reduce heat to low.

2 When garlic begins to release its aroma (before it turns color), add tomatoes.

3 Stir and allow mixture to come to a boil.

4 Add salt, pepper, and fresh parsley; stir and cover. Reduce heat to low, and simmer for 10–20 minutes, or until it has thickened slightly. Taste and adjust seasonings. Serve with grated cheese, if desired.

TIP: If you are using fresh tomatoes, place them in boiling water until their skins peel (just a few minutes), strain, and allow to cool to touch. Peel them, remove the seeds, and cut them into chunks. Then use them in place of boxed or jarred tomatoes in Step 2.

NOTE: *Arrabbiata* means "angry" in Italian, and this sauce is called that because of the addition of fiery chilies, which also make someone's face turn red like anger does. This sauce, which hails from Italy's Lazio region, is meant to be intentionally spicy, so if you or your guests don't like heat, just serve a simple tomato sauce instead. Many people do not serve cheese with this recipe, but you can if you like it.

VARY IT! While this sauce is traditionally served with *penne* pasta, a little bit of it goes a long way to enliven leftover chicken and meat recipes, too! Try stirring leftover beans, legumes, and vegetables into the sauce for your own improvisational pasta dish.

Salsa Amatriciana/Sauce from Amatrice

PREP TIME: 5 MIN	COOK TIME: 20 MIN	YIELD: 4 SERVINGS

INGREDIENTS

¾ cup Amy Riolo Selections or other good-quality extra virgin olive oil

½ cup aged guanciale, cut into 1-inch strips (see Note)

1 small fresh hot red chile pepper, rinsed, trimmed, and seeded

½ cup dry white wine

¼ cup Pecorino Romano cheese

1¼ cups Italian pomodori pelati (peeled tomatoes) or 4-5 fresh, red, ripe tomatoes if in season

Unrefined sea salt, to taste

Black pepper, freshly ground, to taste

DIRECTIONS

1 In a large skillet, preferably cast iron, heat the olive oil over medium heat, and add the *guanciale* and allow to melt slightly.

2 Add the hot red chili pepper and stir. Brown the *guanciale* on all sides, and increase the heat to high. Add the wine, and allow to evaporate; remove the *guanciale* from the pan, and set aside on a plate.

3 Add the tomatoes to the same pan, and stir to combine. Add salt and pepper, and cook over medium heat. Allow to simmer, covered, for 10 minutes.

4 Add the cheese and return the *guanciale* to the sauce, stir, and taste to adjust the salt and pepper.

TIP: If you are using fresh tomatoes, place them in boiling water until their skins peel (just a few minutes), strain, and allow to cool to touch. Peel them, remove the seeds, and cut them into chunks.

Normally spaghetti or *bucatini* pasta are served with this sauce. They are cooked simultaneously and the pasta is added to the sauce after it is cooked until al dente.

NOTE: *Guanciale* is made from pork cheek, but it can be substituted or omitted if preferred.

This is a typical recipe of Rome, but it takes its name from the town of Amatrice in modern-day Abruzzo. Amatrice suffered greatly from an earthquake in 2016, and Slow Food International, an international organization that promotes local food and traditional cooking founded by Carlo Petrini in Italy in 1986 (www.slowfood.com), ran an international campaign that promoted Italian restaurants around the globe serving this recipe in order to raise funds for the victims and relief efforts.

VARY IT! Many chefs I know (myself included) make what is called *"Amatriciana Finta"* or "Fake Amatriciana" sauce for vegetarians or those who don't eat pork by replacing it with vegetables, such as zucchini or mushrooms cut in to strips, or by beating a few eggs into the cheese and adding that to the sauce instead of the meat.

Ragù alla Bolognese/Bolognese-Style Meat Sauce

PREP TIME: 10 MIN	COOK TIME: 3-4 HOURS	YIELD: 6 SERVINGS

INGREDIENTS

2 tablespoons Amy Riolo Selections or other good-quality extra virgin olive oil

2 tablespoons butter

¼ cup diced yellow onion

¼ cup diced celery

¼ cup diced carrot

1½ pounds ground beef (try to avoid lean varieties), or veal (see Note)

1 cup white wine

4 cups tomato puree, preferably from San Marzano tomatoes

1 cup beef stock (see Chapter 3)

1 dried bay leaf

½ teaspoon unrefined sea salt, plus extra to taste

1 cup whole milk

Black pepper, freshly ground, to taste

DIRECTIONS

1. Heat the oil and butter in a large saucepan over medium heat. Add the onion, celery, and carrot. Sauté, stirring occasionally, until lightly golden, 3–5 minutes.

2. Add the meat and stir, allowing to brown completely. Add the wine, and stir until wine is completely evaporated.

3. Add the tomato puree, stock, bay leaf, and ½ teaspoon of salt, and stir.

4. Reduce heat to low, cover, and simmer for 3 hours, stirring every 30 minutes.

5. Add the milk, stir, and continue simmering for another 10 minutes.

6. The sauce is ready when it reaches a thick consistency (it will have cooked down to about half of its original volume). Stir and add additional salt and pepper to taste, if needed.

TIP: This sauce can be made a day ahead of time, or made in large quantities and frozen until serving. Serve *ragù alla Bolognese* with thick pasta such as *tagliatelle* (as is done in Bologna), *fettucine*, *pappardelle*, or *rigatoni* if you prefer a shorter pasta.

NOTE: Several Italian regions have their own *ragù* (meat sauce) recipes that were traditionally made on Sunday morning and enjoyed after families came home from church. Since the Catholic Church promoted abstaining from meat from Friday until after receiving the Eucharist on Sunday, a meat-based sauce was the ultimate feast-worthy meal to celebrate with.

VARY IT! You can use whatever kind of meat you choose in this recipe. Goat, lamb, pork, beef, veal, or combinations of your favorites all produce a fantastic sauce.

Chapter **8**

Using Dried Pasta in Daily Meals

"This macaroni is to be eaten looking skywards, where its taste brings about ecstasy, with a thought to God for his divine providence."

BARTOLOMEO NARDINI, PARTENOPE IN CUCINA

asta secca, or dried pasta, which is commonly known as *pastasciutta* in Italy, has become such an important staple around the world that it is hard to imagine that prior to 1867, when the Buitoni company set out to mass produce pasta, it had never been produced in mass. Until that time, pasta was a handmade artisanal product that was taught and passed down from generation to generation. While the next chapter focuses on recipes using fresh pasta, this one teaches you how to effectively incorporate dried pasta into your meals on a daily basis, as most modern Italians do. In this chapter, you'll also discover the art of pairing pastas with sauces (*salsa*/simple sauces, *sughi*/more elaborate sauces, and *condimenti*/condiments). Mastering these principles is essential for cooking great Italian food. In addition, you'll also get some tried and true recipes to fill everyone's pasta cravings.

Dried Pasta Basics

Most Italians eat a *primo*, or a first course, as a part of their larger lunch meal. While the *primo* could be a soup, risotto, or gnocchi dish, depending upon where you're eating and when, pasta is the main staple and traditionally is eaten almost every day. To Italians, pasta is a food capable of evoking pride, passion, love, desire, and hunger simultaneously.

Comparing homemade and dried pasta: Separate but equal

While we revere homemade pasta the most, the truth is that nowadays in Italy, it is usually only enjoyed in restaurants and on special occasions. Most people rely on dried pasta on a daily basis, and fewer people know how to make homemade pasta. One of my greatest dreams is that our pasta- making traditions continue to thrive and be passed down to future generations, but I also use dried pasta for certain recipes and achieve great flavor and nutrition in a short amount of time.

You should understand that fresh and dried pasta are separate but equal in the modern Italian kitchen. Some shapes cannot be made with fresh pasta, and some cannot be made with dried pasta. Many dried pasta shapes rely on a machine to cut them; hand extruders were used to create these before the invention of automatic machinery for many, and then others were invented with automation. Some shapes cannot be done by hand. The mixture of the two adds to the incredible diversity of Italian pasta, which is how it can be eaten every day without getting boring.

Dried pasta is perfect for quick lunches at home, weeknight dinners, and unexpected company. It also has a special place in our hearts because it reminds us of certain occasions and memories. Many Italians grew up eating pastina, small round pasta as a first food in childhood and had little star-shaped pasta or ditalini fed to us in soups when we were sick. Few things ever satisfy us as much as a plate of *Spaghetti aglio e olio*, even though it is super easy and inexpensive to make. Whenever I need a mental and physical pick-me-up at mealtime, that's what I prepare! And just like chicken soup, a plate full of spaghetti studded with garlic, chilies, and parsley and drizzled with good-quality EVOO does wonders for my soul.

Considering quality when purchasing dried pasta

Many Americans deem pasta as unhealthful, yet Italians eat pasta almost daily and still enjoy good health as a nation. This is because Italians eat smaller quantities, dress the pasta in healthful ways with herbs, fresh sauces, and vegetables, and use better quality boxed pasta to begin with.

REMEMBER

Not all boxed pastas are created equal. Unfortunately, many brands use subpar wheat and production techniques. I have even heard of companies using chemicals in the process of making the dried pasta.

On a positive note, many artisanal brands of dried pasta are now available in supermarkets along with organic and gluten-free varieties. You should know that in Italy heirloom varieties of wheat, which are lower in gluten than the mass-made varieties, are also being used to produce delicious dried pasta. Of course, it is ultimately your decision which brand(s) of pasta to use.

TIP

Of the readily available pasta brands in U.S. grocery stores, De Cecco and Rummo are reliable. My favorite artisanal brands are Anfosso, Dorazio, and Verrigni because they are made in a smaller production, artisan way and with top-quality ingredients and allow gradual air drying, among other rituals, to ensure better taste and texture. Pasta that is guaranteed to be from the Gragnano (with an IGP marking on the label) is made of excellent wheat in an area that is known for its superior pasta.

Recently, a new law in Italy requires pasta companies to declare on the package the origin of the wheat used in the pasta. Wheat grown in Italy is subject to very strict laws regarding the use of (potentially harmful) pesticides and genetically modified seeds; wheat grown outside the EU less so. Many of the household brands in Italy now have *"100 per cento grano Italiano"* on the packets, while others (De Cecco included) declare a mixture of Italian and non-EU wheat.

Another thing to look for on pasta labels is *"trafilato al bronzo,"* which means that the pasta is extruded from bronze dies, and that makes for fantastic texture and shapes. I always look for them, with the exception of the *Spaghettoro* Spaghetti from Verrigni, which is included in my Amy Riolo Selections Italian Primi Essentials Gift Box at Ditalia.com. This variety of spaghetti is actually cut with gold dies, and I can assure you that it is like none you've ever tasted before. I recommend stocking your pantry with various pasta shapes—the best you can find from your local grocer—and supplementing with the small-production artisan brands that I mentioned earlier. Ditalia.com and ItalianFoodandStyle.com are great sources of pasta online.

Preparing pasta "al dente"

Cooking pasta *al dente* is a common instruction, but you might be wondering what that truly means. The Italian term *al dente* means "to the tooth" and refers to the fact that pasta should be chewy or "toothy" and require more effort to chew than say, a soup noodle, while still providing a pleasant experience. This term is usually applied to dried (packaged) pasta and fresh pastas made with durum wheat because the softer pasta doughs, such as ravioli, cook to a more tender texture.

Cooking pasta *al dente* is not only better because it's the authentic way of cooking it, but it is also more healthful to prepare it this way. *Al dente* pasta retains more nutrients and has a lower glycemic index. Pasta cooked for a shorter amount of time has less time to release into the boiling water, so the starch gets digested more slowly, preventing blood sugar to spike in your body.

TIP

Here are some tips for cooking pasta al dente:

» Always use abundant water – at least three to four times enough to cover the pasta.

» Bring water to a boil, uncovered, on high heat before adding a generous amount of salt (I prefer using unrefined sea salt for its healthful benefits).

» Add pasta, stir, and reduce heat to medium. Stir often while cooking so that it doesn't stick.

» If cooking dried pasta, boil it for a few minutes *less* than the directions on the package and then taste, ensuring that the pasta is cooked until it is still slightly tough to the tooth, yet cooked.

» If cooking fresh pasta, boil it just until it rises to the surface.

» Drain the pasta well using a colander or slotted spoon, but don't rinse it before dressing it or adding it to your sauce or *condimento*.

Pairing Pasta with Sauces

Italy enjoys more than 500 different pasta shapes, with numerous toppings, accompaniments, and sauces to be paired with. The Italian obsession with serving the right pasta with the proper sauce might seem daunting to newcomers, but it is important to learn the magic behind the right combinations that make both the sauce and the pasta better. If you've ever met a lovely couple—people who are fantastic on their own but really bring the best out of each other when they are together—then you get the idea. That is how the right sauce can complement its culinary partner.

Many of us are used to eating pasta a certain way, so we never give it a second thought; linguine with pesto, tagliatelle with ragù, pappardelle with a thick tomato sauce, and so on are all classic combinations of sauces that are paired correctly. As an example, think about light, airy angel hair pasta and how heavenly it tastes tossed simply with EVOO, herbs, and lemon or a fresh tomato sauce. Now imagine that same angel hair pasta weighed down with heavy gobs of a meat sauce; the meat sauce would take over the dish. The same thing can happen conversely. If you have a thick, pappardelle pasta and you dress it with lemon and herbs, the pasta seems too heavy for the dish. The heavy egg taste from the pasta overpowers the lightness of the fresh herbs and citrus. In this case, a meat ragù or a heavier tomato sauce would be the perfect partner.

Italians happily follow rules that have stood the test of time in the kitchen. There are, of course, always exceptions to the rules, and if you really love a combination that is not normally paired together, continue to enjoy it. But if you want to get some of the proper guidelines, here's a quick reference guide to keep you on track (check out Figure 8-1 for a few examples):

>> **Short/small pasta shapes**

- Acine di pepe: Tiny "peppercorn"-shaped pasta added to soups and eaten as a first food, alone, with butter, or EVOO and salt for children.

- Annellini: "Little rings" are usually tossed with tomato sauce and incorporated into more elaborate baked pasta dishes, such as the Sicilian *Timbalo*.

- Campanelle (Gigli): "Little bells" have lots of curves and ridges for holding thick meat and vegetable sauces.

- Cavatelli: The name comes from the Italian verb *cavare*, which means to make hollow; the little cave shaped pastas are perfect for "storing" sauce. Traditional to the Italian South, they are emblematic of the Calabria region, where they are generally served with fresh tomato sauce or a meat ragù.

- Corzetti: These disc-shaped pastas from the Liguria region are made with wooden stamps, which give them a unique design and helps the sauce adhere to the pasta; generally served with light herb and citrus-based sauces.

- Cuscussù: This pasta is named for the Sicilian dialect word for couscous, which was introduced to the island by the Arabs from modern-day Tunisia in the ninth century. In Sicily, couscous is generally prepared with seafood or a fresh tomato and almond pesto.

- Ditalini: Tiny tubular pasta are used in soups and *minestre*.

- Farfalle: Bow-tie pasta, called "butterflies" in Italian, can be paired with cream-based, fresh tomato, or pesto sauces.

- Foglie d'ulivo: Olive-leaf shaped pasta can be served simply with olive oil, herbs, and toasted bread crumbs, or with a pesto or tomato sauce.

- Fusilli: There are various sizes of fusilli in Italy. Some long versions are shaped around a knitting needle and are known as *fusilli al ferro*. They are usually paired with heavier tomato, vegetable, or meat-based sauces that fit into the crevices of the pasta.

- Garganelli: This elongated, ridged, tubular pasta pairs well with loose tomato and meat sauces that coat both the inside and outside of the pasta.

- Gnocchi: Potato and ricotta dumplings are usually categorized with pasta in Italy. They can be dressed with a simple butter and herb sauce or with a traditional tomato sauce. The potato variety can also be topped with fresh pesto sauce.

- Orecchiete: "Little ear"-shaped pastas hail from the Puglia region and are usually served with broccoli, garlic, and chilies. They are also enjoyed with tomato sauce and meat sauce and also used in baked pasta dishes.

- Maltagliati: This "poorly cut" pasta gets its nickname from its ragged edges and is used in *pasta e fagioli* and soup recipes. It is rarely served with sauce on its own.

- Paccheri: Short- or medium-sized, very wide, hollow pasta similar to a bigger *rigatoni* is perfect for hugging thick pasta sauces. Sometimes they are stuffed with fresh mozzarella, breaded, and fried in the Naples area.

- Penne: Called "pens" because they are shaped like the quills once used as writing instruments, *penne* are now more commonly eaten outside of Italy. Their hollow shape is perfect for holding Arrabbiata sauce or tomato sauce and for tossing along with vegetables, cheese, and EVOO.

- Rigatoni: Short, very wide, rectangular pasta is usually ridged. This shape pairs well with Béchamel sauce, thick tomato sauce, and meat sauces, or a combination of sauces, and is often used in baked pasta recipes such as *Rigatoni al forno*/Baked Rigatoni with Besciamella Sauce and Meat Ragù featured in this chapter.

- Tortiglioni: Ridged, twisted, cylindrical-shaped medium-sized, hollow pasta that is best paired with rich tomato and vegetable sauces.

- Trofie: Thin, short, twisted pasta shapes usually served with pesto sauce, potatoes, and green beans in the Liguria region.

- Ziti: This medium-sized hollow pasta is best paired with homemade tomato sauces, spicy sauces, and meat sauce. *Zitoni* are longer *ziti* that pair with the same types of sauce.

» Long pasta shapes

- Bigoli: Long, thick noodle strands from the Veneto region are sometimes made with buckwheat flour; usually paired with onions and salt-cured fish.

- Bucatini: This long, thick pasta with a hole through the center is like a drinking straw; often paired with tomato sauce, meat sauce, *Amatriciana,* or *cacio e pepe.*

- Cappellini: Angel hair pasta is best tossed with EVOO, fresh herbs, and citrus or a very light dressing of fresh tomato and basil sauce.

- Lagane: Very wide, flat noodles that are indigenous to modern-day Calabria and Basilicata were first made in antiquity and are still enjoyed today. They are often paired with a chickpea-based sauce, tomato sauce, or meat sauce.

- Lasagne: Different regions have different lasagna recipes that use different combinations of sauces. The classic "Italian" recipe comes from Bologna in Emilia-Romagna and uses both Béchamel sauce and meat ragù.

- Linguine: Long, flat, narrow "little tongues" can be paired with seafood, an herb sauce, pesto, or a light tomato sauce.

- Pappardelle: This large, wide, ribbon-like pasta is usually served with a thick-ish tomato sauce, mushroom or vegetable ragù, or loose meat sauce.

- Spaghetti: The name of this pasta comes from the word "spago" or "twine" and wraps perfectly around olive oil and vegetables, seafood, and tomato sauce.

- Tagliatelle: These narrow "little cuts" are long, egg-based pasta strands that are traditionally paired with Bolognese sauce, but taste great with other tomato and butter-based sauces as well.

- Tonnarelli: This is the Roman name for *spaghetti alla chitarra*—slightly square-ish spaghetti strands made with a wooden *guitar* pasta cutter. They are usually served with *cacio e pepe* in Rome or with a variety of tomato, pepper, and meat sauces in Abruzzo.

- Trenette: Similar to *linguine, trenette* are narrow, long, flat pasta shapes from Liguria and are often paired with the traditional pesto sauce from the region.

» Stuffed pasta

- Agnolotti: This stuffed pasta is similar to ravioli but folded in half. The sauce used depends upon the filling—usually a butter and herb sauce for a cheese filling or a tomato sauce for a heavier, meat filling, for example.

- Cannelloni: These stuffed pasta tubes can be filled with meat or spinach and cheese filling and are usually topped with tomato sauce.

- Cappelletti: "Little hats" are stuffed pasta that are often served in broth. They are similar to tortellini except tortellini are made from circles and cappelletti are made from squares. Depending upon their filling, cappelletti can also be dressed with a vegetable, tomato, or meat sauce.

- Caramelle: Delicate stuffed "candy" pasta shapes (they look like hard candy wrapped in paper and twisted at the ends) are usually filled with some combination of whipped cheese and tossed in melted butter and sage, or another simple topping.

- Ravioli: Depending on the filling, ravioli are usually topped with a butter and herb sauce or a tomato sauce.

- Tortellini: Tiny stuffed pastas said to be inspired by Venus's belly button, *tortellini* can be stuffed with meat or cheese and are usually served in broth (a traditional Christmas Day first course in Italy) or in a butter, cream, or cheese-based sauce.

FIGURE 8-1:
Example pasta shapes.

Creating a Meal that Compliments Your Pasta Pairing

When you decide on a particular pasta and sauce combination to serve for an Italian meal, you need to make sure that the other items you're serving complement it both in terms of taste and nutrition. As mentioned before, 9 times out of 10 an Italian begins planning their meal with the first course, the *primo*, which is often pasta, instead of planning a meal around the second course, or entrée. There are occasions, however, such as Easter when lamb or goat might be served as a second course, or Christmas Eve, which is all about seafood, when Italians plan the meal around the second course.

Regardless of which dish you plan to build your next Italian meal around, it's imperative that the pasta course shines and pairs well with everything else being served.

Here are some general rules to follow:

>> If your pasta course contains a tomato-based sauce, your second course should not. Choose grilled, roasted, stewed, boiled, fried, or broiled options that are either sauce-free or dressed with a green sauce or citrus and herbs.

>> Conversely, if your second course (*entrée*) contains a heavy tomato sauce, such as a stew, you do not want to serve a pasta with tomato sauce.

>> Heavy meat sauces are reserved for Sundays and especially cold weather.

>> Pesto and fresh herb-based sauces are served in the summer.

>> Seasonal vegetables are always appropriate to serve with pasta.

>> If the pasta you serve is tossed with vegetables or beans and legumes and is free of an actual tomato sauce, it pairs well with a second course made with tomatoes, such as Eggplant Parmesan, Meatballs in Tomato Sauce, Stewed Meat, and so on.

>> Light, delicate proteins such as grilled or roasted fish served as a second course require a lighter pasta to precede them. *Spaghetti al limone, Linguine alle vongole,* and *trenette* with pesto sauce are great choices.

Spaghetti al aglio e olio/Spaghetti with Garlic, Oil, and Chile Pepper

INGREDIENTS

½ teaspoon unrefined sea salt

1 pound spaghetti, preferably made with gold or bronze dyes

¼ cup Amy Riolo Selections or other good-quality extra virgin olive oil, plus extra for drizzling

8 cloves garlic, peeled and minced

¼ teaspoon crushed red chili flakes

1 bunch (roughly ¾ cup) fresh, flat-leaf parsley, finely chopped

Black pepper, freshly ground, to taste

¼ cup freshly grated Pecorino or Parmigiano-Reggiano cheese for serving, if desired

DIRECTIONS

1 Cook the pasta according to package directions until very al dente (about 3 minutes less than if you were serving immediately).

2 Start the garlic/oil mixture immediately after adding the pasta to the boiling water. While the pasta is cooking, heat the olive oil in a large wide skillet over medium heat. Add the garlic and chili flakes, and cook just until they release their aroma, 30 to 60 seconds.

3 Drain the pasta and add the pasta and parsley to the skillet, toss to coat.

4 Drizzle with additional olive oil, if desired. Add black pepper to taste, and serve immediately with cheese.

TIP: Use the best-quality spaghetti, garlic, and EVOO you can find for this dish. With only a few ingredients in this recipe, the difference in quality will shine through.

Pair this dish with a bottle of *Riesling Italico* or similar. The aromatic spectrum, characterized by notes of quince and yellow peach, is finalized in a sip characterized by mineral and slightly bitter hints.

NOTE: This is a go-to "feel better" dish for Italians; I use it to get rid of migraines, and some say it helps with hangovers. This is the pasta to put together quickly after a late night, a long run, or just for the taste of it. Pair it with a tomato-based second course such as *Pollo alla cacciatora* (see Chapter 12), *Vrasciole*/Calabrian Meatballs (see Chapter 13), or Eggplant Parmesan (see Chapter 14).

VARY IT! Fresh broccoli, zucchini, peppers, and cauliflower can be sautéed and cooked to your liking in the EVOO before tossing in the spaghetti.

Orecchiete con cimi di rapa/ Orecchiete Pasta with Broccoli Rabe

PREP TIME: 5 MIN	COOK TIME: 20MIN	YIELD: 6 SERVINGS

INGREDIENTS

⅓ cup good-quality extra virgin olive oil, preferably Puglian

3 cloves garlic, peeled and finely chopped

½ chile pepper, seeded and minced, or ½ teaspoon crushed red chili flakes

¼ cup pine nuts

12 small cherry tomatoes, quartered

½ teaspoon unrefined sea salt or salt

¼ teaspoon black pepper, freshly ground

½ pound broccoli rabe

2 tablespoons freshly chopped basil or Italian parsley

1 pound orecchiette, or any short pasta

¼ cup Pecorino cheese (such as Romano), freshly grated, for serving

DIRECTIONS

1 Heat the olive oil in a large, wide skillet over medium heat.

2 Add the garlic and chile pepper, and sauté about 1 minute, just until they release their aroma.

3 Add the pine nuts and sauté until lightly golden.

4 Add the cherry tomatoes, salt, and pepper. Stir, and cook for 2 minutes.

5 Add the broccoli, basil or parsley, and ½ cup water, stir, and cover. Cook until the broccoli is fork-tender, about 10–minutes.

6 Meanwhile, cook the pasta in a large pot of slightly salted boiling water for about 10–12 minutes, or until al dente.

7 Drain, and add pasta to the finished sauce. Toss to combine. Taste and adjust seasonings, if necessary. Top with Pecorino cheese of your choice.

TIP: Good-quality pasta makes a big difference in the final result of this dish because it will hold its shape and cook to a better texture. Broccoli rabe is called *rapini* in Italian, and while the buds look like broccoli, they don't form a large head. The leaves are eaten as well, and are prized for their bitter taste and health properties. If you can't find them, substitute the best quality broccoli or other cruciferous vegetable you can find.

Pair this dish with a bottle of *Susumaniello* or similar. Made with a black grape variety from Puglia, this wine offers a dry sip. The herbaceous notes of the wine enrich each bite with balance. With aging, its finish adds value to the pairing.

NOTE: A tomato-based second course such as meatballs, *Braciole,* or a stew or roast is a great way to complement this dish.

Tagliatelle con salsa di ricotta e basilico/Tagliatelle with Basil Ricotta Cream Sauce

PREP TIME: 5 MIN | COOK TIME: 20 MIN | YIELD: 6 SERVINGS

INGREDIENTS

1 pound tagliatelle pasta

1 cup fresh ricotta

Bunch fresh basil (roughly ¾ cup), reserving a few leaves for garnish

¼ cup Grana Padano or Parmigiano-Reggiano cheese, freshly grated, plus extra for garnish if desired

¼ cup grated Pecorino Romano cheese

¼ cup Amy Riolo Selections or other good-quality extra virgin olive oil

Salt, to taste

Black pepper, freshly ground, to taste

DIRECTIONS

1 Cook the pasta to al dente, reserving 1 cup of pasta water.

2 While the pasta is cooking, combine the remaining ingredients except for salt and pepper in a food processor, reserving some of the Grana Padano cheese for garnish.

3 Process until smooth. Taste, and adjust salt, pepper, and olive oil to your preference. Add a bit of pasta water if sauce needs to be thinner.

4 Spoon sauce into a large bowl. Using tongs, toss pasta with sauce until combined. Garnish with basil and Grana Padano cheese, if desired.

TIP: You can use your own homemade *tagliatelle* (see Chapter 9), buy fresh *tagliatelle*, or use the dried variety for this recipe. When serving this dish, be sure to pair it with grilled or roasted meat or poultry for a second course.

Pair this dish with a bottle of *Malvasia puntinata* (or *Malvasia del Lazio*) or similar. This wine is characterized by its marked fruity and fresh-savory note, which, when blended with Trebbiao grapes, also gives an almond finish.

NOTE: Be sure to buy the best-quality cheese and freshest basil possible to make this quick sauce.

VARY IT! Other flat, long pastas such as *fettuccine, pappardelle,* and *trenette* also work well with this sauce.

Spaghetti al limone/Lemon Infused Spaghetti

PREP TIME: 5 MIN	COOK TIME: 20 MIN	YIELD: 6 SERVINGS

INGREDIENTS

Zest of 1 lemon

Juice of 1 lemon

1 cup heavy cream

Black pepper, freshly ground, to taste

1 teaspoon salt

1 pound spaghetti

½ cup freshly chopped Italian parsley

1 cup Parmigiano-Reggiano cheese, freshly grated

DIRECTIONS

1 Combine zest, lemon juice, cream, and a small amount of black pepper in a non-reactive medium saucepan over low heat. Simmer, whisking constantly so that the mixture doesn't curdle while preparing the spaghetti.

2 Cook the pasta according to package directions, until al dente. Drain well and return to the pot.

3 Add parsley and Parmigiano-Reggiano to the sauce, and whisk well to combine.

4 Pour sauce over the pasta, and turn well to coat pasta evenly. Serve hot.

TIP: This is the perfect pasta to serve in warm weather, preceding a seafood- or chicken-based second course dish.

Pair this dish with a bottle of *Trebbiano toscano* or similar. Part of the large Trebbiano family, this Tuscan clone is characterized by freshness and flavor, often accompanied by light aromas of yellow fruit.

NOTE: This is a traditional dish of the Amalfi coast, where lemons grow to gigantic proportion. I like to serve it as part of an entire lemon-based menu. I start with an appetizer of *Insalata di mare/*Seafood Salad (see Chapter 6), then serve this pasta followed by *Petto di pollo marinato/*Marinated Chicken Breasts (see Chapter 12).

VARY IT! Farfalle pasta also works well with this sauce.

Cuscussú alla mandorla Trapanese/ Trapani–Style Almond Couscous

PREP TIME: 10 MIN	COOK TIME: 45 MIN	YIELD: 6 SERVINGS

INGREDIENTS

¼ cup plus 2 tablespoons blanched almonds, lightly toasted, divided

1 pint small cherry tomatoes, 12 reserved whole and the rest quartered, divided

¼ cup grated Parmigiano-Reggiano cheese

2 cloves garlic, peeled

1 cup basil leaves, roughly chopped, plus more for garnish

½ teaspoon red chili flakes, crushed in a mortar and pestle or spice grinder

4 tablespoons good-quality extra virgin olive oil, such as Sicilian Nocellara di Belice, divided

1 cup couscous

1¼ cups Homemade Vegetable Stock (see Chapter 3)

DIRECTIONS

1 Put ¼ cup almonds in a food processor fitted with the blade attachment; pulse them 15-20 times until roughly chopped. Add the quartered tomatoes, cheese, garlic, basil, and red chili flakes. Pulse 8-10 times. With the machine running, use the feed tube to slowly add up to 2 tablespoons olive oil in a slow, steady stream. The resulting pesto should be quite grainy but not too chunky and not too wet. You may not need all the oil. Set pesto aside.

2 Heat the remaining 2 tablespoons olive oil in a saucepan over high heat. Add the couscous and cook, stirring often, until toasted, about 2 minutes.

3 Add the stock, cover the pan, and reduce heat to low. Simmer 5-10 minutes until all the liquid has been absorbed. Fluff with a fork, and toss in ¼ cup tomato pesto.

4 Garnish with remaining whole tomatoes, 2 tablespoons chopped almonds, and a few basil leaves. Serve.

TIP: This dish tastes best preceding a seafood-based second course.

NOTE: Trapani, located on Sicily's west coast, inherited the tradition of couscous from the Tunisians in the 9th century. In Sicily, couscous is usually served with seafood. Each year, in San Vito Lo Capo, Sicily, there is a Couscous Fest that brings together chefs, cooks, artisans, musicians, and public figures from the Mediterranean's couscous-making cultures to promote pluralism. Each country that attends prepares their own signature recipe.

VARY IT! The sauce in this recipe also tastes great on fusilli. If you want to make a seafood couscous, simply add scrubbed mussels to the pot during the last 5 minutes of cooking and steam until they open and couscous is cooked through. Discard any unopened mussels.

Pasta con tonno e finocchio/Bucatini with Fresh Tuna and Fennel

PREP TIME: 5 MIN	COOK TIME: 25 MIN	YIELD: 6 SERVINGS

INGREDIENTS

¼ cup plus 3 tablespoons Amy Riolo Selections or other good-quality extra virgin olive oil, divided

¾ pound fresh tuna fillets

16 ounces bucatini pasta, or spaghetti or linguine

2 medium (8-ounce) bulbs fennel

½ cup white wine

Juice from 1 lemon

Zest from 1 lemon

2 tablespoons capers, rinsed and drained

¼ teaspoon unrefined sea salt

¼ teaspoon black pepper, freshly ground

DIRECTIONS

1 Preheat oven to 400 degrees.

2 Heat ¼ cup olive oil in a large, wide skillet over medium-high heat. Add tuna fillets, and sauté until golden on each side, approximately 3 minutes per side if your tuna is cut very thickly, and if you would like it to cook more in the center: transfer to oven, and cook to desired doneness— approximately 5 minutes for medium-well.

3 Cook pasta according to package instructions, omitting salt. Drain, reserving 1 cup pasta water, and return to pot.

4 Trim fennel bulbs, reserving ¼ cup chopped fronds. Quarter, core, and thinly slice bulbs crosswise. Sauté with 1 tablespoon olive oil in a skillet over medium-high heat. Add wine, and reduce heat to low. Cover and cook until tender, stirring occasionally, 10-20 minutes.

5 Add fennel to pasta, along with fennel fronds, lemon juice, capers, remaining 2 tablespoons olive oil, and reserved pasta water. Season with salt and pepper. Flake in the tuna and drizzle with remaining EVOO from the pan.

6 Gently toss and garnish with lemon zest. Serve hot.

TIP: You can prepare the tuna a day ahead of time, or make this recipe with leftover grilled tuna to save time.

Pair this dish with a bottle of *Verdicchio di Matelica Riserva* or similar. This wine has a deep color and a richness and complexity of flavor and aroma that recalls dried fruit, notes of candied fruit, and honey. Excellent length of the finish.

NOTE: This dish is best served prior to another seafood course. In many Calabrian and Sicilian households, this dish is served as a first course on Christmas Eve.

Linguine alle vongole/Linguine with Clams

PREP TIME: 5 MIN | **COOK TIME: 20 MIN** | **YIELD: 6 SERVINGS**

INGREDIENTS

1 tablespoon salt

1 pound linguine

¼ cup Amy Riolo Selections or other good-quality extra virgin olive oil

2 cloves garlic, peeled and sliced thinly

1½ pounds small clams, scrubbed well, and debearded if necessary

½ cup seafood stock, divided (see Chapter 3)

2 tablespoons finely chopped fresh flat-leaf Italian parsley

1 lemon, cut into 6 wedges

DIRECTIONS

1 Cook the pasta according to package directions, until very al dente (about 3 minutes less than if you were serving immediately). Drain, reserving a cup of cooking liquid.

2 While the linguine is cooking, heat the olive oil in a large sauté pan over medium heat. Add the garlic, and cook until it begins to release its aroma.

3 Add the clams and seafood stock. Cover and cook over medium heat until all the clams are open, approximately 2–3 minutes. Discard any broken or unopened clams.

4 Add the linguine to the clams, and toss well with reserved pasta water. Continue to cook for 1–2 minutes to allow the flavors to combine and the linguine to achieve desired tenderness.

5 Toss with tongs to combine. Place pasta on a platter or individual plates and arrange clam shells around the pasta. Top with parsley, and serve immediately with lemon wedges.

TIP: This dish is best served before a fish dish. The second course could include tomatoes.

Pair this dish with a bottle of *Cirò rosato* or similar. From Gaglioppo grapes, this Calabrian rosé, with a complexity of flavor and aroma that recalls blueberries, currants, and Mediterranean scrub, is the perfect aromatic partner for this dish.

NOTE: Be sure to purchase your clams on the day that you are making this dish. Store them in the top of the refrigerator or the coldest part until using. To clean them, scrub them with a clean brush and rinse under cold water until no sand remains. Remove their beards if they have any, and use immediately. Clams open when they are dead, and you need live clams to cook. So, if you have an open clam or mussel, gently tap it on the counter and wait to see if it closes. If it does not, discard it. If it does, use it in your recipe.

VARY IT! You can also use mussels in this recipe instead of clams and spaghetti instead of linguine.

Pasta e fagioli cannellini/Pasta, White Bean, and Tomato Soup

PREP TIME: 5 MIN	COOK TIME: 30 MIN PLUS AT LEAST 1 HOUR SOAKING TIME	YIELD: 6-8 SERVINGS

INGREDIENTS

½ pound (8 ounces) dried borlotti (cranberry) beans, placed in heat-proof bowl of boiling water to soak for 1 hour, or placed in cold water to soak overnight

1 teaspoon salt, plus more to taste

1 bay leaf

⅓ cup Amy Riolo Selections or other good-quality extra virgin olive oil, divided

1 celery stalk, diced

1 carrot, diced

1 small yellow onion, diced

1 garlic clove, peeled and chopped

1 sprig fresh rosemary, finely chopped

Pinch of crushed red chili flakes or pepperoncino

1 cup tomato purée or Fresh Tomato Sauce (see Chapter 7)

Black pepper, freshly ground, to taste

2 cups ditalini pasta

¼ cup grated Parmigiano-Reggiano, Pecorino, or Grana Padano cheese, for garnish

DIRECTIONS

1 Drain the soaked beans, place them in a large saucepan, and cover with almost double the amount of water. Add 1 teaspoon of salt and the bay leaf; bring to a boil. Reduce heat to medium-low, cover, and simmer 45 minutes, or until tender. Do not drain.

2 Carefully transfer half of the beans and a bit of the cooking liquid to a blender and purée until smooth; be sure the lid cap is off and cover it with a clean folded kitchen towel to avoid splashing.

3 Drain the remaining beans and reserve the cooking liquid for Step 6.

4 In a large pot, heat 2 tablespoons of the olive oil over medium heat. Add celery, carrot, and onion. Stir with a wooden spoon and allow to cook for 5-7 minutes until soft and onions are slightly translucent.

5 Add garlic and rosemary, stir to combine, and cook for another minute. When the garlic releases its aroma, add chili flakes and stir.

6 Add tomatoes and reserved liquid from cooking the beans. Season with salt and pepper, and increase heat to high.

7 When mixture boils, add ditalini pasta, reduce heat to medium-low, and heat until pasta is cooked and sauce has thickened. Drizzle with an additional teaspoon of olive oil and garnish with grated cheese, if desired.

TIP: Pair this dish with a bottle of *Montepulciano d'Abruzzo* or similar. With a little aging it expresses itself with a more rounded and defined fruit, able to accompany even the most complex versions of this dish.

Rigatoni al forno/Baked Rigatoni with Besciamella Sauce and Meat Ragù

PREP TIME: 5 MIN	COOK TIME: 20 MIN	YIELD: 8 SERVINGS

INGREDIENTS

1 pound rigatoni pasta

¼ cup butter, cubed

Half recipe Salsa besciamella/ Béchamel Sauce (see Chapter 7)

Half recipe Ragù Bolognese or Fresh Tomato Sauce (see Chapter 7)

1 cup grated Parmigiano-Reggiano cheese

DIRECTIONS

1 Preheat oven to 375 degrees.

2 Cook the pasta according to package directions, until very al dente (about 3 minutes less than if you were serving immediately). Drain.

3 Grease a deep 9x13-inch baking dish with 1 cube of butter and spread a layer of the besciamella sauce on the bottom.

4 Add a layer of rigatoni over the sauce, then a layer of ragù Bolognese, and a few tablespoons of cheese. Continue layering until all of the pasta and sauce are used up.

5 Sprinkle the remaining cheese on the top, dot with remaining butter cubes, and place in the oven. Bake for 20-30 minutes until golden. Allow to cool for at least 15 minutes and slice into large squares to serve.

TIP: Baked dishes can be assembled the night before and baked the morning of serving so they have time to set up. If you are serving this as a first course, you need an equally filling second course that does not have too much sauce, such as roasted meat or fried meatballs.

Pair this dish with a bottle of *Tramonti rosso* or similar. A mix of the ancient Aglianico, Tintore, and Piedirosso vines and a unique terroir create fruity and Mediterranean notes with a fresh, tannic, warm, and spicy sip.

NOTE: These types of dishes are synonymous with Sundays and special occasions in Italy, although, if served on a Wednesday night, that would make it a celebration, too!

VARY IT! You can use just one of the sauces in larger amounts, or swap out the rigatoni for ziti or penne, if you like in this filling dish. Some people like to layer their baked pasta dishes with vegetables or sliced hard-boiled eggs as well.

Chapter 9

Making Fresh Pasta: A Labor of Love

Often dismissed as "poor man's food," real, authentic, pasta is much more than a way to stave off hunger. Homemade pasta is as integral to the Italian cultural landscape as art, fashion, design, opera, and other innovations are. According to legend, when Giuseppe Garibaldi, an Italian general who contributed to the Italian unification, first tasted *Spaghetti al pomodoro* in Mileto di Porto Salvo, Calabria, he declared that it would be the dish that unified all of Italy. (He actually sold pasta in Uruguay before leading his troops to take control of Italy from the Bourbons and unifying the nation himself.) While his claim may seem like an exaggeration to many, it pales in comparison to the 17th century Duke of Bovino stating that "the angels in paradise eat nothing but" the same dish!

I love to share these phrases because they help us to understand just how integral pasta is to the Italian food culture. While typical meals are made up of multiple courses, if they had to, most Italians would renounce all of them, except for the pasta. Pasta often gets a bad rap in the United States and abroad. People view it as carb-heavy and lacking in protein. The recipes in this chapter, however, prove otherwise. When you make pasta by hand, you are ensuring that you are using good-quality flour, eggs, and water. Daily pastas (with the exception of lasagne and stuffed varieties served on holidays) are dressed with fresh vegetables, produce, EVOO, and legumes, making them as nutritious as they are delicious. These types of dishes have been staples in the Mediterranean diet for millennia and are linked to positive health. Enjoy them at midday instead of in the evening and in small portions to keep your health on track. Plus, making homemade pasta is a bit of a workout. Burning some calories while you gear up for a mouthwatering meal allows you to "have your *pasta* and eat it, too!"

In this chapter, you discover how to make authentic regional Italian recipes the way a modern cook would. You also learn their history and the role they play in a typical meal as well as what to pair them with.

Stepping Inside the Pasta Maker's Kitchen

Sfoglia is an Italian word for pastry dough. A *sfoglina* was historically a female dough maker who made all types of dough, including an *impasto* for pasta. Nowadays the word *sfoglina* is used to describe a female pasta maker in Italy whose craft is hand-making pasta (without a machine). There are restaurants by this name around the world that feature homemade pasta. Once specializing only in dough, and now in pasta, these women were single-handedly responsible for passing Italy's culinary patrimony down from generation to generation for millennia.

In the professional Italian kitchen, it is imperative that chefs learn to make pasta in order to prepare traditional dishes. Some restaurants even purchase the pasta from a local *sfoglina* instead of making it onsite, while others hire *sfogline* to work in the dining room or front window, showcasing their creations.

Chef Luigi Diotaiuti, Ambassador of Italian Cuisine to the world and owner of the famed Al Tiramisu Restaurant in Washington, D.C., has a non-profit organization in his native Basilicata, Italy, that dedicates a portion of its events to Pasta Lab, a yearly event that pairs professional chefs with *sfogline* in order to keep the artisan pasta trade going strong.

Italians are not the only ones to appreciate the art of dough making throughout history. During the Ottoman Empire, the Topkapi Palace in Istanbul actually employed 100 dough cooks at any given time. Nowadays, one of the unique facets of Italian cuisine is that it is based on the cooking of women and grandmothers in the home. Even the finest Italian restaurants that re-interpret dishes in modern ways are still working off base recipes and traditions that began in the home.

Fresh pasta is not meant to be made under pressure. It is best when it is prepared with others, as a community effort. The repetitive tasks allow for flowing conversation and inspiration. When you are able to make fresh pasta, you have not only learned a task, but a new way of living. I believe that Sophia Loren said it best when she stated, *"Una donna che sa fare la pasta a regola d'arte ha un prestigio che resiste anche oggi a qualsiasi altro richiamo dei tempi"* ("A woman who knows how to make pasta to perfection has a prestige that resists even today any other lure of the times"). I dare add that the same thing applies to men who make pasta!

Getting the Most Out of Your Pasta-Making Experience

Making fresh pasta is a labor of love—one that can become therapeutic and pleasurable if you allow it. To get the most out of your pasta-making experience, however, allow yourself plenty of time to experiment. Buy the ingredients one day, read through the recipes another, and on the day that you try the recipe, be sure that you have a Plan B for dinner.

Pasta-making, like all other artisan crafts, takes practice and dedication. Your first try might not come out the way you wanted, but that's fine. Skilled pasta-makers have decades of experience. If you stick with it, though, you'll be making delicious and nutritious pasta on your own before you know it. Best of all, you'll enjoy yourself in the process.

With the recipes in this chapter, I have organized them the way that Italian housewives and professional chefs run their kitchens. In most circumstances, cooks do not start out making sauces, pastas, and all of the other courses from scratch before a large meal. Instead, they keep certain staples always on hand (see Chapters 3 and 5). By having sauces and pastas already made and frozen, you can put together more elaborate dishes and meals easily and with great success.

To get the most out of the dishes in this chapter, read the recipes thoroughly at least a day prior to making them so you can be sure to have everything on hand— the pre-made items, the pantry staples, the equipment, and the time needed to make each dish. This way, when you actually set out to create the pasta, you can enjoy the process. Note that the recipes in this chapter, although varied and representing different regions, are still just a small percentage of the types of fresh pasta recipes that are available in Italy. Once you learn these, however, you can easily expand your repertoire as you discover new recipes.

I recommend making large batches of fresh pasta and freezing some to use later. To do that, after you have cut the fresh pasta, wrap a handful at a time of the strands around your hand to form a little nest. Then set those nests in little piles on a baking sheet dusted with the same flour that you used to make the pasta. Set in the freezer for an hour. After the nests are frozen and hard, remove them from the baking sheet and place them in a large plastic container or a double-lined zip top bag for up to a month. When you need fresh pasta simply remove nests from the freezer, drop in salted boiling water, and enjoy with your favorite dressing or sauce.

Meeting Your Pasta Maker: Rolling Pin or Pasta Machine

You don't need a pasta machine or fancy attachments for your mixer in order to make fresh pasta. You can make it by hand using a rolling pin, a knife, a fork, and a clean work surface, as I do. This is the way that the women in my family and in many Italian families make pasta. While this labor of love is nowadays reserved for Sundays and special occasions, there is no reason to be intimidated by it.

Working with a rolling pin to roll out your dough produces a more characteristic texture that is highly appreciated nowadays. There are chefs from around the globe that travel to Italy to learn how to make pasta using this method so that they can include it on their menus in the U.S. While this method takes more time than using a pasta machine, it is highly rewarding and therapeutic, plus you can increase your physical activity while making your meal! So, when the mood strikes, give yourself plenty of time to experiment, and have fun with the process.

Pasta machines are wonderful inventions because they enable you to make large amounts of pasta in a short amount of time. If I am doing an event for more than 30 people, I usually enlist the help of a pasta machine. There are several varieties to choose from for both professional and home use. If you're searching for a pasta machine to use at home, the old-school crank variety has stood the test of time, and, while it requires you to turn it manually, is highly effective. Another favorite is the pasta-making attachments that fit on standing mixers. Electric pasta machines enable you to make many shapes and styles by simply changing the extruders.

If you plan on making fresh pasta often, and in large quantities, or if you want to save your hands and arms the effort, take your time choosing a maker that suits your needs. Then follow the manufacturer's instructions carefully for best results.

Note: Most of the recipe instructions for this book are for pasta which is hand-rolled. If you are using a hand–crank pasta machine or mixer attachment, never fear – the following instructions will help you achieve the best outcome:

1. Set the pasta machine or attachment at the widest setting. Lightly flour each side of the dough and pass it through the pasta machine. If the flour comes off, lightly coat with more flour, fold the dough in half, and run through the machine again.

2. Continue this process until the dough is 2 feet long. Each time you pass the dough through the machine, adjust the settings slightly so you end up on the narrowest setting.

3. Cut the dough into four equal pieces.

4. Run each piece through the machine 4-5 times in the same fashion, dusting with flour as needed, until each piece of the dough is $\frac{1}{16}$-inch thick.

5. Cut the pieces in half width-wise to make two 12-inch-long rectangular pieces out of each.

6. Change the attachment on the pasta machine to create desired shapes and sizes, or cut them by hand when following a particular recipe.

Ricetta base per la pasta/Basic Pasta Dough

PREP TIME: 15 MIN	COOK TIME: 30 MIN RESTING TIME	YIELD: 4 SERVINGS (APPROXIMATELY ½ POUND)

INGREDIENTS

2½ cups 00 (highly refined) flour or all-purpose flour, plus additional 1 cup for work surface

4 jumbo eggs (10 ounces total)

1 teaspoon salt

DIRECTIONS

1 Place the flour in a mound on a clean, dry work surface. Make a hole in the center and break the eggs into the middle. Using a fork, carefully mix the eggs together and incorporate a little flour into the eggs at a time.

2 Add the salt, and mix well by hand to form a solid dough.

3 Lightly flour the work surface, and knead and fold the dough energetically until it forms a smooth ball; see Figure 9-1. Using your hands or a floured rolling pin, flatten out the dough to form a 10-inch diameter disk. Cover and set aside to rest for 30 minutes.

4 Using a rolling pin, roll out the dough to form a rectangle about 12-inches long. Cut the rectangle into four equal pieces. Roll each piece on a lightly floured surface until it is $\frac{1}{16}$-inch thick. Cut pasta sheets into desired shapes called for in your recipe. Refer to individual recipes in the next section for instructions on creating different shapes.

TIP: There are two different base pasta recipes (with eggs) in Italy. This one is used to make fettuccine, tortellini, ravioli, maltagliati, farfalle, and more tender pasta shapes. The following Basic Grano Duro Pasta Dough recipe is used to make other pasta shapes listed there.

NOTE: The standard Italian equation for pasta is 1 egg for every 100 grams (or roughly ¾ cup) of flour, but it is truly just a base because different flours require different amounts of moisture in different temperatures, and eggs can vary in size. This dough should be smooth and supple. If it isn't, add a little bit of water, a tablespoon at a time, until it is more pliable and you can work with it.

In Italy, flour is labeled by how finely-ground it is, and to what degree the bran and germ have been removed. Flour is sold as 1, 0, or 00, with the latter being so highly refined that it almost feels like talcum powder.

VARY IT! You can use heirloom grains such as einkorn, or even all-purpose flour with this recipe, if you prefer. The texture and taste of the pasta will vary depending on what you use, but it will still be delicious! (For example, einkorn flour makes a more substantial, resilient dough, while 00 and all-purpose flour make a more tender dough.)

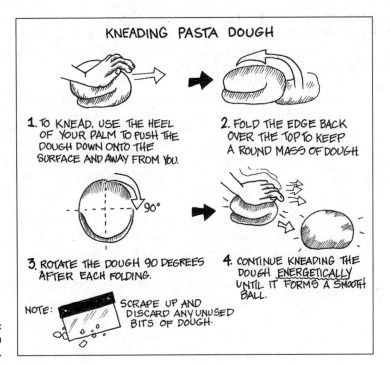

FIGURE 9-1:
Kneading pasta
dough.

Ricetta base per la pasta grano duro/ Basic Grano Duro Pasta Dough

PREP TIME: 25 MIN	COOK TIME: 5 MIN	YIELD: 4 SERVINGS (APPROXIMATELY ½ POUND)

INGREDIENTS

2¾ cups durum wheat flour, plus additional 1 cup for work surface

4 jumbo eggs (10 ounces total)

1 teaspoon salt

DIRECTIONS

1 Place the flour in a mound on a clean, dry work surface. Make a hole in the center and break the eggs into the middle. Using a fork, carefully mix the eggs together and incorporate a little flour into the eggs at a time.

2 Add the salt, and mix well by hand to form a solid dough.

3 Lightly flour the work surface, and knead and fold the dough energetically until it forms a smooth ball (refer to Figure 9-1). Using your hands or a floured rolling pin, flatten out the dough to form a 10-inch diameter disk. Cover and set aside to rest for 30 minutes. Scrape up and discard any unused bits of dough.

4 Using a rolling pin, roll out the dough to form a rectangle about 12-inches long. Cut the rectangle into four equal pieces. Roll each piece on a lightly floured surface until it is $\frac{1}{16}$-inch thick. Cut pasta sheets into desired shapes called for in your recipe. Refer to individual recipes for further instructions.

TIP: This type of dough is used to make taglierini, pappardelle, fusilli, orecchiette, cavatelli, lagane, spaghetti, ziti, and many other traditional pasta shapes.

NOTE: Pasta in most Southern Italian regions is generally made with *grano duro* durum wheat flour, "hard wheat," which is higher in protein than other kinds of wheat and is considered a whole wheat product because it contains the germ, bran, and other parts of the wheat grain. During the milling process, durum wheat can be ground into semolina, and semolina is sometimes used to make these shapes as well. This dough is *not* used for stuffed pasta recipes.

VARY IT! Semolina, einkorn, spelt, and other heirloom varieties of wheat can be used when making this pasta.

Originally this type of dough was made with only flour and water (as in the *Ravioli Capresi* recipe in this book), but nowadays many Italian chefs include eggs. If you prefer to make this type of pasta without eggs, you can use 3 cups of durum wheat flour plus 1 ½ cups tepid water along with 2 tablespoons of lukewarm water and 1 teaspoon salt as ingredients.

Lagane con ceci/Lagane Pasta with Chickpeas

PREP TIME: 10 MIN	COOK TIME: 1 HOUR PLUS OVERNIGHT FOR SOAKING MIN	YIELD: 4 SERVINGS

INGREDIENTS

8 ounces dried chickpeas, covered in water, soaked overnight, and drained

1 bay leaf

1 clove garlic, peeled

3 teaspoons unrefined sea salt or salt, divided

4 tablespoons Amy Riolo Selections or other good-quality extra virgin olive oil

1 small yellow onion, finely chopped

1 small chile pepper, seeded and finely chopped

¾ pound cherry tomatoes, quartered

6 fresh basil leaves, shredded, or 1 tablespoon finely chopped parsley

Black pepper, freshly ground, to taste

1 recipe (roughly 1/2 pound) Basic Grano Duro Pasta Dough (refer to the recipe earlier in this chapter)

Pecorino Crotonese, Pecorino di Moliterno, or Pecorino Romano cheese, freshly grated, for serving

DIRECTIONS

1 Place the prepared chickpeas, bay leaf, garlic clove, and 1 teaspoon salt in a large saucepan, cover with water, and bring to a boil over high heat. Reduce heat to low, and simmer, covered, adding hot water if liquid is absorbed from chickpeas before they are tender, for 30 minutes or until very tender. Drain and remove the bay leaf.

2 While the chickpeas are cooking, lightly flour your work surface and use a rolling pin to roll out the prepared dough until it is about $\frac{1}{16}$-inch thick (or use a pasta machine as directed in the recipe — this setting is usually second to last or last depending upon your machine). Fold the dough over itself in equally spaced quarter folds.

3 With a sharp knife or pasta cutter, slice lengthwise strips of varying lengths, 5-6 inches long, and about ¼-inch wide. Set aside.

4 In a large skillet, heat the olive oil over medium heat. Add the onion, and sauté until soft, 3-5 minutes. Add the chile pepper, tomatoes, and basil or parsley. Stir in 1 teaspoon salt and black pepper to taste. Allow to cook 5 minutes.

5 Add the cooked chickpeas to the tomato mixture, cover, and simmer for 30 minutes, or until chickpeas are tender.

6 Bring a large pot of water to boil over high heat. Season with a teaspoon of salt, add the lagane, stir, and reduce heat to medium-low. Allow to cook for about 10 minutes, or until pasta is al dente.

7 Drain the pasta, and toss it with ladles of the sauce. Garnish with freshly grated Pecorino cheese and serve.

(continued)

TIP: You can make the lagane and/or the sauce a day or up to a week ahead of time in order to pull the dish together at the last minute for an event.

Pair this dish with a bottle of *Guarnaccino rosato* or similar. Produced only in Basilicata, it is a muscular wine with notes of small red fruits supported by acidity and a delicate tannin content that allow the wine to age well.

NOTE: Lagane (or laganelle) is a type of homemade pasta often paired with beans and used primarily in Basilicata, Campania, Calabria, and Puglia. Until recently, few cooks outside of these regions knew how to prepare it. At first glance, it resembles tagliatelle or fettuccine, but lagane are flatter, thinner, and of varying lengths. (If you intend to serve this pasta with a traditional tomato or meat sauce, make strips a uniform 8 inches long instead.)

VARIOUS types of pasta with chickpeas are famous throughout Italy. Chickpeas were once a symbol of rebirth in southern Italy and other areas of the Mediterranean. Local pastas like cavatelli and lagane, which were prepared with whole-grain flour since the fourth century BCE in the region, were paired with chickpeas and served at harvest times. In Calabria, they are usually served on the Festa di San Giuseppe (St. Joseph's Day), which is also Father's Day, and celebrated on March 19 in Italy.

VARY IT! Lagane can be enjoyed with a simple Fresh Tomato Sauce (see Chapter 7), Meat Ragù (see the following recipe), or other legume-based sauce as well as with the chickpeas.

Tagliatelle Bolognese/Tagliatelle with Meat Ragù

PREP TIME: 20 MIN   COOK TIME: 2 HOURS   YIELD: 8 SERVINGS

INGREDIENTS

2 recipes (roughly 1 pound) Basic Pasta Dough (refer to the recipe earlier in this chapter)

1 recipe Ragù alla Bolognese (see Chapter 7)

4 tablespoons Amy Riolo Selections or other good-quality extra virgin olive oil

⅓ cup freshly grated Parmigiano-Reggiano cheese

DIRECTIONS

1 To cut the tagliatelle, lightly flour a work surface and roll out the dough until it forms a rectangle 2 feet long and about $\frac{1}{16}$-inch thick.

2 Cut the dough in half width-wise to make two 12-inch-long rectangular sheets.

3 Dust each pasta sheet lightly with flour, roll up sheet, and, using a sharp knife, cut into ¼-inch-wide strips; unroll.

4 Bring a large pot of water to a boil. Add 1 tablespoon salt and the tagliatelle.

5 Cook, uncovered, stirring occasionally, until the pasta is al dente. Drain pasta, and return it to the pot.

6 Add the sauce, a ladleful at a time until the tagliatelle are dressed to your taste.

7 Toss gently to combine, and place on a platter. Drizzle with EVOO and sprinkle with cheese before serving.

TIP: You can dry fresh tagliatelle on a floured work surface for 30 minutes and then store in an airtight container for up to 3 days.

Pair this dish with a bottle of *Lambrusco Grasparossa di Castelvetro* or similar. Typically dry to the sip, fruity, and with a spicy finish, this wine has a fine and crisp bubble that is known for its purple hues, its taste, and for its role as a palate regenerator.

Italians like to serve pasta such as tagliatelle in rather neat mounds, instead of dumping it on a plate or platter. To do this, you need long tongs and a fairly wide ladle. With your dominant hand, grab a generous amount of pasta in the tongs, place the bottom of the tongs in the ladle, and twist from the top to make a nest shape. Carefully transfer the mound from the ladle to a plate with the assistance of the tongs to make a compact mound. Figure 9-2 helps you visualize this process.

(continued)

NOTE: Fresh Tagliatelle (which comes from the verb *tagliare* and means "to cut") and Fettuccine (which comes from the word *"fetta"* and means "slice") are very similar in size and shape. In the region of Bologna where this recipe hails from, they are simply called Tagliatelle as they are in some other Northern regions. In Rome and the South, they are usually called Fettuccine. It is believed that this shape was developed in 1501 by court cook to Giovanni II Bentivoglio. His cook, Zaffirino made them for Lucrezia Borgia because he was inspired by her golden hair. Fresh pasta ribbons must be ¼-inch wide, as mandated by the Chamber of Commerce of Bologna.

VARY IT! Tagliatelle also taste great with cream sauces and tomato sauces (see Chapter 7), and even with butter or EVOO and some Parmigiano-Reggiano cheese when you are feeling under the weather.

MAKING PASTA NESTS

1. WITH YOUR DOMINANT HAND, PLACE A GENEROUS AMOUNT OF PASTA IN THE TONGS, PLACE THE BOTTOM OF THE TONGS IN THE LADLE,

2. AND TWIST FROM THE TOP TO MAKE A NEST SHAPE.

3. CAREFULLY TRANSFER THE MOUND FROM THE LADLE TO THE PLATE WITH THE ASSISTANCE OF THE TONGS TO MAKE A COMPACT MOUND.

FIGURE 9-2: Plating pasta mounds or nests.

Ravioli Capresi/Capri-Style Ravioli

PREP TIME: 30 MIN	COOK TIME: 30 MIN	YIELD: 4 SERVINGS

INGREDIENTS

For the Dough:

2 ½ cups all-purpose flour, plus more for dusting

1 cup water

For the Filling:

¾ pound fresh, good-quality ricotta cheese, drained

¼ pound aged Parmigiana-Reggiano cheese, grated

½ cup Provolone cheese, grated, divided

1 egg

Handful of fresh marjoram or oregano leaves, roughly chopped

For the Sauce:

1 tablespoon Amy Riolo Selections or other good-quality extra virgin olive oil

2 garlic cloves, peeled and roughly chopped

14 ounces canned San Marzano tomatoes (crushed by hand); half a 28-ounce can

Fresh basil leaves (about 3 tablespoons), roughly chopped

2 tablespoons butter

DIRECTIONS

1 For the dough, add the water to a small sauce pan and bring to a boil. When the water boils, immediately remove from the heat. In a large bowl, add the flour to the bowl and create a well in the center. Add the hot water to the flour well, and stir together. Let the dough rest for 5 minutes until cool.

2 While the dough rests, make the filling. In a medium bowl, combine the ricotta, Parmigiano-Reggiano, half the Provolone cheese, egg, and the roughly chopped marjoram or oregano. Use your hands to combine well. If you have a pastry bag, you can put the filling in it with a 1-inch tip attached, to make filling the ravioli quicker and easier. You can also use a large zipper lock bag by filling it with the cheese filling, carefully pushing the filling down to the bottom of one side as if it were a pastry bag, and snipping off the end. Otherwise, you can simply spoon the filling on the dough.

3 For the sauce, in a medium sauce pot over medium-high heat, add the olive oil. Add the chopped garlic, and cook until light brown (do not burn!). Add the tomatoes, and simmer over low heat. Cook and reduce the sauce until thick. Add salt and pepper to taste and the basil. Cook a little more until the basil flavor is cooked into the sauce. You can use an immersion blender to make this sauce smoother, if desired.

4 To assemble and cook, roll out the dough into a very large rectangle (approximately 2x3 feet) on a well-floured surface using a well-floured rolling pin until the dough reaches $\frac{1}{16}$-inch thickness.

(continued)

5 Cut 3-inch-wide strips of dough across the width of the entire piece. Using a teaspoon, place dollops of the filling about 1 inch apart along one strip of dough. Leave the next strip empty and use it to cover the strip of dough with the filling. Using a juice glass, a ravioli stamp, or a cookie cutter dipped in flour, cut out each ravioli. Remove the excess dough and, if using a cookie cutter or glass, which don't seal the edges for you, use a fork to gently seal the ravioli all around. Lay out on a sheet pan dusted with ¼ cup flour and cover with a dish-towel to prevent from drying out until ready to cook.

6 Repeat with remaining strips — filling one and using the next one as a cover until all dough is used up. Gather leftover scraps of dough and add a tablespoon or more of boiling water to form a supple dough like the one you started with. Roll that dough out in the same fashion and make more ravioli until all of the dough is used up.

7 Cook the ravioli in salted boiling water until cooked through. Because this pasta doesn't use eggs, it cooks quickly. When the "flour" smell is gone from the pot and the ravioli float to the top, they're done.

8 To serve in a traditional manner, drain the ravioli and place around a plate. Spoon a few tablespoons of tomato sauce in the center of the plate, and garnish with a few basil leaves. Sprinkle with grated Parmigiana-Reggiano or Provolone cheese, and serve.

TIP: If it's your first time making ravioli, a few pieces of equipment, such as a ravioli stamp, or a cookie cutter that is the same size as your desired ravioli size, will make things easier. A ravioli stamp is more convenient because you can cut through two layers of dough with the filling in the middle and save time. If you use a cookie cutter, you have to cut out individual shapes, fill them, and then press their edges together. Be sure to flour your work surface well and to add more flour to your rolling pin if you notice dough sticking to it or pulling back when you try to roll it out.

Pair this dish with a bottle of *Asprinio di Aversa* or similar. A white wine characterized by citrus notes, marked freshness, and light body. This wine will accompany every bite and refresh the taste buds without overpowering the dish.

NOTE: These are not typical Italian ravioli made with the Basic Pasta Dough recipe earlier in this chapter; they are instead the traditional ravioli of the island of Capri (called the Pearl of the Mediterranean by poet Pablo Neruda) made with the ancient technique of combining flour with boiling water and no eggs to make pasta. This recipe was taught to me by Ristorante d'Amore's Executive Chef Pasquale Rinaldo in Capri, and it was the highlight of the "Under the Capri Sun" dinner we served to a sold-out crowd at the James Beard House in 2020. We used heart-shaped cookie cutters to shape the ravioli for Valentine's Day.

VARY IT! If you already have Basic Pasta Dough (see recipe earlier in this chapter), you can use it and this same procedure with the filling and sauce of your choice to make the more commonly known ravioli.

Trofie al pesto/Trofie Pasta with Pesto Sauce

PREP TIME: 1 HOUR | COOK TIME: 20 MIN | YIELD: 4-6 SERVINGS

INGREDIENTS

1 recipe (roughly ½ pound) Grano Duro Pasta Dough (recipe earlier in this chapter — use the egg-free variation to make the dough)

1 tablespoon salt

1 recipe Pesto (see Chapter 7)

¼ cup Anfosso or other good-quality extra virgin olive oil, preferably from Liguria

¼ cup Parmigiano-Reggiano cheese, freshly grated

A handful of fresh basil leaves

DIRECTIONS

1   Start with the Grano Duro Pasta Dough that has rested; cut the dough and shape into six even-haped balls.

2   Using the palm of your hands, roll them on a floured surface to form a long even-sized rope with the thickness of a pencil (the same technique that is used for gnocchi).

3   With a sharp knife or bench scraper, cut even, marble-sized pieces of the dough.

4   Place the marbles, one at a time in the middle of a pastry board or a floured surface.

5   Place the middle of the side of your hand on top of the marble and scrape down in a horizontal fashion, dragging the dough about 4 inches down and to your left on the diagonal to form twisted, elongated pasta shapes that resemble an extremely thin little spiral or corkscrew, with the being ends thinner than the central part (see Figure 9-3).

6   Bring a large pot of water to boil over high heat, and add salt. Add the trofie, and allow them to cook for 4 minutes, or until al dente. Drain, reserving a bit of pasta water to thin the pesto.

7   Gently stir the pesto into the pasta until it is well coated, and add a few tablespoons of the reserved cooking water to make a sauce-like consistency.

8   Pour onto a platter, and garnish with a drizzle of EVOO, cheese, and fresh basil.

TIP: If you've never made or eaten trofie before, I recommend watching a few YouTube videos just to get the gist of the motion and desired shape.

Pair this dish with a bottle of *Pigato* or similar. A little-known Ligurian white wine with a typically fresh, straightforward taste in which the typical savory/slightly salty notes are accentuated in the wines produced by the vineyards higher in the hills.

NOTE: Trofie are an ancient pasta from the Liguria region and were once made around knitting rods, just like the fusilli of Southern Italy was. The main difference in the shape is that trofie are much shorter and often quite a bit thinner than fusilli are.

VARY IT! You can buy good-quality, artisan made trofie at specialty stores if you do not have time to make them from scratch. Fresh pesto also tastes great with linguine and farfalle pasta shapes.

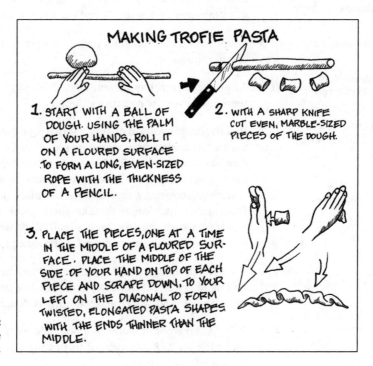

MAKING TROFIE PASTA

1. START WITH A BALL OF DOUGH. USING THE PALM OF YOUR HANDS, ROLL IT ON A FLOURED SURFACE TO FORM A LONG, EVEN-SIZED ROPE WITH THE THICKNESS OF A PENCIL.

2. WITH A SHARP KNIFE CUT EVEN, MARBLE-SIZED PIECES OF THE DOUGH.

3. PLACE THE PIECES, ONE AT A TIME IN THE MIDDLE OF A FLOURED SURFACE. PLACE THE MIDDLE OF THE SIDE OF YOUR HAND ON TOP OF EACH PIECE AND SCRAPE DOWN, TO YOUR LEFT ON THE DIAGONAL TO FORM TWISTED, ELONGATED PASTA SHAPES WITH THE ENDS THINNER THAN THE MIDDLE.

FIGURE 9-3: Making trofie pasta.

Cavatelli con sugo/Calabrian Cavatelli with Spicy Tomato Sauce

| PREP TIME: 1 HOUR | COOK TIME: 20 MIN | YIELD: 6-8 SERVINGS |

INGREDIENTS

2 cups finely ground semolina flour or grano duro, plus extra for dusting

½ teaspoon sea salt

¾ cup water

¼ cup Amy Riolo Selections or other good-quality extra virgin olive oil

1 recipe Fresh Tomato Sauce (see Chapter 7)

Calabrian chile pepper, to taste, or crushed red pepper flakes

¼ cup Pecorino Crotonese, or other Pecorino cheese, freshly grated

DIRECTIONS

1 Place the semolina flour on a work surface, and sprinkle with salt. Make a well in the center.

2 Add the water into the well in the center of the flour. Use a fork to carefully incorporate the water into the flour to form a dough. Add more water if needed. The dough should feel soft and supple. Use your hands to knead the dough well for 5-10 minutes until smooth and elastic; form into a ball.

3 Cover with a clean kitchen towel, and set aside. Allow to rest for 30 minutes.

4 After the dough has rested, cut off ¼ of the dough. While working, cover the remaining dough.

5 Roll the cut off portion of dough into a rope that is the width of a pencil. If it sticks, use a bit more semolina. Cut the dough rope into ¾-inch pieces. Using two fingers (the index and the middle finger), press firmly onto each piece of dough and drag toward you creating a cave-shaped indentation; see Figure 9-4. (Remember that cavatelli take their name from the word *"cavare,"* which means to make hollow and that is our objective—to make more room for the sauce.)

6 Place the pasta in a single layer (but not touching) on a floured baking sheet or parchment paper that has been dusted with semolina. Repeat with the remaining ¾ dough.

7 Bring a large pot of water to a boil, add all the dough pieces, and cook for 4-8 minutes, or until they float to the top and have a tender texture.

8 While pasta cooks, heat 2 tablespoons EVOO in a large, wide skillet. Add Calabrian chile pepper and tomato sauce to the skillet to heat through.

9 Drain the pasta, pour it into the sauce, and toss to coat. Pour onto a serving platter, and top with remaining 2 tablespoons EVOO and the grated cheese.

TIP: If you've never made or eaten cavatelli, also called covatelli in the Calabrian dialect, spend some time looking at pictures of them online so you know how to shape them. If you have extra Basic Grano Duro Pasta Dough already made (see recipe earlier in this chapter), you can also make cavatelli with that instead of with the semolina flour.

Pair this dish with a bottle of *Cirò Rosso* or similar. Chef Amy Riolo's family traditionally pairs this heirloom recipe with wine made from the Calabrian Gaglioppo grape, which was served to Greek Olympic champions in antiquity.

NOTE: Cavatelli are the typical pasta of my ancestral homeland of Calabria, but they are also enjoyed in the neighboring regions of Puglia and Basilicata as well. This is an excellent first course to precede roasted meat, meatballs, or a vegetarian main course such as *Melanzane alla parmigiana*/Eggplant Parmesan (see Chapter 14).

VARY IT! In Calabria, this pasta is also served with vegetables and legumes, but it is most often served with a slow simmering pork-based sauce that contains a combination of fresh meat and aged bits of sopressata and other sausages. It tastes fantastic with *Ragù alla Bolognese*/Bolognese-Style Meat Sauce as well (see Chapter 7).

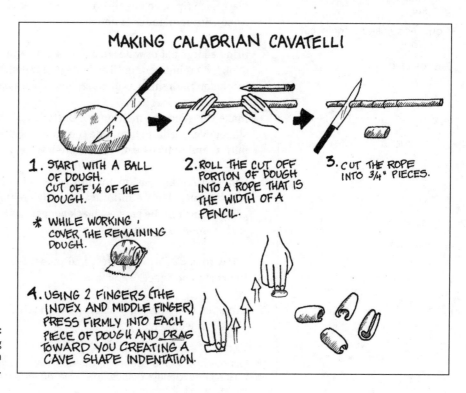

FIGURE 9-4:
Shaping Calabrian cavatelli pasta.

MAKING CALABRIAN CAVATELLI

1. START WITH A BALL OF DOUGH. CUT OFF ¼ OF THE DOUGH.

* WHILE WORKING, COVER THE REMAINING DOUGH.

2. ROLL THE CUT OFF PORTION OF DOUGH INTO A ROPE THAT IS THE WIDTH OF A PENCIL.

3. CUT THE ROPE INTO ¾" PIECES.

4. USING 2 FINGERS (THE INDEX AND MIDDLE FINGER) PRESS FIRMLY INTO EACH PIECE OF DOUGH AND DRAG TOWARD YOU CREATING A CAVE SHAPE INDENTATION.

Farfalle con salmone/Bowtie Pasta with Smoked Salmon and Cream Sauce

PREP TIME: 50 MIN	COOK TIME: 15 MIN	YIELD: 4 SERVINGS

INGREDIENTS

1 recipe (roughly ½ pound) Basic Pasta Dough (refer to the recipe earlier in this chapter)

1 teaspoon sea salt

¼ cup butter

1 small yellow onion, diced

½ cup cream

Handful of fresh parsley, finely chopped

Black pepper, freshly ground, to taste

4 ounces smoked salmon, cut into strips

Zest of 1 lemon

DIRECTIONS

1 Start with pasta dough that has rested for at least 20 minutes. Roll out pasta dough to a $\frac{1}{16}$-inch thickness on a lightly floured surface using a rolling pin. (See the "Meeting Your Pasta Maker: Rolling Pin or Pasta Machine" section earlier in this chapter if you're using a pasta machine instead.)

2 Using a fluted-edge pastry wheel or a pizza cutter, cut the dough into 2½-inch squares.

3 To shape the farfalle, pinch each square in the middle with your thumb and index finger so they look like little bowties. Place each finished bowtie on a floured baking sheet and continue with remainder of dough.

4 Bring a large pot of water to a boil, salt it, and add the farfalle. Cook for 2 minutes or until al dente (they should float to the top when done). Drain in a colander, and shake away excess water.

5 Make the sauce by melting the butter in a large, wide, deep skillet over medium heat. Add the onion, stir well to coat with butter, and reduce heat to medium-low.

6 Sauté, stirring occasionally, until the onion is very soft and translucent, about 5 minutes. Add the cream, and whisk to combine. Stir in the parsley, black pepper, and smoked salmon with a wooden spoon.

7 Allow to cook for 2 minutes, and take off the heat. Combine the pasta and sauce.

8 Transfer to a serving platter, garnish with lemon zest, and serve immediately.

TIP: Pair this dish with a bottle of *Pignoletto Classico Superiore* or similar. From Grechetto Gentile grapes, this wine offers subtle floral aromas underlined by a full, fresh sip.

Maltagliati con fagioli/Hand-Cut Pasta with Beans

PREP TIME: 40 MIN	COOK TIME: 10 MIN	YIELD: 4 SERVINGS

INGREDIENTS

1 recipe (roughly ½ pound) Basic Pasta Dough or Basic Grano Duro Pasta Dough (refer to the recipes earlier in this chapter)

½ cup Amy Riolo Selections or other good-quality extra virgin olive oil

1 garlic clove, peeled

1 sprig rosemary, whole

1 small onion, finely chopped

2 teaspoons tomato paste

1 cup cooked borlotti or cannellini beans (see Chapter 3)

Unrefined sea salt

Black pepper, freshly ground, to taste

2 cups baby kale, roughly chopped

¼ cup grated Parmigiano-Reggiano cheese

DIRECTIONS

1   Start with pasta dough that has rested for at least 20 minutes. Roll out pasta dough to form a rectangle about 12-inches long.

2   Divide the dough into six balls, and use a rolling pin to roll each ball out to approximately 24 inches long and $\frac{1}{16}$-inch thickness. (See the "Meeting Your Maker: Rolling Pin or Pasta Machine" section earlier in this chapter if you're using a pasta machine instead.)

3   Cut the pieces in half width-wise to make two 12-inch-long rectangular pieces out of each.

4   Cut the pasta with a knife or tear with your hands to obtain irregular shapes about 1-inch long. Place pieces in a single layer on floured cookie sheets until ready to cook.

5   To make the sauce, heat 2 tablespoons EVOO in a large, wide saucepan over medium heat. Add the garlic, rosemary, and onion, and cook until the onion turns golden, stirring occasionally, approximately 5 minutes.

6   Stir the tomato paste into the pan with a wooden spoon, allowing it to caramelize by cooking on the bottom. After the tomato paste begins to sizzle, thoroughly stir it into the other ingredients and add the beans and salt and pepper to taste.

7   Add water to about 1 inch short of covering the beans, and increase heat to high.

(continued)

8 Bring to a boil, stir, and reduce heat to medium–low. Allow to simmer for 20 minutes, and then remove the rosemary and garlic. Carefully remove half of the soup with a ladle, and blend it until smooth in a blender or food processor. (Or use an immersion blender to slightly thicken the mixture right in the pot.)

9 Return the mixture to the heat, and stir in the kale. If needed, add water until the mixture is a creamy, soup-like texture.

10 Taste, and adjust salt and pepper. Increase heat to high, and after it boils, add the pasta pieces (or *maltagliati*) and cook for 5 minutes more, or until they are very tender.

11 Garnish with additional EVOO and cheese, and serve.

TIP: Making the beans in advance saves time with this dish. You could also make the pasta in advance and put everything together at the last minute. This dish is one of the few pasta dishes that actually tastes better the next day, so you could make the whole thing in advance. Just add additional liquid or vegetable stock, adjust seasoning, and reheat to serve.

Pair this dish with a bottle of *Montepulciano d'Abruzzo* or similar. With a little aging it expresses itself with an even more encompassing and defined fruit flavor, able to accompany even the most complex versions of this dish.

NOTE: Some people use whole wheat flour or a combination of whole wheat and semolina flour when making maltagliati. Others use 00 (or highly refined) flour, so you can experiment and see which you like the best.

Maltagliati means poorly cut, and this pasta is traditional in the Emilia Romagna region of Italy, where it is especially appreciated in fall and winter.

This dish can be eaten by itself as a light supper, or in smaller quantities as a first course in a large, multi-course lunch, perhaps followed by roasted chicken or meat dishes.

VARY IT! You can add your own favorite beans or swap out the kale for another green in this dish. Many people add pieces of pancetta (cured pork belly) to the mix while browning the onion as well. You could substitute your favorite cured meat, if desired, but the recipe would no longer be traditional.

Lasagne classica/Homemade Lasagna Bolognese-Style

PREP TIME: 45 MIN	COOK TIME: 1 HOUR (2 HOURS IF YOU NEED TO MAKE SAUCES FROM SCRATCH)	YIELD: 9 SERVINGS

INGREDIENTS

1 recipe (roughly ½ pound) Basic Pasta Dough (refer to the recipe earlier in this chapter)

1 teaspoon salt

½ cup unsalted butter, divided

1 recipe *Ragù alla Bolognese* (see Chapter 7)

1 recipe *Salsa besciamella* (see Chapter 7)

1 cup Parmigiano-Reggiano cheese, freshly grated

DIRECTIONS

1 Start with pasta dough that has rested. Divide the dough in four, and roll each quarter to $\frac{1}{16}$-inch thickness. Cut into 16 (8-inch long) rectangles or sheets.

2 Line a tray with clean kitchen towels.

3 Bring a large pot of water to a boil over high heat. Salt and add 4 of the lasagna sheets at a time, and cook until just tender—less than a minute. Use tongs to transfer sheets to the towel-lined tray.

4 Preheat the oven to 350 degrees.

5 Grease a 9x13-inch baking dish with some of the butter, and top with a layer of 4 lasagna sheets, then a layer of ¼ of the *Ragù alla Bolognese* sauce, then a layer of ¼ of the *Salsa besciamella,* and top with a spoonful of Parmigiano cheese.

6 Repeat the same steps until all of the pasta sheets have been used.

7 Cover the final layer with the remaining *Salsa besciamella,* scatter chunks of butter over the top, sprinkle with additional cheese, and bake for around 30–45 minutes, or until bubbly and golden.

8 Remove from the oven, and allow to set for a few minutes before cutting and serving.

(continued)

TIP: Having the sauces made a day or two in advance and stored in the refrigerator cuts down on last-minute cooking time when making this dish.

Pair this dish with a bottle of *Sangiovese di Romagna* or similar. Typically elegant, the wines produced in the hilly area have a more slender and defined fruit and an acid content that accompanies the savory-chalky vein on a pleasantly spicy finish.

NOTE: Every region in Italy has its own signature lasagne dish(es). This one is based on the style of Bologna. This dish can be assembled the night before baking, or baked, cooled, refrigerated, and reheated on the day of serving. It is important to point out that even though this is a labor-intensive recipe, Italians do not eat lasagne on a daily or weekly basis. It is usually only eaten a few times a year, and for celebratory or entertaining purposes.

Chapter **10**

More Delicious First-Course Dishes

Your mind might automatically gravitate toward pasta and pizza when you think of Italian food in general, but other traditional first courses are integral to both Italy's cuisine and culture. Risotto, soups, and gnocchi dishes are the other *primi*, or first courses, that begin classic Italian meals.

In this chapter, you discover how to make them properly and pair nutritious and mouth-watering first courses with other courses in a typical Italian meal. Follow the simple strategies and techniques contained in this chapter, and you can become the envy of your friends with your accomplished Italian *primi*.

If you would like to make vegetarian versions of any of these recipes that call for chicken, beef, or seafood stock, just substitute vegetable stock. *Buon appetite!*

Moving Beyond Pasta: A Primo Primer

Primi piatti, literally "first dishes," also commonly referred to as *primi,* are the backbone of the Italian kitchen. Learning to make pasta, risotto, soups, polenta, and gnocchi like an Italian grandmother and culinary professional enables you to take a trip to Italy without ever leaving your kitchen. Best of all, you can enjoy them at a fraction of the price that it would cost to eat them in restaurants.

In addition to understanding the techniques needed to make each style of first course, it's important to also master the recipes themselves as well as how to pair them in a meal. Although Italian restaurants offer an array of all types to choose from anytime, in Italy there are cultural and regional factors that determine what to serve and when. You should take into consideration the people you are serving, the time of day, and the season when selecting a primo.

REMEMBER

Keep in mind it is appropriate to serve only one *primo* at a time during normal meals, so you would not have a pasta and then a soup, or vice versa, in the same meal, as is often seen on so called "Italian" menus outside of Italy.

REMEMBER

Pasta is always an appropriate first course at lunch time or as a part of the later Sunday lunch that takes place at the end of the day. It can be served to guests at dinner or eaten in a restaurant, but part of Italian culture is to enjoy pasta at lunch, not later, even though exceptions occur, especially when Italians are entertaining outside of Italy. When time permits, homemade pasta is always seen as more appropriate for special occasions and honoring distinguished guests. When time is of the essence, however, especially for late-night entertaining, boxed pasta is appropriate. For pasta pairing instructions, refer to Chapters 8 and 9 on dried and fresh pasta.

The following sections explore other traditional first-course options.

Risotto

Risotto is an Italian dish made out of short, starchy Italian rice (*riso*) such as *carnaroli, vialone nano,* or Arborio. In order for the *riso* to be considered risotto it must be cooked in a certain manner in which liquid is slowly added to the rice bit by bit until it is cooked to a firm-to-the-bite texture. In order to master making risotto, you must learn how to make it *all'onda* or "by the wave," meaning that it will have a creamy, firm, yet fluid consistency that resembles the strong waves of the ocean.

Risotto was once enjoyed only in the northern regions of Italy where rice grew. But thanks to the unification of Italy in the 19th century, the increased modes of transportation, as well as the expat community that introduced it to the rest of the world, risotto is now considered a mainstream "Italian" food. Italian culinary students are even judged on their risotto making skills.

Risotto is often served as a first course at lunch in the Veneto, Piemonte, and Lombardia regions, where various types of rice are grown, and it is a staple. Pasta is enjoyed as well in these regions, but not when risotto is served.

In other regions of Italy, it might be enjoyed once a week or once a month, if that. In areas where rice is not grown in Italy, risotto is seen as more of a gourmet-type dish appropriate for serving to business colleagues, or when you want to impress someone. It has a slightly more elegant image in those regions, because it is not part of the traditional local diet. Eating them is loosely associated with cooler temperatures, because of the warming ritual of the time spent stirring broth into the rice to make risotto. Because of its creamy texture, risotto usually precedes roasted, grilled, or fried main courses, not those with sauces.

The manner of making risotto—sautéing an onion in butter gently, coating a grain, adding wine to evaporate, slowly ladling in stock, resting, and mixing in butter or cheese—produces such a creamy dish, when done properly, that the same process is used to make other grains or vegetables instead of rice now as well. *Farrotto* (farro cooked in the manner of risotto), *orzotto* (barley cooked in the manner of risotto), and other dishes are also becoming increasingly popular.

While risotto is best eaten the moment it is prepared (so that the starches don't congeal), some completely mouthwatering recipes—such as Roman Risotto Croquettes (later in this chapter) and Baked Risotto "Cakes" make good use of leftovers.

TIP

If you've never made risotto before, take your time with the first recipe. Choose a time when you have some flexibility with your schedule to make it. Risotto is best to make on a cold or rainy day, when you are home anyway, or on an evening when you want to immerse yourself in the joys of cooking and forget about the world. Each recipe in this chapter includes a pairing suggestion so you know when to pair it.

Soups

Soups are appreciated the whole world over, and Italy is no exception. In my ancestral homeland of Calabria there is a proverb (in dialect) that says soups are capable of doing seven things; *"cura famaa, e sete attuta, riempie il ventre, netta il dente, fa' dormire, fa' smaltire, e da la guancia calorire,"* which means they can "satisfy hunger, quench thirst, fill the stomach, clean the teeth, help you to sleep, aid with digestion, and put color in the cheeks."

THE HISTORY OF RISOTTO

"La storia del risotto e lungo quanto e il mondo" is an Italian proverb that means "The history of risotto is as long as that of the world itself."

Italy is now the largest producer of rice in Europe. Rice is grown predominately in the regions of Lombardy, Piedmont, and Veneto. While arborio is the most widely known variety of Italian rice in the U.S., *carnaroli* and *vialone nano* are prized and popular varieties grown in Italy. The short, stubby grains of Italian rice varieties are ideal for slowly absorbing liquid and maintaining a firm-to-the-bite texture.

Carnaroli rice is widely known as the "king of rice" in Italian cuisine. Vialone Nano rice hails from the Verona area, where it has been grown since 1937 and was developed by crossing the Vialone rice variety with another called Nano, which means "dwarf" in Italian, noting the plant's low height. In 1996, Vialone Nano rice from the Verona area was given the Protected Geographical Indication (IGP), under the name of Riso Nano Vialone Veronese IGP.

Risotto was once enjoyed only in the northern regions of Italy where rice grew. But thanks to the unification of Italy in the 19th century, the increased modes of transportation, as well as the expat community that introduced it to the rest of the world, risotto is now considered a mainstream "Italian" food. Risotto, in fact, is one of the foods that Italian chefs are judged on.

There are several types of Italian soups, most of which are enjoyed in fall, winter, and spring, although some cold soups are served in summer. When those are made, however, it is more of a novelty and not something that all people partake in regularly. Various types of soup are a traditional way to start an Italian dinner, when meals are smaller and lighter.

The season determines the type of soups, as well as their ingredients:

>> Mushrooms, pumpkin, and broccoli usually make their way into fall soups.

>> Winter soups include more pantry items like beans, legumes, and dried porcini mushrooms, with grains such as pasta, barely, rice, and more. These items could be used throughout the year, but winter soups relied on them for millennia because there was no fresh produce available in the cold months.

>> Spring soups usually include new vegetables—peas, spinach, carrots, new potatoes, and fresh tender lettuces and herbs.

>> Summer soups include fresh tomato, eggplant, zucchini, basil, bell peppers, as well as copious amounts of herbs.

It is appropriate to entertain with soups as a first course, even for special occasions. Soups are a unique Italian *primo* because especially in the evening, they can be served alone or with a salad. Heavier soups, called *minestre*, are a meal in a bowl and can be enjoyed by themselves, although they may be served in a series of courses during a large meal.

In Italy, soup can be a light, elegant way to open an evening meal or large banquet. Some soup recipes in this book are thick and chock full of hearty beans, legumes, chestnuts, and pasta, while others are creamy, smooth purées that can take even leftover ingredients to new heights.

TECHNICAL STUFF

Italian soups fall into four main categories—*minestre, zuppe, crème,* and *vellutate*—and, in the Italian language, the correct terms are used to refer to each type of soup. For example, while *Vellutata di castagne,* or Cream of Chestnut, would be called a soup in English, it would only be called a *vellutata* in Italian. Note that these three terms can end with either an "a" or an "e" depending on whether the term is singular or plural; ending in an "e" denotes the plural form of a feminine word in the Italian language.

Here are the different types of Italian soups:

>> *Minestra/e:* In Italy, a *minestra* is a thick soup made from a multitude of ingredients. The suffix "-one" on the end means that it is a "large or big" minestra, which explains why there are so many ingredients in minestrone.

>> *Zuppa/e:* A soup, in Italy, is something made from a clear stock base with ingredients added to it. It's a rather "loose" soup, where the ingredients are perceivable and separate from the stock. A vegetable soup or consommé-type soup would fall into this category.

>> *Crema/e:* A *crema* was traditionally a thicker, cream-based soup. It always has a creamy, puréed texture. Nowadays, a *crema* may omit the actual cream for health reasons, but it should still have a luxurious, velvety mouth feel.

>> *Vellutata/e:* A *vellutata* is a *veloutè*—a soup, usually made from vegetables, that has been puréed to make it creamy and smooth.

Polenta

Polenta is cornmeal cooked and often enhanced with butter and cheese in the Italian kitchen. It is normally a cold weather treat and served at dinner or a Sunday lunch in winter, when it is a base for stewed meat, meat sauces, or other heavy second courses. Topping polenta with a meat sauce or stew makes a heavy meal that is crave-worthy during the winter months. I avoid putting those dishes on summer menus unless someone is requesting it.

In warmer weather, polenta can also be grilled and served as an appetizer, or opt for grilled polenta with light toppings. You also can use polenta in baked goods. In the past, in rural communities, farmers ate polenta and hearty meats for breakfast (which is in stark contrast to typical Italian breakfasts) before heading out to work in the fields.

Polenta is usually not served as a first course when entertaining or for a holiday, unless it is a very informal, familial gathering, or it is part of a theme dinner in which you are inviting guests specifically for the pleasure of eating creamy polenta. Polenta can also be served as a side dish to grilled and roasted meats, poultry, or seafood as well.

Although corn was originally a New World crop that was not immediately embraced by Italians, it was popularized by the Jewish community in Venice and is now a staple ingredient throughout Italy. In addition to the Veneto region, Lombardia, Valle d'Aosta, Piemonte, Liguria, Trentino, Emilia-Romagna, and Friuli-Venezia Giulia all have deep polenta traditions as well.

Polenta, when served hot, pairs perfectly with seafood stews or grilled fish, and can also accompany meaty and vegetarian stews. It is often used as a "bed" for saucy dishes or served as a side dish for proteins. Polenta can also be cooled and cut into sticks, cubes, or large squares that are then topped or served with sauces, spreads, or dipped as appetizers. One of the most common ways to do this is to grill cooled polenta and top it as you would bruschetta. For this reason, I always recommend making extra polenta. That way, some can be eaten hot with a topping immediately and the other portion can be sliced and grilled for use on another day.

There are even desserts, cookies, and cakes made with cornmeal that are an important part of the sweet traditions in the Veneto region and nowadays throughout Italy. Cornmeal is a good gluten-free alternative to flour in many recipes. It adds a characteristic sandy texture to baked goods.

As with many other Italian grains, olives, grapes, and other ingredients, there is a major push to use heirloom varieties that are native to different regions. One of the cornmeal varieties that I love the most is Biancoperla's stone ground white corn polenta from the Veneto region of Italy; it is a rare and prized corn varietal with a distinct sweetness and delicate flavor. It is known for its low yield, fineness, and delicate flavor. This pearl-white variety is obtained from an ancient quality of maize that now risks becoming extinct, thus making it a protected and recognized Slow Food Presidium product.

Gnocchi

Gnocchi is the Italian word for dumplings. In Italy, gnocchi are made from potatoes, pumpkin, semolina, spinach, and ricotta cheese.

While potato gnocchi are now the most known, different Italian regions have their own specialties as well. Gnocchi are a home-cooking staple, but can be enjoyed in restaurants as well. Many people place gnocchi in the "pasta" category on menus, because they are a *primo* and contain some form of flour, but I believe that they deserve their own category.

In Italian *trattorie* (family-style restaurants), it is traditional to serve gnocchi on Thursdays, and to this day many households have the tradition of enjoying them on that day. Gnocchi can be used for familial gatherings, traditional lunches, and entertaining as well.

Although they are not difficult to make, it is very hard to find good potato gnocchi in Italian restaurants in America. The main reason is that the amount of flour needed for gnocchi always varies. The type of potato you use, its freshness, how it is cooked, and whether you use eggs are factors that determine the taste of the gnocchi you make.

Risotto allo zafferano/Risotto Milanese

PREP TIME: 5 MIN	COOK TIME: 30 MIN	YIELD: 6 SERVINGS

INGREDIENTS

5 tablespoons unsalted butter, divided

1 medium yellow onion, finely chopped

2 ½ cups Carnaroli rice, Vialone Nano, or Arborio

½ cup white wine

6-8 cups chicken stock (see Chapter 3), heated

¼ teaspoon saffron

½ cup Parmigiano-Reggiano cheese, freshly grated

DIRECTIONS

1 Melt 4 tablespoons butter in a large saucepan. When butter foams, add onion, and cook on low until soft and translucent, approximately 5 minutes. Stir in Arborio rice, and cook until coated with butter.

2 Add the wine, and increase the heat to high. Cook until the wine has evaporated.

3 Add a ladle of stock, stir, and reduce heat to medium. Stir slowly and consistently until stock has evaporated. Continue adding stock, cooking, and stirring over medium heat until most of the stock is used, and the rice has an "al-dente" consistency. Resist the urge to add more than a ladleful of stock at a time. It will be worth the wait.

4 When the rice has an al dente consistency and the liquid is thick enough to make a wave formation as you stir it, add the remaining tablespoon of butter, the saffron, and the Parmigiano-Reggiano cheese. Give it a good stir.

5 Serve immediately in individual bowls.

TIP: The traditional Milanese dish that accompanies the *Risotto allo zafferano* is *Ossobuco,* or braised veal shanks. Other braised meat dishes or *Scaloppine di vitello*/Veal Cutlets (see Chapter 13) are also a great second course for this dish.

Pair this dish with a bottle of *Lugana Superiore* or similar. From Turbiana grapes, a wine with flavor, citrus freshness, volume, and good mineral structure which in this version is accentuated.

NOTE: It is said that this recipe was invented when there was a royal marriage about to take place in the courts of Milan. The bride was being made to marry a man whom she did not love, who had red hair. Her boyfriend entered the kitchen where the wedding meal was being prepared and added large amounts of saffron to the rice to make it orange in color in order to mock the groom. Both the color and the flavor of the rice were a hit, and even though we don't know what happened at the end of the love story, the recipe became the most famous risotto recipe in the world.

VARY IT! Fresh peas, seafood, and seasonal vegetables are all great add-ins to risotto.

Farrotto/Farro "Risotto"

PREP TIME: 10 MIN	COOK TIME: 55 MIN PLUS 1 HOUR SOAKING TIME	YIELD: 4 SERVINGS

INGREDIENTS

4 tablespoons unsalted butter, plus 1 teaspoon for dressing

1 small yellow onion, finely diced

½ teaspoon kosher salt

1 cup farro, soaked in boiling water to cover for 1 hour

1 cup dry white wine

3 cups homemade or low-sodium chicken or vegetable broth

1 cup cherry tomatoes, quartered

1 bunch (approximately ¾ cup) fresh basil, finely chopped

⅓ cup freshly grated Parmigiano-Reggiano cheese

⅓ cup freshly grated Pecorino Romano cheese

DIRECTIONS

1 Melt 4 tablespoons butter in a 3 ½-quart pan over medium-high heat. Add the onion, and stir to coat with butter. Reduce the heat to medium, and cook the onion, stirring often, until soft and fragrant, about 3–5 minutes. Add the farro to the pan, and stir to coat the grains in the butter and toast slightly, 2–3 minutes.

2 Increase the heat to high, and add the wine, and stir. Cook the farro, stirring occasionally, until the wine evaporates almost completely, about 6 minutes. Add the broth in 1-cup increments, stirring often, and cooking until the liquid almost completely evaporates before adding the next increment; this takes about 45 minutes to complete.

3 When the farro is tender and absorbs most of the liquid, stir in the tomatoes, basil, Parmigiano-Reggiano, Pecorino Romano, and remaining teaspoon of butter. Continue to stir until the butter is melted in and the mixture is creamy.

4 Serve immediately in individual bowls.

TIP: You can buy presoaked farro that cooks in only 18 minutes and does not need to be soaked, or you can soak it yourself. I usually soak more farro than I need and store the excess in the refrigerator for a week. That way, if I want to cook with it, I don't have to wait until the following day.

Pair this dish with a bottle of *Vernaccia di San Gimignano* or similar. Delicate, fruity, and floral. In the reserve version, strong, pleasant mineral notes broaden the aromatic spectrum, giving length and taste persistence.

NOTE: Farro, which is becoming more popular by the minute, is an ancient grain similar to spelt. Full of protein and vitamins, it's a nutritious whole grain that adds fiber to your diet. It is believed that farro was cultivated in 7,000 BCE near the Tuscan town of Lucca.

VARY IT! Farro can be served in many ways — with chicken or shrimp as a main course, with milk and fruit as a breakfast cereal, or in pastries for special occasions.

Orzotto/Pearl Barley Risotto with Radicchio and Taleggio Cheese Fondue

PREP TIME: 10 MIN | **COOK TIME: 45 MIN** | **YIELD: 6 SERVINGS**

INGREDIENTS

8 tablespoons butter, divided

1 shallot, finely minced

1 head radicchio, leaves roughly chopped, leaving a few whole for garnish

2 cups pearl barley, soaked in cold water for 20 minutes

1 cup red wine (any kind that you would drink with dinner)

4 ½ cups vegetable broth, divided

¼ cup Parmigiana-Reggiano cheese

Salt, to taste

Freshly ground black pepper, to taste

¼ cup flour

Approximately 1 cup Taleggio cheese, cubed

½ cup marsala or sweet red wine

2 tablespoons finely chopped fresh Italian parsley

DIRECTIONS

1 Melt 2 tablespoons butter in a large saucepan over medium high heat. Add the shallot, and cook until lightly golden and tender, stirring often. Add the radicchio, and cook until wilted.

2 Add the barley, and stir to coat well. Pour in the wine. Increase heat to high, stir, and allow alcohol to evaporate.

3 Reduce heat to medium, add a ladleful of stock. Stir often, until stock evaporates. Continue adding stock, a ladleful at a time, until barley is al dente. Stir in 2 tablespoons butter and Parmigiana-Reggiano cheese.

4 Taste and season with salt and pepper according to your preference.

5 In a separate saucepan, prepare the Taleggio fondue. Melt 4 tablespoons butter, and stir in flour with a wooden spoon to create a roux. Allow mixture to turn light golden. Add Taleggio cheese cubes, and stir to incorporate. When cheese starts to melt, stir in marsala or sweet red wine and cook for a few minutes longer. Fondue is done when it is creamy and incorporated.

6 Place the *orzotto* in serving plates, and make a well in the center. Fill with the Taleggio fondue. Garnish with chopped parsley and serve immediately.

TIP: If you soak the farro in water for an hour prior to cooking, it will cut down on the cooking time in this recipe.

Pair this dish with a bottle of *Chiaretto del Garda* or similar. A wine with light colors, a slender body, and delicate aromas of rose petals. The characteristic pleasantness of the wine when it is savored in the mouth offers contrast to the sweetness of the dish.

NOTE: Italians now cook pearl barley in the fashion of risotto. A traditional and healthful recipe, the addition of Taleggio cheese from the Lombardy region makes it especially alluring. Barley is believed to be the oldest grain consumed by humans and was very popular in ancient Greece, Rome, and Egypt. Whole grain barley is a very good source of molybdenum, manganese, dietary fiber, and selenium, and a good source of copper, vitamin B1, chromium, phosphorus, magnesium, and niacin.

VARY IT! You can substitute another grain, such as fresh corn or whole wheat for the barley in this dish and another creamy cheese such as mascarpone for the Taleggio, if desired.

Suppli al telefono/Roman Risotto Croquettes

PREP TIME: 30 MIN | COOK TIME: 20MIN | YIELD: 8 SERVINGS

INGREDIENTS

½ recipe *Risotto allo zafferano* (earlier in this chapter), or leftovers

2 eggs

1 cup plain bread crumbs (see Chapter 3)

¼ cup Parmigiano-Reggiano or Pecorino Romano cheese, grated

Black pepper, freshly ground, to taste

8 ounces fresh mozzarella, cut into ¼-inch cubes

Extra virgin olive oil, for frying

¼ cup Fresh Tomato Sauce (see Chapter 7)

DIRECTIONS

1 Allow risotto to cool completely, and set up a breading station by whisking the eggs together in one small shallow bowl and mixing the bread crumbs, pepper, and cheese together in medium-sized shallow bowl.

2 Form risotto croquettes into equal-sized balls; they can range from the size of a small to large ice cream scoop (I usually make them into egg-size shapes); they need to be the same size for frying.

3 Stuff a cube of mozzarella into the center of each ball (cut the mozzarella in half if making mini-sized balls). Store in the refrigerator until ready to fry.

4 Heat 2 inches of oil in a large shallow frying pan to 325 degrees. Carefully lower one ball into oil and monitor the browning process. If it becomes golden right away, proceed; if not increase heat before continuing. If it becomes too dark too quickly, lower the heat and proceed.

5 Lower 4-6 croquettes into the oil at a time being careful not to crowd the pan. Adding the cold croquettes lowers the oil temperature, so check the oil and increase the heat to medium-high, if needed, to keep the temperature at 325 degrees.

6 Fry each regular sized croquette for approximately 2-minutes (or until golden on one side), carefully turn using a slotted spoon, and fry the other side for a minute until equally golden. Smaller, mini croquettes can be turned a few times in the oil and should cook up evenly in just under 2 minutes.

7 When croquettes are golden, drain them on a platter or tray lined with paper towels. Serve hot or at room temperature with Fresh Tomato Sauce.

TIP: In Rome and other places in Italy, these croquettes are sold as a street food in little pieces of waxed paper and are eaten on the street along with pizza sold by the slice. They are also sold in *pizzerie* as an appetizer before pizza and are sometimes included as an appetizer in home buffets.

Pair this dish with a bottle of *Cesanese del Piglio* (Vintage and Steel varieties only) or similar. A local wine that in the basic version has an average structure with vermilion color and delicate fruity notes and delicate tannins.

NOTE: Roman Risotto Croquettes are best when accompanied by or when preceding pizza, roasted chicken and potatoes, or enjoyed with other fried treats such as artichokes.

Many people confuse Rice Croquettes/*supplì* with *arancini*, another variation of rice balls or croquettes made in Sicily.

VARY IT! Risotto croquettes are a great way to use up a variety of leftover vegetables, cheese, and meats and shaped into larger balls or pear shapes.

Short on time but want to make something tasty with leftover risotto? Line a deep, greased 9-inch baking pan with half of your risotto. Top with cheese, meat, and vegetables of your choice. Top with another layer of risotto to cover. Dot with butter and sprinkle with grated cheese. Bake at 425 degrees until golden. Cut into slices and serve warm.

Pasta e fagioli/Pasta, White Bean, and Tomato Soup

PREP TIME: 5 MIN | COOK TIME: 30 MIN | YIELD: 4 SERVINGS

INGREDIENTS

1 tablespoon Amy Riolo Selections or other good-quality extra virgin olive oil

3 garlic cloves, peeled and minced

1 cup tomato puree or Fresh Tomato Sauce (see Chapter 7)

Kosher salt, to taste

Black pepper, freshly ground, to taste

¼ cup parsley or basil, freshly chopped

3 cups reduced-sodium vegetable or chicken stock (see Chapter 3)

1 ½ cups cooked cannellini or borlotti beans (see Chapter 3)

½ cup orzo or other small pasta

¼ cup Pecorino Romano cheese, freshly grated

DIRECTIONS

1 Heat oil in a large saucepan over medium heat. Add garlic, and sauté until it releases its aroma.

2 Add tomato puree, salt, and pepper. Increase heat to high, and bring to a boil.

3 Add parsley or basil, stir, reduce heat to low, and cover. Simmer for 15 minutes.

4 Remove the lid carefully, stir in stock, and cannellini beans.

5 Bring to a boil, uncovered, over high heat.

6 Reduce heat to low, stir in orzo, and cook 10–15 minutes until pasta is al dente. Garnish with cheese and serve hot.

TIP: When making the Fresh Tomato Sauce from Chapter 7, you can make a double batch and reserve half of it to make this soup. In a pinch, you can use a good-quality, low-sodium jarred tomato puree to make the recipe. This soup is so simple, however, there's no need. Making your own stock will also improve the flavor and make the soup more nutritious.

This soup can be served by itself with a salad and bread any time of day. As a part of a multicourse lunch, follow it with roasted chicken or meat.

Pair this dish with a bottle of *Montepulciano d'Abruzzo* or similar. With a little aging it expresses itself with an even more encompassing and defined fruit flavor, able to accompany even the most complex versions of this dish.

NOTE: In Italy, the rinds of hard cheeses like Parmesan and Romano are added to soups and stews to give them extra flavor. You can buy a block of cheese, grate it yourself, and reserve the rinds to slowly simmer in sauces and stews. If you have rinds at home, you can substitute them for the grated cheese in this recipe. If you prefer not to grind your own cheese, many specialty food stores now sell rinds alone.

Crema di ceci/Chickpea Soup

PREP TIME: 5 MIN	COOK TIME: 60 MIN	YIELD: 4 SERVINGS

INGREDIENTS

2 cups cooked chickpeas (see the Dried Beans recipe in Chapter 3) or 1 can (15 ounces) chickpeas, drained and rinsed

1 ½ cups Vegetable Stock (see Chapter 3)

1 large yellow onion, quartered

1 dried bay leaf

½ teaspoon chopped fresh rosemary

1 lemon, juiced

Unrefined sea salt or salt, to taste

Black pepper, freshly ground, to taste

2 tablespoons Amy Riolo Selections or other good-quality extra virgin olive oil, for garnish

DIRECTIONS

1 Place the chickpeas in a large saucepan or stockpot with stock, onion, bay leaf, and rosemary. Simmer, covered, on medium-low for 5 minutes.

2 Remove from the heat and drain, reserving cooking liquid. Remove bay leaf and rosemary.

3 Place the chickpeas and the reserved liquid in blender. Add lemon juice and salt and pepper to taste. Blend well until a purée is formed.

4 Return the mixture to the pot. Taste again, and adjust salt and add pepper if necessary. If the soup is too thick, stir in a few tablespoons of water.

5 Stir and simmer on low heat until serving. To serve, ladle into bowls and drizzle with additional EVOO.

TIP: Using chickpeas that you've cooked and stock that you've made gives you the most nutritious and best-tasting results.

Pair this dish with a bottle of *Frappato di Vittoria rosato* or similar. A delicate wine in colors and clear in flavors. Floral and soft blueberry notes accompany a typically fresh-savory sip with medium structure that remains pleasanty on the palate after sipping.

NOTE: This cream soup can also be served over croutons made out of grilled bread or with sautéed shrimp added in. Because it is made with a legume, this soup is very versatile and can precede poultry, meat, seafood, or vegetarian mains.

VARY IT! Experiment with preparing your favorite beans and legumes this way. Rice, thin noodles, or short pasta also can be stirred into the soup during Step 5 and cooked until done.

Millecosedde/Calabrian Minestrone

PREP TIME: 15 MIN | COOK TIME: 50 MIN | YIELD: 8 SERVINGS

INGREDIENTS

2 tablespoons Amy Riolo Selections or other good-quality extra virgin olive oil

1 stalk celery, diced

1 carrot, diced

1 large yellow onion, diced

2 cloves garlic, peeled and finely diced

¼ cup dried porcini mushrooms, soaked in water for 20 minutes, drained, and rinsed

2 cups Fresh Tomato Sauce (see Chapter 7) or boxed chopped tomatoes or canned reduced-sodium diced tomatoes

2 cups chopped savoy cabbage

¼ cup brown lentils, rinsed and sorted

½ teaspoon unrefined sea salt

¼ teaspoon black pepper, freshly ground

1 cup cooked cannellini beans (see Chapter 3)

1 cup cooked chickpeas (see the Fagioli secchi/Dried Beans recipe in Chapter 3)

4 cups Homemade Chicken Stock or Vegetable Stock (see Chapter 3), reduced-sodium stock, or water

½ teaspoon crushed red chili flakes

1 cup ditalini or gluten-free pasta

DIRECTIONS

1 Add olive oil to a large, heavy-bottomed saucepan or Dutch oven over medium heat. Add celery, carrot, onion, and garlic.

2 Sauté until golden, approximately 5 minutes. Stir in mushrooms, and sauté for another 2-3 minutes. Add tomatoes, cabbage, lentils, salt, and pepper. Stir and simmer for 5 minutes.

3 Add cannellini beans and chickpeas to the vegetable mixture along with stock or water and the crushed red chili flakes. Bring to a boil over high heat; reduce heat to medium–low and simmer, covered, for 40 minutes.

4 Add pasta, and cook until pasta is done and beans are tender, approximately 10 more minutes. Serve hot.

TIP: This soup gets better as it sits, making it the perfect cook-ahead dish. You can also freeze it in individual containers to reheat later. This soup can be served by itself with bruschetta and salad or precede a hearty winter roast.

Pair this dish with a bottle of *Gravello IGT Calabria* or similar. The Gaglioppo and Cabernet Sauvignon blend with delicate fruit notes and a soft sip accompanied by a delicatley spicy finish.

NOTE: Called *millecosedde* or *millecuselle,* or "a thousand little things" in dialect. It is made on New Year's Eve to clean out the pantry.

VARY IT! This recipe is just a base. In Italy, they literally use what is on hand. The only guideline is that this soup contains a mixture of legumes, vegetables, and grains.

Zuppa di zucchini /Zucchini Soup

PREP TIME: 10 MIN	COOK TIME: 30 MIN	YIELD: 6 SERVINGS

INGREDIENTS

¼ cup Amy Riolo Selections or other good-quality extra virgin olive oil

2 cloves garlic, peeled and thinly sliced

4 medium zucchinis, washed and finely diced

6 cups Homemade Chicken Stock or Vegetable Stock (see Chapter 3) or 3 cups reduced-sodium chicken stock mixed with 3 cups water

⅛ teaspoon unrefined sea salt

¼ teaspoon black pepper, freshly ground

1 tablespoon freshly chopped mint

1 tablespoon freshly chopped basil

½ cup Pecorino Romano or Parmigiano-Reggiano cheese, freshly grated, divided

¼ cup heavy cream

6 very thin slices Italian bread, toasted on both sides until golden

DIRECTIONS

1 Heat the olive oil in a large saucepan over medium heat. Add garlic and zucchini, stir, and cook until golden, approximately 3–5 minutes. Add the stock, and season with salt and pepper.

2 Cover the saucepan, reduce heat to medium-low, and cook until zucchini is tender, approximately 20–30 minutes. Remove from heat.

3 In a small bowl, combine the mint, basil, 2 tablespoons cheese, and cream. Whisk well to combine. Slowly pour the cream mixture into the hot soup, whisking constantly.

4 Place a slice of bread in the bottom of each individual soup bowl. Ladle the soup over the bread. Sprinkle with remaining cheese and serve.

TIP: This is the perfect summer soup to serve with salad and cheese for a simple supper or prior to grilled seafood, poultry, or meat in a larger meal.

Pair this dish with a bottle of *Gewürztraminer* or similar. A south Tyrolean wine, reminiscent of tropical fruits, aromas of roses, and refined spices, delivers a typically fresh, captivating sip with full savory mineral notes.

NOTE: You can also serve this soup puréed and/or at room temperature. It can also be prepared by puréeing half of the ingredients and leaving the other half whole for a unique texture.

VARY IT! Carrots, potatoes, and mushrooms can be used in place of the zucchini. Rice or thin noodles also can be added during the last 10 minutes of cooking in Step 2.

Zuppa di lenticchie/Rustic Lentil Soup

| PREP TIME: 10 MIN | COOK TIME: 50MIN | YIELD: 6 SERVINGS |

INGREDIENTS

1 tablespoon Amy Riolo Selections or other good-quality extra virgin olive oil

2 carrots, diced

1 medium yellow onion, diced

2 stalks celery, diced

2 cloves garlic, peeled and sliced

Pinch crushed red pepper flakes

1½ cups brown lentils, rinsed and sorted

⅛ teaspoon unrefined sea salt

¼ teaspoon black pepper, freshly ground

4 cups Homemade Chicken Stock or Vegetable Stock (see Chapter 3) or reduced-sodium vegetable or chicken stock

2 cups Fresh Tomato Sauce (see Chapter 7)

¼ cup plus 2 tablespoons freshly chopped flat-leaf parsley, divided

¼ cup Parmigiano-Reggiano or Pecorino Romano cheese, grated

DIRECTIONS

1 Heat olive oil in a large saucepan over medium heat. Add carrots, onion, celery, garlic and crushed red chili flakes.

2 Sauté until vegetables are translucent, about 3–5 minutes. Stir and add lentils. Cook for 1 minute, and season with salt and pepper.

3 Add stock, tomato sauce, and ¼ cup parsley. Stir and increase the heat to high. When the stock begins to boil, reduce heat to medium-low and stir. Cover and allow to simmer 45–60 minutes, or until lentils are tender.

4 Place half of the lentil mixture in a blender or food processor (be sure to remove the cap from the center spout and cover it with a clean kitchen towel to prevent mixture from bursting out). Purée for a few minutes until smooth. Or use an immersion blender to blend half of the mixture until smooth.

5 Return the purée to the pot with the rest of the lentils. Cook over medium heat for an additional 10 minutes. Garnish with remaining parsley and the cheese, and serve.

TIP: Make large batches of Rustic Lentil Soup and freeze single servings to reheat later. That way, you'll have a nutritious alternative to canned soup on hand whenever you need it.

Pair this dish with a bottle of *Ciliegiolo* or similar. A wine from the Tuscan Maremma, the local soil and environment provide a moderate alcohol content, freshness, harmony, and strong vinous notes.

NOTE: Since lentils were traded as currency in ancient times and their shape is reminiscent of small coins, they are often associated with wealth. Italians like to serve lentils during New Year's celebrations.

VARY IT! You can swap out the lentils for any kind of legume in this soup. Noodles also can be added in Step 5 and cooked until done.

Vellutata di castagne/Cream of Chestnut Soup

PREP TIME: 10 MIN | COOK TIME: 40 MIN | YIELD: 4 SERVINGS

INGREDIENTS

2 tablespoons Amy Riolo Selections or other good-quality extra virgin olive oil

1 pound roasted or steamed jarred chestnuts

1 small carrot, peeled and coarsely chopped

1 stalk celery, coarsely chopped

1 small yellow onion, coarsely chopped

2 cloves garlic, peeled and sliced

4 cups Homemade Vegetable or Chicken Stock (see Chapter 3) or low-sodium chicken or vegetable stock

1 dried bay leaf

1 teaspoon fresh rosemary, minced OR ½ teaspoon dried thyme

⅛ teaspoon kosher salt

¼ cup cream

¼ teaspoon black pepper, freshly ground

½ cup Parmigiano-Reggiano cheese, grated

DIRECTIONS

1 Heat oil in a large saucepan over medium heat. Add chestnuts, carrot, celery, and onion, stirring to mix well. Sauté until tender, about 7 minutes. Stir in garlic.

2 Add the stock to the vegetables, increase heat to high, and bring to a boil. Reduce heat to medium-low and add bay leaf, rosemary or thyme, salt, and pepper. Simmer, covered, for 20–30 minutes, or until vegetables are tender.

3 Purée the soup in a food processor fitted with a metal blade (carefully remove the core of the lid, and cover it with a kitchen towel, so that mixture will not burst out). Process for 20 seconds, and stir in cream.

4 Pour the purée into the bowls. Sprinkle fresh black pepper and Parmigiano-Reggiano cheese, and serve hot

TIP: Serve this creamy, cozy soup in the fall. It is an excellent first course and pairs well with poultry and meat. I like to serve it with turkey, and it makes an unexpected way to start the Thanksgiving meal.

Pair this dish with a bottle of *Terrano del Carso* or similar. A lively ruby red wine that is known for the exuberance of its acid verve and for the fragrant notes of blackberry, currant, and raspberry.

NOTE: The scent of roasted chestnuts instantly transports me to Rome, where during the winter months fresh chestnuts are roasted on many streets. Despite the health virtues of this soup, its luxurious flavors and creamy texture make it perfect for a family winter holiday.

VARY IT! Freshly roasted chestnuts are traditionally used in this soup, but since that is not an option for many, the jarred variety can be substituted. You can puree all of this soup and serve it that way as well, perhaps with short pasta or rice added in Step 3 and cooked until done before serving.

Polenta

PREP TIME: 5 MIN | COOK TIME: 30 MIN | YIELD: 8 SERVINGS

INGREDIENTS

4 cups water (or more, if needed)

1 cup dried polenta (classic or instant)

¼ teaspoon unrefined sea salt

¼ teaspoon black pepper, freshly ground

DIRECTIONS

1 Add 4 cups water to a medium saucepan, and bring to a boil over high heat. Slowly pour in the polenta in a gentle stream, stirring and whisking simultaneously with a whisk or wooden spoon to avoid lumps. Continue stirring until mixture starts to thicken, about 3 minutes.

Note: If you are cooking instant polenta, it will already be finished at this time, and you can season with salt and pepper and move to Step 3. Otherwise, if using regular polenta, continue to the next step.

2 Lower heat to medium-low (or a temperature that allows a very low simmer) and cook for at least 20-25 minutes, stirring about every 5 minutes. Be sure to crush any lumps that may form against the side of the pan. If the polenta is too thick, add ½ cup water to soften it. Polenta is done when it easily comes away from the sides of the pan. Add sea salt and pepper.

3 Remove saucepan from heat and cool, allowing polenta to solidify. If not using right away, store polenta in an airtight container in the refrigerator for up to 1 week.

TIP: Make double portions of polenta so that you can serve the extra portion grilled, as in the next recipe.

Pair this dish with a bottle of *Valtellina Superiore* or similar. From Nebbiolo grapes, this is a wine that is dependant on the area it is grown in for its characteristic rich aromas, especially in the reserve version. It has a full, harmoious sip with a delicately spicy finish.

NOTE: For a fun alternative to mashed potatoes, stir your favorite cheese, such as Parmigiano-Reggiano, into the polenta.

VARY IT! You can prepare the polenta with milk or stock instead of water, if you like.

Polenta grigliata/Grilled Polenta

PREP TIME: 5 MIN	COOK TIME: 10 MIN PLUS AT LEAST 4 HOURS REFRIGERATION TIME	YIELD: 4 SERVINGS

INGREDIENTS

1 cup water

1 cup milk or stock

¾ cup quick-cooking polenta

½ cup Parmigiano-Reggiano cheese, grated

Salt, to taste

¼ cup Amy Riolo Selections or other good quality extra virgin olive oil

DIRECTIONS

1 Place 3 cups water and 1 cup milk or stock in a large saucepan, and bring to a boil over high heat. Reduce heat to medium-low, and add the polenta, stirring slowly.

2 Cook, uncovered, stirring slowly and steadily until polenta is smooth and creamy, about 3-5 minutes.

3 Stir in the Parmigiano-Reggiano and salt to taste. Remove from heat.

4 Spoon the polenta into a heat-proof dish, about 8x6x2 ½-inches. Let cool.

5 Cover and refrigerate for at least 4 hours or overnight.

6 Remove the polenta from the refrigerator and slice it into 3 ½-inch pieces (or the size you prefer).

7 Preheat a grill or broiler on high. Brush polenta lightly with olive oil on both sides. If using a grill, place the polenta slices on it for a few minutes, or until grill marks appear. Flip over and grill on other side.

8 If using a broiler, grill marks won't appear, but keep the polenta under the flame until it turns golden.

TIP: You can use leftover polenta to make this recipe the next day.

Pair this dish with a bottle of *Valtellina Superiore* or similar. From Nebbiolo grapes, this is a wine that is dependant on the area it is grown in for its characteristic rich aromas, especially in the reserve version. It has a full, harmonious sip with a delicately spicy finish.

NOTE: Grilled polenta makes a fantastic appetizer. Top it with your favorite toppings such as whipped goat cheese and herbs, a mushroom medley, grilled vegetables, or whatever combination appeals to you.

VARY IT! Stir in the cheese or herb of your choice to give this recipe your own unique flavor.

Gnocchi di patate/Potato Gnocchi

PREP TIME: 30 MIN | COOK TIME: 60 MIN | YIELD: 8 SERVINGS

INGREDIENTS

8 medium-sized russet potatoes (about 4 pounds)

1 egg

1 tablespoon salt

1 ½ to 2 cups unbleached all-purpose flour

Fresh Tomato Sauce, Pesto, or Bolognese-Style Meat Sauce (see Chapter 7), to serve

¼ cup Parmigiano-Reggiano cheese, grated, for serving

¼ cup Amy Riolo Selections or other good-quality extra virgin olive oil, for drizzling

DIRECTIONS

1   Preheat oven to 375 degrees. Wash and dry potatoes. Make a long incision in the potatoes lengthwise about ½ inch deep. Bake the potatoes 45-60 minutes until tender.

2   When cool enough to handle, peel the potatoes and pass them through a potato ricer (see Tip). Add the egg and salt. Add the flour, little by little. You may not need all of the flour. Mix with your hands until the dough begins to stick together.

3   Transfer the mixture to a wooden board. If the dough sticks to the board, add a little more flour. When the dough is soft, pliable, and a little sticky, it is ready.

4   Cut the dough into plum-sized pieces. Flour your hands. Gently roll out each piece of dough with quick back and forth motions until you have created a long thin rope (it should be about the width of your thumb). Cut into 1-inch pieces.

5   Hold a fork with the curved part parallel to the wood board. Starting from the bottom of the backside of the fork, press each piece of dough firmly upward along the length of the tines. Let the gnocchi fall back onto the surface. Place gnocchi onto a lightly floured baking sheet.

6   Repeat with remaining dough until all of it has been cut and shaped.

7   Bring a large pot with 6 quarts of water to a boil. Salt water. Reduce heat to medium. Gently add half of the gnocchi. Remove gnocchi with a slotted spoon when they float to the top (3-4 minutes).

8 Carefully shake off excess water. Place directly into a pan of your favorite sauce and turn to coat, or place on a large platter or tray to finish saucing later.

9 Bring water back to a boil. Repeat with remaining gnocchi. To serve, add a few large tablespoons full of tomato, pesto, or meat sauce to the undressed gnocchi, and toss to coat. Plate, garnished with extra cheese and a drizzle of EVOO, if desired. Serve immediately.

TIP: Always use a potato ricer instead of a potato masher when making the dough. If you use a masher, you will end up with a paste that is too heavy to be authentic gnocchi.

Pair with a bottle of Soave Superiore or another delicate bodied white Italian wine.

Gnocchi di ricotta/Ricotta gnocchi

PREP TIME: 30 MIN | COOK TIME: 3 MIN | YIELD: 4 SERVINGS

INGREDIENTS

1 ½ cups flour, plus extra for dusting

1 egg

1 cup whole milk ricotta cheese, well drained (see Tip)

½ cup freshly grated Pecorino-Romano cheese, plus extra for sprinkling

Salt, to taste

Black pepper, freshly ground, to taste

1 teaspoon olive oil

4 cups Fresh Tomato Sauce (see Chapter 7)

DIRECTIONS

1   Place 1 ¼ cups of flour in a large bowl. Lightly beat the egg with a fork, and add it to the flour along with the Ricotta and Pecorino Romano; season with salt and pepper. Mix ingredients together with your hands to form a dough.

2   Transfer the dough to a lightly floured working surface, and knead lightly for 2–3 more minutes, gradually adding remaining flour if the dough sticks to the board or your hands. The dough is ready when it no longer sticks but is still somewhat tacky to the touch and soft.

3   Divide the dough into four pieces, and roll into balls. Using both hands, roll out each ball of dough into a log about the width of your index finger. Cut each log into ¼-inch pieces. Place on a large cutting board or a large piece of parchment or wax paper.

4   Bring a large pot of water to a boil. Add a teaspoon of olive oil and the gnocchi. Cook, uncovered over high heat until the gnocchi rise to the surface of the water, about 2–3 minutes. While the gnocchi are cooking, heat the Fresh Tomato Sauce in a large sauté pan over medium heat.

5   Remove the gnocchi from the water with a slotted spoon and transfer to the sauté pan with the Fresh Tomato Sauce. Turn to coat, and serve warm, with additional Pecorino Romano cheese.

TIP: Drain the Ricotta in a fine mesh colander over a bowl or in a cheese-cloth overnight for best results.

Pair this dish with a bottle of *Grechetto di Todi* or similar. A white wine with a straw color and floral and golden apple aromas. Fresh, savory, and with a mineral taste, it envelops the palate with harmony and balance.

NOTE: Even though potato gnocchi are much more prevalent in the United States, ricotta gnocchi actually have a longer history. Potatoes only arrived in Italy in the 16th century from the New World, so it was this recipe that people made prior to that. Many gourmands prefer to make them in tiny "pearls" instead of larger sizes, and they taste great served with tomato and pesto sauce.

VARY IT! Serve with pesto instead of tomato sauce, if preferred.

Gnocchi alla Romana/Semolina Gnocchi

PREP TIME: 20 MIN | COOK TIME: 20 MIN | YIELD: 4 SERVINGS

INGREDIENTS

For the Gnocchi

2 cups whole milk

1 teaspoon salt

¾ cup coarse semolina

¼ cup Parmigiano-Reggiano cheese, grated

Dash of nutmeg

2 large egg yolks

1 tablespoon unsalted butter

For the Topping

3 tablespoons unsalted butter, melted, divided

2 tablespoons grated Parmigiano-Reggiano cheese

DIRECTIONS

1 Place the milk and salt in a medium saucepan, and bring to a boil, uncovered, over high heat. Reduce heat to medium.

2 Add the semolina in 3 additions (¼ cup at a time), stirring with a wooden spoon until you reach a paste-like consistency. Add the grated Parmigiano-Reggiano cheese, egg yolks, and nutmeg.

3 Transfer the mixture onto a large smooth working surface (drizzling a little olive oil on the surface makes the process easier). With a spatula, spread it out to a ¼-inch thickness. Let cool.

4 Preheat oven to 350 degrees. After the gnocchi sheet has cooled, use a glass, mold, or cookie cutter to cut into circles about 2 ½ inches in diameter. Set aside the leftover odds and ends.

5 Butter a 9x13-inch baking dish with 1 tablespoon melted butter. Place some of the leftover odds and ends vertically in the center of the dish.

6 Arrange the gnocchi disks evenly around the sides and on top of the center mound of odds and ends, in an overlapping fashion.

7 Sprinkle with Parmigiano-Reggiano cheese and bake in preheated oven until lightly golden, about 10-15 minutes. Serve immediately.

TIP: Serve Semolina Gnocchi in a meal with a second course that is in a tomato sauce, such as a stew or cacciatore-style chicken.

Pair this dish with a bottle of *Castelli Romani bianco* or similar fresh and balanced wine with fruity and floral notes.

Canederli/Bread Gnocchi from Alto Adige

| PREP TIME: 15 MIN | COOK TIME: 30 MIN | YIELD: 4 SERVINGS |

INGREDIENTS

1 tablespoon unsalted butter

1 small yellow onion, finely chopped

2 cups cubed stale bread

½ cup milk

2 eggs, lightly beaten

½ teaspoon salt

¼ teaspoon black pepper, freshly ground

¼ teaspoon nutmeg

1 ¾ cups all-purpose flour, divided

½ cup flat leaf parsley, finely chopped, divided

½ cup Fontina cheese, finely diced

6 cups Vegetable Stock (see Chapter 3)

¼ cup Parmigiano-Reggiano cheese, grated, to serve

DIRECTIONS

1 Melt the butter in a large skillet over medium heat, and sauté the onion until lightly golden. Let the onion cool to room temperature.

2 Place the bread cubes, milk, eggs, salt, pepper, and nutmeg in a large mixing bowl. Mix well, and press down mixture with the back of a fork to incorporate milk with bread well.

3 Add 1 cup of flour, half the parsley, and Fontina cheese, and mix well to combine. Add cooled sautéed onion, and mix well.

4 Let the mixture rest for another half an hour covered with a tea towel. It should look uniformly moist and slightly sticky.

5 Using your hands, form the *canederli* by pressing together enough of the mix to make balls the size of a small tangerine (about 2 inches in diameter). You should be able to produce 10 or 11 balls out of the entire mix.

6 Place remaining ¾ cup flour on a platter. After making each ball, roll it in flour to seal the outside and prevent the *canederli* from sticking to each other. Place on a large sheet of aluminum foil, wax paper, or cutting board. When all the *canederli* are ready, re-roll them into flour and reform them a second time.

7 Bring the vegetable stock to a boil in a large pot over high heat. Taste it and adjust salt, if necessary. Place the *canederli* gently into the pot, reduce heat to medium-high. Boil the *canederli* for 12-15 minutes or until firm and floating.

8 To serve them "dry" or plain as they are called in Italy, transfer two or three *canederli* into each bowl. Finish with some grated Parmigiano-Reggiano cheese and remaining parsley. See Tip to learn how to serve them in broth, or *in brodo*, as they are often enjoyed.

TIP: You can serve the *canederli* in stock. Simply prepare more vegetable stock (the one used for boiling will be cloudy because of the flour). Place one or two *canederli* into each bowl, and pour the clear stock over them. Finish with some grated Parmigiano-Reggiano cheese and remaining parsley.

Some Southern Italian regions offer similar dumplings, but they are called "bread meatballs" and are usually served with tomato sauce or fried. Once boiled, the *canederli* can be stored in the fridge for up to three days, or in the freezer for up to two weeks.

Pair this dish with a bottle of *Teroldego* or similar. With a dark and dense color and fruity aromas of morello cherry and wild berries. The sip is broad, decisive, and dynamic with intense fruit flavor and a spicy, balsamic finish.

NOTE: Many regions of Northern Italy have strong Austrian roots. In the province of Trentino–Alto Adige, for example, 40 percent of the residents still speak German as a first language. Similar to Matzo Balls but made with bread, *canederli* are bread dumplings only found in the north-east of Italy (Trentino-Alto Adige, Friuli, and part of Veneto), where they are served as a first course or as a main entree. They are usually served in homemade broth, or pan fried and dressed in melted butter and chives.

VARY IT! Variations of this dish are common in all south-eastern Europe, where they are also served as an accompaniment to meat stews and roasts. The word *canederli*, in fact, derives from the German and Austrian *knödel* (dumplings).

3

Main Courses, Side Dishes, and Salads

IN THIS PART . . .

Get to the core of what Italian main courses look like and the importance of seasonality.

Discover which side dishes play an important role on Italian tables and how they are paired with main courses.

Embrace the many ways of serving Italian salads as well as their place in a typical Italian meal pattern.

Master main course recipes and learn the role that each dish plays in authentic Mediterranean meals.

Learn the most popular fish, seafood, egg, poultry, meat, and vegetable recipes.

Insalata di mare/Seafood Salad (Chapter 6)

Polpette di melanzane/Eggplant Croquettes (Chapter 6)

*Pesto/*Fresh Basil and Pine Nut "Sauce" (Chapter 7)

*Salsa di pomodoro/*Fresh Tomato Sauce (Chapter 7)

*Tagliatelle con salsa di ricotta e basilico/*Tagliatelle with Basil Ricotta Cream Sauce (Chapter 8)

*Rigatoni al forno/*Baked Rigatoni with Besciamella Sauce and Meat Ragù (Chapter 8)

Lagane con ceci/Pasta with Chickpeas (Chapter 9)

Farfalle con salmone/Bowtie Pasta with Smoked Salmon and Cream Sauce (Chapter 9)

Cotolette d'agnello alla griglia/Grilled Lamb Chops (Chapter 13)

Filetto di manzo marinato/Rosemary and Balsamic Marinated Filet of Beef (Chapter 13)
Verdure grigliate/Grilled Mixed Vegetables (Chapter 14)
Peperonata/Roasted Mixed Pepper Medley (Chapter 14)

Insalata Caprese/Caprese Salad (Chapter 15)

Macedonia/Fruit Salad (Chapter 15)

Taralli dolci al vino rosso/Sweet Red Wine Biscuits (Chapter 19)

Mostaccioli/Chocolate Holiday Cookies (Chapter 19)

*Pizza bianca con rucola e salmone affumicato/*White Pizza with Smoked Salmon and Arugula (Chapter 20)

*Sfincione/*Sicilian "Sponge" Pizza (Chapter 20)

Chapter **11**

Secondi/Main Courses: Fish and Seafood

Second courses, or *secondi*, as they are known in Italian, are called entrees or main courses in English. The only difference is that in English-speaking countries, the meal is planned around the main course, while in Italy the meal is usually planned around the first course, which precedes the main. This is particularly interesting because even though the second course comes after the *integral primo*, it is equally as important. I like to think of the *primo* and *secondo* as being like spouses or parents — they both have equally important parts to play, but with different roles.

When planning an Italian menu, choose your *primo* first, no pun intended, so that you are menu-making like an Italian. Then choose the *secondo* that best complements it. The exception to this rule, of course, is when you may have a great piece of fresh fish, or some just-caught seafood that you need to cook. In that case, it is perfectly acceptable to build a menu around that.

From a nutritional standpoint, Italian second courses need to fill in the nutritional gaps to make a complete meal out of the *primo* and salad courses, so they need to contain protein and be accompanied by vegetables, or side dishes called *contorni* (see Chapter 14). As mentioned in Chapters 8, 9, and 10, if your first course contains a heavy tomato-based sauce, your second course should be grilled or roasted, and free of a thick sauce.

Additionally, it is important to remember that Italians usually do not create surf and turf meals, so if your first course is linguine with clams, then your *secondo* should contain fish or seafood as well. If you are planning to serve Adriatic-Style Fish Stew from this chapter for a second course, you do not want to start out with *Tagliatelle al ragù Bolognese* or with anything that contains meat or cheese. Instead, opt for a simple vegetable or herb-based sauce to set the stage for the seafood and tomatoes that will follow it.

In this chapter, you read about the types of fish and seafood available in Italy, learn how to pair them in menus, as well as find out authentic ways to prepare them. In addition, you find how to select and store them so seafood can be a part of your healthful and delicious lifestyle.

Appreciating the Importance of Fish and Seafood in Italian Cuisine

"*Pisci cottu e carni cruda*" is a Calabrian proverb that means "Fish should be well cooked and meat has more flavor when it's cooked less."

Surrounded by the Adriatic, Ionian, Tyrrhenian, and Mediterranean Seas, Italy has one of the richest ranges of seafood in the world. Seafaring and fishing have been important parts of the Italian economic, cultural, and culinary scene since the beginning of time. Nowadays marine biologists use sophisticated technology to track the migratory patterns of fish off the coast of the Mediterranean — a modern trend that the ancient Romans began over two thousand years ago.

The Italian approach to selecting, buying, and storing fish and seafood is the same as it is with every other raw ingredient. Choose the freshest, most ethically and locally sourced fish possible, and cook it in a simple way that enhances its flavor and texture. It's worth mentioning that what is considered fresh in Italy and in the rest of the world is relative. In Italy, coastal cities have marinas that sell freshly caught fish daily. Purchasing something that was caught the day before (perhaps because it was a national holiday and the fishermen didn't work) makes an Italian think that what they are buying is "old."

In addition to fresh fish, dried and later salt cod (known as *stoccafisso* or *baccala* in Italian) have been an integral part of the Italian food scene. The *stoccafisso* comes from Norway and the *baccala* from the northern Atlantic. You find both of them all over Italy especially in the Veneto and in the south of Italy from Rome down. In more recent times Atlantic cod (*merluzzo*) has become increasingly popular and is found in many traditional Italian restaurants and a freezer staple in supermarkets. *Baccala* is often a part of Christmas Eve menus in Italy (see Chapter 4 for more info about cooking with an eye on the calendar).

In the United States, fish usually comes from more than a few miles away, and it is most likely that more than a day has passed between the time it was caught and the time it's available to eat. That said, there are some steps you can take to make sure that you're eating the best and freshest seafood possible. Here are my suggestions:

>> Purchase from a store that tells you where the fish was caught and how it was raised.

>> Download the Monterrey Bay Aquarium Seafood Watch app or visit their website to check the health and sustainability of the fish you are about to consume.

>> Avoid "fishy" smelling fish. Fresh fish should smell like the body of water it came from — the fishy smell of iodine is actually from fish decaying.

>> If you are buying whole fish, look for bright white eyes around the pupil, bright red, moist gills, and a shiny coat.

The Mediterranean Diet recommends eating fish and seafood a minimum of two times per week. Unfortunately, even accomplished home cooks are often intimidated when it comes to cooking seafood and pairing it in courses, but you don't need to be intimidated. Each recipe in this chapter includes serving tips, storage techniques, and other dishes to pair it with.

TIP

Adding an additional single serving of fish to your diet has been shown to reduce risk of heart disease by up to 49 percent! Plus, fish contains so many healthful fatty acids and nutrients to boost brain power that Italians consider it a secret to the longevity that their citizens enjoy. The recipes in this chapter were chosen to give you easy, tasty dishes to prepare that can benefit your health and please your palate.

The Feast of the Seven Fishes: An Italian American tradition

"Chi dorme nun pija pesce" means "who sleeps doesn't catch fish" and is the Roman way of saying "the early bird gets the worm." Fish are mentioned often in common Italian expressions because they are a part of the lifestyle. It is not

uncommon to see three- and four-year-old children with a knife and fork skill-fully de-boning fish better than most adults around the world, because it is something that they do often.

Many Americans are introduced to Italian fish recipes through a popular Italian American tradition called "The Feast of the Seven Fishes," a tradition with roots in Italy; it uses many Italian recipes, but has become a phenomenon of its own in the U.S. One of the reasons fish is eaten on a regular basis has to do with religion. In the Catholic tradition, it was forbidden to eat meat prior to receiving Holy Communion on Sunday, special days, and holidays. Therefore, communities and with families who wanted to enjoy a large Christmas Eve *cenone* (or dinner) before taking communion at Midnight Mass, created a feast, but with fish and seafood instead of meat.

There are no preset types of fish or seafood that must be included; cooks can use any fish they choose. *Prezzo fisso* restaurant menus, which offer several courses at a fixed price, are causing a renaissance of the custom, and many younger Italian-Americans, and non-Italians are happy to reclaim it. The number 7 was significant even in pre-Christian times. When celebrating Christmas, it is used to signify the seven Sacraments. Some people make nine courses to represent the Holy Trinity times three. Others make 13 to represent the 12 apostles plus Jesus. My theory is that the tradition of seven courses is more widespread because it is the easiest to prepare. As I tell my students, while seven courses seem daunting to many Americans, it is a small number, especially for a holiday meal by my Calabrian family's standards.

Celebrating Italian-style seafood recipes

In addition to fish itself, many types of seafood, including squid (which the whole world now refers to by its Italian name, *calamari*), octopus, mussels, clams, crabs, sea urchins, scallops, shrimp, prawns, eels, and mollusks, just to name a few, are all celebrated in the Italian kitchen. Because those foods weren't always readily available in the U.S., they are often viewed as fine-dining foods to be enjoyed in Italian restaurants. Few American home cooks know how to cook Italian-style seafood with ease, but it doesn't need to be that way!

Seafood is nutritious, tastes great, and cooks up very quickly. With the recipes in this chapter as a guide, you can create restaurant-worthy dishes anytime the mood strikes! Just be sure to always purchase fresh seafood on the day of preparation, or use frozen items as a backup plan. Selecting the best-quality ingredients you can find means not only that they are safe and sustainable, but also that you can have the best-tasting results.

Brodetto di pesce/Adriatic Fish Stew

PREP TIME: 5 MIN	COOK TIME: 15MIN	YIELD: 4 SERVINGS AS A MAIN COURSE, 6 SERVINGS AS A FIRST COURSE

INGREDIENTS

¼ cup Amy Riolo Selections or other good-quality extra virgin olive oil

2 garlic cloves, peeled and sliced

Pinch of crushed red chili flakes

1 pound peeled tomatoes (fresh or canned), roughly crushed with a masher or by hand

¼ teaspoon black pepper, freshly ground

½ teaspoon unrefined sea salt

2 pounds mixed fresh fish (monkfish, mullet, or other white fish works well), cut into 2-inch pieces

1 cup Homemade Seafood Stock (see Chapter 3) or water

¼ cup parsley, minced

DIRECTIONS

1 Heat oil in a 6-quart saucepan over medium heat. Add garlic, and cook until fragrant, about 1 minute.

2 Add crushed red chili flakes, and stir. Add tomatoes along with their juice, season with pepper and salt, and cook, stirring occasionally, about 10 minutes. Stir in stock, cover, and simmer for 10 minutes.

3 Add fish and cook, covered, until fish is just firm and opaque about 5 minutes.

4 Ladle stew into bowls, garnish with parsley, and serve.

TIP: This stew can be a main course, served after a simple pasta dish such as *Spaghetti al aglio e olio* (see Chapter 8), or as a first course in a series of fish dishes.

Pair this dish with a bottle of *Vermentino di Gallura* from Sardinia or similar. A full-bodied white, this wine intrigues for its typical aromas of white blossoms. The sip is broad, full, and delicately spiced.

NOTE: Each coastal town and region in Italy has its own version of fish and seafood stews. Let the daily catch be your guide when recreating this dish.

VARY IT! This recipe often includes mussels, shrimp, octopus, or a medley of whatever fresh seafood appeals to the cook along with the fish.

Pesce in acqua pazza/Neapolitan–Style Fish in Crazy Water

PREP TIME: 5 MIN | COOK TIME: 20 MIN | YIELD: 4 SERVINGS

INGREDIENTS

¼ cup Amy Riolo Selections or other good-quality extra virgin olive oil

4 cloves garlic, peeled and roughly chopped

1 small red chile pepper, seeded and finely chopped

2 cups cherry tomatoes

1 handful of fresh basil leaves, roughly torn

½ teaspoon unrefined sea salt or salt

Black pepper, freshly ground, to taste

4 boneless white fish fillets, such as cod or halibut, 4 ounces each

DIRECTIONS

1 Heat the olive oil in a large, heavy-bottomed skillet over medium-high heat. Add the garlic, chile pepper, cherry tomatoes, basil, salt, and pepper. Pour in 1 ¾ cups of water, and bring to a boil over high heat.

2 Reduce the heat to medium-low, and cook for 10 minutes until a sauce has formed.

3 Add the fish, spoon sauce over to cover, and cook about 7-10 minutes, until the fish is opaque and cooked through.

4 Remove the fish from the pan, and place on a large serving dish. Raise the heat, cook the sauce for 30 seconds to concentrate the flavors slightly. Taste and adjust salt and pepper. Pour sauce over the fish, and serve immediately.

TIP: The sauce for this dish is called "Crazy Water" because it uses a chile pepper for heat. You can omit it, or replace it with another herb or diced sweet bell pepper, if preferred.

Pair this dish with a bottle of *Verduzzo Friulano* or similar. Greenish in color, it is distinguished by floral scents and intense fruity notes. The sip is delicate, dry, and fresh with a medium-length finish.

NOTE: Fish in Crazy Water is a traditional Neapolitan dish. It pairs well as a second course with *Linguine alle Vongole* (see Chapter 8), pasta with Fresh Tomato Sauce (see Chapter 7), and *Spaghetti al aglio e olio* (see Chapter 8).

VARY IT! Shrimp, mussels, and scallops also taste great cooked this way and can be swapped out for the fish, or added to it; just be sure to adjust the cooking times for the types of seafood you add.

Spiedini di pesce/Grilled Fish Skewers

PREP TIME: 10 MIN	COOK TIME: 15 MIN	YIELD: 4 SERVINGS

INGREDIENTS

8 sturdy sprigs of rosemary (see Note)

1 ¼ pounds skinless firm fish, such as swordfish, tuna, or mahi mahi, cut into 1 ½-inch cubes

24 grape tomatoes

2 tablespoons Amy Riolo Selections or other good-quality extra virgin olive oil

1 clove garlic, peeled

Juice of 1 lemon

¼ teaspoon unrefined sea salt

¼ teaspoon black pepper, freshly ground

Crushed red chili flakes, to taste

DIRECTIONS

1 Heat grill or broiler on high. Peel leaves from the rosemary branches (reserve for another use) and thread fish onto them like skewers, alternating with tomatoes, being careful to divide the fish and tomato pieces evenly among the eight rosemary skewers.

2 Place 1 teaspoon reserved rosemary leaves, oil, garlic, and lemon in a blender, and purée until smooth. Season with salt, pepper, and crushed red chili flakes. Reserve half the oil mixture in a separate container.

3 Brush kabobs with half of the oil mixture. Grill until fish is opaque, 6–10 minutes, turning occasionally.

4 With a clean brush, coat cooked kabobs with reserved oil mixture. Serve immediately.

TIP: Rosemary gives the fish additional flavor and nutritional benefits because it is great for increasing memory and concentration, but if sprigs are hard to come by, you can use metal or wooden skewers instead. Be sure to soak wooden skewers in water for an hour prior to grilling so they don't burn.

Pair this dish with a bottle of *Verdicchio dei Castelli di Jesi* or similar. A white wine with a greenish hue, it offers a harmonious taste and aroma in which floral and herbaceous notes emerge on a pleasantly bitter finish.

NOTE: For additional flavor, marinate the fish in the oil, garlic, and lemon mixture for 20 minutes prior to grilling. This recipe is a great appetizer or main course. It pairs well with Seafood Soup, Seafood Risotto, or *Spaghetti al limone*/Lemon-Infused Spaghetti (see Chapter 8) for first courses.

VARY IT! You can use chicken or beef in this recipe in place of fish, being sure to cook them to the appropriate doneness (temperature) for each recipe.

Pesce spada alla griglia/Calabrian–Style Grilled Swordfish

PREP TIME: 10 MIN | COOK TIME: 20 MIN | YIELD: 4 SERVINGS

INGREDIENTS

¼ cup Amy Riolo Selections or other good-quality extra virgin olive oil

4 swordfish steaks, 4 ounces each

1 yellow onion, thinly sliced

¼ teaspoon Calabrian chili paste, or your favorite chili paste

2 bulbs fennel, thinly sliced, a few fronds reserved for garnish, finely chopped

1 cup Seafood Stock (see Chapter 3)

¼ teaspoon black pepper, freshly ground

DIRECTIONS

1 Heat olive oil in a very large skillet over medium–high heat. Add swordfish steaks and cook 2–3 minutes per side until golden. Remove the fish from the pan, and place on a platter. Set aside.

2 Add onions and chili paste to the skillet. Stir the paste around the base of the pan with a wooden spoon. Add fennel slices. Sauté, uncovered, over medium heat until onions begin to caramelize, about 10–12 minutes. Add stock and pepper. Stir well to combine, and cook, uncovered, for 3–4 minutes.

3 Add the fish back to the skillet, cover, and cook for 3 minutes per side until done.

4 Remove the fish from the skillet to a serving platter. Pour sauce over the swordfish, and arrange onions around the top and sides of the platter. Sprinkle finely chopped fennel fronds over the top of the dish. Serve warm.

TIP: Serve this dish as a second course with *Cavatelli con sugo*/Calabrian Cavatelli with Spicy Tomato Sauce (see Chapter 9) for lunch or with a side dish of sautéed greens and a salad for dinner.

Pair this dish with a bottle of *Vernacia di San Gimignano* or similar. A white wine with fine fruity aromas combined with notes of Mediterranean scrub, a wild bush native to the Mediterranean. The sip is full, ample, and fresh with a bitter finish.

NOTE: Calabria is famous for its Peperoncini, spicy red chile peppers. Many of the local varieties are preserved as chili flakes and ground into a fine powder, or made into a paste. Nowadays, many of these products are available on the international market, but if you can't find them, you can substitute your own favorite chili paste, crushed red chili flakes, or whatever source of heat you prefer.

VARY IT! Fresh tuna and grilled chicken also taste great prepared this way!

Involtini di tonno melanzane/Fresh Tuna and Eggplant Roulades

PREP TIME: 10 MIN COOK TIME: 25 MIN YIELD: 4 SERVINGS

INGREDIENTS

4 tablespoons extra virgin olive oil, divided

2 cloves garlic, peeled and minced

2 cups crushed tomatoes, fresh or canned

2 tablespoons freshly chopped basil

4 tablespoons pine nuts, divided

½ teaspoon unrefined sea salt or salt, divided

Black pepper, freshly ground

Dash of crushed dried red chili flakes

2 tuna fillets (¾ pound), placed in freezer for 30 minutes for easier slicing

2 tablespoons Fresh Bread Crumbs (see Chapter 3)

2 tablespoons Pecorino cheese, grated

2 tablespoons raisins, soaked in warm water for 20 minutes and drained

1 tablespoon finely chopped yellow onion

2 tablespoons chopped fresh, flat-leaf Italian parsley, divided

½ cup finely chopped roasted eggplant or boiled eggplant cubes

DIRECTIONS

1   Heat 2 tablespoons of olive oil in a large skillet over medium heat. Add the garlic and cook until it releases its aroma, 30–60 seconds; do not let garlic turn brown.

2   Add the tomatoes, basil, 2 tablespoons pine nuts, ¼ teaspoon salt, pepper, and chili flakes; stir, and cover. Reduce heat to medium-low, and simmer for 5 minutes.

3   With a filleting knife, carefully and neatly slice the tuna fillets crosswise once into about ⅛-inch-thick slices. Cut each piece in half to make 4 pieces. Place fish between 2 pieces of wax paper and lightly pound on it, using a meat hammer, to flatten it out a few extra inches.

4   Combine the remaining 2 tablespoons of olive oil, bread crumbs, Pecorino cheese, raisins, remaining pine nuts, onion, parsley, and eggplant in a small bowl, and mix well to combine.

5   Remove the top piece of wax paper from the fish and spread 1 tablespoon of the bread crumb mixture on each piece of fish. Press down firmly with your hands, so the filling sticks.

6   Carefully tuck in the sides of fish. The sides must be firmly tucked in so that the filling doesn't escape. Starting at the wide end, roll up the fish, completely encasing the filling. Use toothpicks or skewers to secure the rolls.

7   Slowly remove the lid from tomato sauce and add the rolls into simmering sauce. Cover and cook for 15–20 minutes, turning once, or until fish is cooked through.

8   Transfer the fish to a serving platter, remove skewers, and top with the remaining sauce. Serve immediately.

(continued)

TIP: Stuffing fish and shaping into rolls is a popular Italian second course. Because there are so many ingredients in this dish, it is best paired with a simple first course, such as Roman Style Gnocchi, a vegetable-based soup, or *Spaghetti al aglio e olio* (see Chapter 8).

PAIR this dish with a bottle of *Salice Salentino Rosato* or similar. A rosé blend of Negroamaro and Malvasia Nera (and/or Primitivo!), its olfactory notes include blueberry, strawberry, and rose petals. Its sip is fresh and delicately salty on a long and persistent finish.

NOTE: When I make this dish, I always double the quantity and serve the leftovers tossed into pasta. I cut the stuffed fish into slices and toss it, along with the sauce into large, wide pasta such as rigatoni, ziti, or paccheri. I spoon extra sauce over the top and garnish with fresh parsley and/or basil.

VARY IT! Fresh swordfish fillets also taste great prepared this way. For vegetarians, try using this same filling and sauce with bell pepper halves to make a unique and delicious stuffed pepper recipe.

Gamberi al limone e rosmarino/ Lemon and Rosemary Scented Shrimp

| PREP TIME: 10 MIN | COOK TIME: 5 MIN | YIELD: 4 SERVINGS |

INGREDIENTS

2 tablespoons Amy Riolo Selections or other good-quality extra virgin olive oil

1 ½ pounds shrimp, peeled and deveined (save the peels for Seafood Stock; see Chapter 3)

1 teaspoon finely chopped fresh rosemary

½ teaspoon kosher salt

¼ teaspoon freshly ground black pepper

Crushed red chili flakes, to taste

Juice from 1 lemon

Zest from 1 lemon

DIRECTIONS

1 Heat olive oil in a large skillet over medium-high heat.

2 When olive oil begins to release its aroma, add shrimp, rosemary, salt, black pepper, and crushed red chili flakes. Cook shrimp on one side just until it is bright pink, approximately 1–2 minutes.

3 Turn shrimp over, and squeeze lemon juice over top. Cook shrimp until all gray color is gone and they are pink and cooked through, approximately 1–2 more minutes. At this point, shrimp should be coiled slightly tighter than when they were raw. Shrimp will continue to sizzle in the pan.

4 Transfer shrimp to a serving platter, garnish with lemon zest, and serve immediately.

TIP: You can buy peeled shrimp in a pinch, but the peel-on are usually cheaper, fresher, and give you the option of freezing the shells until you are ready to make a homemade Seafood Stock (see Chapter 3), which elevates all of your seafood recipes.

Pair this dish with a bottle of *Asolo Prosecco extra brut* or similar. A balanced prosecco with a fine bubble and marked freshness. The scents of lemon and cedar mixed with a delicate floral accompany every bite well.

NOTE: Even though this is in the *secondi* chapter, this recipe is also a popular appetizer and a crowd-pleaser at parties. I like to serve these shrimp over a bed of polenta (see Chapter 10), or following a vegetable-based soup or pasta such as *Sugo alla norma*/Sicilian Tomato and Eggplant Sauce (see Chapter 7)

VARY IT! Chunks of tender white fish fillet and scallops can be prepared this way in place of the shrimp.

Cozze in brodo con pomodori e zafferano/Mussels in Tomato Saffron Broth

PREP TIME: 15MIN	COOK TIME: 20MIN	YIELD: 4 SERVINGS

INGREDIENTS

4 tablespoons Amy Riolo Selections, or other good-quality extra virgin olive oil

¼ teaspoon saffron stamens

2 cloves garlic, peeled and minced

1 teaspoon fresh thyme

1 teaspoon fresh oregano

7 ounces fresh or canned reduced-sodium diced tomatoes

1 teaspoon tomato paste

2 cups Homemade Seafood Stock (see Chapter 3) or water

⅛ teaspoon unrefined sea salt

¼ teaspoon freshly ground black pepper

½ pound fresh mussels, scrubbed and beards removed

2 tablespoons finely chopped fresh flat-leaf parsley (for garnish)

DIRECTIONS

1 Heat the olive oil in a large stock pot over medium heat. Add the saffron, garlic, thyme, and oregano, and cook for 2–3 minutes.

2 Stir in the tomatoes, tomato paste, stock, salt, and pepper, and bring to a boil over high heat. Reduce heat to low, and simmer, covered, for 10 minutes.

3 Stir, add the mussels, cover, and cook for 7–10 minutes until mussels are open completely. (Resist the urge to open and close the lid often, because this causes steam to escape, making it harder for the mussels to open and creating a firmer texture.) Discard any unopened mussels.

4 Pour into individual cups or bowls. Sprinkle with fresh parsley, and serve.

TIP: When choosing mussels, look for ones that are closed (this means they are alive and fresh) and completely smooth (not broken). It is best to purchase mussels from sources that sell them individually, so you can be guaranteed of their freshness. Those sold in bags often seem fresh in the store, but when you take them home, you may realize that some are actually open (meaning they are dead) and need to be discarded.

To scrub mussels, wash them with a clean brush, and rinse them with cold water until the water runs clear and no sand or debris remains. You may need to do this multiple times.

Pair this dish with a bottle of *Ortrugo dei Colli Piacentini* or similar. A white wine with a slender body and soft and delicate floral aromas that is appreciated for its fresh and balanced taste on the bitter finish.

NOTE: While the addition of saffron to an Italian recipe might surprise some, many Italian regions, such as Abruzzo, Basilicata, and Calabria, produce award-winning saffron now, and it is becoming increasingly popular in recipes.

Capesante con salsa di balsamico bianco /Scallops with White Balsamic Sauce

PREP TIME: 10 MIN	COOK TIME: 15 MIN	YIELD: 4 SERVINGS

INGREDIENTS

4 tablespoons Amy Riolo Selections or other good-quality extra virgin olive oil, divided

1 medium yellow onion, diced

1 pound dry sea scallops, about 20-30

⅓ cup Amy Riolo Selections White Balsamic Dressing, or your favorite balsamic vinegar

½ teaspoon unrefined sea salt

¼ teaspoon black pepper, finely ground

¼ cup fresh flat-leaf parsley, finely chopped

2 tablespoons fresh basil, finely chopped

1 pound fresh baby spinach

DIRECTIONS

1 Heat 2 tablespoons of olive oil in a large, wide skillet over medium heat. Add the onion, and sauté until lightly golden, 5 minutes, stirring occasionally.

2 Add the scallops, and brown on each side, approximately 1-2 minutes.

3 Season with salt and pepper, and pour Balsamic Dressing over the scallops. Increase heat to high until two-thirds of the liquid is evaporated.

4 Remove from heat, gently stir in parsley and basil, and cover scallops to keep them warm.

5 While the scallops are resting, heat a large, wide skillet to medium-high heat and add remaining olive oil. Add the spinach, and stir to combine. Season with salt and pepper, and stir every minute or so, until spinach is wilted and cooked through, approximately 3 minutes,

6 Transfer spinach to a platter, or divide among individual dishes. Place scallops on top, and serve immediately.

TIP: Regardless of scallops' symbolism, Italians love to cook them because they are both decadent and easy to prepare. When shopping, always choose "dry" scallops, which are free of chemical additives.

This dish pairs perfectly when served after Bucatini with Fresh Tuna and Fennel as a first course. *Spaghetti al limone* and *Linguine alle vongole* (see Chapter 8) are other great options.

Pair this dish with a bottle of *Pinot Grigio Alto Adige* or similar. A Burgundy vine from north-eastern Italy, this wine has a decidedly fruity olfactory profile and a fresh, savory sip with mineral notes.

NOTE: The Italian name for scallops, *capesante*, is a derivative of the French term for scallops — *coquille Saint Jacques.* The scallop shell is a symbol of the pilgrims who visited the famous cathedral of Saint James in Spain and a symbol of Pope Benedict XVI. The scallop shell was also used in the infamous Botticelli painting of Venus.

Polpo alla griglia/Grilled Octopus

PREP TIME: 10 MIN	COOK TIME: 50 MIN	YIELD: 4 SERVINGS

INGREDIENTS

2 pounds octopus, divided into 4 pieces

½ lemon

½ yellow onion

1 dry bay leaf

1 tablespoon black peppercorns

Unrefined sea salt

4 tablespoons Amy Riolo Selections or other good-quality extra virgin olive oil

2 tablespoons Amy Riolo Selections White Balsamic Dressing, or fresh lemon juice

Handful of parsley, finely chopped

Freshly ground black pepper

½ pound Baby Romaine or Mixed Field Greens

DIRECTIONS

1 Place the octopus parts, lemon, onion, bay leaf, peppercorns, and 1 tablespoon of salt in a large pot. Add enough water to cover plus 2 inches.

2 Bring to a boil over high heat, reduce to medium-high, and let boil, uncovered, for 40 minutes. Remove the octopus from the water, drain, and let cool.

3 Preheat the grill or a broiler to high.

4 Place the octopus parts on the grill until cooked through, about 3 minutes per side. Octopus is finished cooking when the thickest part yields to the sharp point of a small knife with little resistance.

5 Whisk the olive oil, balsamic dressing or lemon juice, and parsley together in a small bowl. Season with salt and pepper.

6 When octopus is finished, scatter the greens over a plate and top with octopus and dressing. Serve immediately.

TIP: It is traditional to serve octopus on a bed of greens, or pureed chickpeas, or a vegetable puree as a second course. Farro Risotto (see Chapter 10), *Zuppa di pesce* (see recipe in this chapter), and even pasta with Fresh Tomato Sauce (see Chapter 7) would make good first course options for this dish.

Pair this dish with a bottle of *Aleatico* or similar. A red wine with a great aromatic complexity that articulates floral and fruity with balance and harmony. The sip is full, round, soft, and persistent with a long and delicately spiced finish.

VARY IT! There are many ways to cook octopus—and it doesn't need to be finished on the grill as in this recipe. Boiled octopus (see Step 2) can be cut into small pieces and added directly into a risotto or sauce for pasta.

Chapter **12**

Secondi/Main Courses Take Two: Eggs and Poultry

Probably some of the most popular of the Italian *secondi* recipe options fall into the egg and poultry category. Italians don't usually eat eggs or anything savory for breakfast (except, of course, for the ones that make their way into traditional *biscotti* and pastries), but they enjoy them immensely at lunch and dinner. Chicken, turkey, and duck meat are also prized and part of the typical regional Italian meal plan, but they are not served alongside pasta, as they are in the U.S. In Italy, poultry is its own second course, with the exception of a few lesser-known dishes.

In this chapter, you discover how to create genuine Italian egg, chicken, turkey, and duck dishes, as well as how to pair them in a meal and what to serve with them.

Enjoying Eggs the Italian Way

"Meglio un uovo oggi che una gallina domani." "Better to have an egg today than a chicken tomorrow" is a popular Italian phrase similar to the English "better a bird in the hand than two in a bush." From a culinary standpoint, however, the phrase can be taken literally. Through the centuries, one did not expect to eat meat as a protein on a daily basis the way that we do today. Having "a bird in the pot" was once only limited to special occasions, and by the Renaissance was more of a Sunday treat. Eggs, however, could be and were enjoyed more frequently because they were more plentiful and for their nutritional value.

TECHNICAL STUFF

One egg contains 7 grams of high-quality protein, only 75 calories and 1.6 grams of saturated fat and many nutrients such as minerals, vitamins, iron, lutein, and carotenoids. Eggs are a staple in the Mediterranean diet. Although they were traditionally viewed as a meat substitute in many countries because of their lower cost, there are many Mediterranean egg dishes that are so savory, that they are often preferred over meat.

TIP

For best results, use organic eggs from pasture-raised chickens.

Frittate, the plural form of the word *frittata*, which are often called Italian omelets, are the most popular Italian way of serving eggs for lunch and dinner. While many Americans serve frittata for breakfast and brunch, in Italy they are not enjoyed that way, except perhaps in the farming communities of the past when workers hit the fields early and needed something hearty to eat at the time similar to the American brunch.

Other than frittate, there are a few egg dishes that are traditional, such as *Uova in purgatorio*, or Eggs in Purgatory (called this because the eggs are "suspended" in tomato sauce). Hard-boiled eggs are sometimes eaten by the extremely health conscious or those who are following diets for a workout regime, or at Easter time when they are served alongside asparagus and other greens or buried in Easter breads (see Chapter 19). Scrambled eggs, poached eggs, and fried eggs that Americans and English enjoy for breakfast may be offered in hotels or in lodgings that cater to tourists, but are not traditional Italian breakfast items. That said, many Italians who have travelled to the States and England occasionally make them for a light supper in a theme meal of sorts, which reminds them of their trip.

Preparing Poultry Dishes Fit for an Italian Table

The term poultry refers to fowl such as chicken, turkeys, ducks, and geese. While these are eaten in Italy, chicken is by far the most popular today, and I have focused on chicken meat in this section. Interestingly though, Italians eat turkey breast quite regularly, much more than Americans do. Duck also plays an important role on menus and elegant dinners, just like it did during the Renaissance when Catherine de Medici introduced *Anatra all'Arancia*, or Duck a'l'orange to the French courts.

TECHNICAL STUFF

Chicken is a high-quality protein with a relatively low amount of fat. A three-ounce serving contains just 1 gram of saturated fat and less than 4 grams of total fat, yet is packed with 31 grams of protein, which is more than half of the daily recommended allowance for adult females. Chicken meat contains a significant amount of B vitamins, which aid in metabolism, immune system and blood sugar level maintenance, cell growth, and nerve cell and red blood cell maintenance. For these reasons, chicken is a favorite among athletes, dieters, and the health conscious alike.

Chicken has been enjoyed in Italy since pre-Roman times, and the Arabic name for turkey is "Roman bird," which suggests that it was a meat that was introduced with the Italians. Like any other quality staple, these poultry recipes can be dressed up or down according to the occasion. The recipes in this collection hail from a wide range of Italian regions and feature roasted, grilled, sautéed, and stewed poultry dishes that can be part of a healthful and delicious Italian meal plan.

EGG-CELLENT SECOND COURSES

"Non si può fare una frittata senza rompere le uova." "You can't make an omelet without breaking eggs." (Meaning) You have to take action, if you want to bring about change.

Unfortunately, the egg has gotten a bad nutritional rap during the last few decades when it was linked to increased cholesterol, heart attacks, and strokes. Fortunately, several studies, including one in the American Journal of Clinical Nutrition, found no correlation between eggs and heart attack or stroke risks in healthy people. On the contrary, it found that the nutrient choline, found predominantly in egg yolks, may reduce cancer risk.

Egg yolks also contain antioxidants known to prevent macular degeneration. The high protein content in eggs makes you feel full and satisfied longer than other foods, which contributes to weight loss and enables your muscles to repair after a workout. With large eggs containing only 72 calories each and suited to a variety of cooking styles, eggs are a natural choice for the health conscious and for budget-conscious food lovers.

Frittata di verdure/Mixed Vegetable Frittata

PREP TIME: 10 MIN	COOK TIME: 20-25 MIN	YIELD: 4 SERVINGS FOR MAIN, 6-8 SERVINGS AS AN APPETIZER

INGREDIENTS

¼ cup Amy Riolo Selections or other good-quality extra virgin olive oil

½ medium yellow onion, cut into very thin slices

1 large zucchini, trimmed and cut into very thin (⅛-inch) slices

1 large tomato or 2 Roma tomatoes, diced

8 basil leaves, hand torn

6 large organic eggs, beaten in a bowl until foamy

¼ cup Pecorino Romano or Parmigiano-Reggiano cheese, grated

1 teaspoon unrefined sea salt or salt

½ cup Amy Riolo Selections Sundried Red Pesto, if desired, for serving

DIRECTIONS

1 Preheat the oven to 350 degrees. Heat the oil in a large, wide, ovenproof skillet over medium–high heat.

2 Add the onion and sauté, stirring occasionally, until softened and golden, about 4 minutes. Add the zucchini, and stir to combine. Sauté them, until golden, approximately 5 minutes. Add the tomatoes, stir, and cook for another 4 minutes.

3 Add the basil leaves, beaten eggs, cheese, and salt. Mix well, and reduce heat to medium–low. Cook, undisturbed, for 4 to 5 minutes, or until the eggs are cooked through.

4 Finish off the frittata by putting the skillet in the oven until the frittata top is golden and the eggs are set. Cut into 4 pieces, and serve with a dollop of Amy Riolo Selections Sundried Red Pesto on top, if desired.

TIP: Frittate set up well overnight, so you can make this a day ahead and reheat before serving.

Pair this dish with a bottle of *Pagadebit di Romagna* or similar. From Bombino bianco grapes, it expresses itself with a characteristic scent of hawthorn and a dry, delicate, fresh flavor with a short finish.

NOTE: This dish is best served by itself with bread, salad, and a cheese selection for a light dinner, or preceded by a vegetable- or legume-based soup at lunch. In addition to being served as a second course, it can be an appetizer or an item at a buffet. To serve it this way, cut strips or narrow wedges of the frittata (or use a cookie cutter to cut shapes out of the pan) and serve on a bed of baby greens.

VARY IT! Frittate should be made with the best seasonal produce, so you can substitute what is in season for the zucchini and tomatoes. In the winter, swap them out for potatoes and cabbage. In the fall, use fennel and mushrooms; in the spring, use fresh artichokes and baby spinach or peas. You can even make frittata with leftover spaghetti as the main ingredient!

Uova in purgatorio/Eggs in Purgatory

PREP TIME: 10 MIN	COOK TIME: 20 MIN	YIELD: 4 SERVINGS

INGREDIENTS

4 tablespoons Amy Riolo Selections or other good-quality extra virgin olive oil, divided

Crushed red chili pepper flakes, to taste

2 tablespoons tomato paste

1 small yellow onion, diced

2 large red peppers, trimmed, seeded, and diced

3 cups very ripe tomatoes. chopped

Handful of fresh basil, finely chopped

Unrefined sea salt, to taste

Black pepper, freshly ground, to taste

6 large organic eggs

Parmigiano-Reggiano cheese, to serve

Crusty Italian bread, to serve

DIRECTIONS

1 Heat 2 tablespoons of olive oil in a large skillet over medium heat. Add the chili flakes, tomato paste, paprika, onion, and peppers. Stir well to combine, and allow to cook until peppers are tender, 5 to 7 minutes.

2 Add the tomatoes, stir, add most of the basil, reserving a bit for garnish, and increase heat to high. When mixture begins to boil, reduce heat to low and simmer until sauce thickens, about 10 minutes. Taste, and adjust the salt and pepper.

3 Make six wells in the sauce. Break eggs into the wells. Using a fork, gently swirl the egg whites into the sauce. Simmer, uncovered, until the egg whites are set but the egg yolks are not.

4 Drizzle with remaining EVOO, sprinkle remaining basil on top, and serve with bread.

TIP: This dish is the Italian version of the popular North African and Middle Eastern dish known as Shakshouka. It is typically served as a fast, casual dinner, so bread alone would be enough of an accompaniment for it. You can expand the meal with salad afterward, followed by cheese and fruit, but it is not necessary. If you want to serve this as a main in a multi-course Italian meal, I recommend starting with *Spaghetti al aglio e olio* (see Chapter 8) or *Zuppa di lenticchie* (see Chapter 10) as a first course.

Pair this dish with a bottle of *Pallagrello nero* or similar. From an ancient Caserta grape variety, this ruby red wine gives a scent of blackberries and plums and a fresh, dry, and spicy taste.

NOTE: Eggs in Purgatory is a very homey dish to eat among family and those who are very close to you. I have never seen it on a restaurant menu. They take their name from the idea of being suspended in the tomato sauce, just as Catholics believe that souls wait in purgatory.

VARY IT! To make an even faster *Uova in purgatorio* dish, simply substitute the paste, onion, peppers, tomatoes, and basil for 3 cups of Fresh Tomato Sauce (see Chapter 7) and poach the eggs in it. Top with Parmigiano-Reggiano cheese to serve.

Pollo al forno con patate e carrote/Roasted Chicken with Potatoes and Carrots

| PREP TIME: 15 MIN | COOK TIME: 90 MIN | YIELD: 8 SERVINGS |

INGREDIENTS

1 whole chicken, cleaned and rinsed well

¼ cup Amy Riolo Selections or other good-quality extra virgin olive oil

1 teaspoon unrefined sea salt or salt

½ teaspoon freshly ground pepper

1 tablespoon finely chopped fresh rosemary

6 sage leaves, shredded

1 head garlic, peeled stem sliced off, left intact

1 lemon, cut in half

1 ½ pounds Yukon gold or other potatoes, peeled and cut into 1-inch pieces

1 pound carrots, peeled and cut into 2-inch pieces on the diagonal

DIRECTIONS

1 Preheat the oven to 425 degrees. Place the chicken in a roasting pan, and drizzle olive oil over the chicken, turning to make sure that both the pan and chicken are coated. Season with sea salt, freshly ground pepper, rosemary, and sage by rubbing them into the top and sides of the chicken.

2 Place garlic and half the lemon inside the chicken cavity, and squeeze the remaining lemon over the chicken. Bake, uncovered, for 45 minutes. Carefully (oil tends to splatter) remove the chicken from the oven and scatter potatoes and carrots around the edges, turning to coat in olive oil.

3 Return the pan to the oven to bake for another 45 minutes, or until chicken is done and potatoes are tender. Chicken is done when clear juices run from the thickest part of the thigh after being pierced with a fork, or when the internal temperature of the meat reaches 165 degrees.

4 Cover the chicken, and allow to rest for 10 minutes before carving. Discard the garlic and lemon from the chicken cavity before serving.

TIP: You can make the same dish with chicken legs only and cut the roasting time in half.

Pair this dish with a bottle of *Nero di Troia riserva* or similar. A characteristic vine of the high Apulia in the province of Foggia, which produces a wine of marked color and good body, with soft tannins and an elegantly spicy finish.

NOTE: This is a traditional second course. There is an Italian song by Fred Bongusto that said *"Spaghetti, pollo e insalatina e una tazzina di caffe. . .,"* which means "Spaghetti, chicken, a little salad, and a small cup of coffee," and refers to the most typical of Italian meals. Spaghetti or any pasta with Fresh Tomato Sauce (see Chapter 7), *Spaghetti al limone* (see Chapter 8), *sugo alla norma* (in Chapter 7), and (see sauce recipe in Chapter 7) Béchamel Sauce would be great first courses for this dish. Or enjoy it in the evening with salad and bread alone.

VARY IT! Carrots and potatoes are the standard roasted vegetables that should accompany this dish, and work well all year round, but in the summer, you can swap them out for eggplant, zucchini, and tomatoes; in the fall for a variety of mushrooms or broccoli and cauliflower; and in the spring for artichokes and baby vegetables.

Pollo in umido/Chicken, Tomato, and Pepper Stew

PREP TIME: 15 MIN	COOK TIME: 90 MIN	YIELD: 4 SERVINGS

INGREDIENTS

4 tablespoons Amy Riolo Selections or other good-quality extra virgin olive oil, divided

2 pounds chicken pieces

1 large yellow onion, roughly chopped

2 large red bell pepper, trimmed, seeded, and cut into 1-inch pieces

2 large green bell pepper, trimmed, seeded, and cut into 1-inch pieces

2 cloves garlic, peeled and minced

2 cups diced tomatoes

2 tablespoons finely chopped fresh flat-leaf parsley

2 tablespoons finely chopped fresh basil

½ teaspoon unrefined sea salt or salt

¼ teaspoon freshly ground black pepper

¼ teaspoon crushed red pepper, or to taste

DIRECTIONS

1 Heat 3 tablespoons of olive oil in a large, heavy-bottomed Dutch oven over medium heat. Add the chicken, and brown on all sides.

2 Remove the chicken from the Dutch oven, and set on a plate. Add the remaining tablespoon of olive oil, onion, and peppers, and sauté, stirring occasionally, until onion is light golden, 3–4 minutes. Add garlic and stir. Add the chicken back to the Dutch oven, along with tomatoes, parsley, basil, salt, pepper, and crushed red pepper.

3 Stir, increase heat to high, and bring to a boil. Reduce heat to medium-low, stir, and cover. Simmer for 20 minutes. Remove the lid, stir, and continue cooking until the meat is cooked through and vegetables are tender, 45–60 minutes.

TIP: This is a delicious and hearty dish to serve on cooler days. It is a good accompaniment for Risotto Milanese (see Chapter 10) and *Spaghetti al aglio e olio* (see Chapter 8).

Pair this dish with a bottle of *Primitivo di Manduria* or similar. A muscular and full-bodied red wine from Puglia capable of skillfully combining high alcohol content, freshness, delicate tannins, and long persistence.

NOTE: Choose organic, free-range chicken, if possible, for best results.

VARY IT! Swap out the bell peppers for mushrooms, and add potatoes to this dish if you'd like. Instead of chicken, you can also make this dish with veal, beef, or lamb cubes; adjust the cooking time to fit whatever meat you are cooking.

Petto di pollo marinato/Marinated Chicken Breasts

PREP TIME: 10 MIN	COOK TIME: 10 MIN PLUS AT LEAST 1 HOUR MARINATING TIME	YIELD: 4 SERVINGS

INGREDIENTS

½ cup fresh lemon juice

¼ cup Amy Riolo Selections or other good-quality extra virgin olive oil

1 small yellow onion, thinly sliced

4 cloves garlic, peeled and minced

¼ cup chopped fresh basil

1 tablespoon chopped fresh oregano

1 tablespoon chopped fresh mint

Pinch of crushed red chili pepper

2 pounds chicken breast tenders

½ teaspoon unrefined sea salt or salt

¼ teaspoon freshly ground black pepper

DIRECTIONS

1 In a small bowl, whisk the lemon juice, olive oil, onion, garlic, basil, oregano, mint, and red chili, and mix well to combine. Place the chicken breasts in a large shallow bowl or glass baking pan, and pour dressing over the top.

2 Cover, place in the refrigerator, and allow to marinate for 1-2 hours. Remove from the refrigerator, and season with salt and pepper.

3 Heat a large, wide skillet over medium-high heat. Using tongs, place chicken tenders evenly in the bottom of the skillet. Pour the remaining marinade over the chicken.

4 Allow to cook for 3-5 minutes on each side, or until chicken is golden, juices have been absorbed, and meat is cooked to an internal temperature of 160 degrees.

TIP: Marinate the chicken the night before cooking so you don't have to wait on the day of serving.

Pair this dish with a bottle of *Pecorino di Offida* or similar. Pleasantly rich in color, it has strong floral and aromatic herbal notes on the nose: sage, mint, and star anise with a little refinement. The sip is fresh, round, persistent, and with lasting finish.

NOTE: If you don't have fresh basil, oregano, and mint on hand, substitute a handful of whatever fresh herbs you do have. This dish is meant to be made in the spring, summer, and early fall when herbs are plentiful. It is a good second course to accompany *Spaghetti al limone* (see Chapter 8) or any pasta with Fresh Tomato Sauce (see Chapter 7), *Trofie al pesto* or a vegetable- or legume-based soup. It can also be served without a first course for dinner, along with vegetables and salad.

VARY IT! Everything from Portobello mushrooms to shrimp and fish taste great cooked in this manner with the same marinade.

Scallopine di pollo/Chicken Breasts with Citrus and Capers

PREP TIME: 10 MIN	COOK TIME: 25 MIN	YIELD: 4 SERVINGS

INGREDIENTS

2 boneless, skinless chicken breasts, sliced in half width-wise and pounded thin

2 organic eggs, beaten together in a shallow bowl

1 cup Plain Bread crumbs (see Chapter 3) mixed in a shallow bowl with 2 tablespoons Parmigiano-Reggiano cheese

2 tablespoons Amy Riolo Selections or other good-quality extra virgin olive oil

1 cup Homemade Chicken Stock (see Chapter 3) or white wine

2 teaspoons capers, rinsed and drained

Zest of 1 lemon

½ cup freshly squeezed lemon juice

⅛ teaspoon unrefined sea salt

¼ teaspoon freshly ground black pepper

¼ cup finely chopped fresh flat-leaf parsley, for garnish

DIRECTIONS

1 Bread chicken breasts by first dipping them in the egg mixture and then coating in the bread crumb mixture. Set on a large plate or platter.

2 Heat the olive oil in a large, wide skillet over medium-high heat. Add chicken breasts, and brown for approximately 5 minutes per side, or until slightly golden (turning only once).

3 In a medium bowl, stir together the chicken stock, capers, lemon zest, and lemon juice.

4 When the chicken is browned, pour stock mixture over the top. Reduce heat to low. Season with salt and pepper. Cover, and simmer for 10 minutes, or until sauce has reduced by about three-quarters and meat is cooked to an internal temperature of 160°F.

5 To serve, place chicken breasts on platter or individual plates, spoon sauce over the top, and garnish with parsley.

TIP: This recipe is the perfect accompaniment to *Spaghetti al limone* (see Chapter 8) or *Trofie al pesto* (see Chapter 9).

Pair this dish with a bottle of *Verdeca* or similar. This Apulian vine presents itself to the nose with marked herbaceous, citrus, and tropical fruit hints. The taste is fresh, savory, and with a good persistence.

NOTE: Leftover chicken prepared this way is great to serve sliced on top of salads for a light lunch or dinner.

VARY IT! Fish, veal, and turkey breast can also be prepared this way. To make *Scallopine alla Milanese,* don't make the sauce; simply transfer browned chicken breasts to a heated oven to cook through and serve with lemon wedges to squeeze on top before eating. Serve with arugula and tomato salad.

Pollo alla cacciatora/Cacciatore-Style Chicken

PREP TIME: 10 MIN	COOK TIME: 60 MIN	YIELD: 4 SERVINGS

INGREDIENTS

1 cup unbleached, all-purpose flour

2 pounds boneless, skinless chicken breasts, cut into 8 pieces

¼ cup Amy Riolo Selections or other good-quality extra virgin olive oil

1 tablespoon finely chopped fresh rosemary OR ½ teaspoon dried rosemary, crushed

1 medium yellow onion, diced

3 cloves garlic, peeled and minced

¼ cup dried porcini mushrooms, soaked in water for at least 20 minutes, drained, and chopped

1 cup dry sweet red wine

2 cups diced tomatoes, or whole tomatoes, crushed

⅛ teaspoon unrefined sea salt

¼ teaspoon freshly ground black pepper

1 dried bay leaf

Crushed red chili flakes (optional)

DIRECTIONS

1 Place flour in a shallow dish. Coat the chicken liberally with flour, and shake off excess.

2 Heat oil in large skillet over medium-high heat. Add the chicken, making sure not to crowd the skillet (work in batches if necessary). Cook until chicken is golden on all sides, 5-6 minutes. Transfer the chicken to a platter, and set aside.

3 Reduce the heat under the skillet to medium, and add the rosemary and onion. Cook, stirring, until the mixture begins to color and onion softens, 4-5 minutes. Stir in the garlic and mushrooms, and cook for 1 more minute.

4 Return the chicken to the skillet, raise the heat to high, and add the wine. Cook and stir until the wine is almost all reduced, 5-6 minutes.

5 Add the tomatoes, and season with salt, pepper, bay leaf, and crushed red chile flakes (if using). Bring the tomatoes to a boil, and then reduce the heat to medium-low and cover the skillet, leaving the lid slightly askew. Cook until the chicken is tender, 40-50 minutes, and reaches an internal temperature of 160 degrees. Stir and turn the chicken a few times during cooking.

6 When the chicken is cooked, discard bay leaf and serve.

TIP: Serve this fall favorite with crusty bread and salad for dinner or with *Spaghetti al aglio e olio* (see Chapter 8) for lunch.

Pair this dish with a bottle of *Rosso Conero* or similar. A full-bodied red wine with aromas of mature cherries and plums up to licorice and tobacco. The sip is full, warm, ample, and with a lasting finish.

VARY IT! Rabbit and turkey can also be substituted for the chicken in this recipe.

Scallopine di tacchino/Turkey Cutlets

PREP TIME: 10 MIN	COOK TIME: 25 MIN	YIELD: 4 SERVINGS

INGREDIENTS

4 (4 ounce) turkey breast cutlets (or 1 pound cut into 4-ounce pieces), pounded thin

2 organic eggs, beaten together in a shallow bowl

2 cups Plain Bread crumbs (see Chapter 3) mixed in a shallow bowl with 2 tablespoons Parmigiano-Reggiano cheese

4 tablespoons Amy Riolo Selections or other good-quality extra virgin olive oil, divided

2 tablespoons unsalted butter

Handful of fresh parsley, finely chopped

4 cups baby arugula or other lettuce, for serving

4 Roma tomatoes, or other, to serve

1 lemon, quartered

DIRECTIONS

1 Preheat oven to 425 degrees.

2 Bread turkey breasts by first dipping them in the egg mixture and then coating in the bread crumb mixture. Set on a large plate or platter.

3 Heat 2 tablespoons of olive oil and butter in a large, wide, oven-proof skillet over medium-high heat. Add turkey breasts, and brown for approximately 5 minutes per side, or until slightly golden (turning only once).

4 Transfer turkey to the oven, and roast for 15 minutes, or until cooked through.

5 When turkey reaches 165 degrees in the middle, remove it from the oven and plate on a bed of arugula and scatter tomatoes around the top.

6 Drizzle the remaining olive oil over the top, and place a lemon piece over each turkey breast. Serve immediately.

TIP: Orecchiete with Broccoli, Tagliatelle with Basil Ricotta Sauce, or Cream of Chestnut Soup in the fall are perfect first courses to lead up to this dish, or serve it on its own with bread or crackers, olives, and cheese for dinner.

Pair this dish with a bottle of *Ribolla gialla* or similar. Available in two versions, this white wine from Friuli gives a light body, sustained acidity, and delicate floral. Both versions pair well with this dish.

NOTE: Leftover Turkey Scallopine can be sliced and served in panini or over salad.

VARY IT! Chicken and veal can also be prepared this way.

Anatra brasata al vino rosso con polenta/Braised Duck with Red Wine and Polenta

PREP TIME: 15 MIN	COOK TIME: 3 HOURS PLUS OVERNIGHT MARINADE	YIELD: 8 SERVINGS

INGREDIENTS

1 (approximately 4 pound) duck, cut into 12 equal pieces

1 bottle red wine (or enough to cover the meat as it cooks)

1 carrot, diced

1 celery stalk, diced

½ medium yellow onion, diced

2 garlic cloves, peeled and chopped

1 dry bay leaf

2 sprigs fresh thyme

2 sprigs fresh rosemary

¼ cup Amy Riolo Selections or other good-quality extra virgin olive oil

4 cups Chicken Stock (see Chapter 3)

Unrefined sea salt

Freshly ground black pepper, to taste

1 recipe Polenta (see Chapter 11)

DIRECTIONS

1 Place the duck pieces in a 13x9-inch glass baking dish and cover with red wine. Add the carrot, celery, onion, garlic, bay leaf, thyme, and rosemary. Let mixture marinate overnight in the refrigerator.

2 Drain the duck pieces, reserving the wine and vegetables, and discard the bay leaf.

3 Heat the olive oil in a large Dutch oven over medium heat. Place the duck pieces in the pan, working in batches, if necessary. Brown on both sides, about 3 minutes per side.

4 Increase the heat to high, and pour 1 cup of the reserved wine back over the duck.

5 When two-thirds of the wine has evaporated, add the stock to the pot, cover, and reduce heat to low. Simmer for 2–3 hours, or until duck is tender.

6 Remove duck to a tray or platter, and allow to rest until cool enough to handle. Remove the meat from the bones and shred as you would pulled pork.

7 Heat the remaining liquid in the Dutch oven over high heat to reduce and thicken for a few minutes.

(continued)

8 Heat the polenta, and spread in a serving platter.

9 Place the duck meat on top of the polenta, spoon the thickened sauce on top, and serve.

TIP: Cream of Chestnut Soup, Chickpea Soup, or another mushroom- or legume-based soup (see Chapter 10) is a good first course for this dish, or serve it with green vegetable sides and a salad at dinner time.

Pair this dish with a bottle of *Dolcetto d'Alba* or similar. From the vine of the same name, this ruby red wine has purple hues in the foam, a floral aroma, and a dry, harmonious, medium persistence taste.

NOTE: Not all butchers and markets carry duck; call ahead of time to be sure it is in stock.

VARY IT! Leftover shredded duck can be added to frittate or panini, or used as ravioli stuffing.

Chapter 13

Secondi/Main Courses Take Three: More Meats

There are so many tender and succulent meat dishes in the Italian kitchen that it can be hard to choose which to make. Let the season, your mood, the occasion, and availability inspire you to make these mouthwatering recipes whenever you feel like it.

In this chapter, you discover how to make time-honored meat recipes in a straightforward and simple way. In addition, you find out how to pair them and when to serve them.

Preparing Types of Meat in Traditional Italian Recipes

In traditional Italian life, meat and poultry (served as main courses) were reserved for Sundays and holidays. Because animals served many purposes, such as providing eggs or dairy, working the land, or used as currency, eating their meat was of secondary importance. It was costly to eat meats and poultry because it meant losing a part of a flock, so these proteins weren't eaten daily, except with smaller portions of cured meats in sandwiches or appetizers. Luckily, this created a culinary culture that was predominately centered around plant-based foods, which are more healthful anyway.

It's important to point out, though, that contrary to popular belief, red meat wasn't just reserved for special occasions because it was expensive and people couldn't afford to eat it daily. Unlike the United States, Italy never had a culture of eating meat daily, so people did not purposely need to omit it from their diets in order to consume smaller amounts of it. The tradition of enjoying meat was typically reserved for Sundays after Holy Communion and then on holidays and special occasions. Typical meals on ordinary days, on the other hand, relied on beans and legumes, eggs, with moderate additions of fish and seafood, and poultry (instead of red meat) for protein.

Another difference between the way meat was customarily eaten in Italy versus the U.S. is that in Italy people ate meat according to the season in which the animals were slaughtered. Sheep and goat, for example, were usually born in winter, so they were ready to be slaughtered for Easter. Most families usually kept a specific pig to be slaughtered at Christmas. If turkeys were raised, they could also be slaughtered in fall and winter. These rituals, up until the last century, mandated what was eaten and when. Nowadays, of course, there are supermarkets and butchers that stock various types of meats at different times in the year, and so the selection is much larger. That said, many Italians still associate certain meats with special holidays for these reasons.

Curing meat into prosciutto, salami, and sausages is also an ancient craft that is still very much in demand in Italy today. New artisan *salumierie*, or cured meat shops, are opening up all the time. There is even a new trend to produce cured fish and seafood in the same manner as pork was traditionally cured. In addition to being popular on antipasti trays and sandwiches, bits of these cured meats are often incorporated into pasta dishes, sauces, and meat recipes for enhanced depth and flavor. In the ancient world, curing meat was a means of making it shelf-stable and edible all year round, because freezers and refrigerators didn't exist.

Modern Italians have deviated from the traditional Mediterranean diet tenant of eating meat only once a week. Their meals, unless they are vegetarian, do usually contain poultry or some form of meat on a daily basis, even if the quantities and servings are much smaller than those of American standards.

Goat

While it is no longer as widely available as it once was, goat meat was historically very significant in the Italian diet. Today it is still eaten, especially around Spring and Easter holidays in the Southern Italian regions of Calabria, Sicily, Basilicata, and the Central region of Abruzzo.

TECHNICAL STUFF

Goats are known for their hardiness and ability to adapt to difficult conditions. Domesticated in Syria around 8,000 B.C.E., goats underwent an evolution that significantly changed their morphology before goat farming was introduced to Europe and then the rest of the world. As the animals took to various terrains, different types of breeds developed; there are currently more than 300 varieties worldwide.

Goat meat is the leanest of all meats other than ostrich, and it is very easy to digest. Its protein is said to help with muscle recovery after intense workouts. From a culinary standpoint, goat is very neutral, can be cooked in the same applications as lamb, and is very tasty. Goats are also good for the environment, thanks to their eco-friendly grazing patterns. While offering a significant amount of protein, goat meat has the lowest amount of cholesterol and offers generous amounts of iron and other nutrients.

Because not all butchers in the United States carry goat, I tend to source mine from Halal, Indian, Caribbean, and other international markets. Place your order ahead of time so you can be sure that they have it in stock.

Veal

Veal is extremely popular in Italy and the rest of the Mediterranean region. Milk-fed veal is prized in Italy for its tender texture, and some cooks use it exclusively on their menus and in their homes. Veal can be created from either sex of cows, but it usually comes from the male.

More veal is consumed in Italy than beef. Both veal and beef have similar amounts of protein (approximately 30 grams per 3-ounce serving). Beef has slightly less fat, cholesterol, and calories than veal, but both meats are good sources of B vitamins that are needed for energy. They are also significant sources of riboflavin, niacin, and pantothenic acid.

Both beef and veal contain approximately one quarter of the daily recommended value of zinc. Red meat, in general, offers more B12, iron, and zinc than white meat, as well as a higher amount of healthful fatty acids. Goat, sheep, and beef fat (as well as that of other ruminants) contains about equal parts saturated and monounsaturated fat with only a small quantity of polyunsaturated fat.

Check with your local butcher or supermarket before making a trip, because veal often needs to be special ordered.

Lamb

Lamb is very popular in Italian cuisine, because raising sheep has been a way of life in Italy since pre-Roman times. *Abbacchio,* or Suckling Lamb, is a specialty of Roman cuisine known for its characteristic tenderness. In order to be labelled as *abbacchio,* the animal must weigh less than 11 pounds when slaughtered and its meat should be pale pink. A dark shade of meat indicates an older animal, which is also consumed but not as prized. The best season for *abbacchio* is the spring, and it is traditionally eaten at Easter, even if it can be found throughout the year.

Lamb cubes, chops, ground meat, legs, and shanks are all served in Italy. Lamb has only 175 calories per 3-ounce serving, making it a lean, yet nutrient-rich meat choice. Although people in Italy don't eat lamb daily, it is a delicious and healthful weekly indulgence that makes a great alternative to fattier beef. Lean cuts include the leg, loin, and rack. Lamb provides vitamins and minerals and is an excellent source of protein, which helps keep hunger at bay, preserves lean body mass, and regulates blood sugar. A 3-ounce serving has 23 grams of protein — nearly half of the daily recommended intake. The same serving size also offers a good dose of heart-healthy monounsaturated fat and almost five times the amount of omega-3 fatty acids as found in beef.

Because it can sometimes be hard to source lamb in the U.S., I recommend calling ahead to make sure it is in stock or ordering it from your store or butcher.

Beef

Both beef and veal contain approximately one quarter of the daily recommended value of zinc. Red meat, in general, offers more B12, iron, and zinc than white meat, as well as a higher amount of healthful fatty acids. Goat, sheep, and beef fat (as well as that of other ruminants) contains about equal parts saturated and monounsaturated fat with only a small quantity of polyunsaturated fat.

Quality is definitely more important than quantity when dealing with Italian beef recipes. Until the last few decades, beef was not eaten very often in Italy. Nowadays, however, that is changing. Steaks are popular, American burgers are a trendy treat, and beef is often used in meatballs and sauces that were once reserved for pork or veal meat.

The Italian breeds of cows for meat include *Chianina, Marchigiana, Piemontese, Maremmana, Podolica,* and *Romagnola.* There are many initiatives in place in Italy to protect these breeds, and they are raised using ancient methods that produce superior flavor and texture while protecting the environment. When making Italian beef recipes, use the best quality beef you can.

Pignata di capra/Goat, Potato, and Pepper Stew

PREP TIME: 15 MIN	COOK TIME: 75 MIN	YIELD: 8 SERVINGS

INGREDIENTS

¼ cup plus 2 tablespoons Amy Riolo Selections or other good-quality extra virgin olive oil, divided

1 large yellow onion, diced

2 pounds boneless goat shoulder, cut into 2-inch cubes (3 pounds if using bone-in)

4 cloves garlic, peeled and minced

1 pound crushed or diced tomatoes

½ teaspoon unrefined sea salt

⅛ teaspoon freshly ground black pepper

Pinch crushed red chili flakes (preferably Calabrian)

1 large red bell pepper, seeded and cut into 1-inch cubes

1 large green bell pepper, seeded and cut into 1-inch cubes

2 Yukon gold potatoes, scrubbed, peeled and cut into 1-inch cubes

2 tablespoons finely chopped fresh flat-leaf parsley

2 tablespoons finely chopped fresh basil

DIRECTIONS

1 Heat ¼ cup olive oil in a large, deep skillet over medium heat. Add onion and sauté for 3-4 minutes, or until light golden brown. Add goat, and brown on all sides. Stir in garlic, tomatoes, salt, pepper, and chili flakes. Cover, reduce heat to low, and simmer for 1 hour, (1 hour 30 minutes if using bone-in) or until goat is almost tender.

2 Meanwhile, in a Dutch oven or large, wide saucepan, heat 2 tablespoons olive oil over medium heat. Add bell peppers, potatoes, and parsley. Stir and sauté, uncovered, just until vegetables are tender, approximately 12-15 minutes. Stir in basil.

3 After goat has cooked for an hour, and registers approximately 160 degrees, add pepper/potato mixture and stir. Cover and cook until all ingredients are tender and flavors have blended, approximately 30 minutes. Serve hot.

TIP: Serve this recipe with hearty *Risotto allo zafferano* or *Lagane con ceci* as a first course, or for dinner with bread and salad.

Pair this dish with a bottle of *Aglianico del Vulture Superiore Riserva* or similar. A full-bodied wine with notes of blackberry, herbs, licorice root, leather, and tobacco. The taste is full, broad, tactile, elegantly tannic on a long finish, and pleasantly persistent.

VARY IT! Lamb or beef also works really well with this recipe; be sure to add an additional 30 minutes to cooking time if using those instead of goat.

Capretto al forno/Roasted Kid

PREP TIME: 15 MIN | COOK TIME: 90 MIN | YIELD: 8 SERVINGS

INGREDIENTS

¼ cup Amy Riolo Selections or other good-quality extra virgin olive oil

½ pound yellow onion, peeled and roughly chopped

½ pound carrots, peeled and cut into 2-inch pieces

1 stalk celery, cut into 1-inch pieces

6 cloves garlic, peeled and sliced

2 ½ pounds goat or meat cubes, from the thigh or shoulder, about 1 ½ inches each

1 teaspoon unrefined sea salt or salt

3 sprigs fresh rosemary, leaves finely chopped

1 bunch fresh thyme, finely chopped

1 bay leaf

1 ½ cup Chicken Stock or Meat Stock (see Chapter 3)

1 pound Yukon gold potatoes, scrubbed, peeled, and cut into 2-inch pieces

1 cup crushed peeled tomatoes

¼ teaspoon crushed red chile pepper

DIRECTIONS

1 Preheat oven to 400 degrees.

2 Heat the olive oil in a large, ovenproof heavy-bottomed saucepan or Dutch oven over medium-high heat.

3 Add the onions, carrot, and celery, and turn to coat in oil. Reduce heat to medium-low, and sauté until tender, about 5 minutes. Add the garlic, stir, and cook for 1 minute, or until it releases its aroma.

4 Add the goat meat, and cook 3-5 minutes, until browned on all sides.

5 Season with salt, and stir in rosemary and thyme. Add the stock and bay leaf. Increase heat to high, and bring to a boil.

6 Add the potatoes, tomatoes, and crushed red chile pepper. Stir, and cover. Place in the oven, and cook for 1 hour.

7 Carefully remove cover, stir, taste, and adjust seasoning. Cook for another 30 minutes or until the meat is very tender. Goat meat is cooked thoroughly when it registers 160 degrees, but in this recipe, it should be cooked beyond that point and until very tender. Taste and adjust seasonings again; remove the bay leaf before serving.

TIP: Serve this hearty main dish with *Gnocchi alla romana* or Farro Risotto (see Chapter 10), or *Cavatelli con sugo* (see Chapter 9) as a first course.

Pair this dish with a bottle of *Tintilia del Molise* or similar. With a bright ruby color, the taste-smell has notes of black cherry and small, red fruits that end in a spicy and finely ethereal finish after aging.

NOTE: Sealing and roasting the goat helps it to cook quickly and evenly. This recipe may only require 1 hour in the oven if it is tender.

VARY IT! Beef or lamb meat also can be cooked this way.

Arrosto di vitello/Roasted Veal

PREP TIME: 10 MIN	COOK TIME: 2 HOURS	YIELD: 8 SERVINGS

INGREDIENTS

¼ cup Amy Riolo Selections or other good-quality extra virgin olive oil, divided

1 cup fresh flat-leaf Italian parsley

10 ounces pitted green olives, Sicilian Colossal variety, if possible

¼ cup Parmigiano-Reggiano cheese

2 cloves garlic, peeled

1 boneless breast of veal roast (3 pounds)

1 teaspoon unrefined sea salt or salt

½ teaspoon freshly ground black pepper

3 carrots, peeled and chopped

3 stalks celery, chopped

1 medium yellow onion, chopped

2 cups Chicken Stock (see Chapter 3), divided

1 cup chopped or diced tomatoes

DIRECTIONS

1 Preheat the oven to 400 degrees. Combine 2 tablespoons of olive oil, parsley, olives, Parmigiano-Reggiano, and garlic cloves in a food processor, and pulse on and off until you obtain a paste. Remove lid and blade.

2 Season both sides of the veal with salt and pepper. Spread the stuffing paste evenly over the surface of the veal, generously covering it. Roll the roast, and tie it with butcher's twine just tightly enough to secure; don't tie too tightly or the filling may ooze out.

3 Heat the remaining 2 tablespoons of olive oil in an ovenproof pan over medium-high heat. Add the veal roast, and brown on all sides. Add the carrots, celery, and onion, and stir. Add ½ cup of the chicken stock, and tomatoes to the pan. Stir, remove from heat, and cover.

4 Place the roast in the oven, and cook for 2 hours (basting with ½ cup stock every 30 minutes) or until veal is tender. When the veal is ready, remove from the oven; carefully place the meat on a cutting board, and allow to rest for 10 minutes. The safe minimum cooking temperature for veal is 160 degrees, but it should register much higher than that after cooking this way. To serve, slice the veal and pour sauce over the top.

TIP: This is a typical *Pranzo domenicale* (Sunday supper) recipe; serve pasta with Fresh Tomato Sauce (see Chapter 7) or *Cavatelli con sugo* (see Chapter 9) to start.

Pair this dish with a bottle of *Raboso* or similar. A dark red wine with intense blackberry bush aromas, the aged versions, or with a little over-ripening, provide a sip that's soft with a delicate spice.

NOTE: This recipe takes time to roast, so get it into the oven and use the time to do other things.

VARY IT! Turkey breast also can be prepared in this manner.

Scaloppine di vitello/Veal Cutlets

PREP TIME: 15 MIN	COOK TIME: 10 MIN	YIELD: 4 SERVINGS

INGREDIENTS

4 veal breast cutlets, pounded thin

2 eggs, beaten together in a shallow bowl

2 cups Plain Bread crumbs (see Chapter 3) mixed in a shallow bowl with 2 tablespoons Parmigiano-Reggiano cheese

2 tablespoons Amy Riolo Selections or other good-quality extra virgin olive oil

2 tablespoons unsalted butter

Handful of fresh parsley, finely chopped

1 lemon, quartered

DIRECTIONS

1 Preheat oven to 425 degrees.

2 Bread the veal cutlets by first dipping them in the egg mixture and then coating in the bread crumb mixture. Set on a large plate or platter.

3 Heat 2 tablespoons olive oil in a large, wide, ovenproof skillet over medium–high heat. Add veal, and brown for approximately 5 minutes per side, or until slightly golden (turning only once).

4 Transfer veal to the oven, and roast for 15 minutes, or until cooked through.

5 When veal reaches 165 degrees in the middle, remove it from the oven, transfer to a platter, and place a lemon piece over each veal cutlet. Serve immediately.

TIP: This is an iconic dish that has stood the test of time. It pairs well with pasta with Fresh Tomato Sauce or Pesto Sauce (see Chapter 7), *Sugo alla norma, Cavatelli con sugo (*see Chapter 9), and any gnocchi recipe.

Pair this dish with a bottle of *Chianti Classico* or similar. The pleasant floral notes combined with small, red fruits and balsamic nuances underlie a harmonious sip, with good tannins and an elegant finish.

NOTE: *Veal scaloppine* are the base for the Italian-American classic — *Veal alla parmigiana.*

VARY IT! Chicken, fish, and turkey also can be prepared this way.

Agnello al forno/Roasted Lamb

PREP TIME: 15 MIN | COOK TIME: 2.5 HOURS | YIELD: 12 SERVINGS

INGREDIENTS

1 leg of lamb (5 pounds)

1 head of garlic, peeled

½ teaspoon unrefined sea salt or salt, plus to taste

¼ teaspoon freshly ground black pepper, plus to taste

2 cups Chicken Stock (see Chapter 3), or water, divided

Juice of 1 lemon

2 large yellow onions, sliced into rings

2 tablespoons Amy Riolo Selections or other good-quality extra virgin olive oil

2 large tomatoes, chopped, or ½ cup chopped canned tomatoes

DIRECTIONS

1 Preheat the oven to 350 degrees. With a paring knife, make 1-inch slits in various places around leg of lamb. Sliver garlic cloves, and insert them into the slits in the lamb.

2 Massage salt and pepper into the leg of the lamb. Place lamb in a large roasting pan. Pour 1 cup of the chicken stock or water into the pan. Bake for 1 hour, uncovered, basting every 20 minutes.

3 Pour lemon juice over the lamb. Place the onion rings over the top and drizzle olive oil over the onions. Scatter the tomatoes around the sides of the pan. Add the remaining 1 cup of stock to the pan. Return to the oven and bake, uncovered, an additional 2 hours, basting every 20 minutes, until lamb begins to fall off the bone.

4 Remove from the oven, and cover the pan with a lid or aluminum foil. Allow the lamb meat to stand at room temperature for 10 minutes before carving. Place the lamb on a serving platter, and carve. Serve warm, with tomatoes and onions spooned over the top.

TIP: Because this is a holiday or celebratory dish, it can be paired with an equally prominent first course such as *Lasagne classica* or *Ravioli capresi* (see Chapter 9).

Pair this dish with a bottle of *Barbaresco* or similar. With its characteristic garnet red color, the olfactory spectrum is clear and defined. The taste is dry, delicately tannic, and harmonious.

NOTE: Leftover lamb meat can be made into a panini, used to top salads or fill ravioli, or transformed into a frittata or baked pasta dish.

Polpette d'agnello/Lamb Meatballs

PREP TIME: 30 MIN	COOK TIME: 30 MIN	YIELD: 6 SERVINGS

INGREDIENTS

2 pounds ground lamb

1 medium yellow onion, quartered

6 cloves garlic, peeled and roughly chopped

1 teaspoon chopped fresh basil

1 teaspoon chopped fresh parsley

1 egg

¼ cup Parmigiano-Reggiano cheese

½ teaspoon unrefined sea salt or salt

¼ teaspoon freshly ground black pepper

1 recipe Fresh Tomato Sauce (see Chapter 7)

DIRECTIONS

1 Preheat the broiler. Combine the lamb, onion, garlic, basil, parsley, egg, cheese, salt, and pepper in a food processor. Pulse until mixture turns into a rough paste. Turn the mixture out onto a work surface. Form 24 meatballs that are about 2 ½ inches long and 1 inch wide in the center, tapering off to blunted tips at each end.

2 Place the meatballs on a baking sheet. Brown for about 10 minutes per side, turning after every 2–3 minutes. Turn and brown until they are golden on the outside and cooked through on the inside.

3 Heat the Fresh Tomato Sauce over medium heat.

4 Gently add the meatballs to the sauce, and turn to coat. Cover, reduce heat to low, and simmer until sauce has thickened by half, about 15–20 minutes. Lamb is considered safe to consume at 160 degrees, but these meatballs should register higher than that after simmering in the sauce.

TIP: Serve these meatballs with *Cavatelli con sugo, Lagane con ceci,* Tagliatelle with Basil Cream Sauce, or *Orecchiete con cime di rapa* (see Chapter 8), or *Spaghetti al aglio e olio* (see Chapter 8).

Pair this dish with a bottle of *Montefalco rosso* or similar. A ruby red wine with olfactory vinous notes of cherry combine with a dry, harmonius sip with good body.

NOTE: You can skip the step of baking the meatballs in the oven and instead cook them in the sauce by bringing the sauce to a light boil, carefully adding in the meatballs, and cooking the mixture for 30 minutes or until cooked through.

VARY IT! The amount of sauce used in this recipe is just enough to coat the meatballs, which is the way they are served in Italy. If you would like to serve your meatballs American style with lots of sauce, you can double the quantity of tomato sauce in the ingredients list. You can use beef, turkey, or veal in this recipe as well.

Cotolette d'agnello alla griglia / Grilled Lamb Chops

PREP TIME: 5 MIN | COOK TIME: 25 MIN | YIELD: 5 SERVINGS

INGREDIENTS

4 cloves garlic, peeled and minced

3 tablespoons Amy Riolo Selections or other good-quality extra virgin olive oil

Juice of 1 lemon

1 teaspoon finely chopped fresh rosemary or thyme

1 teaspoon unrefined sea salt

½ teaspoon freshly ground black pepper

2 ½ pounds lamb loin chops (or 10 loin chops)

DIRECTIONS

1 Combine garlic, olive oil, lemon, rosemary, salt, and pepper in a small bowl. Place lamb chops on s large tray, and rub garlic oil mixture all over the chops; set aside while the grill heats.

2 On the gas grill, turn all burners to high, close the lid, and heat until the grates are hot, about 15 minutes. Scrape grates clean. Grill lamb chops for about 6 minutes per side or until cooked to 145 degrees or until desired doneness. Move to a clean plate, and let rest for 5 minutes, covered with aluminum foil before eating.

TIP: Serve this dish with any fresh or spicy tomato sauce except meat ragu. Use leftover meat on salads, in soups, panini, and pasta dishes.

Pair this dish with a bottle of *Sagrantino di Montefalco* or similar. Dark in color, it has a captivating sense of smell where the variety of forest scents are concentrated. The sip is broad, thick or "chewable," dry, and with a long and persistent finish.

NOTE: Rubbing the lamb with the marinade prior to grilling helps protect it from the carcinogens that are associated with grilling, in addition to giving it great flavor.

VARY IT! Goat and veal can also be prepared this way.

Vrasciole/Calabrian Meatballs

PREP TIME: 15 MIN	COOK TIME: 20 MIN	YIELD: 6 SERVINGS

INGREDIENTS

1 cup dried Italian bread mixed with ¼ cup skim milk, drained, and squeezed of excess liquid

1 pound ground beef (85% or higher fat content)

1 egg, lightly beaten

½ cup fresh flat-leaf parsley or basil, finely chopped

½ teaspoon salt

¼ teaspoon freshly ground black pepper

¼ cup Pecorino-Romano cheese

Pinch crushed red chile flakes (preferably Calabrian; see Where to Buy Guide)

Good quality extra virgin olive oil, for frying

2 cups Fresh Tomato Sauce (see Chapter 7)

DIRECTIONS

1 In a large bowl, combine all ingredients except for the Fresh Tomato Sauce. Mix well with hands.

2 Shape mixture into uniform ½-inch meatballs, roll them into an egg (croquette shape), and then rub them between your hands to make them slightly more elongated, (the desired shape should be a cross between a football and a cylinder), and set on a clean baking sheet or cutting board.

3 Heat 2 inches of oil in a large, wide skillet over medium-high heat to 375 degrees.

4 With a slotted spoon, carefully lower meatballs into the oil and cook, turning once, a few minutes on each side until golden.

5 Carefully remove from the oil using a slotted spoon, and transfer to a paper towel-lined tray or platter.

6 Bring Fresh Tomato Sauce to a light boil in a large saucepan over medium heat. Add the meatballs, stir, and cover. Reduce heat to medium-low, and simmer for 30 minutes, or until meatballs are cooked through and tender. Minimum safe internal temperature for the meatballs is 160 degrees, but they should register much higher on a thermometer at the end of this recipe.

TIP: A Calabrian Sunday staple, serve this recipe with *Cavatelli al ragu* or *Lagane con ceci* (see Chapter 9) for a first course or with Risotto Croquettes for appetizers (see Chapter 10).

Pair this dish with a bottle of *Savuto* or similar. A blend of Gaglioppo, Aglianico, Greco nero, and Nerello Cappuccio from the valley of the Calabrian river of the same name. The characteristic ruby red is underscored by a fruity scent and a full, dry, and harmonious sip.

NOTE: The meatballs can be baked instead of fried or cooked directly in the sauce. Leftover meatballs can be sliced onto Ciabatta bread, topped with sauce and provolone cheese, and put under the boiler until the cheese melts for a tasty lunch or dinner.

VARY IT! Veal or pork meat, or a combination, can be used instead of beef in this recipe.

Stufato di manzo/Beef Stew

PREP TIME: 15 MIN	COOK TIME: 2 HOURS MIN	YIELD: 6 SERVINGS

INGREDIENTS

1 ½ pounds beef stew cubes, approximately 2-inches, if desired

10 cloves garlic, peeled and sliced into thin slivers

1 ½ teaspoons unrefined sea salt or salt, divided

¾ teaspoon freshly ground black pepper, divided

3 tablespoons Amy Riolo Selections or other good-quality olive oil

2 small or 1 large yellow onion, thinly sliced

½ cup dry red wine

3 green bell peppers, seeded and cut into 4-inch strips

2 cups diced tomatoes

1 bay leaf

DIRECTIONS

1 With a sharp knife, make slits into each piece of beef and stuff with a few of the garlic slivers. Season the meat with 1 teaspoon salt and ½ teaspoon pepper.

2 Heat the oil in a Dutch oven or large, heavy-bottomed saucepan over medium heat. Working in batches, brown the meat on all sides. Transfer to a plate. Add the sliced onions to the pan, and sauté until lightly golden and soft, about 5 minutes.

3 Pour the wine into the pan, and stir in the meat. Increase heat to high, and cook, stirring often, until the wine almost disappears, 3-5 minutes. Add the peppers and any remaining garlic to the pan, and turn to coat. Add the tomatoes, bay leaf, remaining salt and pepper, and stir to combine.

4 Cover, reduce heat to low, and simmer for 1 ½ hours, or until the meat is extremely tender, stirring every half hour, and adding water ½ cup at a time if sauce seems too dry. Meat is done when it is tender. A safe/minimum internal temp for beef is 160 degrees, but it usually registers higher than that when cooked to this level of tenderness. Remove the bay leaf before serving.

TIP: This rustic dish is best served over creamy Polenta or with *Gnocchi alla Romana* (see Chapter 10). This stew also can be served over thick, medium-sized pasta such as rigatoni, ziti, or paccheri.

Pair this dish with a bottle of *Sfurzat della Valtellina* or similar. Ruby red with garnet reflections, this wine offers rich aromas with intense hints of fully ripe fruit and a sip of great body and softness, dry, and with a long finish.

NOTE: Making slits in the meat and inserting the garlic adds flavor to the sauce and tenderness to the meat.

VARY IT! Lamb, goat, or veal also can be prepared this way.

Filetto di manzo marinato/Rosemary and Balsamic Marinated Filet of Beef

PREP TIME: 10 MIN	COOK TIME: 50 MINS PLUS OVERNIGHT MARINADE	YIELD: 12 SERVINGS

INGREDIENTS

½ cup Amy Riolo Selections White Balsamic Dressing, or your favorite balsamic vinegar

¼ cup Amy Riolo Selections or other good-quality extra virgin olive oil

4 sprigs rosemary, needles finely chopped

6 garlic cloves, peeled and sliced

Unrefined sea salt

Freshly ground black pepper

1 whole filet of beef (6 pounds), (ask butcher to tie the meat so that individual pieces are separated for easier portioning, if desired)

DIRECTIONS

1 Whisk together the first four ingredients in a medium bowl. Add salt and pepper to taste.

2 Place filet in a large, glass baking pan, and pour marinade over the top. Cover with plastic and marinate overnight.

3 Preheat oven to 500 degrees (you can roast the meat at a lower temperature, but it will add a bit more cooking time to the recipe).

4 Roast the filet 30 minutes for rare, 40 minutes for medium, and 50 minutes for well done, using a meat thermometer to check that the thickest part is at least 160 degrees.

5 When the meat has finished cooking, remove from the oven, and cover with foil.

6 Allow to rest for 10 minutes, and then transfer to a cutting board. Remove twine, and cut into individual steaks. Using a fine mesh sieve, strain the marinade liquid over top.

TIP: A fantastic holiday or party dish, serve with Barley Risotto or Cream of Chestnut Soup (see Chapter 10), *Cavatelli con sugo*, or Farfalle with Smoked Salmon and Cream Sauce (see Chapter 9) for a first course.

Leftover beef is great to use in panini and to stuff ravioli.

Pair this dish with a bottle of *Barolo* or similar. Garnet-red in color, the nose offers intense and persistent notes of violets and vanilla berries. The sip is balanced, harmonious, and delicately dry with a pleasantly spicy finish.

NOTE: You can add sliced potatoes, carrots, and other root vegetables, cut into 1-inch pieces, into the bottom of the pan while cooking, if desired.

VARY IT! Veal or lamb also can be cooked this way.

Chapter **14**

Adding Contorni: Authentic Vegetable Side Dishes

Contorno is the Italian word for "side dish." In Italian cuisine, sides are always made up of vegetables. Side orders of spaghetti, garlic bread, gnocchi, and risotto that are served in "Italian" restaurants abroad do not exist in Italy. In the traditional cuisine, side dishes were a way to transform seasonal produce into culinary masterpieces that complement and enhance the flavor and nutritional profile of the main dishes they are served with.

REMEMBER

The recipes in this chapter don't include wine pairings because they accompany a main dish, and usually it's the main dish that gets paired.

Making the Most of Seasonal Produce

In a typical Italian meal, a main course consisting of fish, meat, or poultry would be accompanied by a green vegetable or two and perhaps a root vegetable or carrots. The *contorni* are always served alongside the main course and are therefore a part of the Secondo course and need to be planned accordingly.

REMEMBER

It is important to use seasonal produce in Italian side dishes, not only because eating local food is good for the environment, but also because it is better for us. Our bodies naturally crave the nutrients in produce that is in season in the area that we live in. So, for example, in the fall when broccoli and squash are plentiful, it does our body more good to eat them at that time than it would to eat them in June.

Italian-style side dishes are among the most delectable, simplest to prepare, and healthiest in the world. Many Italian contorno recipes were originally created to take advantage of the abundance of various harvests. Before modern times, food was preserved in salt or olive oil, but it was most often consumed when it was fresh and in season. For the sake of variety, different recipes using the same vegetables were created.

The Mediterranean diet, which has deep roots in Italy, promotes basing our meals around plant-based foods. The USDA recommends getting 5-9 servings of fresh fruit and vegetables a day, and by planning accordingly with the *contorni* at each meal, you are guaranteed of getting at least four servings during your main course at lunch and dinner. Add in a serving as an appetizer, a few with the first course, and a few more with your salad and you get nine servings a day just by following a delectable Italian meal plan, and without any fad diets.

TIP

» Grilled and broiled vegetables: Grilled and broiled vegetables are the perfect natural partners for grilled and broiled fish, meat, and poultry. They also taste great with pan-fried meat dishes such as Scaloppine (see Chapter 13) and with roasted main courses.

Leftover grilled vegetables are perfect for topping pizza and tossing into salads, soups, dips, and purees.

» Roasted vegetables: Few aromas add warmth and comfort to our surroundings as the scent of roasted vegetables, garlic, and herbs do. Walking into a kitchen full of these traditional smells transports most Italians to their youth. From a culinary standpoint, roasting vegetables is a great way of cooking them because it helps to coax out their natural sweetness. A healthful and low-fat method as well, roasting vegetables in the oven saves time, effort, and stovetop space.

TIP

When preparing the roasted vegetable recipes in this chapter, I highly recommend that you make double or triple quantities. Leftovers can be frozen for up to a month or stored in the refrigerator for up to a week. I always choose the latter option. That way, I can add the vegetables to *frittate* and pasta dishes, purée them into soups, or serve them alongside other mains whenever I'm short on time.

>> Pan-fried vegetables, parmigiane, and gratins: Additional ways that Italians love to serve vegetables are by pan-frying them, preparing them *"alla parmigiana"* like eggplant, and making them into gratins. These slightly more complex recipes, found toward the end of this chapter, are so full of flavor that they are often capable of taking center stage from simpler *contorni*. Use them as appetizers, side dishes, or vegetarian main courses when you want to make a great, long-lasting culinary impression.

Verdure grigliate/Grilled Mixed Vegetables

PREP TIME: 20 MIN	COOK TIME: 10 MIN	YIELD: 6 SERVINGS

INGREDIENTS

¼ cup Amy Riolo Selections White Balsamic Dressing or your favorite balsamic vinegar

½ cup Amy Riolo Selections or other good-quality extra virgin olive oil

2 cloves garlic, peeled and finely minced

¼ teaspoon freshly ground black pepper, plus extra, to taste

¼ cup fresh basil, finely chopped

2 large red bell peppers

1 small, firm eggplant, cut into ½-inch-thick slices

4 small zucchini, trimmed and cut in half lengthwise

1 pint cherry tomatoes

1 bulb fennel, cored and quartered

Unrefined sea salt

DIRECTIONS

1 Combine balsamic vinegar, olive oil, garlic, black pepper, and basil in a small bowl and set aside.

2 Hold (with tongs) whole red peppers over an open flame of a gas grill, or broil under the broiler, until blackened and blistered. Place peppers in a paper lunch bag, and seal shut. In a few minutes, open the bag carefully (let steam escape), remove peppers, peel off the skin, and cut into slices.

3 Preheat broiler to high or grill. Place eggplant, zucchini, cherry tomatoes, and fennel on a large baking tray and broil or grill, turning once or twice as brown, until caramelized, tender, and cooked on all sides (approximately 3–5 minutes). Remove grilled vegetables to a large bowl.

4 Stir in sliced peppers, pour balsamic dressing over all, and mix together. Season with salt and pepper to taste. Serve hot or at room temperature.

TIP: This colorful confetti of a side dish is perfect for serving alongside Marinated Chicken Breasts, Grilled Fish Kabobs, any grilled meat or protein, and pan-friend items such as Scaloppine or fish fillets.

NOTE: These are all summer vegetables meant to accompany grilled proteins in the warmer months.

VARY IT! Make a meal out of the leftover grilled vegetables by tossing them with hot pasta and some shredded mozzarella cheese, piling them high on panini, or by puréeing them with a little bit of homemade stock (see Chapter 3) to make a soup.

In the fall, different types of pumpkin, squash, and mushrooms can replace the peppers, eggplant, and tomatoes.

Asparagi grigliati con balsamico bianco e parmigiano/Chargrilled Asparagus with White Balsamic and Parmesan

PREP TIME: 5 MIN	COOK TIME: 10 MIN	YIELD: 4 SERVINGS

INGREDIENTS

24 asparagus spears, trimmed

¼ cup Amy Riolo Selections or other good-quality extra virgin olive oil

2 tablespoons Amy Riolo Selections White Balsamic Dressing or your favorite balsamic vinegar

¼ cup Parmigiano-Reggiano cheese, shaved

DIRECTIONS

1 Preheat a grill or griddle to high heat (you should be able to hold your hand above the grates for just 1–2 seconds).

2 On a large platter or baking sheet, brush asparagus with olive oil to coat easily. Place asparagus directly on grill, cover, and cook for 4 minutes. Lift lid, turn, and continue to cook until al dente, approximately 4–5 more minutes, turning often.

3 Remove from grill, drizzle with balsamic, and garnish with Parmigiano–Reggiano cheese to serve.

TIP: This is another perfect accompaniment for grilled, roasted, or pan-fried chicken, turkey, veal, or beef. Try this recipe with Grilled Lamb Chops, Rosemary and Balsamic Marinated Filet of Beef, or any of the Scaloppine recipes in this book.

NOTE: White, green, and purple asparagus all work well with this recipe. I always make leftover grilled asparagus so I can purée the rest and serve the next day thinned out with a little homemade stock as a soup or folded into hot farfalle or penne pasta as a sauce.

VARY IT! Zucchini or squash slices can be prepared the same way.

Verdure d'estate arrostite/Roasted Summer Vegetables

PREP TIME: 15 MIN	COOK TIME: 45 MIN	YIELD: 4 SERVINGS

INGREDIENTS

¼ cup Amy Riolo Selections or other good-quality extra virgin olive oil

1 medium sized (8 to 9-inch) eggplant, cut into 1-inch pieces

2 zucchini (½ pound), cut into 1-inch rounds

2 red peppers (4 ounces), seeded and cut into 1-inch pieces

1 tablespoon finely chopped fresh oregano or thyme

1 teaspoon Kosher salt

½ teaspoon freshly ground black pepper

1 head of garlic, top peeled off, left whole

Juice of 1 lemon

DIRECTIONS

1 Preheat oven to 425 degrees.

2 Coat a 9x13-inch baking dish with olive oil.

3 Add eggplant, zucchini, and red peppers, and toss to combine.

4 Sprinkle oregano, salt, and black pepper over the top.

5 Place garlic, peeled side down, in the middle of the pan.

6 Squeeze lemon juice over the top.

7 Roast, uncovered, for 30 minutes, or until vegetables are tender.

8 Remove from oven, and, using oven mitts, remove garlic. Cut off the base of the bulb (about ¼ inches) and squeeze the roasted garlic cloves into the vegetables. Stir to combine, and serve on a platter.

TIP: Serve this recipe with Chicken, Turkey, or Veal Scaloppine, roasted fish, or any other roasted meat, fish, or chicken.

VARY IT! To make this recipe appropriate for fall, substitute broccoli and squash or mushrooms for the peppers, zucchini, and eggplant. In the spring, use artichokes, spinach, and baby onions. In the winter, use potatoes, carrots, and turnips.

You can turn this dish into a fabulous sheet dinner by preparing the vegetables on a large sheet pan. After toasting halfway, add fish fillets, such as salmon or cod to the pan. Drizzle with additional EVOO, lemon, salt, and pepper, and finish baking until fish flakes and vegetables are tender, approximately 20-25 minutes, depending upon the thickness of the fish.

Zucchine al forno/Roasted Zucchini with Tomatoes and Olives

PREP TIME: 10 MIN	COOK TIME: 35 MIN	YIELD: 4 SERVINGS

INGREDIENTS

1 cup quartered cherry tomatoes

2 large zucchini, diced

1 yellow onion, sliced

½ teaspoon unrefined sea salt, divided

⅛ teaspoon freshly ground black pepper, plus extra

2 tablespoons Amy Riolo Selections or other good-quality extra virgin olive oil

2 garlic cloves, peeled and chopped

¼ cup Castelvetrano, Taggiasca, or other Italian olives, pitted and diced

Juice of 1 lemon

Zest of 1 lemon

¼ cup basil, finely chopped

DIRECTIONS

1 Preheat oven to 425 degrees.

2 Place tomatoes, zucchini, and onion in a large baking dish, and season with ¼ teaspoon salt and ⅛ teaspoon pepper.

3 Drizzle with olive oil, and roast approximately 20 minutes, or until vegetables are tender.

4 Remove from oven, stir in garlic, olives, and lemon juice. Sprinkle with remaining ¼ teaspoon salt and pepper to taste.

5 Return to oven, and bake for approximately 15 minutes, or until vegetables are tender.

6 Garnish with lemon zest and basil, and serve.

TIP: Serve this tasty and simple-to-make *contorno* with Roasted Chicken with Potatoes and Carrots or Turkey Cutlets (see Chapter 12), Calabrian Meatballs, or Roasted Veal (see Chapter 13) for a perfect pairing.

NOTE: I often stretch this contorno into an entrée by roasting cod fillets along with the vegetables. Add them with the garlic and olives in step 4, and continue with the recipe, roasting until vegetables are cooked and fish flakes.

VARY IT! When zucchini are not in season, use root vegetables, broccoli, cauliflower, or fresh fennel in their place. Leftovers make a luscious way to dress pasta and rice.

Patate al forno/Roasted Potatoes

PREP TIME: 10 MIN	COOK TIME: 30 MIN	YIELD: 4-6 SERVINGS

INGREDIENTS

¼ cup Amy Riolo Selections or other good-quality extra virgin olive oil, divided

4 Idaho potatoes, peeled and cut into 1-inch cubes

½ teaspoon unrefined sea salt

Freshly ground black pepper

2 cloves garlic, peeled and finely chopped

1 tablespoon fresh rosemary, finely chopped

1 teaspoon fresh sage, finely chopped

1 tablespoon fresh parsley, finely chopped

DIRECTIONS

1 Preheat oven to 425 degrees. Grease a sheet pan or large baking dish with a teaspoon of olive oil.

2 Place potatoes on the pan, and season with salt, pepper, garlic, rosemary, and sage.

3 Mix potatoes with remaining olive oil and roast approximately 30 minutes, or until vegetables are tender. Garnish with fresh parsley and serve.

TIP: This dish is a natural partner for main courses with a saucy component, such as Lamb Meatballs, Calabrian Meatballs, Roasted Lamb, or Lamb Chops (see Chapter 13), and Chicken Scalloppine (see Chapter 12)

NOTE: It is your choice whether to peel the potatoes; I normally do not for nutritional reasons, but it is common to serve them peeled in restaurants.

VARY IT! Try this recipe with various types of potatoes, including sweet potatoes and baby potatoes. You can roast any root vegetable (carrots, turnips, parsnips, rutabaga and more) this way. Leftovers make a great base for *frittata*.

SAGRE: ITALIAN HARVEST FESTIVALS

One ancient Italian custom that is still in practice today allows Italians to celebrate the vegetable harvest and learn multitudes of ways to prepare these vegetables: the agricultural festivals known as *sagre*. The word *sagra*, meaning "sacred," descends from the Latin word *sacrum*, which referred to the gods or anything in their power. In ancient Rome, there were 182 "sacred" days, and many of them had their own foods! In pre-Christian times, the sagre were held to pay tribute to the Agrarian gods — namely Saturn, who was the god of both agriculture and commerce (which is fitting since food was used as currency back then). With the advent of Christianity, the festivals were held on saints' days or Christian holidays, especially if they coincided with the harvest. Sagre are celebrated not only for the vegetable harvest, but also for the harvest of various types of fruits, legumes, beans, nuts, animal products, fish, seafood, and, of course, the grape or wine harvest.

Peperonata/Roasted Mixed Pepper Medley

PREP TIME: 5 MIN	COOK TIME: 20 MIN	YIELD: 4 SERVINGS

INGREDIENTS

¼ cup Amy Riolo Selections or other good-quality extra virgin olive oil

2 pounds mixed red, yellow, and green bell peppers, cut into ½-inch strips

6 garlic cloves, peeled and sliced

¼ cup green olives, pitted and halved

Unrefined sea salt, to taste

Freshly ground black pepper

2 tablespoons Amy Riolo Selections White Balsamic Dressing or your favorite balsamic vinegar

¼ cup finely chopped parsley

DIRECTIONS

1 Preheat oven to 425 degrees, and grease a baking sheet with a teaspoon of olive oil.

2 Add peppers, garlic, olives, remaining olive oil, and a pinch of salt and pepper. Mix to combine.

3 Roast for 20 minutes or until peppers are tender.

4 Transfer to a bowl or platter, and stir in balsamic vinegar. Taste, and add salt if necessary.

5 Garnish with parsley to serve.

TIP: Serve this piquant and tasty side with Lamb Chops, or Turkey or Veal Scalloppine (see Chapter 12), or Herb-Marinated Chicken Breasts, or Roasted Chicken with Potatoes and Carrots (see Chapter 12).

NOTE: I recommend making a double batch so the leftovers can be puréed into a sauce or thinned out with stock to make a nutritious and creamy soup.

VARY IT! You can also add thinly sliced potatoes to this recipe for a heartier side dish, or cook fish, such as fresh tuna fillets in the same pan.

Finocchio in padella con scalogni e castagne/Pan-fried Fennel, Shallots, and Chestnuts

PREP TIME: 10 MIN | **COOK TIME: 20MIN** | **YIELD: 4 SERVINGS**

INGREDIENTS

2 tablespoons Amy Riolo Selections or other good-quality extra virgin olive oil

4 shallots, peeled and quartered

3 pounds fennel, bulbs quartered, stalks reserved for stock

1 cup peeled and boiled chestnuts (jarred is fine)

½ teaspoon salt

½ teaspoon freshly ground black pepper

1 cup Vegetable Stock (see Chapter 3)

½ cup freshly chopped Italian parsley

DIRECTIONS

1 Heat oil in a 12-inch skillet over medium heat.

2 Add the shallots, and sauté until golden and slightly soft. Add the fennel bulbs, working in batches to accommodate the fennel, if necessary. Stir, and cook for 5 minutes on each side, or until golden.

3 Add the chestnuts, stir, and season with salt and pepper.

4 Increase the heat to high, add the vegetable stock, and bring to a boil.

5 Reduce heat to low, cover, and simmer for 10-20 minutes, or until fennel is tender and most of the liquid has reduced.

6 Transfer to a serving platter, and sprinkle with parsley. Serve warm.

TIP: This contorno is the perfect complement to roasted turkey, veal, and chicken dishes with the warm, fall-like flavors from the chestnuts and shallots.

NOTE: In Italy, people munch on raw fennel the way Americans may enjoy crunchy celery sticks. A single cup of fennel is a significant source of Vitamin C and potassium, and it is known to ease the stomach and aid digestion.

VARY IT! Purée leftovers of this dish to make a delicious and creamy fall soup. Butternut squash can be substituted for the fennel.

Patate Raganate/Calabrian Potato Gratin

PREP TIME: 15 MIN	COOK TIME: 45 MIN	YIELD: 6 SERVINGS

INGREDIENTS

¼ cup Amy Riolo Selections or other good-quality extra virgin olive oil, divided

2 pounds Yukon Gold potatoes, peeled and cut into ⅓-inch slices

2 medium red onions, thinly sliced

2 teaspoons finely chopped fresh oregano OR ½ teaspoon dried oregano

Pinch crushed red chili flakes or chili paste

1 teaspoon unrefined sea salt

¼ teaspoon freshly ground black pepper

⅓ cup Fresh Bread Crumbs (see Chapter 3)

½ cup grated Pecorino Crotonese, Ricotta Salata, or Pecorino-Romano cheese

¼ cup unsalted butter, cubed

DIRECTIONS

1 Preheat oven to 425 degrees.

2 Grease a 9x12-inch baking dish with 1 tablespoon olive oil. Add potatoes, onions, oregano, chili flakes, salt, and pepper.

3 Drizzle with remaining olive oil and toss well to combine. Sprinkle bread crumbs and cheese over the top.

4 Scatter the butter over the top.

5 Bake, uncovered, until potatoes are tender and topping is golden, approximately 45 minutes. Serve.

TIP: Because this dish has a dry texture, it is a good accompaniment for main courses that contain tomato or another type of sauce, such as Calabrian Meatballs or Lamb Meatballs (see Chapter 13), and Chicken, Tomato, and Pepper Stew (see Chapter 12).

NOTE: This recipe is actually an authentic Calabrian dish known in the region as *Patate raganate*. The word *raganate*, meaning "gratin," is a dialect word from the neighboring Basilicata region that is now used throughout Calabria. This is important to remember because the recipe varies from what Americans identify with as a French gratin.

VARY IT! Sweet potatoes and other root vegetables also can be prepared this way.

Verdure in aglio, olio, e peperoncino/ Greens Sautéed in Garlic, Oil, and Peperoncino

PREP TIME: 5 MIN	COOK TIME: 5 MIN	YIELD: 4 SERVINGS

INGREDIENTS

¼ cup Amy Riolo Selections or other good-quality extra virgin olive oil

2 ¼ pounds spinach, Swiss chard, dandelion greens, or baby kale. trimmed, washed, and dried

3 cloves garlic, peeled and minced

Pinch crushed red chili flakes

⅛ teaspoon kosher salt

¼ teaspoon freshly ground black pepper

1 lemon, halved, for garnish, if desired

DIRECTIONS

1 Heat the oil over high heat in a very large skillet until very hot.

2 Add the greens (you may need to work in batches) and cook, stirring, for about 1–2 minutes; the greens should turn bright green and wilt slightly. Add the garlic and red chili flakes, and continue to cook, stirring constantly, until the garlic begins to release its aroma, approximately 30 seconds.

3 Remove the greens from the heat, and season with salt and pepper. Toss well to combine, and serve with lemon on the side (for squeezing juice over the greens).

TIP: Serve this *contorno* along with any dish that contains tomatoes, peppers, and/or potatoes.

NOTE: This recipe is one of the backbones of the Mediterranean diet. Cooking nutritional powerhouses such as spinach, Swiss chard, dandelion greens, and baby kale with powerful anti-inflammatory ingredients like EVOO, garlic, and chiles amps up their health benefits and flavor. This dish is a shining example of culinary medicine at its best.

VARY IT! Broccoli, cauliflower, zucchini, squash, Brussels sprouts, and most other vegetables can be prepared this way. Toss leftovers into pasta, soups, or stews.

Melanzane alla parmigiana/ Eggplant Parmesan

PREP TIME: 20 MIN	COOK TIME: 40 MIN	YIELD: 8 SERVINGS

INGREDIENTS

2 pounds eggplant, trimmed, and cut into ¼-inch thin slices

¼ cup Amy Riolo Selections or other good-quality extra virgin olive oil

Unrefined sea salt

1 recipe Fresh Tomato Sauce (see Chapter 7)

½ pound fresh mozzarella, grated

Freshly ground black pepper

Handful of fresh basil, chopped

⅓ cup grated Pecorino, Parmigiano-Reggiano, or Grana Padano cheese

DIRECTIONS

1 Preheat broiler.

2 Place eggplant on a metal baking sheet, and brush each side of each piece lightly with olive oil. Broil a few minutes per side until golden. Sprinkle with salt.

3 Preheat oven to 425 degrees.

4 In a 9x12–inch baking dish, spoon a thin layer of tomato sauce onto the bottom.

5 Top with a layer of broiled eggplant, scatter a few tablespoons of mozzarella cheese over the top, along with a bit of basil.

6 Continue layering in the same order until all the ingredients are used, reserving a thin layer of sauce and grated cheese for the top.

7 Bake uncovered for 30 minutes or until cheese is golden, sauce is bubbly, and eggplant is cooked through.

TIP: This all-time favorite dish can be served in smaller quantities as an appetizer, as part of a buffet, as a vegetarian main course, or, in this case, as a side dish. It pairs well with roasted and grilled meats and poultry. This is the original recipe for the dish, which is made without breading the eggplant slices. If you prefer to flour and fry the eggplant, see the following Note.

NOTE: Traditionally, the eggplant in this recipe would be fried in extra virgin olive oil instead of put under the broiler before baking. If you prefer to make them that way, place the eggplant slices in a large colander and sprinkle ¼ cup salt over them. Allow to sit for an hour to draw out excess moisture. Then rinse and dry the eggplant well. Lightly dredge them in flour, and fry them in a heavy bottomed skillet or pot with 1 inch of EVOO heated to 375 degrees. Fry until golden, and drain on a paper towel-lined tray. Then proceed with Step 4 of this recipe.

VARY IT! You can make a *Parmigiana bianca* or "white parmesan" by substituting the eggplant for zucchini and the Fresh Tomato Sauce for Béchamel Sauce (see Chapter 7).

Chapter **15**

Insalate/Salads

While the debate on where and when to eat Italian salads still exists, I prefer eating them in a separate course after a meal, the way I did growing up. This ensures that salads aren't an oversight and that they are given the attention they deserve.

Salads are an afterthought in many homes and restaurants today, including Italian ones abroad. The average American eats only 57% of the recommended daily amount of vegetables. Only 6% of Americans eat the amount of vegetables they should. This is a shame, because eating vegetables is one of the easiest ways to stay healthy and in shape. The greatest benefit of creating a variety of salads is that it is an easy and tasty way to "eat the rainbow."

In this chapter, you discover ways to expand your salad repertoire with classic Italian salads that are as fun to make as they are mouthwatering to eat.

REMEMBER The recipes in this chapter don't include wine pairings because, traditionally, Italian Sommeliers believe the lemon/vinegar content in salad dressings clashes with the acidity of wine, and, therefore, they never pair salads with wine.

Enjoying Italian Salads and Authentic Dressings

It is not uncommon for Italians to eat salads twice a day, once with lunch and once with dinner. Most Italians (myself included) eat an *insalata verde* (a mixture of fresh greens drizzled with olive oil and vinegar) or an *insalata mista* (a lettuce-based salad with tomatoes, carrots, and maybe a few other vegetables, drizzled with olive oil and vinegar). These are by far the most ubiquitous of Italian salads, similar to what Americans would call a "side salad."

The main differences, however, are that Italian salads usually are eaten at the end of meals, and often they're dressed more healthfully.

Dressing to impress

The term "salad dressing" doesn't exist in Italian, because Italians do not use them. Instead, Italians dress their salads with wine vinegars, balsamic vinegar, or lemon juice and extra virgin olive oil as they have for millennia. *Olio ed aceto*, or oil and vinegar, is a healthful combination that has stood the test of time. In addition to being easy to do, dressing a salad this way ensures more antioxidant power from the extra virgin olive oil, as well as antimicrobial and astringent benefits of the vinegar or lemon juice. That seemingly simple combination is one of the healthiest around, and consuming it twice a day is a powerful tonic for our bodies.

In stark contrast, many Americans dress their salads with heavy, chemical, sugar, and unhealthy, fat-loaded dressings, which do their health a huge disservice. Even the dressings labeled "Italian" on supermarket shelves are not. They often are made of other oils, not extra virgin olive oil, dried herbs, ingredients I can't pronounce, additives, far too much sodium, and sugar.

TIP

If you're ever at a loss for which salad to serve with an authentic Italian meal, you can simply dress any chopped greens with good-quality extra virgin olive oil, balsamic or wine vinegar or lemon juice, sprinkle it with a bit of sea salt and freshly ground pepper, and you are doing your health and your palate a favor.

Adding variety to your salad course

The salad course always follows the second course and side dish in Italy. Salads are not paired with wine because the vinegar used to dress salads clashes with the flavor of the wine. During Roman times, however, salads were eaten before and during meals, much as they are in the U.S. today. Lettuce was actually believed to be an aphrodisiac by the Romans, but not all Italian salads are lettuce-based. Some are made of legumes, grains, rice, and a variety of cooked vegetables and fruits.

TIP

For delicious and nutritious entertaining menus, try preparing a variety of salads from this chapter and serving them with artisan bread, aged Italian cheeses, and olives.

Basic green salads and mixed salads

Vegetables naturally have high water content, making them virtually fat-free and low in calories. Consuming vegetables helps to maintain blood pressure levels and promotes health of the digestive, skeletal, and excretory systems. The antioxidants in vegetables help keep cancer, cardiovascular problems, and strokes at bay and deliver vitamins A, K, B6, folate, and carotenoids — like beta carotene from carrots, zeaxanthin from greens, and lutein from spinach and collard greens.

It's important to try to eat vegetables when they are in season locally; it is at those times of year that our bodies especially require the nutrients they possess. When ripe, in-season, organic vegetables are cooked to perfection — with their natural sugars coaxed out of them and combined with other savory ingredients — eating healthfully becomes a joy!

Cooked and preserved vegetable salads

Some Italian salads don't just contain fresh, raw vegetables, but a mixture of produce and cooked pantry staples as well. Rice, barley, farro, potatoes, pasta, beans, and legumes all make their way into Italian salads at times. In addition to tasting great, these salads also do double duty as light, yet healthy meals and snacks when needed. Hardboiled eggs, leftover shredded chicken and meat, and nuts can transform these simple salads into meals in a bowl. While the concept of eating large salads for an entire *pasto*, or meal, is not traditionally Italian, it can help busy people stay in shape while eating deliciously.

Fruit-based salads

Insalate di frutte, or fruit salads, are popular in Italy, especially during the spring and summer. These sweet plates are the perfect way to showcase seasonal bounty. Whether it's spring berries, summer melons, peaches, plums, and figs, fall apples, grapes, and pears, or the citrus enjoyed in winter, Italians have a "zero kilometer" approach to food, meaning that they try to use what grows in their backyard or buy from the local farmers' market. This mentality ensures that the fruit is not only at peak ripeness, but also that it contains beneficial nutrients needed for good health. Italians also love to preserve fresh fruit in wine in order to enjoy it all year long.

Insalata verde/Green Salad

PREP TIME: 5 MIN | COOK TIME: 0 MIN | YIELD: 6 SERVINGS

INGREDIENTS

½ head radicchio or Treviso, leaves separated and torn into bite-size pieces

1 head chicory, romaine, or frisee, washed, trimmed, and roughly chopped

¼ cup Amy Riolo Sections or other good-quality extra virgin olive oil

2 tablespoons red or white wine vinegar

⅛ teaspoon unrefined sea salt

¼ teaspoon freshly ground black pepper

DIRECTIONS

1 Place the radicchio and lettuce on a platter.

2 Drizzle with the olive oil and vinegar. Season with salt and pepper, toss, and serve.

NOTE: This is the most typical type of Italian salad eaten after meals.

TIP: Use this salad as a bed for grilled chicken or fish when you are in the mood for a light meal.

VARY IT! Swap out spinach or dandelion greens, or any kind of seasonal lettuce that you prefer.

Insalata mista/Mixed Salad

PREP TIME: 5 MIN | COOK TIME: 0 MIN | YIELD: 4 SERVINGS

INGREDIENTS

1 ⅓ cups shredded romaine lettuce

⅓ cup grated carrots

1 ⅓ cups shredded radicchio

2 medium plum or Roma tomatoes, quartered

¼ cup Amy Riolo Selections or other good-quality extra virgin olive oil

2 tablespoons balsamic vinegar

⅛ teaspoon unrefined sea salt

⅛ teaspoon freshly ground black pepper

DIRECTIONS

1 Combine romaine, carrots, radicchio, and tomatoes in a large salad bowl.

2 Place olive oil in a small bowl and vigorously whisk in balsamic vinegar until dressing is incorporated and thick.

3 Pour dressing over lettuce, sprinkle with salt and pepper, toss, and serve.

TIP: This typical Italian salad generally follows meals and is similar to what Americans consider a "side salad."

NOTE: Instead of dressing any Italian salad, you can simply bring the undressed salad to the table with bottles or cruets of oil and vinegar for guests to dress their own.

VARY IT! Add mozzarella balls and hardboiled eggs for an Italian spin on a chef's salad.

Insalata di pomodori e peperoni/ Tomato and Roasted Pepper Salad

PREP TIME: 10 MIN	COOK TIME: 0 MIN	YIELD: 4 SERVINGS

INGREDIENTS

2 Roasted Yellow Peppers (see Chapter 3), cut into strips

2 Roasted Red Peppers, cut into strips

2 Roasted Green Peppers, cut into strips

1 large tomato, thinly sliced

2 tablespoons capers, rinsed and drained

2 tablespoons freshly chopped Italian parsley

1 garlic clove, peeled

2 tablespoons Amy Riolo Selections or other good-quality extra virgin olive oil

2 tablespoons Amy Riolo Selections White Balsamic Dressing or balsamic vinegar

Unrefined sea salt

Freshly ground black pepper

DIRECTIONS

1 Place peppers and tomatoes in a salad bowl, and add the capers and parsley.

2 In a small bowl, whisk together the olive oil and balsamic vinegar.

3 Drizzle dressing over salad. Stir gently to coat.

4 Taste, and season with salt and pepper as needed. Serve at room temperature.

TIP: This tasty and colorful salad can double as an appetizer. It pairs well with grilled and marinated fish, poultry, and meat.

You can use jarred roasted peppers if you don't have time to roast them yourselves.

VARY IT! Toss this mixture into cooked, rinsed, and chilled pasta or rice for a succulent pasta or rice salad dish.

Insalata Caprese/Caprese Salad

PREP TIME: 5 MIN   COOK TIME: 0 MIN   YIELD: 4 SERVINGS

INGREDIENTS

1 (8 ounce) fresh mozzarella ball, preferably from Buffalo-Milk, drained, sliced into 10 even-sized slices

4 large, ripe tomatoes, sliced

¼ cup Amy Riolo Selections or other good-quality extra virgin olive oil

10 fresh basil leaves

Unrefined sea salt

DIRECTIONS

1 Slice mozzarella balls into four thin slices each.

2 Arrange in an artistic pattern on a plate, alternating with the tomato slices.

3 Drizzle olive oil over the top, and scatter basil on top of the plate.

4 Sprinkle with salt, and serve.

NOTE: This popular Italian salad is so simple to make that the recipe reminds us what *not* to put in more than what to use.

TIP: Reserve this salad for the height of summer, when tomatoes and basil are at their peak and use the best-quality mozzarella you can find.

VARY IT! The ubiquitous Caprese Salad recipe often includes balsamic vinegar, various types of lettuce, olives, and more, which are not typical on the island of Capri. You can add other ingredients to this salad, or serve it in a different way, but you can no longer call it a Caprese Salad. I like to toss this mixture into baby spinach as well.

Insalata di riso/Sicilian Rice Salad

PREP TIME: 10 MIN   COOK TIME: 20 MIN   YIELD: 4 SERVINGS

INGREDIENTS

½ teaspoon sea salt

¾ cup Arborio rice

3 tablespoons *Nocellare del Belice, Biancolilla,* or other good-quality Sicilian olive oil, divided

1 small yellow onion, finely chopped

1 tablespoon red wine vinegar

⅓ cup cherry tomatoes, quartered

Juice and zest of 2 lemons

1 teaspoon capers, rinsed and drained

½ cup fresh mint, finely chopped

¼ cup Sicilian olives, pitted and cut into quarters

1 English cucumber, diced

DIRECTIONS

1 Bring a medium saucepan of water to a boil over high heat, and add salt.

2 Add rice, lower heat to medium, and cook for 10–15 minutes, until tender, yet still firm to the bite.

3 Drain rice, and rinse with cold water. Transfer to a bowl, and stir in 1 tablespoon of olive oil.

4 Heat remaining 2 tablespoons oil in a large skillet over medium heat. Add onion, and sauté until golden, approximately 5 minutes.

5 Add vinegar, tomatoes, lemon juice and zest, capers, mint, and olives. Cook for 1 minute.

6 Remove from heat, and allow to cool to room temperature.

7 Stir in cooked rice and cucumber. Serve at room temperature, or refrigerate for up to 1 day and serve cold.

TIP: This salad is typically brought to the beach to eat in summer and included as part of picnics and outdoor gatherings.

NOTE: Rice salad can do double duty as a side dish for grilled fish, seafood, and chicken dishes.

VARY IT! You can substitute the rice for barley, farro, or quinoa, if preferred.

Insalata Siciliana con le patate/ Sicilian Salad with Potatoes

PREP TIME: 15 MIN	COOK TIME: 15 MIN	YIELD: 4 SERVINGS

INGREDIENTS

1 pound golden potatoes, scrubbed, peeled, and cut into 1-inch pieces

1 medium English cucumber, peeled and diced

2 large vine-ripened tomatoes, quartered

1 small red onion, thinly sliced

12 Sicilian olives, pitted and halved

2 tablespoons capers, rinsed and dried

¼ cup freshly squeezed lemon juice

¼ cup good-quality Sicilian extra virgin olive oil

1 teaspoon dried oregano

½ teaspoon kosher salt

¼ teaspoon freshly ground black pepper

Pinch of red chili flakes, if desired

DIRECTIONS

1 Place potatoes in a medium saucepan, and cover with water.

2 Bring to boil over high heat, and cook until fork tender, about 5 minutes.

3 Drain well, and place in a large bowl three-fourths full of cold water and ice.

4 Allow potatoes to cool, drain well, and place in a large salad bowl.

5 Add cucumber, tomatoes, onion, olives, and capers, and mix to combine.

6 Pour lemon juice in a small bowl, and slowly add olive oil while whisking.

7 Add oregano, salt, pepper, and red chili flakes, if using. Whisk well to combine.

8 Pour dressing over salad, and serve.

TIP: This filling salad is perfect to enjoy with a soup at suppertime.

NOTE: Many people are surprised to learn that the potato's fiber, potassium, vitamin C, and vitamin B-6 content combined with its lack of cholesterol promote heart health. Potatoes contain significant amounts of fiber and vitamin B6, and are a good source of potassium, copper, vitamin C, manganese, phosphorus, niacin, dietary fiber, and pantothenic acid. Potatoes also contain a variety of phytonutrients that have antioxidant power.

VARY IT! Adding a cooked potato to a green salad is a typical Southern Italian touch. Slice them into your favorite salad for added nutrients whenever you need a filling meal fast.

Insalata di ceci/Chickpea Salad

PREP TIME: 10 MIN	COOK TIME: 0 MIN	YIELD: 8 SERVINGS

INGREDIENTS

2 cups cooked chickpeas (see Chapter 3)

2 Roasted Red Peppers (see Chapter 3), finely chopped

½ cup Italian parsley, washed, dried, and finely chopped

Juice of 1 lemon

2 tablespoons Amy Riolo Selections White Balsamic Dressing or white wine vinegar

½ teaspoon unrefined sea salt or salt

½ cup Amy Riolo Selections or other good-quality extra virgin olive oil

DIRECTIONS

1 Place the chickpeas in a large bowl, and add peppers and parsley. Mix well.

2 In a small bowl, whisk together the lemon juice, vinegar, salt, and olive oil.

3 Pour over the chickpea mixture, and toss to mix.

TIP: This salad can be served as an appetizer or alongside a green salad at the end of a meal.

NOTE: Some people garnish this salad with hard-boiled egg wedges.

VARY IT! You can substitute cannellini beans for the chickpeas, if you prefer.

Insalata di cetrioli, fagiolini, ed olive/Cucumber, String Bean, and Olive Salad

PREP TIME: 10 MIN | COOK TIME: 10 MIN | YIELD: 4 SERVINGS

INGREDIENTS

½ pound string beans, trimmed

1 ¼ pounds cucumbers

¼ cup black olives such as Taggiasca or Castevetrano, pitted

¼ teaspoon freshly ground pepper

¼ cup Amy Riolo Selections or other good-quality extra virgin olive oil

2 tablespoons Amy Riolo Selections White Balsamic Dressing or balsamic vinegar

DIRECTIONS

1 Bring a pot of water to a boil over high heat, and add the string beans.

2 Cook until tender, drain, and place beans in a bowl of cold water.

3 Split the cucumbers lengthwise; remove and discard the seeds using a spoon.

4 Dice the cucumbers, and place in a large bowl.

5 Place olives, pepper, and olive oil in food processor, and blend to combine.

6 Add string beans to the cucumbers, and spoon olive paste over the top.

7 Add White Balsamic Dressing, mix to combine, and serve.

TIP: This fun salad is a great accompaniment or successor to grilled poultry, fish, and meat.

NOTE: This salad can be stretched into a meal with some leftover cheese, hard-boiled eggs, or shredded meat or chicken.

VARY IT! Cherry tomatoes and cauliflower flowerets also work well instead of cucumbers and string beans in this salad.

Macedonia/Fruit Salad

PREP TIME: 10 MIN	COOK TIME: 5 HOURS FOR OVERNIGHT MARINADE	YIELD: 4 SERVINGS

INGREDIENTS

1 cup pineapple, papaya, or mango chunks

½ cup raspberries

½ cup strawberries, thinly sliced

½ cup blueberries

½ cup sliced kiwi

¼ cup sugar

Juice of half a lemon

4 tablespoons finely chopped fresh mint, plus 4 whole mint leaves

1 cup freshly whipped cream

DIRECTIONS

1 Combine all the fruit in a large salad bowl. Mix the sugar, lemon juice, and mint together in a small bowl.

2 Drizzle the sugar mixture over fruit, and mix gently to combine.

3 Cover the bowl, and store in refrigerator for a minimum of 5 hours or maximum of overnight.

4 Transfer to individual bowls before serving. Garnish with whipped cream and a mint leaf, if desired.

TIP: This salad can pass for a dessert or snack and can even follow a traditional green salad in a meal.

NOTE: There are many types and species of fruit that grow in Italy's many different microclimates, and it is important to always use seasonal fruit in this recipe.

VARY IT! Any combination of fruit you like can be used in this recipe. When berries are not in season, for example, substitute apples, pears, and oranges.

4

Breakfast and Other Sweet Treats, Baked Goods, and Desserts

Learn what Italian breakfasts look like and how to make them.

Discover the role of fruit and nuts in Italian meals.

Enjoy making authentic Italian desserts.

Explore the world of Italian cheeses.

Master Italian pastry shop favorites and how to serve them.

Embrace special occasion baked goods recipes.

Recreate Italian bread, pizza, and focaccia recipes in your kitchen with joy and ease.

Chapter **16**

Starting Your Day with Colazione: Italian Breakfast

In the world's love affair with Italian food, breakfast often goes unmentioned, perhaps because it's not as big a deal as lunch and dinner are. Perhaps this is because tourists to Italy don't experience true Italian breakfasts, or because, to newcomers, Italian breakfasts might not seem so special. *Cornetti*, to the naked eye, look like everyday croissants, *bomboloni* look like common doughnuts, and the idea of eating *biscotti* (cookies) for breakfast might seem strange for some non-Italians. But, if you want to enjoy an authentic Italian eating plan, doing as the Romans do will set you up for success.

Keeping It Short and Sweet: What Italian Breakfasts Look Like

Typical Italian breakfasts can, at first glance, seem very different from traditional American or English options. (Tourists visiting Italy don't always get an authentic glimpse into traditional ways of starting the day because hotel buffets often cater to foreign tourists.)

In order to truly appreciate Italian breakfasts, you have to understand their place in the overall scheme of Italian meals. Because the daily dining crescendo takes place at lunch, breakfast is perfectly positioned to help people break their overnight fast on a sweet note, and fuel them up with just enough energy, and caffeine, to allow lunch to steal the show at approximately 1 p.m. Too large of a breakfast would just mean extra calories and take away from the daily highlight that lunch promises. A pastry (usually a *cornetto*) + a *caffé* + orange juice = the standard Italian breakfast.

Eating breakfast out in Italy usually means standing elbow to elbow in a neighborhood bar to enjoy a perfectly prepared cappuccino or *caffé* (which is what Americans refer to as an espresso) in one hand and a *cornetto* (Italian sourdough croissant) in the other one. *Bomboloni*, or Italian doughnuts, or *Plum Cake* (similar to what Americans refer to as pound cake) are other possibilities. In urban areas, muffins are now a popular import, but that was not always the case. Each Italian city and town also has its own local sweet treats, such as Napoli's *sfogliatelle*, and other cream-filled delicacies such as the *Maritozzi* in Rome and the brioche known as *Veneziane* from Venice.

Many regions and towns have their own versions of sweet breads eaten in the mornings as well. In Italian homes, *biscotti* (the Italian word for cookies as well as the twice-baked variety for dunking) and *fette biscottate*, rusks that look like extra-dry toast, are enjoyed alongside an espresso, cappuccino, caffé macchiato, or a caffé latte most mornings. Most modern Italian households buy the biscotti and the rusks from stores. Supermarkets are full of them just in the way American stores are full of cereal.

On occasion, and especially in rural settings, traditional cakes and breads are served at breakfast. These are especially popular in *agroturismi* and hotels as well; they are the types of recipes I always turn to when entertaining. Another exception to the rule of lighter Italian breakfasts was historically enjoyed by farmers and those who worked the land. Because their days started earlier and required a great deal of physical stamina to carry out the day's labor, Italians who grew up on farms will remember heartier breakfasts made out of polenta, sausage, cheeses, bread, fruit, and more.

Biscotti and rusks

The word biscotti means "twice-cooked," and refers to a type of cookie for which the dough is cooked twice: usually first in a log, which is then sliced; the slices are cooked again until dry and crisp. Some of the versions in this chapter have been around since antiquity and were enjoyed by the ancient Egyptians, Greeks, and Romans. You can still find Anise Biscotti served with tea or coffee in the afternoon and at breakfast everywhere from the South of Italy to Morocco, Greece, and Egypt. I love to keep biscotti on hand for whenever the mood strikes, as well as for entertaining, just like many households in the Mediterranean region do. Also, giving them as homemade gifts is fun. Why not give a batch of the biscotti in this chapter as an edible gift? The recipient is sure to be delighted.

Biscotti is also the generic term for "cookie" in the Italian language, and Italians also eat what Americans would consider to be cookies for breakfast. Supermarket shelves are full of them, and sometimes people make their own as well. Unlike Christmas cookies, however, these are usually drier, unfrosted varieties that make the perfect partner to Italian-style coffee.

Rusks, or *fette biscottate*, are thin slices of bread that have been baked until very crisp, like the twice-baked cookies are. They are plain and can come in a variety of sizes. Some might be made out of whole wheat flour, and they are all low in calories. Most people top them with honey or fresh preserves at breakfast time. I have never seen or heard of anyone making *fette biscottate* at home, although you could certainly do so. I created my own honey-enhanced version years ago when I couldn't find the imported variety from Italy, and that is the recipe I share in this chapter.

Breakfast cakes

Italians have been honing their cake-making skills since the Renaissance. In the Italian kitchen, some cakes do double duty as dessert. Often times, classic recipes, such as Italian Sponge Cake, which was invented by a Genovese pastry chef in Spain, is eaten plain or with fruit preserves in the morning, and then gets dolled up with more exciting ingredients to transform into a decadent dessert such as a layered cake, a *Florentine zuccotto*, or a *Sicilian cassata*. Sometimes, sponge cake is used instead of lady fingers in trifles or tiramisù recipes as well.

If you do prepare one of these cake recipes, just a slice is all that is needed to accompany your caffé or cappuccino for a delicious breakfast. I like to make two or three of them at a time. That way, they can be wrapped in plastic and frozen until I need them.

Bomboloni and fried treats

Bomboloni, or "big bombs," and *ciambelle* (this word can be used for doughnuts, buns, and in some places, cakes) are typical Italian doughnut varieties that can be found throughout Italy. I must admit that it doesn't take much effort to warm up to them, and even though they look just like their American cousins, Italian doughnuts have their own unique appeal. Their pillow texture combines with the sweet bready flavor of the dough to create a combination that can't be beat. When making *bomboloni* for the first time, be sure to have all your ingredients ready when you start, and try making them in stages if necessary.

Caffé to Go: An Italian Coffee Primer

Coffee plays an important role in the Italian diet. When discussing Italian coffee, it's always about espresso, called *caffé* in Italian. Italian espresso is made from the Arabica style of bean and roasted to different degrees of doneness. Most Italian towns have their own *torrefazione,* or coffee roaster, which blends and roasts their own beans on site. Larger cities have several, and my favorites are Caffé Tazza D'oro in Rome and Caffé Falcone in Lagonegro, Basilicata, along with Guglielmo caffé from Calabria; my relatives will not let me leave my ancestral homeland without a suitcase full.

In 1638, coffee traveled to Venice with the Ottomans, where it became popular with the courtesans and intellectuals. Venice's Caffé Florian is the oldest still operated coffeehouse in the world and is still in operation today. Nowadays, coffee is the world's most widely consumed beverage and the second largest trading commodity in global business!

Many people have their own favorite brand of beans, along with those of the larger industrial varieties such as Illy and Lavazza. Luckily, great quality espresso beans are easy to find in the U.S. nowadays. *"Prendiamo un caffé"* means "let's have a coffee," and it is a quick and easy invitation that you might get several times a day from friends or colleagues. These very short breaks are a way to bond and punctuate a happy event.

REMEMBER

Whether you choose to use a traditional Moka pot (see Figure 16-1) to make yours on the stovetop or an espresso machine, here are a few things to remember:

>> Coffee is always a part of breakfast in Italy.

>> Italian meals are followed by coffee; we like to think of it as a period at the end of sentence — something would be missing without it!

- People do not linger over drinking their coffee, the way they do in the U.S. An espresso should be consumed quickly — one or two swallows.

- Coffee is taken with milk only in the a.m. and as part of breakfast. No milk is added to coffee in afternoon or evening, except for a teeny splash over an espresso to make a macchiato.

- Espresso has less caffeine than American coffee, and some Italian research suggests it is good for the heart, so most Italians enjoy several per day.

- Decaf coffee, although available, is not enjoyed the way it is in the U.S.

ITALIAN COFFEE DRINKS

The abundance of Italian coffee drinks made from espresso are now so prevalent around the world that they don't take as much explanation as they once did. That said, sometimes Italian words are used to describe these concoctions. This list helps translate popular coffee drink names so you can order confidently at any *café* in Italy or your hometown.

Caffé — espresso

Caffé lungo — a *doppio* (double) espresso

Caffé corto — a shorter espresso

Caffé Americano — espresso with lots of hot water added to mimic American coffee

Caffé macchiato — "stained coffee," a shot of espresso with a splash of milk and foam

Caffé latte — espresso with a significant amount of warm milk

Caffé corretto — espresso with a shot of liquor, usually grappa known as "corrected coffee"

Caffé con panna — espresso with a dollop of fresh whipped cream

Caffé decafinato (also called *deca*) — decaf espresso

Caffé ristretto — less water, stronger espresso than usual

Cappuccino — shot of espresso with a bit of milk to form a "hood" *(capuccio)* of foam

» A glass of water is always served on a tray along with coffee when serving guests. The old etiquette of coffee drinking suggests that you drink a few sips of water prior to drinking the coffee. Drinking water after coffee is frowned upon because it's said to "wash away the friendship" that you shared with the coffee.

FIGURE 16-1: Traditional Moka stovetop espresso maker and demitasse "half cups" for serving.

Biscotti d'anice/Anise Biscotti

PREP TIME: 15 MIN	COOK TIME: 35 MIN	YIELD: 2 DOZEN (12 SERVINGS OF 2)

INGREDIENTS

4 large eggs, at room temperature

¾ cup sugar

2 cups unbleached, all-purpose flour

2 teaspoons anise seeds

1 teaspoon vanilla or anise extract

DIRECTIONS

1 Preheat the oven to 375 degrees. Grease and flour two 8 ½x4 ½x2 ½-inch loaf pans.

2 In a large bowl, add eggs and whisk by hand or with an electric mixer on high speed until the mixture turns light yellow, about 3 minutes.

3 Slowly add the sugar, and continue to beat until incorporated.

4 With the mixer running on low speed, add the flour, anise seeds, and vanilla. Mix well to incorporate.

5 Pour half the batter into each pan, and smooth out the top of the batter.

6 Bake in the middle of the oven for 25 minutes, or until dough turns golden.

7 Remove from the oven, and reduce temperature to 325 degrees.

8 Let biscotti cool for 10 minutes in the pan. Using oven mitts, turn over loaf pans to unmold cookies. Allow to cool for an additional 10 minutes.

(continued)

9 Cut each loaf crosswise into 1-inch sections. Lay each slice on its side on a cookie sheet.

10 Bake for 8-10 minutes, remove from oven, turn biscotti over, and bake for another 8-10 minutes until cookies are light brown. Cool thoroughly.

TIP: Enjoy these simple cookies dunked into espresso, cappuccino, or caffé latte for breakfast, or with a bottle of *Passito di Vigoleno* or similar if serving later in the day.

THESE cookies will keep in an airtight container for up to a month.

NOTE: These crunchy cookies were first introduced in the U.S. by Italian immigrants. Italians had enjoyed these cookies since ancient times in Egypt and Rome.

VARY IT! Almond, citrus zest, or the flavoring of your choice can be used instead of anise. You also can add chopped nuts, chocolate chips, or dried fruit to this base recipe.

Biscotti di miele/Honey Breakfast Biscuits

INGREDIENTS

2 large eggs

⅓ cup pure honey

1 cup unbleached all-purpose flour

2 teaspoons pure vanilla

1 teaspoon yeast

½ cup extra virgin olive oil

DIRECTIONS

1 Preheat oven to 400 degrees. Line a baking sheet with parchment paper or silicone mat.

2 Combine eggs and honey in a bowl with a wooden spoon. Add flour, vanilla, and yeast. Mix well to combine. Stir in the olive oil, mixing well to incorporate.

3 Spoon the dough into a pastry bag fitted with a 1-inch round tip, or a plastic sandwich bag with the corner tip cut off. Twist the ends to seal the bag, and press down, making cookies that are 2 ½ inches long and 1 inch wide.

4 Bake until golden, approximately 15 minutes. Cool and serve.

TIP: You can make the dough in advance and store it in the refrigerator to be piped at the time of baking and serving.

NOTE: This is strictly a breakfast cookie, a homemade version of the boxed varieties that line Italian supermarket shelves. These types of cookies are enjoyed by Italians the way that Americans eat cereal on everyday mornings and are not meant to be served as dessert. They can also be eaten with afternoon tea.

VARY IT! You can substitute almond or whole-wheat for the all-purpose flour to make a more nutritious cookie.

Cantucci/Tuscan Almond Biscotti

PREP TIME: 10 MIN   **COOK TIME: 30 MIN**   **YIELD: 12 SERVINGS**

INGREDIENTS

2 ¼ cups unbleached all-purpose flour

¾ cup plus 1 tablespoon sugar

2 teaspoons baking powder

¾ teaspoon salt

4 large eggs

2 tablespoons honey

2 tablespoons lemon juice

1 tablespoon lemon zest

2 teaspoons vanilla extract

1 teaspoon almond extract

1 cup blanched whole almonds, toasted

DIRECTIONS

1 Preheat oven to 375 degrees.

2 Line a large baking sheet with parchment paper or silicone mats.

3 Stir flour, ¾ cup sugar, baking powder, and salt in a large bowl to combine.

4 In a separate bowl, combine eggs, honey, lemon juice, lemon zest, vanilla extract, and almond extract, and mix well.

5 Pour egg mixture into flour mixture, and stir until incorporated. Stir in almonds.

6 Shape dough into two 14x4 inch logs, and place them on the baking sheet 2-3 inches apart.

7 Wet your fingertips, and smooth out the logs to even shapes.

8 Sprinkle logs with remaining tablespoon of sugar.

9 Bake for 20-25 minutes, or until logs are golden.

10 Remove logs from oven, and cool on the baking sheet for 10 minutes.

11 Reduce oven temperature to 325 degrees. Locate a clean, cool baking sheet.

12 Carefully transfer baked logs to your work surface and, using a serrated knife, cut them into ½-inch-thick slices.

13 Arrange slices on their sides on the clean baking sheet. Bake for about 10 minutes, or until *cantucci* are golden. Cool completely and serve.

TIP: Store in an airtight container. Because of their crisp, twice baked exterior, these gems last for weeks. Serve with espresso, cappuccino, or caffé latte for dunking, or with a bottle of *Vin Santo Toscano* or similar if enjoying later in the day.

NOTE: *Cantucci* are what Americans call "biscotti" — twice baked cookies can do double duty, as they're served at breakfast and for dessert and snacks.

VARY IT! These mini-biscotti taste great with other nuts instead of almonds and with dried fruit as well. If you change the recipe, however, don't call them *cantucci*, though — just regular biscotti.

Pan di Spagna/Italian Sponge Cake

PREP TIME: 10 MIN	COOK TIME: 40 MIN	YIELD: 8 SERVINGS

INGREDIENTS

Butter or oil spray for greasing pan

6 large eggs, separated

1 cup sugar

2 teaspoons vanilla

1 ⅛ cup unbleached all-purpose flour

½ cup good-quality apricot preserves, if desired

¼ cup powdered sugar, if desired

DIRECTIONS

1 Preheat oven to 350 degrees. Grease a 1.5-quart loaf pan (8.25x9x2.75 inches) with spray oil.

2 Beat egg whites in a large bowl until stiff, and set aside.

3 Cream sugar and egg yolks together, and continue beating until they are very light yellow in color.

4 Stir in the vanilla. Gently fold the egg whites into the batter.

5 Sprinkle flour on top of mixture, and carefully incorporate into the batter until just combined.

6 Pour into prepared baking pan, and bake for 40 minutes or until cake is golden and sides begin to pull away from the pan. You can also test the doneness with a toothpick. If it is inserted into the center of the cake and comes out clean, it is done.

7 Remove from the oven, and allow to cool completely. Serve with apricot preserves and sprinkled with powdered sugar, if desired.

TIP: You can double the recipe and freeze one cake wrapped in plastic wrap for another time.

NOTE: *Pan di Spagna,* or Bread from Spain, is the Italian name for what Americans call Sponge Cake and the French spell Genoise. It was first created in the 17th century in Madrid by a Ligurian cook, *Giovan Battista Cabona* (also known as Giobatta). The cook to the Spanish courts was inspired by Portuguese biscuits and ladyfingers, and came up with the "new" dessert, which the Spanish royal courts baptized as a Genoise cake (or cake from Genova, the capital of Giobatta's region). To this day, the rest of the world calls the cake Genoise, while Italians refer to it as *Pan di Spagna.* This popular classic Italian cake often is eaten for breakfast or as a snack.

VARY IT! *Pan di Spagna* makes a delicious base for shortcakes and sundaes, or for more elaborate holiday desserts such as *Zuccotto, Zuppa inglese,* and *Tiramisù* (see Chapter 18).

Quattro quarti/Italian Pound Cake

PREP TIME: 15 MIN	COOK TIME: 40 MIN	YIELD: 8 SERVINGS

INGREDIENTS

1 cup sugar

1 cup unsalted butter, at room temperature, plus extra for buttering pan

Zest of 1 orange

1 teaspoon vanilla extract

4 large eggs

1 ¾ cup unbleached all-purpose baking flour, plus extra for pan

2 teaspoons baking powder

½ cup organic non-fat French Vanilla Yogurt

DIRECTIONS

1 Preheat oven to 350 degrees. Butter the bottom and sides of a 1.5-quart loaf pan (8.25x9x2.75 inches).

2 Line the bottom of the pan with parchment paper, and butter and flour the top of it. Turn over, and tap off excess flour.

3 Combine sugar, butter, orange zest, and vanilla in a large bowl, and beat until the mixture is light and fluffy.

4 In a separate bowl, beat the eggs until light and foamy. Add the beaten eggs to the sugar mixture, and mix until well combined. Place the flour and baking powder into a sifter or strainer, and sift into the mixture. Using a wooden spoon, mix well just until ingredients are incorporated.

5 Stir in the yogurt. Pour into the loaf pan, and smooth out the top. Hit the bottom of the pan on the counter a few times to remove any air bubbles.

6 Bake on a rack in the middle of the oven for 35-40 minutes, or until the top is golden and a toothpick inserted into the center comes out clean. Remove the cake from the oven. Let it cool for 5 minutes in the pan.

7 Remove from the pan, and place on a cake rack to cool completely; then slice and serve.

TIP: This is the perfect cake to travel with because it's sturdy. I wrap it in plastic wrap and bring it to people I'm visiting. If you're invited to dinner, you can bring it as a host/ hostess gift for breakfast the next morning. In Italy, this cake is sliced and eaten plain for breakfast, or topped with fruit and whipped cream for dessert. This cake can be cut up and used as a base for more sophisticated deserts like shortcakes and trifles as well.

NOTE: This moist, dense pound cake is an Italian classic. North of Rome, it's often referred to as a *Ciambellone;* south of Rome, it's called *Quattro quarti,* meaning four quarters, because the original recipe required ¼ kilo of butter, ¼ kilo of flour, ¼ kilo of sugar, and ¼ kilo of eggs.

VARY IT! Add ½ cup cocoa to the batter to make a chocolate version.

Torta di frutta stagionale/Seasonal Fruit Cake

PREP TIME: 15 MIN | COOK TIME: 40 MIN | YIELD: 8 SERVINGS

INGREDIENTS

7 tablespoons unsalted butter, at room temperature, divided

⅓ cup plus 1 tablespoon sugar, divided

2 large eggs, separated

1 cup unbleached all-purpose flour or almond flour, plus extra for pan

2 ½ teaspoons baking powder

¼ cup heavy cream

2 teaspoons almond extract

2 teaspoons vanilla extract

2 ripe plums, apricots, or nectarines, peeled, pitted, and sliced

Confectioners' sugar for dusting

DIRECTIONS

1 Preheat the oven to 350 degrees. Butter a 9-inch tart pan with a removable bottom. Add a round of parchment, butter the parchment, and flour it.

2 Place 6 tablespoons of butter and ⅓ cup sugar in the bowl of an electric mixer fitted with the paddle attachment. Beat together on low speed until smooth and fluffy. Add the egg yolks, and beat well until combined.

3 In a small bowl, stir together the flour and the baking powder. In another small bowl, stir together the cream, ¼ cup water, almond extract, and vanilla extract. Stir the mixtures into the butter mixture by alternating the flour mixture with the cream mixture — adding one-third of each at a time until they are used up.

4 In a clean bowl fitted to an electric mixer using a whisk attachment, whip the egg whites until stiff peaks form. (If the eggs are not stiff enough, the cake will not rise properly.)

5 Using a rubber spatula, gently fold the beaten egg whites into the batter to eliminate all of the white and break up any lumps. Then stir once in the opposite direction to make sure that all white has been incorporated.

6 Pour the batter into the prepared tart pan, and level the surface. Arrange the plums or other fruit in a circle pattern on top of the batter. Sprinkle the remaining tablespoon of sugar on top of the fruit.

7 Bake until a toothpick inserted into the middle of the cake comes out clean and cake begins to pull away from the sides of the pan, 35-40 minutes.

8 Transfer to a cooling rack. Allow cake to cool for at least 30 minutes.

9 Invert onto a cooling rack and remove sides of pan, then bottom and parchment paper. Turn over to cool completely.

10 Invert the cake onto another plate and then back over onto a serving platter. Dust with confectioners' sugar. Serve at room temperature.

TIP: If you're not serving this cake the day you bake it, then refrigerate it once it cools so it won't spoil.

NOTE: This traditional European cake is a favorite of my family. Light and airy, it's a great way to start the day or end a meal, and can be made with a variety of fruits. This cake is perfect to bring to a potluck or give as a hostess gift.

VARY IT! You can substitute pears, apples, peaches, blueberries, raspberries, or blackberries for the fruit in this recipe, or use a variety of fruits.

Bomboloni alla crema/Cream-Filled Doughnuts

PREP TIME: 20 MIN	COOK TIME: 30 MIN PLUS 2 HOURS RISING TIME	YIELD: 7 SERVINGS (2 DONUTS EACH)

INGREDIENTS

For the donuts

2 ½ teaspoons fresh yeast

¼ cup lukewarm milk (110 degrees)

¼ cup sugar, plus extra for dusting

¼ teaspoon salt

1 cup unbleached all-purpose flour, plus extra for rolling out the dough

1 teaspoon vanilla

1 ¼ tablespoons unsalted butter, melted

3 cups peanut or sunflower oil

For the cream filling

3 egg yolks

3 tablespoons sugar

Zest of 1 lemon

⅛ cup unbleached all -purpose flour

1 cup whole milk

DIRECTIONS

1 To make the dough: In a large bowl, dissolve the yeast in the milk; add 2 tablespoons of sugar and the salt. Stir well to incorporate.

2 Add the flour, vanilla, and butter. Stir well to form a dough.

3 Turn the dough out onto a lightly floured counter, and knead for 5-10 minutes until the dough is smooth. Roll the dough out until it is 1/8-inch thick.

4 Using a 3-inch round cookie cutter, or the rim of a glass, cut into disks.

5 Move the disks to another clean work surface dusted lightly with flour.

6 Bring together the leftover scraps of dough, roll them out, and cut out the remaining disks. You should end up with 14 disks.

7 Cover the disks with a kitchen towel, and allow them to rise for 1 hour, or until doubled.

8 To make the custard: In a large bowl or the bowl to a standing mixer, beat the egg yolks, granulated sugar, and lemon zest on medium speed, until they become lemon colored and thick.

9 Reduce speed to low, and slowly add the flour; beat until well blended.

10 In a medium saucepan, heat milk almost to a boil over medium heat. Turn off heat just before milk boils.

11 Add 2 tablespoons of the hot milk to the egg mixture, while beating on low heat.

12 Continue beating the mixture, and slowly add the remaining warm milk in a steady stream. (Adding the milk too fast or not beating the mixture while adding the milk will cause the eggs to curdle.)

13 After all the milk has been added, increase the speed to medium and beat for 1 minute.

14 Pour the custard back into the medium saucepan, and cook for 5 minutes over medium heat, stirring constantly. The custard is done when it coats the back of a spoon and you can run your finger through it without the edges running into the middle.

15 Cover the top of the cream with plastic wrap so it does not form a skin, and allow the custard to cool. Refrigerate until the *bomboloni* are ready to be filled.

16 To fry the *bomboloni:* Heat the oil in a large, deep pan over medium heat to 325 degrees.

17 Fry the *bomboloni* four at a time, for 2–3 minutes each side, or until golden.

18 Remove them with a slotted spoon, and place on a plate lined with paper towels.

19 Dust with sugar on each side. Continue with remaining dough.

20 With a small knife, make a hole halfway through the *bomboloni*, being careful not to puncture the sides.

21 Fill a pastry bag with the cream. Pipe the cream into the center of each pastry, taking care not to overstuff it. Serve warm.

TIP: This is a time-consuming recipe that is best done in stages the first time. Make the pastry cream a day in advance, and make the dough the night before, letting it rise in the refrigerator. In the morning, all you have to do is fry and fill the doughnuts before eating.

NOTE: These are my favorite Italian breakfast food. They are sold in bars, croissant shops, and *cornetterie* for breakfast. They are the Italian cousins of the American cream-filled doughnut. They taste their best served fresh and warm.

VARY IT! You can fill *bomboloni* with chocolate cream, Nutella, or Sicilian pistachio cream instead of pastry cream, if you like.

Caffè/Classic Espresso

PREP TIME: 1 MIN	COOK TIME: 7 MIN	YIELD: 4 SERVINGS

INGREDIENTS

4 demitasse cups full of cold, filtered water

Approximately 2 tablespoons ground Arabica beans (for espresso)

Sugar, if desired

DIRECTIONS

1 Holding the handle of the stovetop espresso maker with your right thumb, turn the top of espresso maker counter-clockwise to open.

2 Use your fingers to lift out the basket, which holds the espresso.

3 Fill the bottom of the espresso maker about three-fourths full of cold water, or to just underneath the knob on the side.

4 Place basket back into the bottom of the espresso maker, and fill with espresso.

5 Carefully twist the top of maker back on, making sure that it is positioned properly.

6 Place maker over the lowest heat possible.

7 Allow to brew for approximately 5–7 minutes, or until steam begins to come out of the spout of the espresso maker.

8 Remove from heat immediately, and set aside.

9 Pour espresso into demitasse cups, and serve hot.

TIP: Moka stovetop espresso makers (refer to Figure 16-1) come in various sizes ranging from single-serving to others that make 12 cups at a time. While this recipe calls for a Moka stovetop coffee maker, which is present in nearly all Italian homes, you can also make espresso in electric machines at home.

NOTE: Most Italians start and end their day with a cup of espresso. A serving of espresso contains only half of the caffeine of regular American coffee. Coffee drinking has become an important ritual in Italian culture. Italian friends will offer each other an espresso to celebrate all aspects of life — promotions, transfers, marriages, engagements, business deals, and more.

Caffé Latte

PREP TIME: 1 MIN	COOK TIME: 5 MIN	YIELD: 4 SERVINGS

INGREDIENTS

2 cups warm milk

4 servings espresso

Sugar, to taste

DIRECTIONS

1 Pour equal amounts of warm milk into four coffee cups.

2 Pour equal amounts of espresso over the milk.

3 Stir and serve with sugar to taste.

TIP: This is the way Italians make caffé latte at home for breakfast only. If you like froth in your milk and don't have an espresso machine, you can use a handheld frother and have great results.

A cup of espresso requires 40 coffee beans, and experts say that the ideal heat on which to brew espresso is the flame of a match! With that in mind, be sure to brew your espresso slowly, in order to produce a light brown foam on the top known as "crema" or cream.

VARY IT! Instead of using lots of milk, some people prefer a *macchiato* (or "stained coffee") with just a bit of milk. In bars and restaurants, a *caffé macchiato* refers to an espresso topped with just a dot of foamed milk.

Chapter 17

Fruit, Cheese, and Nuts: Bridging the Gap Between Dinner and Dessert

Fruit, cheese, and nuts form a course of their own that follows traditional meals in Italy. Typical daily meals in Italy end with fruit and nuts or a variety of cheeses that are nutritious and delicious opportunities to sample local flavors.

Historically fruit, nuts, and cheese were the "desserts" or the last course served during daily meals. "Modern" desserts sweetened with cane sugar were popular during the Renaissance and enjoyed by the upper classes until only a few centuries ago in Europe. Even as sugar became more readily available and inexpensive, having dessert after dinner or lunch was not a part of the daily ritual. Desserts are typically reserved for Sundays, holidays, and special occasions by most Italians.

While fancier desserts are always available at restaurants, most Italians don't eat them daily. The recipes in this chapter aren't elaborate in the traditional sense, but I have included them to spark creativity and help to promote the tradition of consuming fresh, local, ripe fruit, cheese, and nuts to end meals at home. What these dishes lack in intricacy, they make up for with Mother Nature's luster.

In this chapter, you learn the role that fruit, nuts, cheese, and desserts play in an Italian meal. You can easily put together your own versions to add flavor and health-boosting benefits to your own meals.

Fruit and Nut Plates

Fresh, lush, seasonal fruit and fresh local nuts always grace Italian tables and are brought out to enjoy leisurely after a meal while talking and visiting with loved ones. Even though this is the simplest of courses in the culinary sense, it is one of my favorites. Fresh fruit and nuts after a meal symbolizes family, health, and the luxury of being together.

TECHNICAL STUFF

The high amount of fiber and other nutrients in fruit make it the perfect food for ending a meal. According to Catherine Itsiopoulos, A.P.D., A.N., head of the Department of Dietetics and Human Nutrition at La Trobe University in Melbourne, who has conducted numerous research studies on the Mediterranean diet, "fresh fruit should be eaten daily," and "dried fruit and nuts should be consumed as snacks and desserts."

In my family's homes, each season comes with its own favorite combinations. Fresh figs, apricots, and almonds in spring; berries, peaches, and pistachios in summer; apples, pears, and walnuts in the fall; and clementines and mandarins with hazelnuts or chestnuts in the winter are classic combinations that never go out of style.

REMEMBER

When shopping, be sure to pick up the best, freshest fruit from your area as possible. Stock up on good-quality almonds, walnuts, chestnuts, and pistachios when you can; store them in airtight containers in the refrigerator until needed.

With Cheese: An Italian Cheese Primer

Italy is a gourmet paradise for cheese lovers. Luckily for Americans, good-quality Italian cheese is becoming more readily available on a daily basis. The Mediterranean Diet Pyramid recommends eating cheese and other dairy in moderate portions, daily to weekly.

Exploring Italian cheese categories and types

There are more than 1,400 classified types of cheese in the world, approximately 480 of which are Italian. Out of all those Italian cheeses, the ones that are most widely used and appreciated in both restaurants and homes around the globe are *mozzarella* and *ricotta*. Despite their Italian names, they have become so commonplace in global kitchens that there's no longer a need to use the word "cheese" after their names, because international consumers are already familiar with them.

In Italy, goat, sheep, cow, and buffalo milk is made into a wide variety of cheeses, which fall into three basic categories:

» Fresh and soft (water content between 45 percent and 70 percent with a lower sodium content): This type of cheese is lighter in texture and melts easily.

» Semi-hard (water content between 40 percent and 45 percent): These are popular table cheeses and are often included on cheese boards.

» Hard and aged (water content below 40 percent and higher sodium content): These cheeses are grated, shaved, and sprinkled on finished dishes as well as eaten as chunks any time of day. The high sodium content helps them to last longer as well.

These Italian cheeses are some of the most highly prized on the world market today:

» **Pecorino:** This sheep's milk cheese is an important part of many regions' cuisines. In Basilicata, for example, *the Pecorino di Moliterno* and *Pecorino di Filano* are well known. In Calabria, the *Pecorino Crotonese* is the most coveted. Rome's Lazio is known for *Pecorino Romano,* and the Sardinians have *Pecorino Sardo.* Each has its own distinct taste and texture (depending on the breed of sheep, what they graze on, and the local territory), and the differences are worth exploring. It's worth noting that while the ancient Romans developed the technique for *Pecorino Romano,* it is produced in three regions today: Lazio, Sardinia, and parts of Tuscany, and most of it is produced in Sardinia.

» **Formaggio di capra:** This goat's milk cheese has a similar composition to cow's milk, yet it possesses less lactose and has more elastic fibers than other dairy products, which helps with muscle recovery, making it a great choice for athletes in training. Milk, cultured milk, buttermilk, ricotta, yogurt, and yogurt cheese are all made from goat's milk, and wonderful varieties are available in many U.S. farmers markets.

>> **Mozzarella di bufala:** Luckily, you don't have to try too hard to get people to like buffalo milk mozzarella; it's creamier, richer, and much more flavorful than the version made from cow's milk.

>> **Caciocavallo podoloco:** Named one of the "five highest priced cheeses in the world" in 2013, authentic *caciocavallo podolico* is a craft cheese made exclusively from the milk of the Podolico cow found only in the Appenine Mountains between Basilicata and Calabria, which are now at risk of extinction. Traditional methods of caring for these cows include the ancient process of taking them to cooler pastures in the summer. Though they have a smaller milk yield than other cows, it is higher in flavor and nutrients. Imitation *caciocavallo* cheese is made from other cow's milk using non-traditional techniques. It has a very different flavor and is lower in nutrients.

Other cow's milk cheeses include:

>> **Asiago:** This firm cheese has a sweet, nutty flavor.

>> **Asiago Fresco:** This softer and creamier Asiago cheese has a mild, sweet flavor.

>> **Burrata:** Its name comes from the word "burro," which means butter. This cheese is fresh mozzarella filled with shreds of mozzarella soaked in cream. It is currently one of the trendiest Italian cheeses in America.

>> **Gorgonzola:** This is Italian Blue Cheese.

>> **Fontina:** This soft cheese has a sweet, buttery flavor.

>> **Fresh mozzarella:** Called *Fior di latte* in Italy, this cheese has a delicate, milky flavor.

>> **Grana Padano:** Known as just "grana," this cheese is one of the most widely used in Italy, but it's not readily available in the U.S. Culinarily speaking, it can be used wherever Parmigiano-Reggiano is used. In terms of production, the differences are that Grana Padano originated in the Po River Valley in northern Italy, and while it is made in a similar way to Parmigiano-Reggiano, there are fewer strict regulations governing the production of grana, so it is made outside of the mandated geographical area.

>> **Smoked fresh mozzarella:** Smoked with natural wood and added into vegetarian dishes, this cheese is especially good in baked pastas, giving them depth.

>> **Mascarpone:** This fresh, creamy, spreadable soft cheese has a sweet, creamy flavor.

- >> **Parmigiano-Reggiano:** This hard, aged table cheese has a full, nutty flavor. As a successful GI (Geographic Indicator) product with an eight-century history, Parmigiano-Reggiano is the most widely consumed Italian cheese in the world.

- >> **Provolone:** This semi-hard cheese comes in flavors ranging from mild to sharp and is known for its classic oval shape.

- >> **Ricotta:** "Re-cooked" cheese is made from the whey left over from making aged cheeses. It was traditionally made in handmade reed baskets. In Italy, it is often made of sheep's milk. It can be used in desserts, eaten with honey at breakfast, or served as a dollop on the side of some traditional pasta recipes.

- >> **Ricotta Salata:** This crumbly cheese has a milky flavor and a hint of salt added into fillings and shaved on pasta. Some call it "the Italian Feta" because of its flavor and texture.

- >> **Stracciatella:** This cheese comprises *Burrata's* creamy filling — shreds of Mozzarella soaked in sweet cream, which is becoming increasingly popular in restaurants.

Making a (cheese) course of it

The manner in which cheese is consumed varies from place to place. In Italy, cheese courses were once customarily served after a meal. Through the ages, the cheese course came after the salad and prior to a sweet dessert on special occasions. Because historically most meals were vegetarian, this ensured more protein and variety in a meal. It also goes without saying that cheese is a much more healthful alternative to sugar–laden desserts with little nutritional value.

AUTHENTIC PARMIGIANO-REGGIANO

Authentic Parmigiano-Reggiano cheese is made with the milk from cows that have been fed only on fodder, rennet, and salt. It's made in the same traditional process and in the same places as it has been made for centuries. Additives are prohibited, and it must be aged a minimum of 12 months, but is typically aged 20-24 months. This industry currently provides work to over 50,000 people. In 2012, it created roughly $2,555,800 in revenue in consumption turnover. Production is regulated by the Consorzio del Formaggio Parmigiano-Reggiano. In order to be authentic, it must be labeled as Parmigiano-Reggiano and have its name spelled out in stenciled dots, which are visible on the rind. Other names, such as "Italian," "organic," and "Parmesan," are not authentic.

Nowadays, however, the cheese course is at risk of being forgotten. Instead, I'm starting to see a new trend of serving cheese as an *antipasto* or appetizer, the way it is in the United States, or during an *aperitivo* or light meal at the end of the workday. A cheese course is sometimes used as a vegetarian main course in modern menus. Italian nutritionists and dieticians have started to recommend against the cheese course, because it adds "unnecessary" fat and protein to a meal that may already contain meat or other sources of protein as a second course.

Personally, I feel that the cheese course is an important part of our culinary patrimony, and that it deserves to be preserved. A cheese course is the perfect opportunity to sample the wonderful varieties of nutrient-rich artisan cheeses on the market, and it helps to fill you up so you won't need more "sinful" desserts afterward. A happy medium, in my mind, would be to preserve the tradition on two occasions: when enjoying a large, celebratory meal on occasion, and after a lighter vegetarian meal (which the Mediterranean diet/lifestyle recommends you eat often anyway). In other words, you can skip the cheese course in meals when you enjoy fish-, poultry-, or meat-based second courses.

But, after a delightfully flavorful light meal of *Pasta e fagioli*, *Spaghetti al pomodoro*, pureed fava beans with greens, or a soup and salad, a cheese plate (especially one enhanced with fruit and nuts), makes a fabulous addition. You can also afford the splurge on holidays and for Sunday suppers. When I visit my family in Calabria, we often have a cheese theme night to celebrate our love of dairy and the local culinary masterpieces. That night, our dinner consists of the best local cheeses, bread, and preserved vegetables as the main event, and it is one of the most magical meals I have ever experienced.

Buying in to quality cheese production

Like other genuine products, the quality of cheese, the way it is made, the ingredients used (as well as those not used), maturation time, the transformation process, and storage all play a role in its overall taste, texture, and health benefits.

Many cheeses have been made in the same artisanal fashion for centuries, ensuring authenticity, flavor, and environmentally sound practices. Great care goes into making artisan cheese. Ancient farming practices that emphasize the well-being of the animals include high-quality feed, grazing in cooler pastures in the hot summer months, and hand milking.

Quality cheese production, in addition to maintaining culinary traditions, also provides a sense of community to those involved in making it, and when promoted properly, can be a strong boost to local economies. Those who weren't raised with an affinity for cheese, or the understanding of what goes into making an honest product, often choose sub-par products in order to save money. This trend, paired with the widespread availability of non-authentic cheeses on the market today, has made it increasingly difficult for small producers all over the world to stay in business. Luckily, due to the educational efforts of organizations like Slow Food, nutritionists, and promotional campaigns led by major cheese-producing nations, this is beginning to change. Educated consumers are now seeking out the best quality cheeses, not only for the taste and tradition they offer, but for their nutritional benefits and to support honest producers as well.

TIP

When purchasing Italian cheeses, look for DOP, IGP, or PAT designations, which indicate the cheese has a protected status of origin and is guaranteed authentic. (The nearby sidebar explores these certifications in more detail.) If you cannot find good-quality, imported Italian cheese, choose the best-quality local cheese from farmers in your area, which is always the best substitute. Many award-winning Italian chefs and restaurateurs in the U.S. turn to local farmers markets to find cheeses that remind them of Italy, such as the *toma* cheese produced by the Amish community.

ITALIAN CHEESE CERTIFICATIONS

The Italian government and the European Union go to great lengths to ensure that quality is upheld in the preparation of food items including cheese. In order to obtain one of the following Geographic Indicators (GIs), Italian producers must be able to demonstrate and document the breeds of animals they use, how and when they milk them, how they store and cook the milk, how they age the cheese, how long they age the cheese, and much more. There are currently hundreds of types of Italian cheeses that meet these regulations.

Each type of cheese has its own set of rules, but here is an example of how a specific type of cheese meets these regulations as well as how it is labeled. The protected term for true Buffalo Milk Mozzarella, for example, is *Mozzarella di Bufala Campana DOP*, where DOP stands for *Denominazione di origine protetta* (Protected Designation of Origin, or PDO, in English). Since 2008, the legislations surrounding the cheese determine where the buffalos themselves come from and the region in which the cheese is made. The race of buffalos and their feed are also determining factors. The cheese must be made of fresh, whole buffalo's milk with a minimum of 7.2 percent fat content. The milk must be filtered in traditional methods within 60 hours of milking, plus natural veal rennet must be used and additives omitted. The cooking temperatures, shapes, taste, fat content, and humidity levels present in the cheese are all pre-determined as well.

Refer to Chapter 5 for more information about important food certifications and requirements.

Pesche al forno con pistacchi e crema di basilico/Roasted Peaches with Pistachios and Basil Cream

PREP TIME: 5 MIN	COOK TIME: 25 MIN	YIELD: 4 SERVINGS

INGREDIENTS

1 teaspoon Amy Riolo Selections or other good-quality extra virgin olive oil

4 ripe peaches, pitted and halved

4 teaspoons sugar

1 cup vanilla yogurt or whipped cream

2 tablespoons finely chopped fresh basil

¼ cup local honey

4 teaspoons finely chopped pistachios

DIRECTIONS

1 Preheat oven to 400 degrees.

2 Oil a large baking dish; place peaches, cut side up, in the dish and sprinkle 1 teaspoon sugar over each.

3 Bake, uncovered, for 25 minutes.

4 While the peaches are baking, stir together drained yogurt, basil, and honey.

5 Divide half of yogurt mixture among four plates, or spread in a large serving platter.

6 When the peaches are finished baking, remove from the oven and place two halves over yogurt on each plate.

7 Fill the holes in the peaches with yogurt mixture, sprinkle with pistachios, and serve warm.

TIP: Choose fruit that is ripe but still a bit firm for this recipe, so it doesn't break down in the oven.

NOTE: Baking fruit brings out its natural sweetness to create a delightful dessert without the guilt.

VARY IT! Nectarines, plums, and apricots also can be prepared this way.

Pere cotte al cioccolato/Poached Pears in Chocolate

PREP TIME: 5 MIN	COOK TIME: 25 MIN	YIELD: 4 SERVINGS

INGREDIENTS

4 bosc pears, peeled

2 tablespoons lemon juice

2 tablespoons sugar

½ cup 60% dark chocolate, Fair Trade Certified, if possible

⅓ cup sliced almonds

DIRECTIONS

1 Place pears in a medium saucepan, and cover with water.

2 Add lemon juice and sugar, and bring to boil over high heat. Reduce heat to medium–low, and simmer for 20 minutes, or until pears are tender.

3 Turn off heat, and drain pears.

4 In the meantime, break chocolate into pieces and melt it over a double boiler or in the microwave.

5 When pears are cool enough to handle, stand them upright in the middle of dessert plates.

6 If pears fall over, slice off the bottoms to make them stand firmly.

7 Drizzle melted chocolate over the tops and sides of the pears.

8 Allow to stand for 5 minutes at room temperature, top with almonds, and serve.

NOTE: Poached pears are a classic Italian dessert that has stood the test of time.

VARY IT! Pears also can be poached in red wine or sweet wine such as Kerner.

Apples also can be prepared this way; they could be topped with caramel sauce instead of chocolate and topped with walnuts.

Macedonia di frutta con noci/Fruit Salad with Walnuts

PREP TIME: 5 MIN	COOK TIME: 60 MIN REFRIGERATION	YIELD: 4 SERVINGS

INGREDIENTS

2 bananas, sliced

2 clementines, peeled and segmented

2 kiwi, sliced

1 cup blueberries

¼ cup sugar

2 tablespoons lemon juice

4 tablespoons finely chopped walnuts

DIRECTIONS

1 Combine all fruit in a large salad bowl. Mix sugar and lemon juice together in a small bowl.

2 Drizzle sugar mixture over fruit, and mix gently to combine.

3 Cover bowl, and store in refrigerator for an hour.

4 Transfer to individual bowls before serving. Garnish with nuts.

TIP: When cooking a meal, make this salad first so it will be ready by the time you are finished eating.

VARY IT! Any seasonal fruit, such as melons in summer and berries in spring, can be substituted. Fruit salads also are served with whipped cream or ice cream in Italy.

Ficchi secchi al cioccolato/Almond–Stuffed Dried Figs in Chocolate

INGREDIENTS

20 fresh ripe figs or good-quality dried white figs (see Tip)

¼ cup slivered almonds

Zest of 1 orange, or ¼ cup candied citrus peel

1 teaspoon ground pure cinnamon

½ teaspoon ground cloves

4 ounces good-quality dark chocolate, Fair Trade Certified, if possible

DIRECTIONS

1 Preheat the oven to 350 degrees. Line two baking sheets with parchment paper.

2 With the fig upright, make an incision halfway down to the bottom, and open with your fingers. In a small bowl, combine the almonds, orange zest or peel, cinnamon, and cloves. Stuff each fig with some of the filling. Press the figs closed and place them an inch apart on one baking sheet. Bake until slightly softened and darkened, 5–8 minutes.

3 Break chocolate into pieces, and melt it in the top of a double boiler over low heat, stirring constantly, just until chocolate is melted, 2–3 minutes, or melt in the microwave.

4 Remove the figs from the oven, and using tongs or holding figs by the stem, dip them quickly into the warm chocolate. Place on the second lined baking sheet to cool.

5 Allow to stand at room temperature for at least 20 minutes before serving.

TIP: White figs are used for this recipe because they are usually more tender. If you cannot find dried white figs, you can substitute another type, but it is worth seeking out the best quality you can find. If the figs are very hard, be sure to soak them in water for a few hours to "plump" them before proceeding with the recipe. Store stuffed figs in an airtight container in the refrigerator.

NOTE: This is a traditional Christmas treat in Calabria. As far as sweets are concerned, it combines lots of nutrient-dense ingredients like almonds, figs, and spices with antioxidant-rich dark chocolate, which is known to balance blood sugar in those with diabetes. I like to serve these on a platter, garnished with more chopped almonds, sprinkles, or gold leaf for special occasions.

VARY IT! Dried dates and apricots also can be prepared this way. Remember to soak them in water for a bit to soften them before proceeding with the recipe.

Frutta estiva/Summer Fruit Platter

PREP TIME: 10 MIN	COOK TIME: 0 MIN	YIELD: 4 SERVINGS

INGREDIENTS

1 cup cubed watermelon

1 cup cubed cantaloupe

1 cup cubed honeydew melon

1 cup chopped fresh pineapple (peeled, cored, and diced into 1-inch wedges)

8 kiwi, peeled and sliced into ¼-inch rounds

½ cup fresh coconut shards, if desired

DIRECTIONS

1 Arrange the fruit in a pleasing pattern on a serving plate, sprinkle with coconut if desired, and serve with cocktail forks or cocktail toothpicks.

TIP: For maximum flavor and health benefits, use the best-quality, locally grown fruit you can find.

NOTE: Eating seasonal fruits is healthier because it contains the nutrients your body needs during that specific time of year.

VARY IT! Peaches, plums, and nectarines also make delicious desserts. Try serving a plate of fresh oranges in the spring; fresh figs, dates, and grapes in the fall; or apples and pears in the winter.

Vassoio di formaggi/Cheese Platter

PREP TIME: 10 MIN	COOK TIME: 0 MIN	YIELD: 8 SERVINGS

INGREDIENTS

1 wedge (about 4 ounces) Pecorino cheese

1 wedge (about 4 ounces) Taleggio cheese

1 wedge (about 4 ounces) Provola or other semi-hard cow's milk cheese

1 wedge (about 4 ounces) Goat cheese

1 bunch red grapes, divided into small clusters

1 cup dried Medjool dates

8 dried figs

1 cup blanched almonds, toasted

DIRECTIONS

1 Arrange the cheeses together on a very large platter.

2 Arrange the fresh and dried fruits, and almonds around the cheese on the platter. Or arrange the fruit and nuts on another platter.

TIP: The cheeses you serve should be a reflection of your tastes and what is available. To make an interesting cheese platter, try to offer a variety of textures — creamy, semi-hard, and aged cheeses, preferably from a combination of goat, cow, and sheep milk, if possible.

NOTE: This platter does double duty as an appetizer, during an aperitivo, or as a snack.

VARY IT! Use whichever cheeses, nuts, and dried fruits compliment your meal or what you have on hand. Even one type of cheese along with fruit and nuts can be a delicious finale or appetizer to a meal.

Susine grigliate con ricotta e miele/ Grilled Plums with Ricotta and Honey

PREP TIME: 5 MIN	COOK TIME: 10 MIN	YIELD: 4 SERVINGS

INGREDIENTS

4 ripe plums, halved and pitted

1 teaspoon Amy Riolo Selections or other good-quality extra virgin olive oil

4 teaspoons sugar

1 cup good-quality ricotta cheese

2 tablespoons fresh, local honey (Eucalyptus and wild flower are best)

¼ cup chopped pistachios or almonds

DIRECTIONS

1 Preheat the grill or grill pan over medium high heat.

2 Brush the plums with olive oil; place them in a pan, cut side up, and sprinkle ½ teaspoon sugar over each. Grill until marks appear and flesh is soft, turning once, approximately 3–5 minutes total.

3 Place plums on a platter, cut side up.

4 Divide the ricotta evenly onto each plum half.

5 Drizzle ½ tablespoon of honey on top of each, and sprinkle nuts on top. Serve warm.

TIP: This is the dessert to make when the grill is heated up in the summertime. Otherwise, use a grill pan in the kitchen.

NOTE: Good-quality ricotta makes all the difference in this dish. In Italy, ricotta is often made with sheep's milk, which I highly recommend if you can find it.

VARY IT! Peaches can be used instead of plums, and mascarpone cheese can be used in place of ricotta, as can yogurt, if preferred.

Mele al forno con crema ed amaretti/ Roasted Apples with Cream and Amaretti

PREP TIME: 5 MIN	COOK TIME: 30 MIN	YIELD: 6 SERVINGS

INGREDIENTS

1 tablespoon butter

6 apples, cored

1 cup heavy cream, divided

¼ cup sugar

6 ounces amaretti cookies or lady fingers

½ teaspoon Ceylon cinnamon, or your favorite cinnamon

DIRECTIONS

1 Preheat the oven to 425 degrees and grease a 9-inch baking pan with butter.

2 Place the apples in the baking pan, and add water to a depth of ⅛ inch. Place in the oven and bake, uncovered, until the apples are tender but still firm, about 30 minutes. Remove from the oven, and let cool.

3 Whip the cream until firm, adding the sugar halfway through.

4 Arrange the apples in a deep serving dish. Spoon half of the whipped cream around them.

5 Crumble the amaretti cookies or lady fingers. and sprinkle the tops of apples with cinnamon.

6 Bake, uncovered, for 20-30 minutes, and serve with additional whipped cream.

TIP: This is a comforting dish to serve in late fall or winter.

VARY IT! The apples also can be baked without the whipped cream and topped with pastry cream from the *Bomboloni* recipe (see Chapter 16), or with vanilla gelato or yogurt. Pears also can be used in this recipe.

Fragole in aceto balsamico/ Strawberries in Balsamic Vinegar

PREP TIME: 5 MIN	COOK TIME: 30 MIN REST TIME	YIELD: 6 SERVINGS

INGREDIENTS

4 cups fresh strawberries, cleaned, trimmed, and thickly sliced

5 tablespoons good-quality balsamic vinegar, preferably aged *aceto balsamic di Modena* or Amy Riolo Selections White Balsamic

2 tablespoons good-quality local honey

Freshly grated lemon zest or finely chopped fresh mint (for garnish)

DIRECTIONS

1 Thirty minutes to an hour before serving, combine the strawberries, balsamic vinegar, and honey in a bowl. Stir to combine, and set aside at room temperature until ready to serve. (If you're making this dish the night before, cover with plastic wrap and store in the refrigerator.)

2 Spoon into individual ramekins, garnish with lemon zest or mint, and serve.

TIP: This recipe is the time to show off good-quality balsamic and fresh, local or organic strawberries. Because it is so simple, quality ingredients will shine through to make it an event.

If you do not have balsamic vinegar, substitute freshly squeezed lemon juice and ¼ cup of sugar instead.

NOTE: My private label Amy Riolo Selections White Balsamic Dressing is made strictly from Trebbiano grapes in Italy (one of the grapes used in traditional Balsamic recipes) and has an extra, naturally sweet flavor that pairs very well with the strawberries.

VARY IT! Peaches, figs, and other berries can be used.

Chapter **18**

Classic Dolci/Desserts: Elevating the Everyday

talian sweets and desserts are famous the world over for their incredible flavors and varieties — from those eaten at breakfast (see Chapter 16); to fruit, cheese, and nut plates often enjoyed *as* dessert (see Chapter 17); to those reserved for holidays and special occasions (look ahead to Chapter 19). But the most classic examples of Italian sweets often blur the lines between a dessert, a breakfast, and a decadent pick-me-up to be enjoyed anytime, and those amazing dishes are the topic of this chapter.

Whether you're interested in making a comforting classic like rice pudding, a cream-filled cake for an intimate special occasion, trying your hand at authentic cannoli, or making *tiramisù*, the world's most popular Italian dessert in your own kitchen, the recipes in this chapter are for you! The best news of all: They're some of the easiest sweets to make.

TIP

If you aren't used to baking or making sweets, be sure to read the recipes carefully a few times to familiarize yourself with the techniques. Then set aside more than enough time to try the recipe. I don't recommend trying a recipe for the first time when you are hurried or have company. The recipes in this chapter easily can be made a day in advance, if not more. By making them ahead of time you will be less harried when you are serving them, and allow yourself to have fun and experiment with the recipe.

Creating Classic Italian Desserts

Ever since Cleopatra began enticing Mark Antony with marzipan-filled walnuts in elaborate display of her wealth (sugar was extremely expensive and available only to European emperors in antiquity), Italians have had a love affair with sweets. Even though they are thankfully consumed less often than they are in the United States, Italian sweets are edible works of art capable of transforming even the gloomiest of days.

The collection of classic sweets in this chapter falls into three categories: "spoon desserts," cakes, and pastry shop favorites. *Note:* Because cookies are usually served with breakfast or at tea time, I have included those recipes in Chapter 19 along with other special-occasion baked goods served for holidays.

Dolci al cucchiaio/"Spoon desserts"

While the term "spoon desserts" is widely used in Italy, it is relatively unheard of in the U.S. Many Italian desserts, however, fall neatly into this category, such as puddings, trifles, mousses, *tiramisù*, *panna cotta*, *gelato*, and many other desserts enjoyed in Italian restaurants.

Part of the reason of the popularity of these dishes is that historically they could be easily reproduced in professional and home kitchens alike. If an Italian chef, who is not trained in pastries, and cannot afford a pastry chef onsite, opens an Italian restaurant, they can still completely satisfy their customers' sweet cravings by offering desserts such as *budini* (puddings), *tiramisù*, and *panna cotta*, which don't require fancy ovens or baking skills.

Whether you eat your creamy *panna cotta* prepared by a loving mother or grandmother, or from a restaurant, the same delicious and comforting sensations will come over you. Spoon desserts are the perfect entry into the world of Italian desserts because they are easy to make while still offering sensational sweet flavors and heavenly textures.

Cake and pastry shop favorites

Original versions of cakes were made in Italy in antiquity. Originally served as offerings to the gods, they eventually became synonymous with special saints' days and other official occasions. It was during the Renaissance that the art of Italian pastry-making truly skyrocketed as various royal palaces competed with each other in the culinary arts.

THE RISE OF ITALIAN PASTRY-MAKING

For European royalty, having the best cooks and recipes was a symbol of prestige. The House of Savoy (Italian: *Casa di Savoia*) is a royal family that was established in 1003 in the historical Savoy region. Through gradual expansion, the family grew in power from ruling a small county in the Alps of northern Italy to absolute rule of the kingdom of Sicily in 1713.

The biscuits created in this palace were called *Savoiardi,* which is still the Italian name for lady fingers that are used in tiramisù recipes. They were invented around 1350 in Amedeo VI's court for a visit by the king of France, which is when they got their name. During that time period, the Ottoman palaces were at the height of style. One of their common practices was to name dishes after parts of the female anatomy (lady's fingers, lady's thighs, lady's eyelashes, and so on), and the trend spread through Europe and other fashionable courts as well.

When Catherine de' Medici, niece of Lorenzo the Magnificent, Grand Duke of Tuscany, married the French King Henry II (1533), the course of French gastronomic history changed forever. As nobility, Catherine didn't cook for herself, but she enlisted teams of chefs from the Florentine court to escort her to Paris. As a result, the Grande Cuisine of Paris, and even French pastry, was influenced by Italians.

Sponge cake (see Chapter 16) is an Italian creation that was invented in the mid-1700s by a Genovese cook, Giovan Battista Cabona. While visiting Spain in the service of Marquis Domenico Pallavicini, the Ambassador of Genoa, the cook introduced the incredibly light and fluffy cake for the first time during a royal banquet at the court of the King of Spain. The clever dessert creation was an immediate success. Originally called *Pâte Génoise,* or Genovese pastry, as a nod to the nationality of its inventor, the Italian name later changed to *pan di spagna* (Spanish bread) in honor of the Spanish court where it was first presented.

The traditional sponge cake that we know today is actually a variation of the original *Pâte Génoise.* The original recipe called for the same ingredients, but they were combined hot, while the modern version mixes the ingredients cold.

Sponge cake is one of the stars of the Italian dessert world, because it is a basic element of the most popular treats. It can be served with a simple soaking syrup (with or without alcohol), layered with various types of cream (from pastry cream to chocolate ganache), or garnished with fruit and whipped cream. However it is finished, the extraordinary fragrance and softness of sponge cake always make it a hit. The dessert's characteristic features are the result of truly simple ingredients: flour and/or starch (wheat starch, potato flakes, cornstarch), eggs, sugar, and flavorings (such as lemon peel or vanilla beans).

Over the centuries, baking ingredients (flour, sugar, eggs, and butter) slowly became more accessible to the masses. The pastry arts became a truly respected and recognized profession, which enabled everyone to eat the delicious creations from the courts. Each region and town in Italy now has a variety of desserts and pastries to offer. In addition to those, there are the traditional *dolci casalinghi,* or homemade desserts that often followed Sunday lunches and special occasions. With just the right amount of sweetness and wholesome ingredients, these recipes have stood the test of time. Whether you eat them for dessert, at tea time, or for a decadent breakfast, you won't be disappointed.

Budino di riso/Carnaroli Rice Pudding

PREP TIME: 5 MIN | COOK TIME: 30 MIN | YIELD: 4 SERVINGS

INGREDIENTS

⅔ cup Carnaroli rice

4 cups whole milk

1 teaspoon pure vanilla extract

⅔ cup sugar

DIRECTIONS

1 Rinse the rice and drain well. Pour milk into a medium saucepan.

2 Add drained rice, vanilla, and sugar.

3 Stir with a wooden spoon, and bring to a boil over medium-high heat.

4 Once mixture boils, reduce heat to low, stir, and cover.

5 Simmer for 30 minutes, stirring occasionally, until rice is tender and liquid is absorbed.

6 Allow pudding to cool at room temperature. Pour into a serving bowl.

7 Refrigerate leftovers for up to two days.

TIP: This is the perfect dessert for a casual family dinner.

If you'd like to pair this dessert with wine, look for *Moscato d'Asti* or similar.

NOTE: Carnaroli is known as the "King of Rices" in Italy. If you cannot find it, you can substitute Arborio or Calrose rice in this recipe.

VARY IT! Add ½ cup cocoa powder to the recipe to make a chocolate rice pudding.

Panna cotta con lamponi/Cooked Cream with Raspberries

PREP TIME: 10 MIN	COOK TIME: 10 MIN PLUS COOLING TIME	YIELD: 6 SERVINGS

INGREDIENTS

1 ½ cups whole milk

½ cup granulated sugar, plus additional, if needed

1 ½ gelatin sheets, soaked in cold water to cover (10 minutes), and drained

1 ½ cups plain full-fat yogurt, strained in a colander one hour before using

½ pound fresh raspberries or other berries, cleaned and trimmed

DIRECTIONS

1 Place the milk and sugar in a saucepan. Bring almost to a boil over medium heat.

2 Remove from heat, squeeze excess water from gelatin sheets and stir them in. Whisk well to combine so the mixture doesn't curdle.

3 Add the yogurt, whisking vigorously, and mix well to incorporate.

4 Place the panna cotta into a glass or ceramic container (see Note). Cover and refrigerate for at least one hour.

5 To make the raspberry sauce, place raspberries in the food processor and pulse until a sauce is formed. Add sugar to taste. Refrigerate until serving.

6 Drizzle the raspberry sauce over the panna cotta, and serve.

TIP: This recipe combines milk and yogurt for added depth of flavor, but traditional recipes were made with just fresh cream alone. You can try it both ways and decide which one you prefer.

If you'd like to pair this dessert with wine, look for *Moscato di Pantelleria (Zibibbo)* or similar.

NOTE: You can prepare the panna cotta in individual ramekins and unmold and serve them at the table, or make and chill them in wine glasses or other decorative glasses.

VARY IT! You can add a few tablespoons of cocoa to the milk to make a chocolate panna cotta. I often substitute ½ cup of the milk for espresso to make a coffee-laced version.

Tiramisù

PREP TIME: 20 MIN | COOK TIME: 0 MIN PLUS OVERNIGHT CHILLING | YIELD: 8-10 SERVINGS

INGREDIENTS

3 extra large egg yolks, at room temperature

3 tablespoons sugar

1 cup mascarpone cheese, chilled

1 cup heavy cream

24 plain lady fingers, divided

½ cup espresso, at room temperature with 2 tablespoons sugar stirred in

1 ounce dry rum

2 teaspoons pure vanilla extract

Unsweetened cocoa for dusting, Fair Trade Certified if possible

DIRECTIONS

1 In a medium bowl, using an electric mixer set on high speed, beat together the egg yolks and sugar until pale yellow, smooth and shiny, about 5 minutes.

2 Add the mascarpone, and continue to beat another 3-5 minutes until smooth.

3 In another bowl, using clean beaters, whip the cream until soft peaks form.

4 Using a rubber spatula or whisk, fold the whipped cream into the yolk mixture until blended.

5 Arrange 10-12 lady fingers in a single layer in the bottom of a decorative serving bowl (10 inches in diameter).

6 Mix espresso, rum, and vanilla in a medium bowl, and whisk to combine.

7 Brush some of the espresso mixture evenly over the lady fingers.

8 Turn lady fingers over and brush again until each one is soaked through with the espresso mixture.

9 Spoon some of the mascarpone over the lady fingers in an even ½-inch layer.

(continued)

10 Place remaining lady fingers in a single layer over mascarpone mixture.

11 Brush their tops with espresso to soak. Spoon remaining mascarpone over the top. Cover and chill for 6 hours to 2 days before serving. To serve, lightly dust cocoa over the top using a fine-mesh sieve. Scoop individual portions onto top plates.

TIP: If you'd like to pair this dessert with wine, look for *Moscato di Scanzo* or similar.

NOTE: The "father of tiramisù," Ado Campeol, passed away in 2021, and Italians recognized him for creating the recipe at his restaurant, Le Beccherie, alongside his wife, Alba Di Pillo, and Chef Roerto Loli Linguanotto.

VARY IT! This is my variation on classic tiramisù. I omit the egg whites, which are normally whipped to stiff peaks and folded into the mascarpone mixture instead of cream. If you prefer to make it the traditional way, omit the cream, and fold in egg whites instead.

Tiramisù di fragole/Strawberry Tiramisù

PREP TIME: 20 MIN	COOK TIME: 0 MIN PLUS OVERNIGHT CHILLING	YIELD: 12 SERVINGS

INGREDIENTS

3 large egg yolks

1 cup sugar

1 cup mascarpone cheese, chilled

1 cup heavy cream

24 plain lady fingers, divided

½ cup strawberry purée (made from puréeing fresh strawberries)

2 teaspoons pure vanilla extract

1 cup freshly sliced strawberries

DIRECTIONS

1 In a medium bowl, using an electric mixer set on high speed, beat together the egg yolks and sugar until pale yellow, smooth, and shiny, about 5 minutes. Add the mascarpone, and continue to beat until smooth, about 3-5 minutes.

2 In another bowl, using clean beaters, whip the cream until soft peaks form.

3 Using a rubber spatula or whisk, fold the whipped cream into the yolk mixture until blended.

4 Arrange 12 lady fingers in a single layer in the bottom of a decorative serving bowl (10 inches in diameter).

5 Place strawberry purée and vanilla in a medium bowl, and whisk to combine.

6 Brush some of the strawberry purée evenly over the lady fingers. Turn lady fingers over, and brush again until each one is soaked through with the strawberry purée.

7 Spoon some of the mascarpone over the ladyfingers in an even ½-inch layer.

(continued)

8 Place remaining 12 lady fingers in a single layer over mascarpone mixture. Brush the tops with strawberry purée to soak. Spoon remaining mascarpone over the top. Cover and chill for 6 hours to overnight before serving. To serve, place sliced strawberries on top and scoop individual portions onto plates.

TIP: Serve this recipe instead of strawberry shortcake in the summertime.

If you'd like to pair this dessert with wine, look for *Prosecco dry* or similar.

NOTE: Because this version of tiramisù contains no alcohol, in Italy it's often prepared with kids.

VARY IT! You can use any kind of berries you like, or a mixture of berries, in this recipe. I usually make a red-white-and-blue version with the addition of blueberries for 4th of July and Memorial Day celebrations.

Torta di nocciola/Piemontese Hazelnut Cake

| PREP TIME: 20 MIN | COOK TIME: 40 MIN | YIELD: 8 SERVINGS |

INGREDIENTS

1 teaspoon butter

½ cup blanched (peeled) hazelnuts or hazelnut flour

1 cup confectioners' sugar, plus extra for garnish

3 tablespoons potato or corn starch

⅔ cup unbleached all-purpose flour

2 tablespoons unsweetened cocoa, Fair Trade Certified if possible

2 ½ teaspoons baking powder

Pinch of ground cinnamon

½ cup unsalted butter, cut into small pieces

3 large eggs

2 teaspoons pure vanilla extract

1 orange, zested

1 tablespoon orange juice

1 cup semisweet chocolate chips, Fair Trade Certified if possible

DIRECTIONS

1 Preheat oven to 400 degrees. Butter the bottom and sides of a 9-inch cake pan. Line the bottom with a piece of parchment paper, and butter bottom and sides with additional baking spray.

2 Combine hazelnuts and confectioners' sugar in a food processor fitted with a metal blade attachment. Pulse on and off until hazelnuts are finely ground, stopping before they turn to flour.

3 In a large bowl fitted to a standing electric mixer, combine the hazelnut mixture, potato starch, flour, cocoa, baking powder, and cinnamon. Beat over medium speed for a few minutes until combined.

4 Add the unsalted butter, and continue to beat until the mixture resembles bread crumbs.

5 Beat in eggs and vanilla, mixing on low speed until combined.

6 Increase the speed to high, and beat until the mixture is light and fluffy, 2–3 minutes.

7 Stir in orange zest, juice, and chocolate chips.

8 Pour the batter into a prepared pan, and level off the top.

9 Tap the bottom of the pan a few times on the counter to remove any air bubbles.

10 Bake in the center oven rack for 20-30 minutes, or until a tester inserted in the middle of the cake comes out clean.

(continued)

11 Remove the cake from the oven and let it cool in pan on a rack for 5 minutes. Run a sharp knife around the edges to loosen the cake. Invert the cake onto a platter, remove parchment paper, and invert it once again onto a serving platter.

12 Allow to cool completely and sprinkle the top with confectioners' sugar before serving.

TIP: It is possible to buy peeled hazelnuts in stores. I usually find them at organic and Middle Eastern markets, but they aren't always in stock, so it is best to call ahead or order them online. Some specialty flour companies also sell hazelnut flour, which is just ground hazelnuts, in the baking aisle of markets. That can also be substituted.

If you'd like to pair this dessert with wine, look for *Erbaluce di Caluso passito* or similar.

NOTE: The region of Piemonte is known for its prized hazelnuts, which make their way into oils, liqueurs, salads, sauces, candies, and desserts. *Giandiuja* is the Italian word for a mixture of chocolate and at least 30% hazelnut paste, but nowadays the term is used widely to refer to the chocolate-hazelnut flavor combination.

VARY IT! You can swap out any kind of nuts in this recipe — almonds, walnuts, and pistachios also work well — just remember to call it by a different name if you're not using hazelnuts!

Torta Caprese/Capri-Style Chocolate and Almond Cake

PREP TIME: 15 MIN	COOK TIME: 45 MIN	YIELD: 8 SERVINGS

INGREDIENTS

1 cup mixed berries

1 tablespoon good-quality balsamic vinegar

1 cup sugar, divided

⅔ cup melted butter, divided

⅓ cup dark chocolate chips, Fair Trade Certified if possible

¼ cup hot espresso or strong coffee

2 teaspoons pure vanilla extract

2 egg whites

1 egg yolk

½ cup unsweetened cocoa powder, Fair Trade Certified if possible

½ cup almond flour

DIRECTIONS

1 Combine the berries with balsamic vinegar and 2 tablespoons sugar in a medium bowl. Stir to combine, cover, and set aside at room temperature until serving cake. (If you are serving the cake the next day, you can store the berries in the refrigerator.)

2 Preheat oven to 350 degrees. Grease a 9-inch springform pan (with 2 ¾-inch-high sides) with butter. Line bottom of the pan with parchment paper, and grease that with butter as well.

3 In a large glass or metal bowl, stir chocolate chips, hot espresso, and vanilla together until chocolate is melted and mixture is smooth. Allow mixture to cool to lukewarm.

4 Using clean beaters and a standing electric mixer, beat the egg whites until stiff peaks form.

5 In a separate bowl, whisk egg yolk, remaining butter, and remaining sugar until batter is smooth and resembles maple syrup in consistency. Stir in cocoa powder and almond flour, mixing well until incorporated.

6 Fold egg yolk mixture into lukewarm chocolate mixture. Fold in egg whites one-third at a time.

(continued)

7 Place prepared cake pan on a baking sheet. Pour batter into pan. Bake until a cake tester or toothpick inserted into center comes out with moist crumbs attached, about 35–40 minutes.

8 Let cake cool completely in pan. (Cake can be prepared up to one day ahead. If preparing ahead of time, cover with plastic wrap and refrigerate. Let stand at room temperature 1 hour before continuing.) Run knife around pan sides to loosen cake. Remove sides of pan, and then remove parchment paper. Transfer cake to platter, and serve with berries on the side.

TIP: Good-quality chocolate and fresh almonds help to make this iconic cake reach its full potential.

If you'd like to pair this dessert with wine, look for *Ischia Piedirosso passito* or similar.

NOTE: My colleagues at the Ristorante d'Amore on the island of Capri told me that this cake was originally created as a Caprese-inspired version of the Sacher Torte. Anytime you need a flourless chocolate cake option, this is a great solution!

VARY IT! You can use walnut flour instead of the almond flour, just don't call it a Torta Caprese.

Torta di ficchi, noci, e semi di finocchio/Fig, Walnut, and Fennel Seed Cake

PREP TIME: 15 MIN	COOK TIME: 30 MIN	YIELD: 8 SERVINGS

INGREDIENTS

¼ cup plus 1 teaspoon Amy Riolo Selections or other good-quality extra virgin olive oil, divided

⅔ cup unbleached all-purpose flour, plus extra for dusting the pan

2 teaspoons baking powder (use gluten-free, if needed)

1 teaspoon fennel seeds, crushed in a mortar

¼ teaspoon salt

4 large eggs, separated

¾ cup sugar

1 teaspoon pure vanilla extract

5 ounces chopped dried white figs

1 cup walnuts, toasted and chopped, divided

DIRECTIONS

1 Preheat oven to 350 degrees. Grease (with 1 teaspoon extra virgin olive oil) and flour a 9-inch springform pan.

2 Mix flour, baking powder, fennel seeds, and salt in a small bowl.

3 Beat egg yolks and sugar together in another bowl until thick and pale yellow, about 3 minutes. Slowly beat in ¼ cup oil and vanilla. Stir in the flour mixture, and then the figs and ½ cup walnuts.

4 Using clean beaters, beat egg whites in a separate bowl until stiff peaks form. Stir one-third of the egg whites into batter, and then carefully fold in the remaining egg whites.

5 Transfer batter to the prepared pan. Bake cake in the center of the oven until a cake tester or toothpick inserted into center comes out clean, about 25-30 minutes.

6 Cool cake in the pan on a rack. Serve completely cooled.

TIP: If you want a sweeter cake, add honey to the recipe, or drizzle a bit of honey or confectioners' sugar on it before serving.

If you'd like to pair this dessert with wine, look for *Vermentino di Gallura passito* or similar.

NOTE: This is a toothy, slightly dense style of farmhouse cake that also works really well for breakfast.

VARY IT! Dried apricots and pistachios or dates and almonds can be substituted for the figs and walnuts in this recipe. If you are not a fan of fennel, simply omit them and add an extra teaspoon of vanilla or the flavoring of your choice.

Torta di ciliege, mandorle, ed olio d'oliva/Cherry, Almond, and Olive Oil Cake

PREP TIME: 10 MIN	COOK TIME: 45 MIN	YIELD: 9 SERVINGS

INGREDIENTS

½ cup plus 1 teaspoon Anfosso Taggiasca mono-cultivar or other good-quality extra virgin olive oil

2 ⅓ cups almond flour

½ cup sliced almonds

2 eggs, separated

⅔ cup freshly squeezed orange juice

2 teaspoons grated orange zest

1 cup sugar

2 teaspoons pure vanilla extract

1 teaspoon almond extract

1 teaspoon baking powder

½ teaspoon unrefined sea salt or salt

1 cup pitted fresh or frozen cherries or Italian sour cherries (amarene) in syrup, drained

2 tablespoons confectioners' sugar, to serve

DIRECTIONS

1   Preheat the oven to 350 degrees. Grease (with 1 teaspoon extra virgin olive oil) and flour a 9-inch springform pan. Line with parchment paper. Brush the parchment paper with olive oil and sprinkle with sliced almonds.

2   In the bowl of a standing mixer or in a large metal bowl using a hand mixer, beat the egg whites until stiff peaks form. Set aside.

3   In a separate bowl, combine the orange juice, orange zest, remaining olive oil, egg yolks, sugar, vanilla, and almond extract.

4   In a large bowl, sift together the flour, baking powder, salt, and ground almonds. Stir in the orange juice mixture, and fold in the cherries. Fold in the egg whites.

5   Pour the batter into the prepared pan, and smooth out the top with a spatula. Bake until a toothpick inserted into the middle comes out clean and the cake begins to pull away from the sides of the pan, 40–45 minutes.

6   Cool completely. Invert the cake onto a platter, and release the sides of the pan. Remove the parchment paper, sprinkle with confectioners' sugar, and serve.

TIP: Be sure to pit and drain cherries really well before adding them to this recipe.

If you'd like to pair this dessert with wine, look for *Greco di Bianco passito* or similar.

NOTE: The buttery flavor of Anfosso's Taggiasca extra-virgin olive oil is a beautiful compliment to cakes. If you substitute another olive oil, make sure you like the taste before adding it to the recipe.

VARY IT! You can use regular flour instead of almond flour, if you prefer, or a combination of them.

Zuccotto/Florentine Cream–Filled Dome Cake

PREP TIME: 30 MIN	COOK TIME: 0 MIN PLUS AT LEAST 3 HOURS FOR CHILLING	YIELD: 8 SERVINGS

INGREDIENTS

Nonstick baking spray

1 loaf *Quattro quarti*/Italian Pound Cake (see Chapter 16)

¼ cup brandy

6 ounces bittersweet chocolate, preferably Fair Trade Certified, chopped

2 cups chilled whipping cream

½ teaspoon pure almond extract

1 teaspoon espresso

Juice and zest of 1 orange

¼ cup confectioners' sugar

½ cup sliced almonds, toasted, coarsely chopped

Unsweetened cocoa powder, preferably Fair Trade Certified

DIRECTIONS

1 Set a large metal bowl over a saucepan of simmering water, and place the chocolate in the bowl; stir until the chocolate melts. Allow the chocolate to cool slightly. Stir in espresso, orange juice, and zest. Cool to room temperature.

2 Spray a 1 ½-quart bowl with nonstick cooking spray. Line the bowl with plastic wrap. Cut the pound cake crosswise into slices ⅓-inch thick. Cut each slice diagonally in half, forming 2 triangles. Line the bottom and sides of the prepared bowl with the cake triangles. Brush some of the brandy over the cake triangles lining the bowl. Reserve the extra triangles.

3 Using an electric mixer, beat 1 cup of cream in a large bowl until thick and fluffy. Fold one-fourth of the whipped cream into the completely cooled chocolate. Fold half of the remaining whipped cream into the chocolate mixture. Fold in the remaining whipped cream. Spread the chocolate cream over the cake, covering completely and creating a well in the center.

4 In another clean large bowl, add the remaining 1 cup of cream and almond extract. Using an electric mixer with clean beaters, beat on medium speed and gradually add the confectioners' sugar. Beat until firm peaks form. Fold in the nuts. Spoon the cream mixture into the center of the filling.

(continued)

5 Brush the remaining cake slices with brandy, and arrange them over the cake, covering the filling completely and trimming to fit, if necessary. Cover the cake with plastic wrap, and refrigerate at least 3 hours and up to one day.

6 Invert the cake onto a platter. Remove the bowl and the plastic wrap. Sift the cocoa powder over and serve.

TIP: Make pound cake a day (or more) in advance and have all ingredients ready when you go to assemble the dessert so that it is easier.

If you'd like to pair this dessert with wine, look for *Malvasia di Bosa dolce naturale* or similar.

NOTE: Bernardo Buontalenti created this classic, pumpkin shaped dessert in honor of Caterina de Medici. He made it in the shape of Brunelleschi's Dome of the Florence Cathedral Santa Maria del Fiore.

VARY IT! The fillings could be changed in this recipe; for example, pumpkin puree or pudding could be folded into ½ of the amount of filling, but it is not traditional.

Cassata Siciliana/Sicilian Ricotta–Filled Cassata Cake

PREP TIME: 20 MIN	COOK TIME: 0 MIN PLUS AT LEAST 30 MIN CHILLING	YIELD: 8 SERVINGS

INGREDIENTS

1 sponge cake (see Chapter 16)

½ pound whole milk ricotta cheese

½ cup miniature semisweet chocolate chips, Fair Trade Certified if possible

1 ½ cup confectioners' sugar, divided

1 cup shelled pistachios or almonds

1 egg white, lightly beaten

Few drops green food coloring, if desired

2 teaspoons lemon juice

4 whole candied fruits, such as oranges, apricots, and cherries, halved, if desired, for decoration

2 tablespoons Sicilian Candied citron, cut in strips, if desired, for decoration

DIRECTIONS

1 Slice sponge cake into 8 equal-sized pieces. In a large mixing bowl, combine ricotta, chocolate chips, and ½ cup confectioners' sugar together.

2 In a food processor, process pistachios until finely chopped. Add ½ cup confectioners' sugar, and process until finely ground. With processor running, slowly add enough egg white to form a smooth paste-like dough. If desired, add a few drops of green food coloring. Transfer paste to a work surface dusted with confectioners' sugar, and knead until smooth. Using a rolling pin, roll marzipan into an approximate 8-inch square (¼-inch thick), and cut into quarters. Roll the quarters out until they are approximately 4-inches each.

3 Line the bottoms and sides of four 4-inch pie molds or ramekins with plastic wrap, and press one portion of marzipan into the bottom of each mold, using your fingers to press the dough into the bottom and sides so that the entire interior is covered. Place a layer of cake over the marzipan (you may need to break it into pieces to fit into the mold), and top with a thick layer of ricotta mixture. Place another layer of cake on top, making sure to cover the entire surface leaving no exposed ricotta.

4 Wrap the pie molds in plastic wrap, and refrigerate until chilled, 2 hours (or 30 minutes in the freezer). Meanwhile, combine remaining confectioners' sugar and lemon juice in a medium bowl to make a thick glaze. Invert each pie mold onto a small serving dish, and peel off the plastic wrap. Garnish with candied fruits and citron, if desired.

(continued)

TIP: Authentic Sicilian and Italian candied fruit are delicacies and very different from what is found in most American supermarkets. I highly recommend seeking them out from importers such as www.italian foodandstyle.com for the best results.

If you'd like to pair this dessert with wine, look for *Grillo (late-harvest)* or similar.

NOTE: Cassata is every bit as popular in Sicily as cannoli is, but for some reason it is lesser known in the U.S. This is a traditional Easter dessert and one that I love to indulge in for breakfast each Easter Monday.

VARY IT! You can make a simpler, more rustic cassata-type cake by omitting the marzipan and just layering the pound cake with the ricotta filling. You can even drizzle it with chocolate sauce, if desired.

Zeppole di San Giuseppe/St. Joseph's Day Cream Puffs

PREP TIME: 30 MIN	COOK TIME: 30 MIN PLUS AT LEAST 20 MIN FOR CHILLING TIME	YIELD: 6 SERVINGS

INGREDIENTS

For the Dough:

1 pinch salt

2 tablespoons unsalted butter

1 cup all-purpose flour

3 eggs

For the Filling:

1 cup whole milk

Zest of 1 lemon

2 egg yolks

½ cup sugar

2 tablespoons all-purpose flour

To Finish:

Sour cherries in syrup, drained

Confectioners' sugar, to garnish

DIRECTIONS

1 Add 1 cup water to a saucepan, and add the salt and butter. Bring to a boil, while stirring.

2 Add the flour, leaving the pan on the heat, and mix the batter using a spoon until the batter is a smooth, solid mass, all flour is incorporated, and it no longer sticks to the sides of the pan.

3 Remove the pan from the heat, and transfer the batter to a bowl to cool.

4 Once the batter reaches room temperature, approximately 15 minutes, add the eggs, one at a time, and mix together with a wooden spoon.

5 Once the batter is fairly light and airy, place the dough in the refrigerator for at least 20 minutes.

6 To prepare the pastry filling, pour the milk into a saucepan. Add the lemon peel, and bring to a boil.

7 In a bowl, beat the egg yolks and the sugar. Incorporate the flour, whisking continuously.

8 When the milk begins to boil, remove it from the heat, and slowly add the egg, sugar, and flour mixture, whisking as you go. The resulting mixture should be soft and creamy.

9 Transfer the mixture to the stove over medium heat. Stir continuously until the cream becomes fairly dense and coats the back of a spoon. (This could take 10–15 minutes and can be done a day ahead of time.)

(continued)

10 When the cream is ready, transfer it to a bowl; cover with plastic wrap, and place in refrigerator. Be sure to cover the bowl well so that a film doesn't form on the surface of the cream.

11 Preheat the oven to 375 degrees. Line a baking sheet with parchment paper.

12 To shape the puffs, place the batter in a pastry bag with a star-shaped tip (Wilson #4B works well).

13 Pipe batter to form six 4-inch rounds or twelve 2-inch rounds equally spaced apart on the parchment paper. Bake for 15-20 minutes, or until puffed and golden. Remove from the oven.

14 When the puffs are cool enough to handle, fill another pastry bag with the pastry cream. Fill the puffs with pastry cream by inserting the nozzle into the center of the cream puff and piping a bit inside to fill.

15 Decorate each puff with a little cream, and place a cherry on top. Finish with a sprinkle of confectioners' sugar.

TIP: Making the filling a day ahead of time makes this recipe easier to manage.

If you'd like to pair this dessert with wine, look for *Passito Malvasia bianca (Calabria) not aromatic* or similar.

NOTE: This cream puff recipe was traditionally served on March 19, as it still is, in honor of St. Joseph, the patron saint of pastry chefs. I have included it in this chapter because in many places, such as Naples, it can be enjoyed all year round.

The basic dough used in this recipe is what the French call a *Pate a Choux*, which can be used to make profiteroles and eclairs in addition to zeppole. Note that this recipe is different from the fried dough balls also referred to as zeppole that are sold at street festivals. Because food terms are often referred to in dialects, it is not uncommon to find different recipes with the same name in Italy and throughout the Mediterranean.

VARY IT! While the dough in this version of the classic dessert is baked, it is also often fried. To do that, heat 1 inch of oil to 375 degrees in a Dutch oven or heavy bottomed, deep skillet. Pipe choux pastry (see Step 13) into the oil carefully, and turn with a slotted spoon until evenly golden (approximately 2 minutes). Remove and drain on a tray lined with paper towels, sprinkle confectioners' sugar, and enjoy!

Struffoli/Neapolitan Honey-Drenched Fritters

PREP TIME: 15 MIN	COOK TIME: 10 MIN PLUS CHILLING TIME	YIELD: 10 SERVINGS

INGREDIENTS

For Dough:

3 cups flour

4 eggs, lightly beaten

1 lemon, zested

3 oranges, zested

1 ½ teaspoon salt

Canola or peanut oil, for frying

To Finish:

6 cups honey

3 lemons, zested and juiced

Confectioners' sugar, for dusting

Sprinkles, for garnish

DIRECTIONS

1 In a mixing bowl, place flour, eggs, zest of 1 lemon, orange zest, and salt, and mix well to form a firm dough. Place in the refrigerator, and allow to rest 30 minutes.

2 Remove from the refrigerator, and cut golf ball-sized pieces of dough from the main batch. Roll each ball into a ¼-inch-thick dowel (rope), and cut each dowel into ½-inch pieces. Roll each piece into a ball, and continue until finished with all dough.

3 In a 14-inch skillet with at least 3-inch sides, heat the oil to 375 degrees. Drop enough balls in to cover about half of the surface of frying oil, and cook until dark golden brown. Use a slotted spoon to turn them regularly, and expect them to puff up while cooking. As they finish, remove them to a tray covered with paper towels to drain well. This should take at least five batches.

4 When the *struffoli* are cooked, heat the honey, lemon juice, and remaining lemon zest together in a wide 8-quart saucepan until quite warm, about 150 degrees, and substantially thinner. Add *struffoli* to honey, and stir carefully until well coated. Remove from heat and allow to cool for 5 minutes in the pan, stirring regularly. Using a slotted spoon, transfer to a large serving tray, and arrange in the form of a pyramid or a ring. Drizzle remaining honey over the top, or reserve additional honey to refresh *struffoli* if they dry out before serving. Dust with confectioners' sugar and sprinkles, if desired, and serve.

(continued)

TIP: You can make the dough a day ahead of time and refrigerate it if desired.

If you'd like to pair this dessert with wine, look for *Falanghina del Sannio passito* or similar.

NOTE: This traditional Neapolitan dessert is called *Pignolata* in Calabria. It is popular throughout Southern Italy and is a staple in the home of many Italian-Americans at Christmastime. The honey-covered dough balls were originally served during the Carnevale period prior to Lent, and eventually became part of Christmas traditions as well. This recipe is usually kept on hand for unexpected guests during the holiday season; it usually gets drizzled with a bit of leftover honey mixture before serving to freshen it up. It is ubiquitous on holiday tables from December to January and also at Carnevale and when traditional desserts are served.

Cannoli

PREP TIME: 30 MIN	COOK TIME: 30 MIN PLUS 30 MINUTES COOLING TIME PLUS AT LEAST 3 HOURS TO DRAIN RICOTTA	YIELD: 10 SERVINGS (1 CANNOLI EACH)

INGREDIENTS

For the Shells:

1 cup all-purpose flour

1 ounce unsalted butter (lard is often used as well)

1 teaspoon salt

¼ teaspoon ground cinnamon

⅓ cup cold water

For the Filling:

½ cup sugar

1 ounce cornstarch

¼ teaspoon salt

1 large egg

1 large egg yolk

1 cup whole milk

1 tablespoon pure vanilla extract

1 teaspoon lemon zest

2 ⅓ cup fresh whole-milk ricotta, drained for a minimum of 3 hours or overnight

DIRECTIONS

1   For the dough: In the bowl of a food processor, or in a standing mixer, combine flour, butter, salt, and cinnamon. Pulse until the butter disappears, about 30 seconds, and then add water and continue processing until dough rides up on the blade and forms a silky but stringy dough. This takes about 2 minutes, but the timing varies depending on the size and horsepower of the food processor.

2   Transfer to a lightly greased bowl, cover tightly, and allow the dough to relax at least 2 hours at room temperature, or up to 24 hours at cool room temperature.

3   For the filling: In a 3-quart stainless steel saucier, whisk sugar, cornstarch, and salt until well combined. Whisk in the egg, extra yolk, and milk. When it's smooth, place over medium-low heat and cook, whisking constantly but gently until warm to the touch, about 3 minutes.

4   Increase heat to medium and cook, now whisking quite vigorously, until the custard begins to thicken, about 2 minutes more. The custard may seem lumpy, almost like cottage cheese, but continue whisking until emulsified and silky smooth.

5   When the thick custard begins to bubble, set a timer and continue cooking and whisking for exactly 1 minute. Remove from heat, and stir in vanilla extract, lemon zest, and cinnamon.

6   Pour the custard into a large pie dish to form a thin layer (to speed the cooling process), and press a sheet of plastic against the surface to prevent a skin from forming. Refrigerate until thick and cool, about 1 hour, or to a temperature of 68 degrees. (Alternatively, refrigerate the custard up to one week and then return to room temperature until warmed to approximately 68 degrees.)

(continued)

To Fry:

Approx. 6 cups refined coconut oil

1 egg white, well beaten

To Serve (Optional):

½ cup finely chopped dark chocolate

½ cup finely chopped pistachios

Confectioners' sugar

7 In a bowl, beat the cooled pudding until creamy and smooth. (This can be done with an electric mixer or by hand using a flexible spatula, although it may seem impossible at first.) Fold in the drained ricotta. Refrigerate in an airtight container until needed, up to three days.

8 To form the dough: Turn the soft dough onto a well-floured surface and, using as much flour as needed to prevent sticking, roll until approximately $\frac{1}{16}$-inch thick. Brush excess flour from the dough, and lightly brush the surface with egg white. Carefully fold the dough in half, and dust with more flour; continue rolling to $\frac{1}{16}$ inch. Gently lift the dough to make sure it hasn't stuck, and cut into 3 ½-inch rounds using a cookie cutter or a glass of the same diameter; reroll the scraps, and cut as before.

9 Place a cannoli form (see Tip) at the top end of a circle and roll the dough over the form.

10 Use the egg white to seal the edges, and holding the form in one hand, use the other to flair the ends of the dough slightly. Gently press the dough between your fingertips and the side of the mold to slightly elongate the shell. Note that there will be exposed steel on the forms, but that ¾ will be covered. Repeat with remaining dough circles and cannoli forms.

11 Preparing the oil: Melt the refined coconut oil (or other solid fat) in a 5-quart stainless steel or enameled Dutch oven. Clip on a digital thermometer, and warm the oil to 380°F over medium heat. Meanwhile, line a baking sheet with three layers of paper towels.

12 When oil has reached the desired temperature, use tongs to carefully lower in three shells at a time.

13 Allow the shells to fry for approximately 1 minute, or until puffed and golden. Do not allow them to scorch.

14 Using tongs or a metal strainer, carefully remove shells from oil; the tubes will be full of oil, so turn them slightly to release oil before lifting out of the pan or fryer. Place them on the lined baking sheet.

15 Double-check the oil temperature, and increase heat if necessary, ensuring that oil is 380 degrees. Continue frying cannoli shells in the same fashion.

16 Cool the cannoli shells with forms still attached for a few minutes. When cool enough to handle, slide forms off of cannoli shells and reuse with remaining dough.

17 After you have used all the dough circles, gather the scraps of dough and reroll to $\frac{1}{16}$-inch thickness. Make additional circles and continue frying until you have used all the dough. Allow shells to cool.

18 To fill the shells: Place the filling in a pastry bag with a 1-inch nozzle attachment or in a large plastic bag with the edge snipped off.

19 Place the nozzle or edge of the pastry bag in the cannoli shell and squeeze to fill.

20 Place the pistachio shells on a plate and dip the cannoli ends in them.

21 Place cannoli on a platter. Dust with confectioners' sugar using a fine mesh strainer. Refrigerate until ready to serve.

TIP: If you like crispy cannoli, be sure to fill them just before serving. Filling them sooner causes the shells to soften.

Cannoli may seem intimidating to make at first, but a few special techniques and tools make them easy to execute. Keep in mind that you need 10 standard cannoli molds, a rolling pin, a pastry bag with a tip (or a plastic bag with the tip cut-off), a thermometer, a 3 ½-inch round cookie cutter, and a fine mesh strainer for best results. Some cannoli molds are sold in sets of 4, so it's best to get 2 or 3 sets so that you don't have to wait for the cannoli to cool before finishing the batch.

Be sure to allow a minimum of 3 hours to drain the ricotta cheese; if the ricotta you are using is watery, you need to drain it overnight before beginning the recipe.

If you'd like to pair this dessert with wine, look for *Malvasia delle Lipari passito* or similar.

(continued)

NOTE: Cannoli are one of the many recipes that owe their survival to the convents. Many traditional Sicilian sweets were once prepared by the women of the harem in the town of Caltanissetta during Arab rule (827-1091 CE). When the Normans forced the Arabs out of Sicily, many Muslim women took refuge in the convents and introduced their pastry-making techniques to the nuns.

Over the years the recipe took many turns and incorporated local Sicilian ingredients, such as local sheep's milk ricotta, lard, and Marsala — as well as imports from the new world, such as chocolate and the fantastic pistachios of Bronte. This recipe combines simple, good-quality ingredients that are readily available. The use of coconut oil, while not traditional, produces a light and flaky crust that mimics what is actually eaten in Sicily.

VARY IT! You can fill cannoli with Sicilian pistachio paste and chocolate cream as well as the traditional ricotta mixture. My *nonna* used to whip fresh strawberries or pineapple into her pastry cream sometimes. Leftover cannoli cream can be used to make Cassata cakes (see recipe in this chapter).

Chapter **19**

Baking Treats for Holidays and Special Occasions

There's always something to celebrate in Italy, and baked goods are the perfect way to do it!

In this chapter, you discover how to make traditional cookies and sweet treats, such as breads, *crostate* (pies), and biscuits that are emblematic of Italian holidays. These edible time capsules have been passed down from generation to generation and are especially fun to recreate with loved ones.

Baking Is Love Made Edible

In Italy, baking is as much an exercise of the heart and spirit as it is of the mind and body. Many of the cakes, breads, and savory pies that we take for granted today may have originally been created to use as offerings to the gods, edible representations of religious sacraments, ways to commemorate holidays, or demonstrations of affection. The presence of these baked goods on modern tables is a testament to maintaining the few cultural traditions which still have a place on modern tables.

This chapter is full of traditional cookies, some of which have been traced back to antiquity. The ceremonious ritual of eating the same sweets for each holiday adds heart-warming reassurance to the psyche of many Italians. Just as many Americans look forward to pumpkin pie at Thanksgiving, cookies at Christmas, and latkes for Hanukah, Italians have thousands of typical holiday treats that were historically used to celebrate Saints' Days (there's one for every day of the year), religious holidays, agrarian festivals, and so on.

This tiny sample of recipes is just a taste for the types that still exist in Italy today. In my family's *panificio*, or bread shop in Calabria, some of these recipes would be prepared along with daily bread. Others I learned from my maternal grandmother, Nonna Angela, who was an amazing baker, or from friends and family in other places in Italy. Because these recipes are a bit more labor intensive than most, are not widely available in pastry shops, and because not many people observe the smaller religious holidays anymore, they are on the verge of disappearing.

I believe that these recipes should be saved. Regardless of our spiritual and religious beliefs, it is endearing to recreate recipes that have stood the test of time. Growing up, the appearance of these recipes on a table and the sight of them being prepared evoked joyful anticipation. It's my greatest desire that they continue to be passed down to future generations and that home bakers everywhere enjoy baking and eating them as much as I do.

Petrali/Cucidati/Southern Italian Fig Cookies

PREP TIME: 60 MIN	COOK TIME: 20 MIN	YIELD: 3 DOZEN COOKIES

INGREDIENTS

For the Dough:

1 cup butter, at room temperature, plus 2 teaspoons extra for greasing baking pans

1 cup sugar

4 cups unbleached all-purpose flour, plus extra for rolling out dough

½ teaspoon salt

2 teaspoons baking powder

1 teaspoon baking soda

2 large eggs

1 teaspoon pure vanilla extract

Zest of 1 orange

½ cup freshly squeezed orange juice, or as needed

For the Filling:

1 pound dried organic white figs, or any dried figs

1 pound dried pitted dates

Zest and juice of 1 whole orange

Zest and juice of 1 whole lemon

1 pound walnuts or almonds

1 cup honey

1 small jar cherries, maraschino or sour cherries (amarene), drained

1 teaspoon cinnamon

¼ cup sugar

For the Glaze:

2 tablespoons butter

1 cup confectioners' sugar

1 teaspoon pure vanilla extract

Zest and juice of ½ orange

Sprinkles, for decoration

DIRECTIONS

1 Grease two baking sheets, each with 1 teaspoon butter.

2 **For the dough:** In a large mixing bowl, combine the sugar, flour, salt, baking powder, and baking soda.

3 Stir in the remaining 1 cup butter, mixing well to combine.

4 Mix in the eggs, vanilla, and orange zest and juice. Stir well until everything is combined.

5 Knead dough a few times in the bowl to make sure everything is incorporated.

6 **For the filling:** Place the figs in a saucepan, and cover with water. Simmer on low heat until soft, about 5 minutes, and then cut off the stems.

7 Drain the figs, and place them in a food processor with the dates; add orange and lemon zest and juice, and process. Add walnuts, honey, cherries, cinnamon, and sugar. Process until combined.

8 Preheat oven to 350 degrees.

9 **To shape the dough:** On a lightly floured surface, roll out the dough into a rectangle, approximately ⅛-inch thick. The dough should feel soft and buttery, similar to a pie dough, while rolling it out.

10 Make strips 4 inches in length across the diameter of the dough (using the same process as you would for ravioli).

11 Place a 1 ½-inch ribbon of filling down the center of the dough strip.

(continued)

12 Roll the dough over to cover the filling. Press down to seal dough and cut it with a pizza cutter or knife into 1-inch diagonal pieces.

13 Place cookies onto greased or parchment-lined baking sheet leaving ½-inch in between cookies.

14 Bake until lightly golden, about 15-20 minutes.

15 Remove from oven, and allow to cool.

16 **For the glaze:** Whisk butter and confectioners' sugar together in a bowl. Add vanilla and orange zest, and stir well to incorporate.

17 Add orange juice, a bit at a time, until you achieve a glaze consistency.

18 Spoon glaze over cookies as soon as they are cool, and top with sprinkles.

TIP: I usually make larger batches of this cookie, to freeze and share with all of my friends and family, and I always make the filling the day before, if possible.

If the figs or dates that you are using seem hard or dry, soak them in water overnight to plump them up before making these cookies.

If you'd like to pair this dessert with wine, look for *Moscatello di Saracena* or similar.

NOTE: My Nonna Angela always rolled out her dough as thin as possible so the filling would take center stage.

VARY IT! In a pinch, good-quality Mediterranean fig and walnut preserves can be substituted for the homemade filling. It's also a good idea to make extra homemade filling to use as preserves. Serve on toasted Italian bread with cheese for breakfast or a delicious snack.

Mostaccioli/Chocolate Holiday Cookies

PREP TIME: 15 MIN	COOK TIME: 20 MIN	YIELD: APPROXIMATELY 3 DOZEN COOKIES

INGREDIENTS

For the Cookies:

2 eggs

1 ¼ cups sugar

1 ½ cups heavy cream

¾ cup Amy Riolo Selections or other good-quality extra virgin olive oil

2 tablespoons baking powder

1 teaspoon ground cloves

½ teaspoon cinnamon

¼ teaspoon nutmeg

½ teaspoon salt

⅓ cup cocoa powder, Fair Trade Certified if possible

2 teaspoons pure vanilla extract

4 cups unbleached all-purpose flour

½ cup toasted walnuts

1 cup mini chocolate chips, Fair Trade Certified if possible

For the Glaze:

1 cup semisweet chocolate, Fair Trade Certified if possible

3 tablespoons heavy cream

Pinch of salt

DIRECTIONS

1 Preheat the oven to 300 degrees. Spray a large baking tray with cooking spray.

2 In a large mixing bowl, vigorously mix the eggs, sugar, cream, oil, baking powder, cloves, cinnamon, nutmeg, salt, cocoa, and vanilla extract. Slowly add flour to form cookie dough. Stir in the walnuts and chocolate chips.

3 Roll the dough into balls 1 ½ inches in diameter and place on the baking tray. To keep them from rolling, carefully press down on the balls on the baking tray.

4 Bake for 8-10 minutes, or until the cookies are just about to crack. Remove the cookies from the oven, and place on a cooling rack.

5 **For the optional glaze:** Add the chocolate to a heatproof bowl, and place it over a pan of simmering water (creating a double boiler). Whisk the chocolate until melted and smooth. Remove from the heat, and whisk in the heavy cream and salt until the mixture is homogenous.

6 Dip the tip of each cookie into the glaze, and put it back on the cooling rack to dry completely (15-20 minutes). Store in an airtight container for one week or freeze for one month.

TIP: If you'd like to pair this dessert with wine, look for *Primitivo passito* or similar.

NOTE: Every region of Italy from Rome South has its own version of *Mostaccioli*. This is the Roman version.

VARY IT! Skip the glaze, if desired, and add dried fruit, such as cherries, apricots, or dates to the cookies instead.

Occhi di Santa Lucia/Santa Lucia's Eyes Cookies

PREP TIME: 30 MIN | COOK TIME: 20 MIN | YIELD: 4 DOZEN COOKIES

INGREDIENTS

For the Cookies:

¾ cup dry white wine, Puglian if possible

¾ cup Amy Riolo Selections, or other good-quality extra virgin olive oil

5 cups unbleached all-purpose flour

¾ cup sugar

Pinch of salt

1 teaspoon baking powder

For the Glaze:

3 cups confectioners' sugar

Juice of ½ lemon

¼ cup hot water

DIRECTIONS

1 Preheat oven to 350 degrees. Line two large baking sheets with parchment paper.

2 In a large bowl combine wine and olive oil, and stir to combine. Stir in the flour, sugar, salt, and baking powder.

3 Mix well to combine ingredients, and continue mixing until dough forms a ball.

4 Pinch off small pieces of dough to form 1-inch balls. On a clean surface, roll each ball into a 3-inch-long cylinder. Bring two ends together and pinch in center to form a circle.

5 Place cookies ¼-inch apart on the baking sheet. Bake for 15-20 minutes until the cookies are hard and bottoms just begin to turn golden.

6 Remove the cookies from the oven, and allow to cool on baking sheet.

7 **For the glaze:** Mix confectioners' sugar, lemon juice, and hot water in a large bowl. If needed, add more hot water, a tablespoon at a time, until the glaze is smooth and glossy and ready to coat the cookies.

8 Place a piece of aluminum foil or wax paper on a work surface, and set a large cooling rack over it.

9 Dip cookies in the glaze, and set on the cooling rack until the glaze hardens. Store cookies in an airtight container for up to three days or freeze for up to one month.

TIP: If you'd like to pair this dessert with wine, look for *Cartizze* or similar.

NOTE: I love these cookies because, in addition to their satisfying flavor, they are full of Southern Italian staples: flour, olive oil, and wine. In the region of Puglia, traditional *taralli* (which are normally savory) are enrobed in lemon-scented sugar on the occasion of Santa Lucia Day, December 13. St. Lucia of Syracuse (283–304 CE), also known as Saint Lucy or Saint Lucia, was a young Christian martyr born into a noble Sicilian family. St. Lucia was martyred in 304 CE. The most common story told about St. Lucia is that she would secretly bring food to the persecuted Christians in Rome, who lived in hiding in the catacombs under the city. She would wear a candle on her head so she had both her hands free to carry things. The name Lucia is derived from "luce" meaning "light," and she is now known as the patron saint of light. She also is believed to help with healing eye ailments. In Italy, it is believed that even Dante asked for her assistance and was healed. December 13 was also the Winter Solstice, the shortest day of the year, in the old Julian calendar, and a pagan festival of lights in Sweden was turned into St. Lucia's Day. The remains of her body are kept at Santi Germania e Lucia church in Venice.

VARY IT! Omit the sugar and the glaze from this recipe to make savory *taralli* cookies to eat with wine and cheese or as part of an appetizer.

Biscotti di regina/Calabrian Sesame Cookies

PREP TIME: 20 MIN	COOK TIME: 20 MIN	YIELD: 2 DOZEN COOKIES

INGREDIENTS

2 ¼ cups unbleached all-purpose flour, plus extra for work surface

⅓ cup sugar

1 ½ teaspoons baking powder

Pinch of salt

⅓ cup butter, at room temperature

⅓ cup whole milk

2 teaspoons pure vanilla extract

¾ cup sesame seeds, untoasted

DIRECTIONS

1 Preheat oven to 375 degrees. Line two cookie sheets with parchment paper or silicone mats.

2 Combine flour, sugar, baking powder, and salt in a large bowl.

3 Stir in butter, and mix well to combine.

4 Combine milk and vanilla in a small bowl, and stir into mixture. Mix ingredients well to form a dough, and turn out onto a lightly floured work surface.

5 Pour sesame seeds onto a plate. Break off 1-inch pieces of dough, and roll them to create finger shapes.

6 Roll in sesame seeds to coat. Place on baking sheets, and flatten top of cookies slightly with a finger. Bake for 18-20 minutes, or until very light golden. Store cookies in an airtight container at room temperature for one week or in the freezer for up to one month.

TIP: You can make the dough a day in advance and form the cookies the next day.

If you'd like to pair this dessert with wine, look for *Famoso frizzante dry* or similar.

NOTE: These cookies are a family favorite. Since antiquity, sesame seeds were seen as symbols of fertility. For this reason, in the Southern Italian province of Calabria, they are served on Christmas Day and at weddings. Their Italian name means "queen's cookies" in honor of the Virgin Mary.

Cozzupe di Pasqua/Calabrian Easter Bread

PREP TIME: 30 MIN	COOK TIME: 30 MIN PLUS 3 HOURS RISING TIME	YIELD: 2 DOZEN ROLLS

INGREDIENTS

For the Bread:

2 dozen hard-boiled eggs, colored, if desired (see Step 1)

4 (0.6 ounce) fresh yeast loaves, or 3 (0.6 ounce) packets active dry yeast

3 cups lukewarm water

5 pounds all-purpose flour

Zest of 1 orange

Zest of 1 lemon

4 teaspoons salt

¼ cup sugar

3 heaping tablespoons butter, plus extra for greasing pans

6 large eggs, lightly beaten

1 ¾ cup freshly squeezed orange juice

For the Icing:

1 cup confectioners' sugar

Juice and zest of 1 orange

1 teaspoon pure vanilla extract

Whole milk, as needed

DIRECTIONS

1 Prepare hard-boiled eggs, and color them if desired, early on the day you bake the bread or the day before.

2 **For the bread:** Combine yeast and water in a medium bowl. Allow to stand for 15 minutes, or until frothy.

3 Add the flour, orange and lemon zest, salt, and sugar to a large bowl, and stir. Add the butter, eggs, and orange juice. Add the yeast mixture, and mix completely to incorporate. Form dough into a ball, and place on a lightly floured work surface.

4 Knead for 5-10 minutes, or until dough is firm and elastic. Grease a very large bowl with butter, place dough inside, and turn to coat. Cover with greased plastic wrap and clean kitchen towels. Allow to rise for 1 ½ hours.

5 Punch dough down with your hands and allow to rise for another hour.

6 Break off pieces of dough the size of a small tangerine.

7 Roll each piece into a 6-inch rope. Wrap each rope around an egg. The egg should be covered with a 1-inch border all the way around (see Figure 19-1).

8 Break off another small piece of dough to form a ribbon around the base of the egg (forming a barrier between the bread and the egg), and cross the ends over one another.

9 Preheat oven to 350 degrees. Place rolls on a cookie sheet, and allow to rise until doubled in size. Bake 20-30 minutes until golden brown.

10 **For the icing:** Make the icing by combining the confectioners' sugar with the orange juice and vanilla.

(continued)

11 Whisk in milk, a few tablespoons at a time, until a smooth, shiny glaze forms. Set aside. While breads are still slightly warm, brush with glaze and allow to dry. Serve individually at breakfast or as edible centerpieces or place holders on Easter. These are also taken on picnics and eaten with cheese, cured meats, and wine on *la Pasquetta* (Easter Monday).

TIP: When making this recipe, I always color the eggs the day before and prep all the ingredients the night before baking.

If you'd like to pair this dessert with wine, look for *Mantonico passito* or similar.

NOTE: Calabrian *cuzzupe* are one of the most famous regional baked goods. Made only at Easter, I learned this specialty from my Nonna Angela. There are many incorrect articles about the origins of this recipe, but it actually comes from the word *koutsouna,* which means "doll." There are many varieties of Greek Easter breads in addition to the iconic braided *tsoureki.* Some are shaped like dolls, others like Jesus's feet, others are formed into chests and snails, and each one has a special symbolism. My *nonna* always said that the egg in the middle of the bread represented Jesus in the womb of the Madonna.

VARY IT! In Sicily, there is another version of this bread called *pupa cu 'l'ova* in dialect or "doll with an egg." It is a slightly crunchier texture than this dough. It can be made by cutting the egg quantity in half and replacing the orange juice with water. At Step 6, instead of using tangerine-sized balls of dough to cover eggs, break off a smaller piece, the size of a medium egg, to roll and wrap around the egg.

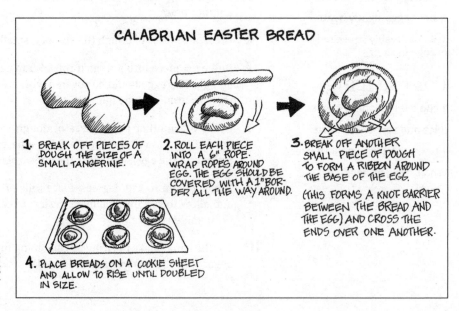

FIGURE 19-1:
Shaping
Calabrian Easter
Bread.

Colomba/Traditional Easter Dove Bread

PREP TIME: 30 MIN	COOK TIME: 3 HOURS RISING TIME PLUS 30 MIN	YIELD: 10 SERVINGS

INGREDIENTS

For the Dough:

½ cup whole milk, warmed to not more than 120 degrees

¼ cup sugar

¼ cup honey

3 eggs

Zest of 1 lemon

Zest of 2 oranges

4 cups all-purpose flour, plus extra if necessary

1 teaspoon salt

2 ½ teaspoons instant or fast acting yeast

4 tablespoons unsalted butter, at room temperature

1 cup chocolate chips (Fair Trade Certified if possible), raisins, dried chopped fruit, or candied citron

For the Glaze:

1 egg white

1 teaspoon almond extract

Handful of whole almonds

DIRECTIONS

1 In the bowl of a stand mixer fitted with a dough hook, combine the milk, sugar, honey, eggs, and both zests. Turn the mixer on low, and add flour, salt, and yeast. Mix until the dough comes together to form a wet ball. If dough does not come together, add an additional ½ cup flour, until you get a dough consistency.

2 Allow the mixer to run on low for 4 minutes, or until the dough is smooth. With the mixer running on low, add the butter, 1 tablespoon at a time, until it is all incorporated. Mix in the chocolate chips, raisins, dried fruit, or candied citron, if using.

3 Cover bowl with plastic wrap, and allow the dough to rise in a warm place until doubled in size, about 1 hour.

4 Line a baking sheet with parchment paper or cooking spray. After the dough has risen, turn it out onto a lightly floured surface and divide it in half.

5 Roll one of the halves into a 12-inch log and place it in the middle of the cookie sheet. Form the other half into a 15-inch-long triangle with a 6-inch-wide base. Place the triangle over the log so the wide end extends 4 inches below the log and the pointed end extends above it (see Figure 19-2).

6 Form the pointed end into the dove's head, and arrange chocolate chips or fruit to be the eye. Cut five incisions in the bottom of the triangle and fan it out to resemble the tail.

7 Cut the sides of the log into wings. Cover the dove and allow to rise for another hour. When the dove has risen, preheat the oven to 350 degrees. Mix the almond extract with the egg white, and brush it over the entire top and sides of the dove.

(continued)

8 Press the almonds along the base of the tail feather and wings in order to outline the design. Bake for 30–40 minutes, or until golden and fluffy. Allow to cool before enjoying.

TIP: The *colomba* can be made ahead of time, wrapped in plastic, and frozen until serving.

If you'd like to pair this dessert with wine, look for *Franciacorta Satén* or similar.

NOTE: This delicious bread, which resembles *brioche,* can be made in cake pans and enjoyed at breakfast throughout the year. The dove shape makes a fantastic centerpiece. Individual baby doves with the guests' names tied around the necks make great table place markers. Traditionally, almonds and large sugar granules are used to decorate the top.

Numerous legends surround this cake. According to one, the Milanese, locked in battle with the Emperor Frederick Barbarossa just after Easter in 1176, saw the struggle turn in their favor when three doves flew from the nearby church. The legend says that ever since, Milanese have celebrated their victory by eating cakes in the shape of a dove.

VARY IT! I like to make miniature c*olombe* at Easter time to eat, as well to give as gifts.

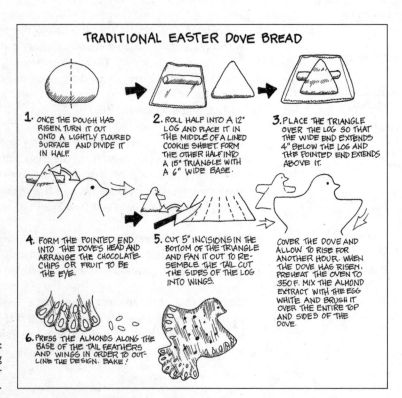

FIGURE 19-2:
Shaping
Traditional Easter
Dove Bread.

TRADITIONAL EASTER DOVE BREAD

1. ONCE THE DOUGH HAS RISEN, TURN IT OUT ONTO A LIGHTLY FLOURED SURFACE AND DIVIDE IT IN HALF.

2. ROLL HALF INTO A 12" LOG AND PLACE IT IN THE MIDDLE OF A LINED COOKIE SHEET. FORM THE OTHER HALF INTO A 15" TRIANGLE WITH A 6" WIDE BASE.

3. PLACE THE TRIANGLE OVER THE LOG SO THAT THE WIDE END EXTENDS 4" BELOW THE LOG AND THE POINTED END EXTENDS ABOVE IT.

4. FORM THE POINTED END INTO THE DOVE'S HEAD AND ARRANGE THE CHOCOLATE CHIPS OR FRUIT TO BE THE EYE.

5. CUT 5" INCISIONS IN THE BOTTOM OF THE TRIANGLE AND FAN IT OUT TO RESEMBLE THE TAIL. CUT THE SIDES OF THE LOG INTO WINGS.

COVER THE DOVE AND ALLOW TO RISE FOR ANOTHER HOUR. WHEN THE DOVE HAS RISEN, PREHEAT THE OVEN TO 350 F. MIX THE ALMOND EXTRACT WITH THE EGG WHITE AND BRUSH IT OVER THE ENTIRE TOP AND SIDES OF THE DOVE.

6. PRESS THE ALMONDS ALONG THE BASE OF THE TAIL FEATHERS AND WINGS IN ORDER TO OUTLINE THE DESIGN. BAKE!

Pastiera Napoletana/Neapolitan Easter Pie

PREP TIME: 30 MIN	COOK TIME: 2 HOURS 45 MIN PLUS 30 MIN CHILL TIME	YIELD: 10 SERVINGS

INGREDIENTS

1 ¼ cups wheat berries

2 cups whole milk

1 tablespoon ground cinnamon

Zest of 1 orange

1 teaspoon pure vanilla extract

4 cups unbleached all-purpose flour

9 ounces unsalted butter divided

1 ⅔ cup sugar, divided

1 ⅔ cups sugar

Pinch of salt

8 large eggs, divided

2 ½ cups whole-milk ricotta cheese (In Italy sheep's milk is used)

¼ cup of candied citron and orange, diced

2 teaspoons orange blossom extract

Zest of 1 lemon

DIRECTIONS

1 Cook wheat berries in a saucepan of boiling water for 2 hours, stirring occasionally. Drain the wheat berries, and place back in the saucepan with milk and cinnamon, orange zest, and vanilla.

2 Bring mixture to a boil, reduce heat, and cook until the milk is absorbed, stirring occasionally, approximately 15 minutes. Let cool.

3 For the dough, mix flour, butter, ⅔ cup sugar, and salt in a large bowl until it resembles bread crumbs. Add 2 eggs, and mix with your hands until combined. Use your hands to shape the dough into a ball. Place in the refrigerator in a bowl sealed with plastic wrap for at least 30 minutes.

4 Mix the ricotta with the remaining 1 cup sugar.

5 Separate 2 eggs, and set the egg whites aside. Beat yolks with the ricotta mixture. Add the remaining 4 whole eggs, and whisk until incorporated. Add the lemon zest, candied fruit, and orange blossom extract.

6 Beat the egg whites until stiff, and fold into the ricotta mixture along with the cooked wheat berry mixture.

7 Preheat the oven to 350 degrees. Grease and flour a 10-inch springform pan. Roll out about two-thirds of the dough on a floured surface until it is about ¼-inch thick. Transfer to the pan. Cut off any overhang. Cover the dough with the ricotta and wheat mixture.

(continued)

8 Roll out remaining dough to about ¼-inch thick, and cut into 10 strips around 1-inch wide. Lay the pastry dough strips across the top of the filling in a crisscross diamond pattern. Press the strips gently to adhere to the edges of the pastry.

9 Bake for 1 hour and 30 minutes until golden. Remove from the oven, and let cool for at least 8 hours in a dry place.

TIP: When I make *pastiera,* I usually make them over a course of three days. On the first day, I cook the grain (you can also buy precooked *grano cotto* in Italian stores). On the second day, I make the dough and filling and bake the pies. I let them cool overnight and serve on the third day for maximum flavor.

If you'd like to pair this dessert with wine, look for *Asprinio di Aversa Spumante Metodo Classico* or similar.

NOTE: This is a classic Easter dessert. Wheat berries are eaten all over the Mediterranean to symbolize spring and rebirth in a custom that has been popular since antiquity.

VARY IT! For a creamier filling, purée some of the cooked wheat berries in Step 6 and then incorporate with the rest of the mixture.

Taralli dolci al vino rosso/Sweet Red Wine Biscuits

PREP TIME: 20 MIN	COOK TIME: 20 MIN	YIELD: 4 DOZEN BISCUITS

INGREDIENTS

¾ cup red wine

¾ cup Amy Riolo Selections, or other good-quality extra virgin olive oil

1 ½ cups unbleached all-purpose flour

¾ cup sugar, plus extra for coating

Pinch of salt

1 teaspoon baking powder

1 teaspoon ground cinnamon

DIRECTIONS

1 Preheat oven to 350 degrees. Line two large baking sheets with parchment paper.

2 In a large bowl combine wine and olive oil, and stir to combine. Stir in the flour, sugar, salt, baking powder, and cinnamon. Mix well to combine ingredients. Continue mixing until dough forms a ball.

3 Pinch off small pieces of dough to form 1-inch balls. On a clean surface, roll each ball into a 3-inch cylinder. Bring two ends together and pinch in center to form a circle.

4 Place ½ cup additional sugar on a plate, and dip cookies in sugar to coat.

5 Place cookies ¼-inch apart on the baking sheet. Bake for 15-20 minutes until the cookies are hard and bottoms just begin to turn golden. Remove the cookies from the oven and allow to cool.

TIP: I always save leftover red wine to make this recipe.

If you'd like to pair this dessert with wine, look for *Burson passito* or similar.

NOTE: *Taralli dolci* are a Puglian specialty. Their crunchy texture is perfect for dipping into coffee or sweet wine.

VARY IT! This recipe also can be made with white wine.

Chapter **20**

Making the Dough You Know and Love: Bread, Pizza, and Focaccia

The ritual of baking is much more important than a means to satisfy hunger — it is a link to our past and a patrimony to pass down to future generations. When we bake, we also lose our worries by engaging in a mindful activity that benefits our psyche as much as our palate.

Whatever your reason for baking is, I can guarantee that like other activities in life, what you put into it is what you get out of it, and if you are willing to get lost in the process, baking can be extremely rewarding and therapeutic.

REMEMBER

Even if you've never baked before, don't be intimidated by the recipes in this chapter. When you are ready to start, decide which recipe interests you and read it over a few times. Have your ingredients ready and dedicate a few hours to what might just become your favorite pastime. You'll be amazed to see what a beautiful recipe you can create with just a few ingredients in the comfort of your own home.

In this chapter, you will learn about the significance of savory baking in the Italian culture, how to make your own dough, and the difference between various types of bread, pizza, and focaccia recipes.

Baking Bread: A Time-Honored Italian Tradition

"Buono come il pane" means that something is "as good as bread," and in the Italian language, that's a huge compliment. Warm like bread, soft like bread, and easily like bread are all expressions that exemplify just how much Italians love bread. For Italians, who, according to a recent news report, consume the most amount of bread of any European nation, bread truly does represent life.

The enticing scent of bread fresh from the oven immediately takes me back to the warmth and home of my Nonna's kitchen and the *centro storico* (historic center) in my ancestral homeland of Calabria.

Some of our Italian relatives owned *panifici*, or bread shops, where, in addition to dozens of everyday breads, bakers prepare ceremonial breads for holidays and special occasions.

Every neighborhood has a bread shop, or *panificio*, in Italy, where you are surrounded by the most beautiful breads, all made with natural leaveners and longer rising times that produce amazing results. Because good bread is so highly prized, bread-making is a craft that is taken seriously. Historically, a community was not complete without a *panificio*, because people did not have ovens at home, so they relied on the local shop for their daily bread. Even though large supermarkets now exist in Italy, most people still prefer to get their bread from an artisan bakery, where top-quality ingredients and traditional techniques provide delicious and wholesome loaves.

During my grandmother's era, home ovens became more popular, and baking bread in the home was a regular activity in Italy. Nowadays, however, most people buy their bread outside of the home, and the ritual has lost much of its appeal. One of the positive side effects of the lockdown due to the Covid-19 pandemic was that people started baking at home again, and we are seeing a renaissance of home bakers both in Italy and the U.S.

TIP

Whenever I bake bread, I always make extra and freeze the remaining loaves in plastic wrap and a plastic bag. Whenever the mood strikes, you can thaw the bread on the counter for a few hours or so and reheat it before serving.

ITALIAN BREAD: COUNT THE WAYS

It is estimated that there are 300 "official" different types of bread in Italy.

Like all other authentic traditional foods in the country, each town, region, and province claims its own types of bread. Some of Italy's historic bread recipes are so interwoven with the culture at large that they are considered part of the nation's intangible cultural heritage and are protected by organizations such as Slow Food.

These are some of the most common types of Italian bread available abroad:

Brioche col tuppo: Brioche with a knot on the top is a typical breakfast pastry.

Ciabatta: This slipper-shaped flattish bread hails from Tuscany originally.

Colomba di Pasqua: The Easter Dove (see Chapter 19 for recipe) is a holiday tradition.

Cornetto: An Italian croissant (made with a sourdough leavener), this is lighter than French varieties.

Farinata: Ligurian chickpea bread.

Filone: Italian-style baguettes.

Focaccia Ligure: This is the commonly found focaccia recipe in the U.S.

Focaccia Pugliese: Made with potatoes; has a different, but equally delicious texture as the Ligurian variety.

Friselle: Twice-baked bread rusks that resemble large bagel chips are reconstituted in water or EVOO and topped with a variety of ingredients (they were originally enjoyed by shepherds in the fields).

Grissini: These long, thin, crunchy cracker-like breadsticks grace many Italian dinner tables.

Michetta (also known as rosetta rolls): Part of many restaurant bread baskets and used to make sandwiches, these rolls have a very crunchy exterior and perfect crumb. I have yet to find anything similar in the U.S.

Panbrioche: This brioche loaf of bread is used for breakfast toast.

(continued)

(continued)

Pan Carrè: Similar to American sandwich bread, very thin slices are used to make *tramezzini*, typical Italian sandwiches and finger food sold in bars.

Pandoro: This brioche-type sweet bread is made for holidays.

Pane Carasau: Very thin Sardinian traditional flatbread that is similar to a large cracker, is perfect for serving with antipasti, on its own, or to sop up sauces.

Pane Sciocco: Saltless bread found in Tuscany, Umbria, and the Marche that is perfect for cured meat and cheese sandwiches (since they contain a great deal of salt). *Sciocco* means foolish in English.

Pane Casareccio: This homemade bread is popular all over Italy.

Pane di Altamura: Puglia's prized artisan bread made from re-milled semolina wheat in the province of Bari and has DOP status (see Chapter 5).

Pane di Cutro: Calabria's prized artisan bread has been nominated for DOP status and is made of 75% durum wheat and 25% tender (spring) wheat. It is prepared in large, round, flattish loaves.

Pane di Matera: Basilicata's prized artisan bread is made from durum wheat, semolina flour, and natural yeast. It has IGP status (see Chapter 5) and is known for its crusty exterior and porous, golden-colored crumb.

Panettone: This Italian Christmas yeast-bread is made from a brioche base and traditionally candied fruit, and is now available in scores of flavors and various filling options.

Panini al latte: Milk rolls that can be eaten at breakfast or with a meal.

Piadina: Griddle bread from Emiglia Romagna that is used to make street food and wrapped snacks.

Pizza Bianca: White pizza that is also similar to focaccia; it can be eaten alone as a bread or topped with other ingredients as a pizza.

Pizza Napoletana: This UNESCO protected recipe is part of the city of Naples' cultural patrimony (see the section dedicated to it in this chapter).

Schiacciata all'uva: This form of focaccia or flatbread is made with grapes during the grape harvest.

Sfincione: This Sicilian-style "sponge"-like pizza with tomato topping that is the ancestor of modern "Sicilian" pizza and Italian-American tomato pies.

Taralli: These traditional bread crackers, originally from Puglia, are now popular everywhere.

Making a Premier Pizza Pie

While many American and international pizzas focus on toppings, the original Italian versions of pizza are all about the dough. The proper level of hydration (water to flour content), right types of flour, water, yeast, and salt, time-honored techniques, and adequate leavening times are just a few of the ingredients needed to make good pizza crust. In Italy, the crust of the pizza is the foundation, and without the right dough, no topping can salvage a poor crust base. For that reason, the art of pizza making and the authentic pizza recipes themselves are protected by the Italian government.

Professionally speaking, making pizza has always been one of the most rewarding recipes for me. As brand ambassador for the Pizza University and Culinary Arts Center, I have learned so much, not only about making pizza in wood-burning and brick pizza ovens, but also about the role of a true *pizzaiolo*.

Like many Italians and Italian-Americans, I used to make pizza with my grandmother. We did not know the techniques and standards that professional pizzaioli use today. For us, as kids growing up, if there was a hot oven and dough on a Saturday night, we knew we were in for a delicious treat — and I think that is still the allure of fresh, homemade pizza today — it turns any old time into a party.

Thanks to the Pizza University and Culinary Arts Center, I was certified with Maestro Pizzaiolo Enzo Coccia's master class on "The Culture of Neapolitan Pizza Cooked in a Wood-Oven" in March 2019. When you study with a master pizzaiolo, you don't just learn about pizza, you get metaphors for life, and that is what pizza is to Neapolitans — life.

You might be surprised to learn that pizza, a food most Americans associate with fast-food or junk food, can be part of a healthy meal plan. Making pizza healthful is simple; it must be prepared according to traditional methods and using the best ingredients. What often is called pizza in the U.S. (where more "pizza" is eaten per capita than in Italy) is very different from what earns the title *Vera Pizza Napoletana* in Naples. A few years ago, UNESCO rightfully granted authentic Neapolitan pizza a place on its cultural heritage list, and to be authentic, there is a list of government-mandated requirements that must be followed.

Nowadays, one of the world's most beloved foods is offered in many different styles, shapes, and flavor profiles (see the nearby sidebar); New York, Chicago, Napoli, Sicily, Rome, and Detroit are each known for their own signature recipes.

Even though the majority of us don't have brick ovens that reach up to 1,000 degrees in our homes, we can still make utterly mouthwatering pies that are much healthier than most delivery options.

Note that the pizza recipes in this chapter are what most professional *pizzaioli* would consider "Grandma style" because they have been adapted for home ovens. In Italy, most households had the tradition of making pizza on Saturday and Sunday nights. What the *pizze* made by the *casalinghe*, or housewives, lacked in uniformity, they more than made up for in flavor, and I am always happy to be invited to partake in them.

TIP

You can make large batches of the dough and freeze it in individual quantities, wrapped loosely in oiled plastic wrap and placed in a freezer bag for up to a month. I usually do this so I can have dough on hand whenever I'm craving a pizza. You can also use the same dough for *calzoni* and *stromboli* as well.

Getting Familiar with Focaccia: A Bread for Many Occasions

In the Italian dictionary, *focaccia* is described as "a flattened bread, often with the addition of a condiment and various ingredients." While focaccia recipes may vary from place to place, and baker to baker, the dough should be similar to a bread dough. *Focaccia* is usually rectangular shaped but can also be served round in certain places, and especially when it is served in a sweet way. Use your *focaccia* to make sandwiches, or cut in thin strips and serve with dinner.

The word *focaccia* is a northern Italian dialect word that refers to a creation that comes from fire. Originally, this type of uneven bread was the result of using dough to test oven temperatures. The way it rose told bakers where the oven was hottest. Eventually, the misshapen loaves grew in popularity and became a tradition of their own. Nowadays, no matter where you buy focaccia, they are almost always sold as uniformly shaped loaves, but I tend to covet the misshapen ones as a nod back to their roots as ancient, edible oven thermometers.

In some areas of Italy, *focaccia* is known as *pizza bianca* (or white pizza). During the grape harvest, it is studded with grapes and referred to as *schiacciata*. The traditional Genovese version of *focaccia* requires making a sponge first, but this is a more straightforward method. The region of Puglia is also known for its *focaccia*, which incorporates mashed potato along with the flour in the recipe, and is usu-ally studded with cherry tomatoes and fresh herbs.

Wrap leftovers in plastic wrap and aluminum foil to freeze.

TYPES OF PIZZA IN ITALY AND AROUND THE WORLD

One of the things we do at the Pizza University and Culinary Arts Center is to categorize and classify different styles of pizza so they don't erroneously get lumped under one category. While there were traces of ancient pizzas in Egypt, Greece, and Rome, our modern pizzas do descend directly from Neapolitan versions. Where we have gone from there, however, is quite different.

We often are asked about the differences between the various styles. This is how we define them:

- **New York-style** pizza is known for having a thin crust and a crunchy texture. Low-moisture and slightly dried fresh mozzarella, along with American or other toma-toes (they don't have to be San Marzano) are preferred. Optimal hydration for this style is 60-63%, while the pizzas should be baked in a 480–550-degree oven.

- **Sicilian** pizza is known for its thick crust, which can be up to 1 inch thick; it's cooked in an oiled pan. Sicilian pizza has up to 70% hydration and is cooked with the bot-tom of the oven set at a higher temperature than the top to create the signature crispy crust. Normally, this is around 540 degrees on top with 570 degrees on bot-tom for a total baking time of 10-12 minutes. Because this pizza has a thicker style, it usually incorporates slightly sweeter tomatoes and low-moisture mozzarella. The Sicilian pizza should be crunchy on the outside and soft on the inside. Another style, "Grandma" pizza, is made from the same dough as Sicilian, but slightly less thick. Both styles are directly influenced by Sicilian immigrants who prepared an adapted version of their traditional *sfincione* in the United States.

- **Detroit-style** pizza uses the same dough as the Sicilian and "Grandma" styles. What distinguishes it, however, is the way in which it is topped and its border. When pre-paring the Detroit-style pizza, Brick Cheese from Wisconsin is sprinkled along the sides of the pan between the pan and the crust to make a very crunchy, slightly charred crust. The pizza dough is first topped with mozzarella and then baked while the tomato sauce is slow-cooked separately and then used to top the pizza after the cheese has already melted.

(continued)

(continued)

- **Chicago-style** pizza is known as *deep dish;* this thick dough (almost double that of other styles) is made with both corn meal and butter to give it a buttery and flaky texture. It uses less than 58% hydration making it drier than the other styles. This is because the crust needs to be firmer in order to hold all the ingredients. Chicago-style dough is rolled out and placed in a pan. A layer of mozzarella is placed on top, followed by all the toppings (such as meat and vegetables). The pizza is finished with a layer of diced tomatoes and Parmesan cheese. Chicago-style pizza should be baked at 420 degrees for 25-30 minutes.

- There are two types of pizza associated with the city of **Rome:** One is long and baked directly on the stones, while the other is square and cut *al taglio* — by the piece in *tavole calde* in Rome. Normally, when Roman pizza styles are discussed, they are talking about the rectangular *pizza al taglio* sold by the slice and weighed to go, or of Pinsa which is oblong and can be sold to go or in *pizzerie*. Pinsa dough, which is becoming increasingly popular in the U.S., is a very moist dough with at least 75% hydration. It is baked in a 480–500-degree oven for approximately 5 minutes to give it its signature (very crunchy) exterior.

- Out of the Neapolitan style, the **Neo-Neapolitan style** was born. This method uses the same dough as the Neapolitan and similar ingredients, but it's cooked in an oven that is heated between 700-730 degrees in 2 to 2 ½ minutes. The higher temperature and shorter cooking time produce a crunchier exterior.

- The **California pizza** boom began in the 1970s and 1980s when California's top chefs began creating gourmet pizzas with unique, fresh, and local ingredients. At that time, the thought of topping a pizza with grilled chicken, red onions, and BBQ sauce or truffles and caviar was unheard of. But when Bay Area chefs, such as Alice Waters, Ed LaDou, and Wolfgang Puck, began transforming wood-fired pizzas into decadent displays of culinary art, the idea spread quickly. Soon chefs and *pizzaioli* (pizza makers) everywhere were inspired to use pizza dough as blank culinary canvases that could become as elegant and luxurious as a classic dish destined for fine dining.

Filoni/Italian Baguettes

PREP TIME: 20 MIN	COOK TIME: 30 MIN PLUS ROUGHLY 2 HOURS RISING TIME	YIELD: 8 SERVINGS

INGREDIENTS

1 tablespoon active dry yeast

1 ½ cups warm water (110–115 degrees), divided

1 tablespoon sugar

4 cups unbleached bread flour, divided, plus extra for work surface

1 teaspoon unrefined sea salt

2 tablespoons olive oil, divided

Sprinkle of cornmeal

DIRECTIONS

1 In a large bowl, mix yeast into ½ cup warm water. Mix well until combined. Let the mixture sit in the bowl for 4-5 minutes, until the yeast is dissolved.

2 Add sugar, 2 cups flour (or gluten-free), and the remaining cup of water to the bowl; mix with mixer or a wooden spoon until smooth. The dough will resemble a batter. Let stand for 10 minutes or so, until mixture rises and bubbles a little in the bowl.

3 Add salt, 1 tablespoon oil, and ½ cup flour, and mix. Continue adding flour, ½ cup at a time, and mixing it in until it is all added. Mix until the dough forms a ball. Dump the ball of dough on the countertop, and gather it into a ball.

4 Lightly dust a work surface, and place the dough on top. Sprinkle flour on the dough and your hands, and knead the dough, adding more flour, if necessary, until the ball is smooth but slightly sticky.

5 Grease another mixing bowl with the remaining 1 tablespoon olive oil. Place the dough into the bowl, and turn to coat. Cover with a kitchen towel, and place in an oven set to the proof setting (about 100 degrees), or cover with additional towels and set in a warm place. Allow the dough to rise until it doubles in size, about 1 hour.

(continued)

6 Turn the risen dough onto a floured surface, and roll and pull until you've shaped a 16-inch-long loaf. (You can also make two 8-inch loaves.) Place the loaf on a greased baking sheet sprinkled with cornmeal.

7 Cover the loaf with a clean kitchen towel, and let it rise until it doubles in size, about 45 minutes. Make 6–8 diagonal slashes in the top of the loaf using a very sharp knife. Bake at 400 degrees for 25–30 minutes, or until nicely browned. Cool on wire rack.

TIP: As you knead the dough, resist the urge to add too much flour; the dough should be slightly sticky but compact enough to work with. Stickier dough, although a bit fastidious to work with, produces a better internal texture of the bread.

For crispier crust, preheat the oven to 425 degrees and spray the inside of the oven with water in a mist bottle before adding the bread and reducing temperature to 400 degrees.

VARY IT! Add your favorite ingredients in Step 6 — ¼ cup of any of the following to give the *filoni* your own touch: chopped, pitted, olives; grated aged cheese; chopped nuts; or sesame seeds.

Pane casareccio/Homestyle Bread

PREP TIME: 20 MIN	COOK TIME: 40 MIN PLUS AT LEAST 2 HOURS RISING TIME	YIELD: 8 SERVINGS

INGREDIENTS

1 package (¼ ounce) or 2 ½ teaspoons active dry yeast

1 ¼ cups warm water (110–115 degrees), divided

3 cups unbleached all-purpose flour

1 teaspoon sugar

1 teaspoon sea salt or kosher salt

3 tablespoons Amy Riolo Selections or other good-quality extra virgin olive oil, divided

2 tablespoons semolina, cornmeal, or regular flour

DIRECTIONS

1 Dissolve yeast in ¼ cup warm water in a small bowl. Let stand for 5 minutes, until it bubbles.

2 Put flour, sugar, and salt into a large mixing bowl. Make a well in the center, and add the dissolved yeast and 1 cup of warm water. Mix well to form a dough. If the dough seems sticky, add more flour, a tablespoon at a time. (Be aware that adding too much flour will make the bread tough.) If the dough seems too dry and will not form a ball, add more water, a tablespoon at a time.

3 Place the dough ball on a lightly floured surface. Knead the dough for approximately 5 minutes, or until you have a smooth, soft, and elastic dough.

4 Grease a large bowl with 1 tablespoon olive oil. Place the dough into the bowl, and turn to coat with the oil. Cover the bowl with plastic wrap and kitchen towels. Place it in a draft-free area, and allow it to rise until double in size. This takes 1–1 ½ hours.

5 When the dough has risen, preheat the oven to 425 degrees. Punch down the dough by pressing down to deflate it.

6 Dust a preheated baking stone or baking sheet with semolina. Divide the dough into two equal-sized pieces. Place the dough pieces on the baking stone or sheet and form them into two 4x12-inch loaves. Make sure that there is at least 4–5 inches between the loaves, so that when they rise they don't stick together. (You may want to use separate baking sheets.) Cover with kitchen towels, and allow to rise for another hour.

(continued)

7 Uncover the bread, make four ⅛-inch slits on the diagonal across each loaf. Brush each loaf with 1 tablespoon of olive oil. Bake for 15 minutes.

8 Lower the temperature to 400 degrees, and bake for 25 minutes, or until bread is golden brown. Allow to cool slightly. Serve warm.

TIP: If you use a pizza stone, handle it with gloves and do not get it wet while it is hot or it will crack.

NOTE: At Step 4, you can cover the dough and place it in the refrigerator to shape the following day.

VARY IT! Make whole wheat loves by swapping ½ of the flour content for whole wheat flour.

Taralli/Bread Rings

PREP TIME: 30 MIN	COOK TIME: 20 MIN PLUS AT LEAST 2 ½ HOURS RISING TIME	YIELD: 8 SERVINGS

INGREDIENTS

1 package (¼ ounce) or 2 ½ teaspoons active dry yeast

¾ cup lukewarm water (approximately 100 degrees), divided

2 cups bread flour, plus extra for work surface

½ teaspoon unrefined sea salt

3 tablespoons plus ½ teaspoon Gerace Nocellara del Belice, or other good-quality extra virgin olive oil, divided

1 egg white, lightly beaten

DIRECTIONS

1 In a small bowl, dissolve the yeast with ¼ cup lukewarm water.

2 Place the flour and salt in a large bowl. Add the yeast mixture, an additional ½ cup lukewarm water, and 3 tablespoons olive oil. Mix well to combine and form a dough.

3 Turn dough out onto a lightly floured surface. Knead energetically, adding a little more flour if needed, for about 8-10 minutes, until the dough is smooth and elastic.

4 Oil a large bowl with remaining ½ teaspoon olive oil, and place the dough inside. Turn dough to coat with oil, and cover with plastic wrap and clean kitchen towels. Allow to rise until doubled in size, approximately 1 ½ hours.

5 Remove dough from bowl, and break off a small, nickel-sized piece. Roll it into a 3-inch rope that is approximately the width of a pencil, and form into a circle. Pinch the ends together tightly, and place the ring on an ungreased baking sheet. Repeat with the rest of the dough. Cover the rings with a clean kitchen towel, and allow to rise until doubled in size, approximately 1/2 hour.

(continued)

6 Preheat oven to 375 degrees. Brush the tops of the rings with the egg white, and bake until light golden, 15–20 minutes. Remove from the oven, and cool on a rack; store in a tightly covered container in the refrigerator for up to a month.

TIP: If you do not have time to make the dough and shape the *taralli* on the same day, you could make the dough a day ahead of time, punch it down, and refrigerate it wrapped lightly in oiled plastic wrap until you have time to make them the next day; then punch down the dough again and begin shaping them.

Taralli are great additions to cheese plates, as part of an appetizer or *aperitivo*, or to enjoy with soup.

NOTE: This recipe makes bread-like *taralli*. If you prefer the crispier cracker-like variety, simply omit the second rising time and bake immediately.

VARY IT! You can add flavorings in Step 2; for example, black pepper, fennel seed, and chili pepper are traditional in Calabria for St. Joseph's Day.

Pizza Napoletana fatta in casa/ Grandma-Style Pizza

PREP TIME: 15 MIN	COOK TIME: 10 MIN PLUS AT LEAST 1 ½ HOURS RISING TIME	YIELD: 2 SERVINGS

INGREDIENTS

For the Dough:

1 package (¼ ounce) or 2 ½ teaspoons active dry yeast

½ cup lukewarm water (approximately 100 degrees)

1 ½ cups 00 flour (highly refined), plus extra for work surface

1 teaspoon unrefined sea salt

2 tablespoons Amy Riolo Selections or other good-quality extra virgin olive oil, divided

For the Sauce:

1 tablespoon Amy Riolo Selections or other good-quality extra virgin olive oil

1 large clove garlic, peeled and sliced

1 cup strained (seeded and skinned) San Marzano tomatoes, crushed (see Note)

10 ounces fresh mozzarella cheese, grated

1 tablespoon finely chopped fresh basil, oregano, or parsley

DIRECTIONS

1 **For the dough:** Place the yeast in a small bowl, and stir in the water. Set aside. Put the flour into a large bowl, and add the yeast mixture to the center. Add the salt and 1 tablespoon olive oil, and stir to combine until it forms a dense dough that is slightly sticky. If the dough does not come together, add more water a tablespoon at a time.

2 Dust a work surface lightly with flour. Knead the dough energetically for 5-10 minutes, or until it is smooth and supple. Shape the dough into a ball, and place it in a lightly oiled bowl. Cover with plastic wrap and a clean kitchen cloth. Allow to rise for 1 ½-2 hours, or until doubled in size.

3 **For the sauce:** Stir together all the sauce ingredients.

4 When the dough has finished rising, preheat the oven to 500-550 degrees. Punch the dough down by pressing it with your fingers to deflate it, and let it rest 5 minutes. Flatten the dough lightly with your hands, and carefully stretch it using a disk motion or by stretching it out and slapping it back onto the surface. (YouTube has videos on the technique called the *schiaffo*, or the slap.) When you have a circle that is 10-12 inches in diameter, transfer it to a pizza stone or paddle from which you can then transfer the pizza to the oven. Alternately, place the pizza circle directly on a pizza sheet and stretch it to fit accordingly.

5 Place the sauce in the middle of the dough, and smooth it out to cover the top using the back of a spoon and leaving a border around the edges for a crust. Scatter the garlic, mozzarella, and the basil over the top, and drizzle with a bit of olive oil. Bake on the second-to-lowest rack for 10-15 minutes or until golden and bubbly. Remove from the oven and allow to stand 5 minutes. Cut and serve.

(continued)

TIP: I recommend watching this video on how to stretch pizza properly before making this recipe: https://www.youtube.com/watch?v=WvHnNfLmHjM.

If you'd like to pair this pizza with wine, look for *Lambrusco Marani/Maestri* or similar.

NOTE: At home, there are *nonne* (or grandmothers) who use a rolling pin to roll out their dough, and you can make a very delicious pie that way, but just be aware that it varies from the Neapolitan hand-shaped tradition. In addition, note that while authentic San Marzano tomatoes can be tricky to find, many supermarkets offer San-Marzano style. While this is not 100% authentic, it will still produce a great tasting pizza in a pinch. The addition of EVOO to pizza dough is not part of the genuine Neapolitan recipe, but many *pizzaioli* have adopted this practice because it works better with the temperatures that home ovens cook at.

VARY IT! You can use whole wheat or other whole grain flours for the dough if you like. And, of course, add your favorite toppings before you bake.

AUTHENTIC PIZZA NAPOLETANA

Authentic Pizza Napoletana is known for being very tender, light, and moist at the same time. It cooks for only 90 seconds in an 800-degree oven and needs 58-65% hydration. Its ingredients must be Italian and come from a specific area such as San Marzano tomatoes. You cannot use more than three ingredients at a time in this type of pizza, because it's about the marriage of ingredients with the proper technique. Pizza Napoletana is always finished with extra virgin olive oil and fresh basil. For more information on the official guidelines of Vera Pizza Napoletana, visit the website (link in the next paragraph) to see the official guidelines and recipe.

Nowadays, more pizza is eaten per capita in the United States (46 slices per year) than in Italy, thanks to delivery. As of December 2017, the art of Neapolitan pizza-making was added to UNESCO's Representative List of the Intangible Cultural Heritage of Humanity. *Pizzaiuoli* (pizza-makers) are a living link for the communities concerned," says UNESCO (the United Nations Educational, Scientific, and Cultural Organization). The European Community granted "Pizza Napoletana" STG or Specialty Tradition Guaranteed status to distinguish it from non-authentic pizzas. The full decree can be read at: https://www.pizzadinapoli.it/images/allegati/stg.pdf

Pizza bianca con rucola e salmone affumicato/White Pizza with Smoked Salmon and Arugula

PREP TIME: 15 MIN	COOK TIME: 20 MIN PLUS AT LEAST 1 ½ HOURS RISING TIME	YIELD: 4 SERVINGS

INGREDIENTS

1 package (¼ ounce) or 2 ½ teaspoons active dry yeast

½ teaspoon salt

3 ½ cups unbleached all-purpose flour, plus extra for work surface

5 tablespoons Amy Riolo Selections or other good-quality extra virgin olive oil, divided

4 ounces fresh mozzarella

4 ounces smoked salmon

2 cups fresh arugula

DIRECTIONS

1 In a small bowl, dissolve yeast with ¼ cup lukewarm water, and let stand 10 minutes, or until bubbly. Put flour and salt into a large bowl, and make a well in the center. Add yeast mixture and 1 cup lukewarm water. Mix well to incorporate and form a ball. Stir in 2 tablespoons extra virgin olive oil. If dough is too sticky, add a little more flour a tablespoon at a time. If dough is too dry, add more water, a tablespoon at a time.

2 Lightly dust a work surface with flour. Knead dough for 10 minutes, or until smooth and elastic.

3 Grease a large bowl with 1 tablespoon olive oil. Place dough inside, and turn to coat. Cover with a few kitchen towels, and allow to rise for 1 hour until doubled in size. After dough has risen, knock it back by deflating the dough by pressing down with your fingers and place on a lightly floured work surface; with a floured rolling pin, roll out into a large rectangular shape.

4 Brush dough with 1 tablespoon olive oil, and use the other tablespoon to grease a 10x13x9-inch baking sheet (or two smaller sheets).

5 Place pizza on the baking sheet. Using your fingers, make dimples all over the dough.

(continued)

6 Cover loosely with kitchen towels, and allow to rise for 30 minutes; preheat oven to 425 degrees during last 10 minutes of rising.

7 Bake 20 minutes, or until golden. Sprinkle mozzarella over the top and return to oven for 5-10 minutes, or until baked through. Drizzle remaining 3 tablespoons of EVOO over pizza and cool slightly before topping with smoked salmon and arugula.

TIP: You can skip the toppings and serve this white pizza simply with extra sea salt or rosemary on top.

If you'd like to pair this pizza with wine, look for *Prosecco* or similar.

NOTE: This recipe was a favorite of mine that I got from a neighborhood *pizza a taglio* shop in the Piazza Fiume neighborhood. Unlike thin-crusted, round versions served in restaurants and *pizzerie* in the evening, it is made in large rectangular pans. This recipe can be made plain, sprinkled simply with sea salt, or with a variety of toppings. It's also a great accompaniment for cheese platters. Wrap leftovers in plastic wrap and aluminum foil and freeze.

VARY IT! Use your imagination to come up with your own topping combinations — sliced potatoes and rosemary, tomatoes and mozzarella, smoked cheese, and cured meat are other popular toppings.

Sfincione/Sicilian "Sponge" Pizza

PREP TIME: 20 MIN

COOK TIME: 25 MIN PLUS
1 ½ HOURS RISING TIME

YIELD: 4 SERVINGS

INGREDIENTS

1 package (¼ ounce) or
2 ½ teaspoons active dry yeast

1 cup lukewarm water
(approximately 100 degrees),
divided

3 cups 00 flour (highly refined),
plus extra for work surface

½ cup unbleached bread flour

½ teaspoon sea salt

3 tablespoons Amy Riolo
Selections extra virgin olive oil,
divided

1 ¼ cups chopped tomatoes
(San Marzano or Pomi brand, if
possible)

2 teaspoons dried oregano,
crushed

DIRECTIONS

1 Dissolve yeast with ¼ cup of the lukewarm water in a small
bowl.

2 Pour both flours into a large bowl, and make a well in the
center. Add the yeast mixture.

3 Add the sea salt and remaining water. Mix well to combine.

4 Dough should form a ball; if it is sticky, add more flour, a
tablespoon at a time.

5 Transfer to a lightly floured work surface. Knead for 5–10
minutes, or until dough is smooth and elastic; shape it into
a ball.

6 Use 1 tablespoon of olive oil to oil a large bowl. Place dough
inside, and turn to coat.

7 Cover with plastic wrap and a kitchen towel, and place in a
draft-free area to rise for 1–1 ½ hours, or until doubled in
bulk.

8 After dough has risen, knock it down by pressing down with
your fingers to deflate, and turn it out onto a lightly floured
work surface.

9 Use 1 tablespoon of olive oil to oil an 11x15-inch rectangle
stone or metal baking pan.

10 Roll the dough out to form an 11x15-inch rectangle.

(continued)

11 Transfer the dough to the pan, and stretch to fit.

12 Brush remaining 1 tablespoon olive oil on top of the pizza dough, and use your fingers to make dimples across the top.

13 Cover with kitchen towels, and allow to rest for 20 minutes.

14 Preheat the oven to 500 degrees, and let dough rest for another 10 minutes.

15 After the 30 minutes has passed, remove towels from the pan and cover the pizza with a thin layer of the tomatoes.

16 Place the oregano in between the palm of your hands, and rub them together over the pizza to break up the oregano and release more of its flavor while scattering it evenly.

17 Bake, uncovered, for 20–25 minutes, or until golden.

18 Remove from the oven, and allow to cool slightly.

19 Cut into 16 equal-size pieces, and serve.

TIP: This pizza is not traditionally served with cheese, although sometimes it is topped with anchovies and olives.

If you'd like to pair this pizza with wine, look for *Nero D'Avola* or similar.

NOTE: Utica Pie, Philadelphia's Tomato Pie, and other Italian-American favorites are the direct descendants of Sicilian *sfincione*, which is derived from the Arabic *sfinj,* which means sponge. The Italian word for sponge is *spugna.*

VARY IT! You can make individual-size versions, if you like.

Focaccia Ligure/Ligurian-Style Focaccia

PREP TIME: 20 MIN	COOK TIME: 25 MIN PLUS 2 HOURS RISING TIME	YIELD: 4 SERVINGS

INGREDIENTS

1 package (¼ ounce) or 2 ½ teaspoons active dry yeast

3 ½ cups unbleached all-purpose flour, plus extra for work surface

1 teaspoon kosher or sea salt

5 tablespoons Anfosso Taggiasca monocultivar or other good-quality extra virgin olive oil, divided

2 tablespoons polenta or cornmeal

2 tablespoons fresh rosemary, finely chopped

DIRECTIONS

1 In a small bowl, dissolve yeast with ¼ cup lukewarm water, and let stand 10 minutes, or until bubbly.

2 Put flour and salt into a large bowl, and make a well in the center. Add yeast mixture and 1 cup lukewarm water.

3 Mix well to incorporate and form a ball. Stir in 2 tablespoons extra virgin olive oil.

4 If dough is too sticky, add a little more flour, a tablespoon at a time. If dough is too dry, add more water, a tablespoon at a time.

5 Lightly dust a work surface with flour. Turn the dough out onto the work surface, and knead it for 10 minutes, or until smooth and elastic.

6 Grease a large bowl with 1 tablespoon olive oil. Place the dough inside, and turn to coat.

7 Cover with kitchen towels, and allow to rise for 1 ½ hours until doubled in size.

8 After the dough has risen, knock it back by pressing down with your fingers to deflate the dough and divide into two balls.

9 Place on a lightly floured work surface, and with a floured rolling pin, roll out into two (1-inch thick) oblongs.

10 Using your fingers, make dimples all over the dough. Brush the dough with remaining 2 tablespoons olive oil.

(continued)

11 Sprinkle two baking sheets with 1 tablespoon each of polenta. Place one focaccia on each sheet.

12 Preheat oven to 425 degrees.

13 Cover focaccia loosely with kitchen towels, and allow to rise for 30 minutes.

14 Sprinkle with rosemary, and bake 20–25 minutes, or until golden. Cool slightly before serving.

TIP: Giving your focaccia a little extra time to rise makes a difference in the flavor and texture.

If you'd like to pair this bread with wine, look for *Cinque Terre* or similar.

NOTE: Top the focaccia with halved cherry tomatoes, olives, or fresh cheese, if you like.

VARY IT! You can use whole wheat flour or a mix of half regular flour and half whole wheat flour to make this focaccia, if you like.

Schiacciata all'uva/Tuscan Grape Harvest Focaccia

PREP TIME: 15 MIN	COOK TIME: 40 MIN PLUS 1 ½ HOURS RISING TIME	YIELD: 8 SERVINGS

INGREDIENTS

1 ½ cups warm water

½ cup Vin Santo Italian dessert wine, at room temperature

1 package (¼ ounce) or 2 ½ teaspoons active dry yeast

½ cup Amy Riolo Selections or other good-quality extra virgin olive oil, divided, plus extra for greasing pan

4 cups bread flour

1 teaspoon unrefined sea salt or salt

2 cups seedless red grapes, cut in half lengthwise (see Note)

DIRECTIONS

1 Pour the water and Vin Santo in the bowl of a standing mixer. Sprinkle the yeast over the top, and mix using the paddle attachment until combined. Let set for 5 minutes. Pour in ¼ cup of olive oil. Add the flour, and mix on low speed; mix until well combined.

2 Switch to the dough hook attachment, and knead the dough on medium speed for 5 minutes. Cover the bowl with plastic wrap, and allow to rest at room temperature until doubled in size, about 1 hour.

3 Oil a 13x17-inch rimmed baking sheet. Turn the dough out from the bowl onto the baking sheet. Using your hands, stretch the dough out and press down until it covers the surface of the pan in an even layer.

4 Using your fingers, press to make dimples in the surface of the focaccia. Cover with oiled plastic wrap, and allow to rise for 30 minutes, or until the dough has doubled in size again.

5 Preheat the oven to 425 degrees. Before baking, remove the plastic wrap and brush the surface of the focaccia with the remaining ¼ cup of olive oil. Scatter the grapes, cut side down over the top, and press them down slightly. Bake for 30-35 minutes, or until the focaccia turns a nice golden brown and is cooked through.

6 Remove from the oven, and allow to cool slightly. Cut and serve immediately. Leftover, cooled pieces can be wrapped in plastic wrap and frozen for up to 1 month.

(continued)

TIP: If you'd like to pair this bread with wine, look for *Prosecco Dry* or similar.

NOTE: *Schiacciata,* the Italian name of this delicious bread, is derived from the verb *schiacciare*, which means "flattened out" or "squashed" — and that's exactly what happens to the dough when freshly harvested grapes are pressed into it. Traditionally made at grape harvest time, this recipe is said to have originated with the Etruscans and was originally baked in the ashes of an open hearth. Luckily, it's simple to make and suits modern palates perfectly. In Tuscany, a specific type of grape, called *uva fregola* (Concord grapes) with the seeds in, are used in making this recipe.

I make this bread with my cooking students during my Grape and Truffle Harvest Tours with Italian Sensory Experience. We pick the grapes from the winery that hosts us, seed them, and use them in making this recipe. Before dinner, I serve it with *prosecco* (and a dollop of whipped cream) to kick off the evening.

VARY IT! Replace the dessert wine with white wine and top this version of focaccia with tomatoes or cheese for a savory option.

5

The Part of Tens

Discover the ten commandments of Italian cuisine.

Enjoy ten fun ways to master Italian cooking.

Chapter **21**

Ten Commandments of Italian Cuisine

C hefs around the globe often describe authentic Italian cuisine as being "simple" and "straightforward" compared to other international cuisines. Like everything else in life, however, simplicity is only desired when it is good. The "commandments" in this chapter will ensure that even the most basic of Italian recipes tastes like a dream. Following them will elevate not only the food you eat, but your overall dining experience.

Honor Thy Food and Those Who Make It

For Italians, food is a gift of the land and is meant to be appreciated and celebrated. Part of good cooking is to respect the ingredients. Italian cooks learn to coax just the right amount of flavor out of each ingredient. Knowing which wine or olive oil pairs best with each dish, in order to create a symphony of flavors, is important. Most Italians also seek out small producers and farmers to buy products from when possible, knowing that it makes a difference in flavor and in the community.

After they have procured the best goods, they attempt to make and serve them in the best way possible, not just to show their own culinary prowess, but to pay homage to the producers, and the ingredients themselves. Italians view not respecting ingredients enough to treat them well as an injustice.

Respect Culture and Tradition

Taking the time to learn about the role that food holds in the various regional cultures of Italy is key to being a good Italian cook. What looks like a simple grain of rice to someone not from the Veneto region of Italy might actually represent the crowning glory of the table to another. Learning how locals view specific foods and why is the first step in cooking authentic Italian food. After you learn this, you are more likely to follow traditions and continue the culinary customs that have been enjoyed for so many years.

Choose Your Ingredients Wisely

Long gone are the days when intensely flavored spice concoctions masked subpar cuisine. While that was common in the Middle Ages in Italy, it is no longer. Instead, cooks choose the best products possible (see Chapter 5) so they have a head start on cooking, After you have great products, a few classic techniques are all you need to turn your food into a masterpiece.

Learning to choose the best ingredients takes time. Get to know your local purveyors, try different things, shop at farmers markets, and learn to read product labels (which often are created to confuse us) so you can stretch your dollar the farthest while enjoying fantastic food.

Waste Not, Want Not

Italians are masters at repurposing food. We learned it from our mothers and grandmothers. Wasting food is considered a sin. To this day, if I drop a piece of bread on the floor, I pick it up and hold it to my mouth as if I were going to kiss it before throwing it away. It is a symbol of respect for the product and gratitude for the food we have.

Part of respecting and honoring the food we eat (Commandment #1) is not wasting it. Italians keep stock of what's on hand and are crafty at inventing something new and delicious from leftovers to avoid waste. Leftover bread becomes bruschetta or bread crumbs; leftover risotto is transformed into cakes and croquettes; other tidbits become soups, sauces, or pasta fillings. My five go-to recipes for leftovers are soups, salads, sandwiches, sauces, and frittate.

Nonna's Always Right in the Kitchen

If you have an Italian grandmother, she is always right in the kitchen — even if you are a top chef. That's just the way it is. Italian cuisine did not evolve solely because restaurant chefs made great dishes. Italian cuisine became renowned because of the tireless work of our *nonne,* who for thousands of years were custodians of the cuisine, making sure regional recipes got passed down from one generation to the next. These women guarded our unique pasta shapes, traditional holiday baked goods, and much more. It is important to remember that modern chefs, no matter how innovative they claim to be, borrowed from the *nonne,* and not the other way around. There are older women in my family who can easily cook a ten-course meal for 100 people or more by themselves. We would be doing ourselves a huge favor to learn as much as they have to teach us.

Choose Whom to Eat with before Choosing What to Eat

The Greek philosopher Epicurus said to "look for someone to eat and drink with before looking for something to eat or drink." Thousands of years later, his sage advice is the basis of the Mediterranean diet. But this is also important to consider in cooking Italian cuisine, because we must always remember that our goal in the kitchen is to please our guests. Having guests and eating communally are the reasons for the large meals and the gorgeous food; this fact can't be overlooked.

Know the Classics

Certain classic dishes, like many of those presented in this book, are what Italian chefs are judged by. You simply cannot take shortcuts when it comes to fresh pasta, authentic sauces, risotto, gnocchi, and pizza. If you don't know the classic techniques to make these dishes properly, you will never master Italian cuisine. Italian chefs are graded on their risotto in culinary school. After you taste how those dishes are supposed to taste, you will know immediately when something is not right.

Part of knowing the classics is also knowing how dishes are supposed to be served. Familiarize yourself with the chapters in Part 1 so you can create the most authentic meals possible.

Learn the Rules of an Italian Kitchen (Even though Occasionally They Are Broken)

Here are a few rules of the Italian kitchen:

>> No milk with coffee after 11 AM.

>> No cheese with seafood (I do see some top chefs starting to do this, but it is not traditional).

>> Pasta, risotto, and gnocchi are served as a first course, not a side dish.

>> A traditional meal contains an appetizer, first course, second course, salad, fruit, nuts, cheese course, dessert course, coffee, and liqueur afterward. (Note that on modern tables the cheese may be omitted from the fruit/nut course).

>> Eggs are for lunch or dinner, not breakfast.

>> Pasta should be dressed lightly in sauce and always *al dente*.

>> Meatballs are part of the second course, unless they are hidden in *lasagne* or in a soup.

>> Chicken is not used in pasta sauce, except for in a few very specific holiday recipes in Abruzzo and Molise.

To Each Recipe his Own Season

Always choose ingredients that are in season while preparing Italian recipes. Whether you need to alter a traditional recipe to fit the season, or just start with a recipe that is meant to be made when you are making it, you will have the best results. Seasonal produce always has the most amount of flavor and nutrition, so using it makes your job in the kitchen easier while keeping your body happy. For this reason, in the description of many recipes in this book, the season in which they are most enjoyed is usually mentioned. Learning to plan menus (see Chapter 4) based on produce is a great way of taking advantage of nature's bounty while enjoying the tastiest and most nutritional foods.

Keep Your Food (Growing) Close

In addition to cutting down on our carbon footprint, consuming food that is grown closest to where you live offers health and flavor benefits. In Italy a "zero kilometer" approach to food has always been promoted. Home cooks and restaurant chefs alike pride themselves on eating and serving what is grown as close to home as possible. In fact, Slow Food International is a non-profit movement based on good, clean, and fair food that was first founded in Italy in the 1980s and continues to promote local food and small-scale producers around the world.

Nutritionally speaking, our bodies naturally crave the vitamins and minerals found in produce that grows in the areas in which we live. By choosing quality foods grown close to home, we can be ensured that we are providing ourselves with the proper nutrients. In addition, as mentioned in the previous section, seasonal items have more flavor and help to create greater variety in the kitchen.

Chapter **22**

Ten Fun Ways to Master Italian Cooking

Mastering Italian cuisine should be a labor of love. In fact, the contents of this book are largely based upon a Mastering Italian Certification Series class that I taught for years. In the 12-week program students learned everything that they needed to know to be a great Italian cook. An Italian ambassador sat in on the final exam that I gave to students. These ten ideas, while not necessary, will add flavor to your dishes and your life alike.

Brush Up on History

In order to truly master Italian cooking, you need to understand the history of Italy through a culinary lens. Knowing which ingredients came first, which indigenous inhabitants lived where, and what foreign power ruled the various regions and when gives you the basic knowledge you need to understand the cuisine. There are books dedicated to the topic, and my YouTube channel videos and blog posts, where I discuss Italian culinary history, are easily accessible.

Go to Italy, Do a Stage with an Italian Chef, or Watch Italian Food Shows

If you've never been to Italy before, the best way to experience the food is to go and sample it. If that is out of the question, consider doing a stage with a chef if you are a professional cook, or spend time in the kitchen with an Italian friend. This is important to familiarize yourself with how food should taste, be presented, and be paired.

I also recommend watching Italian food shows, because they give you lots of ideas for how people eat on a daily basis, presentation, and standards. Anything you can do to familiarize yourself with authentic, genuine cuisine in the early stages is best.

Read Cookbooks by Italians

Nowadays, we have many great Italian cooks and cookbook authors in the U.S. to follow. My favorites were the late Biba Caggiano and Marcella Hazan. Books by Chef Luigi Diotiaiuti and Ale Gambini are also great resources in English. You can also buy the classics, such as the works of Pellegrino Artusi and De Re Coqinaria by Apicius, to get a feel for what was going on throughout history at Italian tables.

Expand Your Italian Kitchen Vocabulary

I often lead workshops with the Italian Embassy in Washington, D.C., to teach the importance of using culinary terminology specific to the type of cuisine you are cooking. If you want to be a good Italian cook, you should use Italian terminology in the kitchen.

Follow Italian Meal Patterns

One of the biggest mistakes I see in Italian kitchens run by non-Italians is the misplacement of dishes. Sometimes they might make a menu with two first courses and no second course, or vice versa. Part of mastering Italian cuisine isn't just cooking specific recipes; it's also putting those recipes together to form a meal and eventually an entire diet. Chapter 4 helps you with this.

Discover How to Pair Food

Italian cooks are constantly striving to come up with the best flavor combinations. Some of them, such as poultry with sage, pasta with tomato sauce, and other classic pairings, have already been taken care of. Within the course of a meal, however, it's important that the first course pairs well with the second, and so on, I have carefully given serving suggestions with each recipe to make this easier for newcomers to the Italian kitchen.

Another layer of pairing to take into consideration is pairing meals and dishes with wine and olive oil. Italians are very careful to make sure that what they are serving is paired with the appropriate wine so the flavors of each can be enhanced. Nowadays, chefs are also pairing various types of extra virgin olive oil from different olive cultivars (there are hundreds in Italy today — each with different flavor profiles), so educating yourself on these products and how to pair them (see Chapter 5) also helps you to master the cuisine.

Cook Your Way through Recipes

One of the great things about cookbooks is that you can literally pick a chapter and cook your way through recipes. (Practice makes delicious!) If you've ever seen the movie *Julie and Julia*, you know what I'm talking about. Of course, you don't have to take it to that extreme, but you can have fun earmarking pages and setting time aside to practice. The more you practice, the better you will be. Italian *nonne* spend their lives perfecting handmade pasta, and professional cooks have built-in on-the-job training. To be truly great, home cooks need to increase their practice.

Learn to Read Labels

Chapter 5 tells you everything you need to know about reading product labels. It helps you to choose the best EVOO, vinegar, salt, chocolate, wine, and so on, so the ingredients in your cooking will shine. Unfortunately, the more marketing dollars a company has to spend on advertising, the more confusing the labels can become.

Counterfeit products and fake foods often sell for nearly the same price (sometimes more) than the real, genuine deal. Familiarizing yourself with government mandates, rules, and regulations helps your shopping to be more informed and your food taste better.

Make It a Priority

Cooking is like anything else in life: The more you put into it, the more you get out of it. One of the things that makes Italian cuisine stand out is that it is a priority by the culture, consumers, government legislators, and producers. Quality seals and certifications are hard to come by and must go through strict regulations. Because there is so much competition in terms of food, it helps to ensure that quality food gets reproduced, because consumers demand it and the government gives incentives to produce it.

In their personal lives, Italians place a high premium on good food, eating well, and nourishing their friends and their families. They are willing to spend extra, work a bit more, and go the extra mile for all of the payoffs that eating well provides. If you make this a priority as well, you will be well on your way to mastering Italian cuisine.

Familiarize Yourself with Authentic Foods

I'm saving the best for last with this list. When learning to cook "Italian" food, it is easy to start out thinking that you know what things should taste like because you've had them before. But it's important to point out that canned pasta, frozen grocery store pizza, and lasagne, while there is a time and a place for them, have *nothing* to do with the real things. If you want to master genuine cuisine, and you have not grown up with it or spent a great deal of time in Italy, you should seek out the most traditional version of the dish you want to make. Once you locate it, taste it, slowly, to pick up the flavors and textures. Take notes on what you are tasting, how it feels, smells, and even sounds while you are eating it. Take pictures of what it looks like, and create a memory of the experience. That way, when you go to make the dish, you will have an accurate benchmark of what you are creating.

If you take cooking classes, or watch shows, or read cookbooks, note the various steps in making a dish. Pay particular attention to what the recipe looks like at each stage as well as the look of the end result so that you'll know what to work toward while cooking. This type of "field research" is one of the most fun aspects of being a food writer and chef, and it can be fun for you, too.

Appendix

Metric Conversion Guide

Note: The recipes in this book weren't developed or tested using metric measurements. There may be some variation in quality when converting to metric units.

Common Abbreviations

Abbreviation(s)	What It Stands For
cm	Centimeter
C., c.	Cup
G, g	Gram
kg	Kilogram
L, l	Liter
lb.	Pound
mL, ml	Milliliter
oz.	Ounce
pt.	Pint
t., tsp.	Teaspoon
T., Tb., Tbsp.	Tablespoon

Volume

U.S. Units	Canadian Metric	Australian Metric
¼ teaspoon	1 milliliter	1 milliliter
½ teaspoon	2 milliliters	2 milliliters
1 teaspoon	5 milliliters	5 milliliters
1 tablespoon	15 milliliters	20 milliliters

U.S. Units	Canadian Metric	Australian Metric
¼ cup	50 milliliters	60 milliliters
⅓ cup	75 milliliters	80 milliliters
½ cup	125 milliliters	125 milliliters
⅔ cup	150 milliliters	170 milliliters
¾ cup	175 milliliters	190 milliliters
1 cup	250 milliliters	250 milliliters
1 quart	1 liter	1 liter
1½ quarts	1.5 liters	1.5 liters
2 quarts	2 liters	2 liters
2½ quarts	2.5 liters	2.5 liters
3 quarts	3 liters	3 liters
4 quarts (1 gallon)	4 liters	4 liters

Weight

U.S. Units	Canadian Metric	Australian Metric
1 ounce	30 grams	30 grams
2 ounces	55 grams	60 grams
3 ounces	85 grams	90 grams
4 ounces (¼ pound)	115 grams	125 grams
8 ounces (½ pound)	225 grams	225 grams
16 ounces (1 pound)	455 grams	500 grams (½ kilogram)

Length

Inches	Centimeters
0.5	1.5
1	2.5
2	5.0
3	7.5

Inches	Centimeters
4	10.0
5	12.5
6	15.0
7	17.5
8	20.5
9	23.0
10	25.5
11	28.0
12	30.5

Temperature (Degrees)

Fahrenheit	Celsius
32	0
212	100
250	120
275	140
300	150
325	160
350	180
375	190
400	200
425	220
450	230
475	240
500	260

Index

H

haddock, 81

halibut, 182

hard wheat, 130

hazelnut flour, 293–294

hazelnuts, 293–294

heavy cream

    Farfalle con salmone/Bowtie Pasta with Smoked Salmon and Cream Sauce, 142

    Macedonia/Fruit Salad, 244

    Mele al forno con crema ed amaretti/ Roasted Apples with Cream and Amaretti, 281

    Mostaccioli/Chocolate Holiday Cookies, 315

    Pesche al forno con pistacchi e crema di basilico/Roasted Peaches with Pistachios and Basil Cream, 274

    Salsa di pomodoro/Fresh Tomato Sauce, 98

    Spaghetti al limone/Lemon Infused Spaghetti, 117

    Tiramisù, 289–290

    Tiramisu di fragole/Strawberry Tiramisù, 291–292

    Torta di frutta stagionale/Seasonal Fruit Cake, 260–261

    Vellutata di castagne/Cream of Chestnut Soup, 165

    Zuccotto/Florentine Cream-Filled Dome Cake, 299–300

    Zuppa di zucchini/Zucchini Soup, 163

herbs, essential, 68

holidays, 13

honey, 255, 256–257, 274, 280, 282, 305–306, 313–314, 321–322

honeydew melon, 278

The House of Savoy, 285

I

icons, explained, 4–5

Il Cuoco Gentiluomo (The Gentleman Cook) (Castegnate), 92

Indicazione geografica protetta/ Protected Geographic Indication (IGP/PGI), 61, 65

ingredients, choosing, 354

insalata, 25

Insalata Caprese/Caprese Salad recipe, 239

Insalata di ceci/Chickpea Salad recipe, 242

Insalata di cetrioli, fagolini, ed olive/ Cucumber, String Bean, and Olive Salad recipe, 243

Insalata di mare/Seafood Salad recipe, 81

Insalata di pomodori e peperoni/ Tomato and Roasted Pepper Salad recipe, 238

Insalata di riso/Sicilian Rice Salad recipe, 240

Insalata mista/Mixed Salad recipe, 237

Insalata Siciliana con le patate/Sicilian Salad with Potatoes recipe, 241

Insalata verde/Green Salad recipe, 236

Involtini di tonno melanzane/Fresh Tuna and Eggplant Roulades recipe, 185–186

Italian cuisine, 10–11, 353–357, 359–362

Italian eateries, antipasto at, 77–78

Italian specialty pantry items, 68

Itsiopoulos, Catherine, 268

J

jalapeños, 83

K

kale, 143–144, 230

Kingdom of the Two Sicilies, 23

kiwi, 244, 276, 278

kneading pasta dough, 129

L

la bella figura, 24

La scienza in cucina e l'arte di mangiare bene (The Science of Cooking and the Art of Eating Well) (Artusi), 92

labeling, 60–61, 361–362

lady fingers, 281, 289–292

Lagane con ceci/Lagane Pasta with Chickpeas recipe, 131–132

lagane pasta, 111, 132

lamb, 103, 198, 208, 209, 210, 213, 214, 215, 217, 218

lasagne, 111

Lasagne classica/Homemade Lasagna Bolognese-Style recipe, 145–146

Laviola, Sante (scientist), 65

legumes, 29–30, 68, 101

lemons

    Agnello al forno/Roasted Lamb, 213

    Bomboloni alla crema/Cream-Filled Doughnuts, 262–263

    Cannoli, 307–310

    Cantucci/Tuscan Almond Biscotti, 256–257

    Cassata Siciliana/Sicilian Ricotta-Filled Cassata Cake, 301–302

    Colomba/Traditional Easter Dove Bread, 321–322

    Cotolette d'agnello alla griglia/Grilled Lamb Chops, 215

    Cozzupe di Pasqua/Calabrian Easter Bread, 319–320

    Crema di ceci/Chickpea Soup, 161

    Crostini con purea di cannellini/ Crostini with Cannellini Bean Purée, 86

    Farfalle con salmone/Bowtie Pasta with Smoked Salmon and Cream Sauce, 142

    Fragole in aceto balsamico/ Strawberries in Balsamic Vinegar, 282

    Funghi ripieni/Stuffed Mushrooms, 82

    Gamberi al limone e rosmarino/ Lemon and Rosemary Scented Shrimp, 187

    Insalata di ceci/Chickpea Salad, 242

    Insalata di mare/Seafood Salad, 81

    Insalata di riso/Sicilian Rice Salad, 240

    Insalata Siciliana con le patate/Sicilian Salad with Potatoes, 241

    Linguine alle vongole/Linguine with Clams, 120

    Macedonia di frutta con noci/Fruit Salad with Walnuts, 276

    Macedonia/Fruit Salad, 244

    Occhi di Santa Lucia/Santa Lucia's Eyes Cookies, 316–317

    Pasta con tonno e finocchio/Bucatini with Fresh Tuna and Fennel, 119

    Pastiera Napoletana/Neapolitan Easter Pie, 323–324

    Pere cotte al cioccolato/Poached Pears in Chocolate, 275

    Petrali/Cucidati/Southern Italian Fig Cookies, 313–314

    Petto di pollo marinato/Marinated Chicken Breasts, 199

About the Author

As an award-winning and best-selling author of 11 books, chef, television personality, and educator, Amy Riolo is one of the world's foremost authorities on culinary culture. She is known for sharing history, culture, and nutrition through global cuisine as well as simplifying recipes for the home cook. A graduate of Cornell University, Amy is considered a culinary thought-leader who enjoys changing the way we think about food and the people who create it. Amy is a food historian, culinary anthropologist, and Mediterranean Diet specialist who makes frequent appearances on numerous television and radio programs both in the United States and abroad, including Fox TV, ABC, CBS, NBC, The Hallmark Channel, Nile TV, The Travel Channel, Martha Stewart Living Radio, and Abu Dhabi Television. She also created and appeared weekly in cooking videos entitled "Culture of Cuisine," which air on nationally syndicated news shows on 28 different channels across the United States, totaling a reach of over 300 million people. One of her videos reached a record of four million hits.

Amy is the brand ambassador for the Maryland University of Integrative Health, Pizza University and Culinary Arts Center, and Ristorante d'Amore in Capri, Italy. In 2019, she launched her private label collection of premium Italian imported culinary ingredients called Amy Riolo Selections, which includes extra virgin olive oil, balsamic vinegar, and pesto sauce from award-winning artisan companies. In 2021, she became a founding member of the international non-profit association A.N.I.T.A (Accademia Nazionale Italiana Tradizioni Alimentari/Italian National Academy of Food Traditions).

Amy is a Chef/Instructor for the Casa Italiana Language School in Washington, D.C., and for Italian Sensory Experience, a company through which she leads Eno-gastronomic tours in Italy, as well as Indigo Gazelle Tours in Morocco and Greece. Her work has appeared in numerous print media, including *USA Today*, *Cooking Light magazine*, *The Washington Post*, CNN.com, *The Wall Street Journal*, *Parade Magazine*, *Gulf News*, *The Jerusalem Post Magazine*, *The UAE National*, and hundreds of other national and international newspapers and magazines.

Amy's previous books include *Mediterranean Lifestyle For Dummies*, the *Diabetes Cookbook* (2 editions), *Creating a Cookbook: How to Write, Publish, and Promote Your Culinary Philosophy*; *The Italian Diabetes Cookbook*; *The Ultimate Mediterranean Diet Cookbook*; *Nile Style*; *Egyptian Cuisine and Culture* (2 editions); and *Arabian Delights — Recipes and Princely Entertaining Ideas from the Arabian Peninsula*. Amy also contributed to *The Food Cultures of the World Encyclopedia* and co-wrote *The Al Tiramisu Restaurant Cookbook: An Elevated Approach to Authentic Italian Cuisine* with award-winning chef/restaurateur Luigi Diotaiuti and edited *The Quick Diabetic Recipes Cookbook*.

For more information on Amy Riolo and to view television appearances, visit her website, amyriolo.com.

Dedication

In loving memory of my dear late friend, healer, inspiration, and spirit sister Kathleen Ammalee Rogers: I would not be here if it weren't for your healing skills, care, support, and friendship. I am eternally grateful to you for my health, career, and overall well-being. May you dwell in eternal bliss.

Author's Acknowledgments

I owe my fluency in all things Italian to my heritage, my family, and the good fortune to spend time living, working, and hanging out with family and friends in Italy. I am grateful to have experienced regional Italian cuisine and culture at its best throughout Italy, but also to have experienced it abroad. I am honored to be able to interpret the time-honored traditions of the Italian kitchen in a straight-forward and simple way that makes them accessible to many more people.

Destiny is also to thank for enabling me to get to know so many people and places in Italy, and at such an intimate level. I believe it truly "takes a village" to make a good chef and a good writer — and in my case, that village is a global one. I am honored and proud to say that I have learned from amazing cooks in places that I never dreamed I would even visit. For all of you who have shared a kitchen or a meal with me, I thank you.

My nonna, Angela Magnone Foti, taught me to cook and bake, as well as valuable lessons that served me outside of the kitchen. Because of her and our heritage, my first tastes of "Italian food" were Calabrian. Those edible time capsules formed a culinary bloodline between us and our relatives in southern Italy. Because of her, I am able to prepare many of the same dishes that my Italian relatives do, even though I am a fourth generation American. Nonna Angela gave me my first cook-book and showed me how cooking was not a mundane chore, but a form of magic that could unite people across distances and time. I owe my career to her, and I would give anything to be able to share more time in the kitchen with her. Cooking was so important to her that a few weeks before she passed, at 91 years old, she refused to go into the hospital because it was Christmastime and she told the doctors that she needed to be home so she could "make cookies with Amy." It is an honor for me to be able to pass her knowledge on to my readers.

My Yia Yia, Mary Michos Riolo, shared her beloved Greek traditions with me, and I am happy to say that they have become woven into my culinary fabric as well — especially since many Italian regions were Greek colonies in antiquity. My earliest memories of cooking were with my mother, Faith Riolo, who would sit me on the counter and roll more meatballs and cookies than I could count. She taught me that food is not just something we eat to nourish ourselves, but an edible gift that can be given to express love. I owe my love of food history and anthropology to my father, Rick Riolo, for planting the desire to answer the question "I wonder how they eat . . ." in my mind since childhood. It's a type of culinary curiosity that is never completely satisfied and gives me the motivation to continue my work each day. To my beloved little brother, Jeremy, you are my why, and I am grateful to be able to pass our family's knowledge down to you.

I would probably never have published a cookbook if it weren't for my mentor Sheilah Kaufman, who patiently taught me much more than I ever planned on learning. I am proud to pass her knowledge on to others. I am very thankful to Chef Luigi Diotaiuti, for always believing in me and for encouraging me to follow my dreams and goals. Your support means the world to me, and I'm blessed to have you in my life.

In Italy, I thank my cousin Franco Riolo and his lovely wife Pina, Tonia Riolo, my beautiful cousin Serena Riolo, with whom I love cooking and attending culinary events, and to her brother Vincenzo Riolo for the bond and memories that we share, as well as to my dear cousin Angela Riolo for sharing my passion and continuously supplying me with authentic Calabrian recipes. In fact, I am immensely grateful to each of my Cugini Calabresi, as I affectionately call them. I am very grateful for their acceptance of me — as a third cousin — who they met later in life, but embrace me wholeheartedly as someone who they grew up with. The sense of peace, happiness, and joy that I feel when we are together is second to none.

To my Italian Sensory Experience partners Antonio Iuliano and Francesco Giovanelli, thank you for making my culinary dreams come true. I am also very grateful to Stefano Ferrari, owner of LIFeSTYLE and Cibo Divino for importing and distributing my private label products along with Vince Di Piazza of DITALIA for distributing them. Additional thanks go to Stellina Pizzeria, The Mediterranean Way, Milan Milan in Bermuda, Tastings Gourmet in Annapolis, and all of the other retailers who carry my products. Grazie mille to all of the fabulous Italian producers who partner with me to create amazing products.

Many heartfelt thanks to the Marra family, especially Francesco Marra and Enzo Marra for including me as an ambassador at the Pizza University and Culinary Arts Center. I am so proud of what you have accomplished and am honored to consider myself your spirit sister. Mille grazie to my Calabrian colleagues, the illustrious Alessandro Cuomo of Stagionello and Valerio Caparelli for enabling me to be a founding member of the international non-profit association A.N.I.T.A (Accademia Nazionale Italiana Tradizioni Alementari). I am also grateful to Marco D'Amore, owner of Ristorante d'Amore in Capri, for naming me as an ambassador. Tante grazie to the internationally recognized journalist, Professor Massimo Lucidi, for including me as the MC at the Premio Eccellenza Italiana Awards Ceremony in D.C. each year. To my dear friend "superwoman" Dr. Antonella Discepolo Chiancone, thank you so much for the enormous amount of generosity and support that you have shown me over the years. Mille grazie to the award winning tailor, Mr. Emilio De Luca for introducing me to so many wonderful Neapolitan people, places, and initiatives, and for making me such beautiful clothes.

Throughout recent years, I have been fortunate to be able to call upon the assistance of many dear friends whom I love like family. Time and time again, they have supported me and my projects in an amazing fashion. My beautiful and talented sorellina Lisa Comento, #TeamAmy founder, marketing diva Gail Broekel, the great Chef Paul Kolze, my favorite molecular gastronomist Edward Donnelly, the multi-talented Stuart Hershey, my friend and kindred spirit Kim Lee, the 5-Star rock star Chef Sedrick Crawley, and our newest recruit. . .Certified Executive Chef Jeff Fritz. I would also like to give a heartfelt thanks to my fantastic producer, Bradley Lewis for being a fantastic mentor and coach. To my Fairy God Sister, Kim Foley, you are the best. Not a day passes that I don't thank my close friend and business partner Alex Safos of Indigo Gazelle Tours for his support and collaborations.

I would also like to thank Dr. John Rosa for recognizing my contributions to the field of culinary medicine and for all the wonderful avenues of collaboration. To Marc Levin, President and CEO of the Maryland University of Integrative Health, thank you very much for the opportunity to work with such an important establishment. I am also very appreciative of my alma maters Cornell University and Montgomery College for recognizing my achievements.

I am very grateful to Dr. Sante Laviola, Italian Research Scientist, professional wine taster, Sommelier, and official wine taster of the *Slow Wine Guide*, published by Slow Food Editore for graciously pairing the dishes in this book with his expert recommendations.

At Wiley, I want to thank Tracy Boggier for being so enthusiastic and great to work with. I truly appreciate the expert and efficient editorial support and guidance of Alissa Schwipps, and thank Kristie Pyles for all of her support as well. Mille grazie to Emily Beisel and Daryl Harris for their fantastic marketing initiatives. Wendy Jo Peterson, thank you for your terrific photography, synergy, and overall appreciation of everything Mediterranean. Grazie mille to food writer, blogger, and Luca's Italy founder, Luca Marchiori for being the technical editor of this book as well.

I am forever indebted to Dr. Norton Fishman for diagnosing me and creating a team of doctors to enable me to heal. I am also forever grateful to Dr. Beth Tedesco, and Dr. Mary Lee Esty for enabling me to overcome my own illness and fulfill my dreams. Thanks to my dear friend Susan Simonet for your love and support. I have dubbed the amazing Monica Bhide "Leading Light" because she is a faithful and trusted friend who always brightens my days. To my trusted friend and colleague Jonathan Bardzik, thank you for helping me create joy daily. And finally, I would like to thank you, the reader, for joining me on this journey into an enjoyable and rewarding way of living and eating with both pleasure and health in mind.

Publisher's Acknowledgments

Senior Acquisitions Editor: Tracy Boggier

Senior Managing Editor: Kristie Pyles

Project Manager & Development Editor: Alissa Schwipps

Copy Editor: Gwenette Gaddis

Technical Editor: Luca Marchiori

Recipe Tester: Emily Nolan

Production Editor: Tamilmani Varadharaj

Photographer: Wendy Jo Peterson

Illustrator: Elizabeth Kurtzman

Cover Image: Wendy Jo Peterson, Grace Geri Goodale